BURNING
QUESTIONS

>><<

BURNING QUESTIONS

>><<

ESSAYS AND OCCASIONAL PIECES

2004 TO 2021

>><<

Margaret Atwood

DOUBLEDAY

NEW YORK

Owing to limitations of space, all acknowledgements to reprint
previously published material appear on pages 452–57.

Jacket photograph © Luis Mora
Jacket design by Michael J. Windsor
Book design by Pei Loi Koay

LIBRARY OF CONGRESS CATALOGING-IN-PUBLICATION DATA
Names: Atwood, Margaret, [date] author.
Title: Burning questions: essays and occasional pieces,
2004 to 2021 / Margaret Atwood.
Description: First edition. | New York: Doubleday, [2022]
Identifiers: LCCN 2021021363 (print) | LCCN 2021021364 (ebook) |
ISBN 9780385547482 (hardcover) | ISBN 9780385547505 (ebook)
Subjects: LCGFT: Essays.
Classification: LCC PR9199.3.A8 B87 2022 (print) |
LCC PR9199.3.A8 (ebook) | DDC 814/.54—dc23
LC record available at https://lccn.loc.gov/2021021363
LC ebook record available at https://lccn.loc.gov/2021021364

MANUFACTURED IN THE UNITED STATES OF AMERICA

1 3 5 7 9 10 8 6 4 2

First Edition

To Graeme—

And for my family

Contents

>>><<<

Introduction

>>><<<

Burning Questions is my third collection of essays and other occasional pieces. The first was *Second Words,* which began in 1960, when I started publishing book reviews, and ended in 1982. The second was *Moving Targets,* which gathered materials from 1983 to mid-2004. *Burning Questions* runs from mid-2004 to mid-2021. So, twenty years, give or take, for each volume.

Each of these time periods has been tumultuous in its own way. Occasional pieces are written for specific occasions and are thus tightly connected to their own time and place—or at least mine are. They are also linked to my age at the time of writing, and to my outward circumstances. (Did I have a job? Was I a student? Did I need the money? Was I already a well-known writer, indulging my interests? Was I doing a freebie in response to a cry for help?)

In 1960, I was twenty, single, unpublished in book form, and a female undergraduate of limited wardrobe. In 2021, I was eighty-one, a fairly well-known writer, a grandmother, and a widow, also of limited wardrobe, having learned through failed experiments that there are some things better left unworn by me.

Naturally I have changed—my hair's a different colour—but so has the world. The past sixty-odd years have been a roller coaster, with many shocks and upheavals, many uproars and reversals. The year 1960 was only a decade and a half after the end of the Second World War. To our generation, that war felt both very close—we'd lived through it, our families contained veterans and casualties, some of our high-school teachers had been in it—and very far away. Between 1950 and 1960 had come both McCarthyism, giving us a peek at the fragility of democracy, and Elvis, upending song and dance. The clothes too had changed radically: the 1940s were sombre, durable, military, boxy; the 1950s, frothy, strapless, bouffant, pastel, beflowered. Femininity was lauded. The cars had gone from the dark, enclosed sedans of the war years to chrome-trimmed convertibles in flamboyant colours. Transistor radios were among us. Drive-in theatres popped up. Plastics arrived.

Then, in 1960, there was another change. Among the earnest young, folk songs replaced formal dances. In the tiny artistic circles that then existed in Toronto coffee houses—inclined as they were to French existentialism rather than Beatniks—black turtlenecks and equally black eyeliner were in vogue.

Still, the early 1960s were the 1950s, in essence. The Cold War was on. Kennedy had not yet been assassinated. There was no birth control pill generally available. There were no miniskirts, though there had just been short shorts. There were no hippies. There was no second-wave women's movement. It was in this period that I wrote my first book reviews, my first collection of poems, my first novel— still in a drawer, happily—and my first published novel, *The Edible Woman*. By the time it came out—in 1969—the world it describes was already gone.

The later 1960s brought uproar. The big civil rights marches in the United States, the anti–Vietnam War protests, the hundreds of thousands of American draft dodgers pouring into Canada. I myself was constantly in transit: for some of these years I was a graduate student in Cambridge, Massachusetts; for others I held minor academic positions in such places as Montreal and Edmonton. I moved sixteen or seventeen times. This period saw the formation of a number of new publishing ventures in Canada, many of them connected with the country's post-colonial struggle to figure itself out. My involvement with one of them gave rise to much essay writing, both at the time and later.

Then came the 1970s: the ferment of the second-wave women's movement, followed by reaction and burnout toward the end; in Canada, Quebec separatism occupied the centre of the political stage. This period saw the arrival of several authoritarian regimes: Pinochet in Chile, and the Argentinian junta, with their murders and disappearances; the Pol Pot regime in Cambodia, with its wholesale slaughters. Some were "right," some were "left," but no ideology, it was clear, had a monopoly on atrocities.

I continued to write book reviews, as well as the novels, stories, and poems I felt were my real work, but I also branched out into articles and speeches. Quite a few of these were about subjects that still occupy my shrinking brain: "women's issues," writing and writers, human rights. I was now a member of Amnesty International, which worked to free "prisoners of conscience," largely through letter-writing campaigns.

By 1972, I had ceased to have academic jobs and had gone freelance, so I was taking any paid work I could pick up. We were living on a farm and had a small child as well as a small budget. We were not poor, though one visitor told people we had "nothing but a goat." (No goats, in reality; they were sheep.) But we were not rolling in cash. We grew a lot of vegetables and kept chickens and other non-human residents. This mini-agribiz took time, and also lost money, so if I could make a bit of cash from writing rather than egg sales, all to the good.

The 1980s began with our move from the farm to Toronto (for school reasons, among others), the election of Ronald Reagan in the United States, and the rise of the religious right. In 1981, I began thinking about *The Handmaid's Tale,* though I put off writing it until 1984 because the concept seemed too far-fetched. My output of "occasional writing" sped up, partly because it could—with a child in school, I had more free time during the day—and partly because I was getting more requests. Looking back at my sporadic, badly kept, and not very informative journals, I note that one of the leitmotifs is a constant moaning about taking on too much. "This has to stop," I find myself saying. Some of the pieces I was writing were in response to pleas for help, and so it has continued.

"Just say no," people told me and I told myself. However, if you're asked to write ten occasional essays a year and say no to 90 per cent of them, that comes to one essay a year. But if you're asked to write four hundred pieces and you still say no to 90 per cent of them—how firm and virtuous you are!—that's still forty pieces a year. I've been averaging forty a year for the past couple of decades. There's a limit. This has to stop.

To resume our chronology: the Cold War and the Soviet system crumbled in 1989, as the Berlin Wall came down. The end of history had occurred, we were told: capitalism was the way forward, shopping was king, your lifestyle choices defined you, and what more could women want? Not to mention "minorities"—referred to in Canada among politicians and government bureaucrats, or so my spies told me, as "multi-eths" (people who spoke languages other than French and English) and "visi-mins" (people who were not "white"). They could both want quite a bit more, it was soon to become evident; but it was not very evident in the 1990s. There were stirrings, there were rumblings; there were wars and political coups and conflicts elsewhere; but there were not yet explosions. "It can't happen here" was still the attitude.

After 2001, with the terrorist attacks on the Twin Towers and the Pentagon, everything changed. Former assumptions were challenged, former comforts flew out the window, former truisms were no longer true. Fear and suspicion were the order of the day.

And that is where *Burning Questions* begins.

Why the title? Possibly because the questions we've been faced with so far in the twenty-first century are more than urgent. Every age thinks that about its own crises, of course, but surely this era feels different. First, the planet. Is the world itself truly burning up? Is it we who've been setting fire to it? Can we put those fires out?

What about the highly unequal distribution of wealth, not only in North America but virtually everywhere? Can such a top-heavy and unstable arrangement possibly last? How soon before the 99 per cent get fed up and set fire to the figurative Bastille?

Then there's democracy. Is it in peril? What do we mean by "democracy" anyway? Has it ever actually existed, in the sense of equal rights for all citizens? Are we serious about *all*? All genders, all religions, all ethnic origins? Is this system we call democracy worth preserving, or else pursuing? What do we mean by freedom? How much speech should be freely uttered, and by whom, and about what? The social media revolution has given unprecedented power to online conglomerations of people that are called "movements" if you like them and "mobs" if you don't. Is this good or bad, or just an extension of old-fashioned crowds in motion?

Does "burn it all down"—a popular slogan in our times—mean all, really?

For instance, does *all* mean all words? What about "the creatives," as some are in the habit of calling them? What about writers and writing? Are they—are we—to be mere mouthpieces, reeling out acceptable platitudes that are supposed to be good for society, or do we have some other function? If it's a function of which others disapprove, shall our books be burned? Why not? It's been done before. There is nothing inherently sacrosanct about a book.

These are some of the burning questions I've been asked, and have asked myself, over the course of the past two decades. Here are some of the answers. Or should I say some of the attempts? That's what *essay* means, after all: an attempt. An effort.

I've arranged this book into five parts. Each is marked by an event or turning point.

Part One begins in 2004. In the aftermath of the Twin Towers and Pentagon attacks, the Iraq War was ongoing. I was still travelling for *Oryx and Crake* (2003), the first book of the MaddAddam trilogy, plotted around a double crisis: the climate crisis and species extinction precipitated by it and a pandemic plague enabled by gene splicing. In 2003–2004, these premises seemed remote; now, not so much. Part One ends in 2009, as the world was still staggering from the big financial crash of October 2008—the very moment at which I was publishing *Payback: Debt and the Shadow Side of Wealth.* (Some people thought I had a crystal ball. I didn't.)

Part Two runs from 2010 to 2013. In these four years Obama was the U.S. president, and the world was slowly recovering from the financial meltdown. I was mostly occupied with the writing of *MaddAddam*, the third novel in the MaddAddam trilogy. Once you've published a book, you are often asked why you did it—as if you've stolen an ashtray—and you will find me, in one of these essays, dutifully trying to account for my crime.

My essay-writing life was varied. I continued to produce reviews, introductions, and, unfortunately, obituaries. The climate crisis was becoming an ever-hotter topic, and I found myself writing about it more often.

In 2012, my partner, Graeme Gibson, was diagnosed with dementia. "What's the prognosis?" he asked. "It will go slowly, it will go quickly, it will stay the same, or we don't know," he was told. It was much the same with the state of the world. It was a restless, unsettled period, without any single overwhelming catastrophe. People were fearful, but their fear was unfocused. We were holding our breath. We were carrying on. We were pretending things were normal. But whiffs of a change for the worse were already in the air.

Part Three gathers essays from 2014 to 2016. The run-up to the 2016 election in the United States was already beginning. At the same time, the television series of *The Handmaid's Tale* was in preparation—it would begin shooting in August 2016—and a miniseries of *Alias Grace,* about a nineteenth-century prisoner and possible murderess, was also being filmed.

Freedom and its opposites were thus much on my mind. Around this time I began work on *The Testaments,* the sequel to *The Handmaid's Tale* that would appear in 2019.

By the end of 2016, a zeitgeist change was surely upon us. With the election of Donald Trump as U.S. president, we had fully entered the strange land of post-truth—a land we would live in until 2020; though some, it appears, are determined to keep living in it.

Part Four begins in 2017, when America feared *The Handmaid's Tale* might not be fiction after all. The inauguration of President Trump was followed immediately by a massive international Women's March. This was a time of much hand-wringing and anguish in the United States: What next? How close to a rollback of women's rights were we? Was an authoritarian regime on the way? When the TV series of *The Handmaid's Tale* launched in April, it found an audience it didn't need to convince. In the same year, the *Alias Grace* miniseries was streamed. *Alias Grace* was how we'd been, *The Handmaid's Tale* was how we might be.

After hackers made a protracted attempt to steal the manuscript online—one of the more bizarre episodes in my writing life—*The Testaments* was published on September 10, 2019.

This period also saw the rise of the #MeToo movement. The overall effect of #MeToo was, I believe, positive, in that notice was given that Harvey Weinsteinish behaviour could no longer expect to pass unreproved. But the pros and cons of social media denunciations are still being debated, and the "culture wars" are ongoing. Against this background, I wrote about the need for truth, fact-checking, and fairness, as did the chroniclers of the Weinstein case, the Bill Cosby case, and many others.

These three years were difficult ones for Graeme and me. Graeme's condition worsened gradually through 2017 and 2018, then more precipitously through the first half of 2019. We knew we had only a limited time left together—months, not years. Graeme wished to depart while he was still himself, and he got his wish. A day and a half after the launch of *The Testaments* at the National Theatre in London, England, he had a massive cerebral hemorrhage, entered a coma, and died five days later.

Some may have been surprised that I carried on with the book tour for *The Testaments* after Graeme's death. But given a choice between hotel rooms and events and people on the one hand, and an empty house and a vacant chair on the other, which would you have chosen, Dear Reader? Of course the empty house and the vacant chair were simply postponed. They came my way later, as such things do.

Part Five begins in 2020. This was an election year in the United States, and a bizarre election year it was—compounded by COVID-19, which struck in earnest in March.

I was asked to write a number of COVID-related pieces—what was I doing all day, what were our prospects?

Totalitarianisms were preoccupying me; the worldwide drift in that direction was alarming, as were various authoritarian moves being made in the United States. Were we yet again witnessing the crumbling of a democracy?

In the fall of 2020, my poetry collection *Dearly* was published; I include one of the pieces I wrote about it. Graeme was much on my mind: it was a pleasure to write the foreword to his *Bedside Book of Birds* and the introduction to his last two novels, both of which were being reissued.

I end *Burning Questions* with pieces about two key conservationists—Barry Lopez and Rachel Carson—whose work, I predict, will become increasingly important as we on Planet Earth face an increasingly uncertain future. The inheritors of Lopez and Carson and the many other early voices who warned us about the growing climate crisis are the young generations of post-millennials whose best-known voice is Greta Thunberg. In the mid-twentieth century, when Rachel Carson was first published, it was convenient to deny, avoid, and postpone, but this is no longer possible. That is, if we want to remain a species on this planet.

The post-millennials will soon grow into positions of power. Let us hope they use their power wisely. And soon.

PART I

>><<

2004 TO 2009

WHAT WILL HAPPEN NEXT?

Scientific Romancing

>>><<<

(2004)

I'm very honoured to have been asked to give the Kesterton Lecture here at Carleton's School of Journalism and Communication.

I note that I'm the fourth in this series, and that I've been preceded by three very eminent men. I have always distrusted the number 4, whereas I do have a preference for the number 3. So I've broken the dubious 4 down into two sets: one of three, a lucky moonstruck set, which includes persons of the male persuasion but excludes me; and a second set of one, which includes persons of the female sort and also, incidentally, me. I am therefore the first in a set that I trust will number many more individuals before long.

That's the feminism for this evening, which, as you can see, I have cunningly combined with the initial fooling around so you won't feel too threatened by it. I've never known why people have some-times felt threatened by me. After all, I'm quite short, and apart from Napoleon, what short person has ever been threatening? Second, I'm an icon, as you've doubtless been told, and once you're an icon you're practically dead, and all you have to do is stand very still in parks, turning to bronze while pigeons and others perch on your shoulders and defecate on your head. Third, I am—astrologically speaking— a Scorpio, one of the kindest and gentlest of astrological signs. We like to lead quiet lives in the dark and peaceful toes of shoes, where we never give any trouble unless someone attempts to cram an aggressively large yellow-toenailed foot in on top of us. And so it is with me: no bother at all unless stepped on, in which case I can't answer for the consequences.

The title of my small talk tonight is "Scientific Romancing." Its cover story is that it's about science fiction. Its subtext is probably *What is fiction for?* or something like that. The subtext under that will be a few paragraphs on the two scientific romances I myself have written. And the sub-sub-subtext might turn out to be *What is a human being?* So this lecture is like those round candies you could once ruin your teeth on for two cents: sugar coating on the outside, with descending layers of various colours, until you come to an odd, indecipherable seed at the very centre.

First, I'll tackle the peculiar form of prose fiction often called "science fiction," a label that brings together two terms you'd think would be mutually exclusive, since *science*—from *scientia,* meaning "knowledge"—is supposed to concern itself with demonstrable facts, and *fiction*—which derives from a root verb meaning "to mould," as in clay—denotes a thing that is feigned or invented. With *science fiction,* one term is often thought to cancel out the other. The book is evaluated as something intended as a statement of truth, with the fiction part—the story, the invention—rendering it useless for any-one who really wants to get a grip on, say, nanotechnology. Or else it's treated the way W.C. Fields treated golf when he spoke of it as a good walk spoiled—that is, the book is seen as a narrative structure cluttered up with too much esoteric geek material when it should have stuck to describing the social and sexual interactions among Bob and Carol and Ted and Alice.

Jules Verne, a granddaddy of science fiction on the paternal side, and the author of such works as *Twenty Thousand Leagues Under the Sea,* was horrified by the liberties taken by H.G. Wells, who, unlike Verne, did not confine himself to machines that were within the realm of possibility—such as the submarine—but cre-ated other machines—such as the Time Machine—that were quite obviously not. "Il invente!" Jules Verne is said to have said, with vast disapproval.

Thus the node of this part of my talk—a node is sometimes a nasty thing you get on your vocal cords from giving too many lectures, but I use it here in its other sense, a point of intersection—its node is that curious locus where science and fiction meet. Where did this kind of stuff come from, and why do people write it and read it, and what's it good for anyway?

Before the term *science fiction* appeared, in America, in the 1930s, during the golden age of bug-eyed monsters and girls in diaphanous outfits, stories such as H.G. Wells's *The War of the Worlds* were called "scientific romances." In both terms—*scientific romance* and *science fiction*—the science element is a qualifier. The nouns are *romance* and *fiction,* and the word *fiction* covers a lot of ground.

We've fallen into the habit of calling all examples of long prose fiction "novels," and of judging them by standards developed for evaluating one particular kind of long prose fiction, namely the kind that treats of individuals embedded in a realistically described social milieu, and which emerged with the work of Daniel Defoe—who tried to pass it off as journalism—and that of Samuel Richardson and Fanny Burney and Jane Austen during the eighteenth and early nineteenth centuries, and which was then developed by George Eliot and Charles Dickens and Flaubert and Tolstoy, and many more, in the mid- and late nineteenth centuries.

This kind of work is found superior if it has "round" characters rather than "flat" ones, round ones being thought to have more psychological depth. Anything that doesn't fit this mode has been shoved into an area of lesser solemnity called "genre fiction," and it is here that the spy thriller and the crime story and the adventure story and the supernatural tale and the science fiction, however excellently written, must reside, sent to their rooms—as it were—for the misdemeanour of being enjoyable in what is considered a frivolous way. They invent, and we all know they invent, at least up to a point, and they are therefore not about Real Life, which ought to lack coincidences and weirdness and action/adventure—unless it is about war, of course—and they are therefore not solid.

The novel proper has always laid claim to a certain kind of truth— the truth about human nature, or how people really behave with all their clothes on except in the bedroom—that is, under observable social conditions. The "genres," it is thought, have other designs on us. They want to entertain, a bad and escapist thing, rather than just rubbing our noses in the daily grit produced by the daily grind. Unhappily for novelists, the larger reading public quite likes being entertained. There's a poverty-stricken writer in George Gissing's masterpiece, *New Grub Street,* who commits suicide after the failure of his slice-of-life realistic novel entitled *Mr. Bailey, Grocer*. *New Grub Street* came out at the height of the craze for such adventure-romance novelties as Rider Haggard's *She* and the scientific romances of H.G. Wells, and *Mr. Bailey, Grocer*—if it had been a real novel—would have had a thin time of it. If you think this can't happen now, take a look at the sales figures of *Life of Pi*—pure adventure-romance— and *The Da Vinci Code,* ditto, and the long-running vampiramas of Anne Rice.

The setting of the realistic novel proper is Middle Earth, and the middle of Middle Earth is the middle class, and the hero and heroine are usually the desirable norms, or could have been in—for instance—tragic versions such as Thomas Hardy, if Fate and society hadn't been so contrary. As publishers' readers say, "We *like* these people." Grotesque variations on the desirable norms appear, of course, but they take the form, not of evil talking clams or werewolves or space aliens, but of people with character defects or strange noses. Ideas about—for instance—novel and untried forms of social organization are introduced through conversations among the characters, or in the form of diary or reverie, rather than being dramatized, as in the utopia and the dystopia. The central characters are placed in social space by being given parents and relatives, however unsatisfactory or dead these may be at the outset of the story. These central characters don't just appear as fully grown adults, but are provided with a past, a history. This sort of fiction concerns itself with the conscious waking state, and if a man changes into an arthropod in such a book, he'll do so only in a nightmare.

But not all prose fictions are novels in this stick-to-realism sense of the word. A book can be a prose fiction without being a novel. *The Pilgrim's Progress,* although a prose narrative and a fiction, was not intended as a "novel"; when it was written, such things did not yet exist. It's a romance—a story about the adventures of a hero— coupled with an allegory—the stages of the Christian life. (It's also one of the precursors of science fiction, although not often recognized as such.) Here are some other prose-fiction forms that are not novels proper. The confession. The symposium. The Menippean satire, or anatomy. The utopia and its evil twin, the dystopia.

Nathaniel Hawthorne deliberately called some of his fictions "romances," to distinguish them from novels. What he might have been thinking of was the tendency of the romance to use a somewhat more obvious form of patterning than the novel was thought to do—the blond heroine versus her dark alter ego, for instance. The French have two words for short stories—*contes* and *nouvelles,* "tales" and "news"—and this is a useful distinction. The tale can be set anywhere, and can move into realms that are off limits for the novel—into the cellars and attics of the mind, where figures that can appear in novels only as dreams and fantasies take actual shape, and walk the earth. The news, however, is news of us; it's the daily news, as in "daily life." There can be car crashes and shipwrecks in the news, but there are not likely to be any Frankenstein monsters; not, that is, until someone in "daily life" actually manages to create one.

But there's more to the news than "the news." Fiction can bring us another kind of news; it can speak of what is past and passing, and also of what's to come. When you're writing about what's to come, you could be engaged in journalism of the dire-warning sort, which used to be known as prophecy and is sometimes termed agit-prop—elect that bastard, build that dam, drop that bomb, and all hell will break loose, or, in its milder form, tut-tut—but as a person who has all too often been asked, "How did you know?," I'd like to make it clear that I don't go in for prophecy, not as such. Nobody can predict the future. There are too many variables. In the nineteenth century, Tennyson wrote a poem called "Locksley Hall," which appeared to predict—among other things—the age of airplanes, and which contains the line, "For I dipt into the future, far as human eye could see"; but no one can really do that. You can, however, dip into the present, which contains the seeds of what might become the future. As William Gibson has said, the future is already with us, it's just unevenly distributed. So you can look at a lamb and make an educated guess, such as, "If nothing unexpected happens to it along the way, that lamb will most likely become (a) a sheep or (b) your dinner," probably excluding (c), a giant wool-covered monster that will crush New York.

If you're writing about the future and you aren't doing forecast journalism, you'll most likely be writing something people will call either science fiction or speculative fiction. I like to make a distinction between science fiction proper—for me, this label denotes books with things in them we can't yet do or begin to do, like going through a wormhole in space to another universe—and speculative fiction, which employs the means already more or less to hand, such as credit cards, and takes place on Planet Earth. But the terms are fluid. Some use *speculative fiction* as an umbrella covering science fiction and all its hybrid forms—science fiction fantasy, and so forth—and others choose the reverse.

Here are some of the things that these kinds of narratives can do that "novels" as usually defined cannot do:

- They can explore the consequences of new and proposed technologies in graphic ways, by showing them as fully operational.
- They can explore the nature and limits of what it means to be human in graphic ways, by pushing the envelope as far as it will go.
- They can explore the relationship of man to the universe, an exploration that often takes us in the direction of religion and can meld easily with mythology—again, an exploration that can happen within the conventions of realism only through conversations, reveries, and soliloquies.
- They can explore proposed changes in social organization, by showing what they might be like for those living within them if we actually did them. Thus, the utopia and the dystopia.
- They can explore the realms of the imagination by taking us boldly where no man has gone before. Thus, the spaceship; the inner space of *Fantastic Voyage;* the cyberspace trips of William Gibson; and *The Matrix*—this last, by the way, an adventure-romance with strong overtones of Christian allegory and thus more closely related to *The Pilgrim's Progress* than to *Pride and Prejudice.*

More than one commentator has mentioned that science fiction as a form is where theological narrative went after *Paradise Lost,* and this is undoubtedly true. Supernatural creatures with wings and burning bushes that speak are unlikely to be encountered in a novel about stockbrokers, unless the stockbrokers have been taking quite a few mind-altering substances, but they are not out of place on Planet X.

I myself have written two works of "science fiction" or, if you prefer, "speculative fiction": *The Handmaid's Tale* and *Oryx and Crake*. Although lumped together by commentators who have spotted those things they have in common—they are not "novels" in the Jane Austen sense, and both are set in the future—they are in fact dissimilar. *The Handmaid's Tale* is a classic dystopia, which takes at least part of its inspiration from George Orwell's *Nineteen Eighty-Four*— particularly the epilogue. In a BBC piece I did in June 2003 on the occasion of Orwell's centenary birthday, I said:

> Orwell has been accused of bitterness and pessimism—of leaving us with a vision of the future in which the individual has no chance, and where the brutal, totalitarian boot of the all-controlling Party will grind into the human face, for ever.
>
> But this view of Orwell is contradicted by the last chapter in the book, an essay on Newspeak—the doublethink language concocted by the regime. By expurgating all words that might be troublesome—"bad" is no longer permitted, but becomes "double-plus-ungood"—and by making other words mean the opposite of what they used to mean—the place where people get tortured is the Ministry of Love, the building where the past is destroyed is the Ministry of Information—the rulers of Airstrip One wish to make it literally impossible for people to think straight.
>
> However, the essay on Newspeak is written in standard English, in the third person, and in the past tense, which can only mean that the regime has fallen, and that language and individuality have survived. For whoever has written the essay on Newspeak, the world of *Nineteen Eighty-Four* is over. Thus, it's my view that Orwell had much more faith in the resilience of the human spirit than he's usually been given credit for.
>
> Orwell became a direct model for me much later in my life—in the real 1984, the year in which I began writing a somewhat different dystopia, *The Handmaid's Tale*.

The majority of dystopias have been written by men, and the point of view has been male. When women have appeared in them, they have been either sexless automatons or rebels who've defied the sex rules of the regime. They've acted as the temptresses of the male protagonists, however welcome this temptation may be to the men themselves: Julia of *Nineteen Eighty-Four;* Lenina, the camiknicker-wearing, orgy-porgy seducer of the Savage in *Brave New World;* I-330, the subversive femme fatale of Yevgeny Zamyatin's 1924 seminal classic, *We.* I wanted to try a dystopia from the female point of view—the world according to Julia, as it were. However, this does not make *The Handmaid's Tale* a "feminist dystopia," except insofar as giving a woman a voice and an inner life will always be considered "feminist" by those who think women ought not to have these things.

In other respects, the despotism I describe is the same as all real ones and most imagined ones. It has a small powerful group at the top that controls—or tries to control—everyone else, and it gets the lion's share of available goodies. The pigs in *Animal Farm* get the milk and the apples, the elite of *The Handmaid's Tale* get the fertile women. The force that opposes the tyranny in my book is one in which Orwell himself—despite his belief in the need for political organization to combat oppression—always put great store: ordinary human decency, of the kind he praised in his essay on Charles Dickens.

At the end of *The Handmaid's Tale,* there's a section that owes much to *Nineteen Eighty-Four.* It's the account of a symposium held several hundred years in the future, in which the repressive government described in the novel is now merely a subject for academic analysis. The parallels with Orwell's essay on Newspeak should be evident.

The Handmaid's Tale, then, is a dystopia. What about *Oryx and Crake?* I would argue that it is not a classic dystopia. Though it has dystopian elements, we don't really get an overview of the structure of the society in it; instead, we see its central characters living their lives within small corners of that society. What they can grasp of the rest of the world comes to them through television and the Internet, and is thus suspect, because edited.

I'd say instead that *Oryx and Crake* is an adventure-romance coupled with a Menippean satire, the literary form that deals in intellectual obsession. The Laputa or floating island portion of *Gulliver's Travels* is one of these. So are the Watson-Crick Institute chapters of *Oryx and Crake.* The fact that Laputa never did and never could exist—though Swift put his finger correctly on the advantage of air superiority—but that the Watson-Crick Institute is very close to being a reality doesn't have much to do with their functions within a literary form.

In *Oryx and Crake,* there are some people who have been designed, and they have been designed as an improvement on the current model: ourselves. Anyone who engages in such design—and designing people is very close to being something we can really do now—such a designer has to ask: How far can you go in the alteration department? What features are at the core of our being? What is it to be human? What a piece of work is man, and now that we ourselves can be the workmen, what bits shall we chop off?

Which brings me back to the node I mentioned earlier—the point of intersection between science and fiction. "Are you against science?" I am sometimes asked. What a curious question. Against science, as opposed to what, and in favour of what? Without that thing we call "science," a lot of us would be dead of smallpox, not to mention tuberculosis. I grew up among scientists; I know their ways. I almost became a scientist myself, and would have done so had I not been kidnapped by literature. Some of my best relatives are scientists. They are not all like Dr. Frankenstein.

But science, as I've said, is about knowledge. Fiction, on the other hand, is about feeling. Science as such is not a person, and does not have a system of morality built into it, any more than a toaster does. It is only a tool—a tool for actualizing what we desire and defending against what we fear—and like any other tool, it can be used for good or ill. You can build a house with a hammer, and you can use the same hammer to murder your neighbour. Human toolmakers always make tools that will help us get what we want, and what we want hasn't changed for thousands of years because, as far as we can tell, human nature hasn't changed either.

How do we know? We know if we consult the myths and stories.

They tell us how and what we feel, and how and what we feel determines what we want.

What do we want? Here's a partial list. We want the purse that will always be filled with gold. We want the Fountain of Youth. We want to fly. We want the table that will cover itself with delicious food whenever we say the word, and that will clean up afterwards. We want invisible servants we'll never have to pay. We want the seven-league boots so we can get places very quickly. We want the Cloak of Invisibility so we can snoop on other people without being seen. We want the weapon that will never miss, and that will destroy our enemies utterly. We want to punish injustice. We want power. We want excitement and adventure; we want safety and security. We want to be immortal. We want to have a large number of sexually attractive partners. We want those we love to love us in return, and to be loyal to us. We want cute, smart children who will treat us with the respect we deserve, and who will not smash up the car. We want to be surrounded by music, and by ravishing scents and attractive visual objects. We don't want to be too hot. We don't want to be too cold. We want to dance. We want to drink a lot without having a hangover. We want to speak with the animals. We want to be envied. We want to be as gods.

We want wisdom. We want hope. We want to be good. Therefore we sometimes tell ourselves stories that deal with the darker side of all our other wants.

An educational system that teaches us only about our tools—the how-to of them, their creation, their maintenance—and not about their function as facilitators of our desires, is, in essence, no more than a school of toaster repair. You can be the best toaster-repair person in the world, but you will cease to have a job if toast is no longer a desirable food item on the human breakfast menu. "The arts"—as we've come to term them—are not a frill. They are the heart of the matter, because they are about our hearts, and our technological inventiveness is generated by our emotions, not just by our minds. A society without the arts would have broken its mirror and cut out its heart. It would no longer be what we now recognize as human.

As William Blake noted long ago, the human imagination drives the world. At first it drove only the human world, which was once very small in comparison to the huge and powerful natural world around it. Now we're next door to being in control of everything except the weather. But it's still the human imagination, in all its diversity, that directs what we do. Literature is an uttering, or outer-ing, of the human imagination. It lets the shadowy forms of thought and feeling—Heaven, Hell, monsters, angels, and all—out into the light, where we can take a good look at them and perhaps come to a better understanding of who we are and what we want, and what the limits to those wants may be. Understanding the imagination is no longer a pastime or even a duty, but a necessity; because increasingly, if we can imagine it, we'll be able to do it.

Or we'll be able to try it, at least. We've always been good at letting cats out of bags and genies out of bottles and plagues out of Pandora's box. We just haven't been very good at putting them back in again. But we're children of narrative, every one of us. Perhaps what impels us forward, and, yes, gets us out of bed and downstairs to read the morning paper, is that simple question every writer of fiction and every journalist—you notice I make a distinction—has to deal with every writing hour. That question is:

What will happen next?

Frozen in Time

>>><<<

INTRODUCTION

(2004)

Frozen in Time by Owen Beattie and John Geiger is one of those books that, having once entered our imaginations, refuse to go away. It made a large impact, devoted as it was to the astonishing revelations made by Dr. Owen Beattie—including the high probability that lead poisoning had contributed to the annihilation of the 1845 Franklin expedition.

I read *Frozen in Time* when it first came out in 1987. I looked at the pictures in it. They gave me nightmares. I incorporated story and pictures as a subtext and extended metaphor in a short story called "The Age of Lead," published in a 1991 collection called *Wilderness Tips*. Then, some nine years later, during a boat trip in the Arctic, I met John Geiger, one of the book's authors. Not only had I read his book, he had read mine, and it had caused him to give further thought to lead as a factor in northern exploration and in unlucky nineteenth-century sea voyages in general.

Franklin, said Geiger, was the canary in the mine, although unrecognized as such at first: until the last years of the nineteenth century, crews on long voyages continued to be fatally sickened by the lead in tinned food. He has included the results of his researches in this expanded version of *Frozen in Time*. The nineteenth century, he said, was truly an "age of lead." Thus do life and art intertwine.

Back to the foreground. In the fall of 1984, a mesmerizing photograph grabbed attention in newspapers around the world. It showed a young man who looked neither fully dead nor entirely alive. He was dressed in archaic clothing and was surrounded by a casing of ice. The whites of his half-open eyes were tea-coloured. His forehead was dark blue. Despite the soothing and respectful adjectives applied to him by the authors of *Frozen in Time,* you would never have confused this man with a lad just drifting off to sleep. Instead, he looked like a blend of *Star Trek* extraterrestrial and B-movie victim-of-a-curse: not someone you'd want as your next-door neighbour, especially if the moon was full.

Every time we find the well-preserved body of someone who died long ago—an Egyptian mummy, a freeze-dried Incan sacrifice, a leathery Scandinavian bog-person, the famous ice-man of the European Alps—there's a similar fascination. Here is someone who has defied the general ashes-to-ashes, dust-to-dust rule, and who has remained recognizable as an individual human being long after most have turned to bone and earth. In the Middle Ages, unnatural results argued unnatural causes, and such a body would have been either revered as saintly or staked through the heart. In our age, try for rationality as we may, something of the horror classic lingers: the mummy walks, the vampire awakes. It's so difficult to believe that one who appears to be so nearly alive is not conscious of us. Surely—we feel—a being like this is a messenger. He has travelled through time, all the way from his age to our own, in order to tell us something we long to know.

The man in the sensational photograph was John Torrington, one of the first three to die during the doomed Franklin expedition of 1845. Its stated goal was to discover the Northwest Passage to the Orient and claim it for Britain; its actual result was the obliteration of all participants. Torrington had been buried in a carefully dug grave, deep in the permafrost on the shore of Beechey Island, Franklin's base during the expedition's first winter. Two others—John Hartnell and William Braine—were given adjacent graves. All three had been painstakingly exhumed by anthropologist Owen Beattie and his team, in an attempt to solve a long-standing mystery: Why had the Franklin expedition ended so disastrously?

Beattie's search for evidence of the rest of the Franklin expedition, his excavation of the three known graves, and his subsequent discoveries gave rise to a television documentary, and then—three years after the photograph first appeared—to *Frozen in Time.* That the story should generate such widespread interest 140 years after Franklin filled his freshwater barrels at Stromness in the Orkney Islands before sailing off to his mysterious fate was a tribute to the extraordinary staying powers of the Franklin legend.

For many years the mysteriousness of that fate was the chief drawing card. At first, Franklin's two ships, the ominously named *Terror* and *Erebus,* appeared to have vanished into nothingness. No trace could be found of them, even after the graves of Torrington, Hartnell, and Braine had been found. There is something unnerving about people who can't be located, dead or alive. They upset our sense of space—surely the missing ones have to be somewhere, but where? Among the ancient Greeks, the dead who had not been retrieved and given proper funeral ceremonies could not reach the Underworld; they lingered in the world of the living as restless ghosts. And so it is, still, with the disappeared: they haunt us. The Victorian age was especially prone to such hauntings, as witness Tennyson's *In Memoriam,* its most exemplary tribute to a man lost at sea.

Adding to the attraction of the Franklin story was the Arctic landscape that had subsumed leader, ships, and men. In the nineteenth century, very few Europeans—apart from whalers—had ever been to the Far North. It was one of those perilous regions attractive to a public still sensitive to the spirit of literary Romanticism—a place where a hero might defy the odds, suffer outrageously, and pit his larger-than-usual soul against overwhelming forces. This Arctic was dreary and lonesome and empty, like the windswept heaths and forbidding mountains favoured by aficionados of the Sublime. But the Arctic was also a potent Otherworld, imagined as a beautiful and alluring but potentially malign fairyland, a Snow Queen's realm complete with otherworldly light effects, glittering ice palaces, fabulous beasts—narwhals, polar bears, walruses—and gnome-like inhabitants dressed in exotic fur outfits. There are numerous drawings of the period that attest to this fascination with the locale. The Victorians were keen on fairies of all sorts; they painted them, wrote stories about them, and sometimes went so far as to believe in them. They knew the rules: going to an Otherworld was a great risk. You might be captured by non-human beings. You might be trapped. You might never get out.

Ever since Franklin's disappearance, each age has created a Franklin suitable to its needs. Prior to the expedition's departure there was someone we might call the "real" Franklin, or even the Ur-Franklin—a man viewed by his peers as perhaps not the crunchiest biscuit in the packet, but solid and experienced, even if some of that experience had been won by bad judgment (as witness the ill-fated Coppermine River voyage of 1819). This Franklin knew his own active career was drawing toward an end, and saw in the chance to discover the Northwest Passage the last possibility for enduring fame. Aging and plump, he was not exactly a dream vision of the Romantic hero.

Then there was Interim Franklin, the one that came into being once the first Franklin failed to return and people in England realized that something must have gone terribly wrong. This Franklin was neither dead nor alive, and the possibility that he might be either caused him to loom large in the minds of the British public. During this period he acquired the adjective *gallant,* as if he'd been engaged in a military exploit. Rewards were offered, search parties were sent out. Some of these men, too, did not return.

The next Franklin, one we might call Franklin Aloft, emerged after it became clear that Franklin and all his men had died. They had not just died, they had perished, and they had not just perished, they had perished miserably. But many Europeans had survived in the Arctic under equally dire conditions. Why had this particular group gone under, especially since the *Terror* and the *Erebus* had been the best-equipped ships of their age, offering the latest in technological advances?

A defeat of such magnitude called for denial of equal magnitude. Reports to the effect that several of Franklin's men had eaten several others were vigorously squelched; those bringing the reports—such as the intrepid John Rae, whose story was told in Kevin McGoogan's 2002 book, *Fatal Passage*—were lambasted in the press; and the Inuit who had seen the gruesome evidence were maligned as wicked savages. The effort to clear Franklin and all who sailed with him of any such charges was led by Lady Jane Franklin, whose social status hung in the balance: the widow of a hero is one thing, but the widow of a cannibal quite another. Due to Lady Jane's lobbying efforts, Franklin, in absentia, swelled to blimp-like size. He was credited—dubiously—with the discovery of the Northwest Passage, and was given a plaque in Westminster Abbey and an epitaph by Tennyson.

After such inflation, reaction was sure to follow. For a time in the second half of the twentieth century we were given Halfwit Franklin, a cluck so dumb he could barely tie his own shoelaces. Franklin was a victim of bad weather (the ice that usually melted in the summer had failed to do so, not in just one year, but in three); however, in the Halfwit Franklin reading, this counted for little. The expedition was framed as a pure example of European hubris in the face of Nature: Sir John was yet another of those Nanoodles of the North who came to grief because they wouldn't live by Indigenous rules and follow Indigenous advice—"Don't go there" being, on such occasions, Advice #1.

But the law of reputations is like a bungee cord: you plunge down, you bounce up, though to diminishing depths and heights each time. In 1983, Sten Nadolny published *The Discovery of Slowness,* a novel that gave us a thoughtful Franklin, not exactly a hero but an unusual talent, and certainly no villain. Rehabilitation was on the way.

Then came Owen Beattie's discoveries, and the description of them in *Frozen in Time.* It was now clear that Franklin was no arrogant idiot. Instead, he became a quintessentially twentieth-century victim: a victim of bad packaging. The tins of food aboard his ships had poisoned his men, weakening them and clouding their judgment. Tins were quite new in 1845, and these tins were sloppily sealed with lead, and the lead had leached into the food. But the symptoms of lead poisoning were not recognized at the time, being easily confused with those of scurvy. Franklin can hardly be blamed for negligence, and Beattie's revelations constituted exoneration of a kind for Franklin.

There was exoneration of two other kinds, as well. By going where Franklin's men had gone, Beattie's team was able to experience the physical conditions faced by the surviving members of Franklin's

crews. Even in summer, King William Island is one of the most difficult and desolate places on earth. No one could have done what
these men were attempting—an overland expedition to safety.
Weakened and addled as they were, they didn't have a hope. They
can't be blamed for not making it.

The third exoneration was perhaps—from the point of view of
historical justice—the most important. After a painstaking, finger-
numbing search, Beattie's team found human bones with knife
marks and skulls with no faces. John Rae and his Inuit witnesses, so
unjustly attacked for having said that the last members of the Franklin crew had been practising cannibalism, had been right after all. A
large part of the Franklin mystery had now been solved.

Another mystery has since arisen: Why has Franklin become such
a Canadian icon? As Geiger and Beattie report, Canadians weren't
much interested at first: Franklin was British, and the North was
far away, and Canadian audiences preferred oddities such as Tom
Thumb. But over the decades, Franklin has been adopted by Canadians as one of their own. For example, there were the folk songs, such
as the traditional and often-sung "Ballad of Sir John Franklin"—a
song not much remembered in England—and Stan Rogers's well-
known "Northwest Passage." Then there were the contributions of
writers. Gwendolyn MacEwen's radio drama, *Terror and Erebus,* was
first broadcast in the early 1960s; the poet Al Purdy was fascinated
by Franklin; the novelist and satirist Mordecai Richler considered
him an icon ripe for iconoclasm, and, in his novel *Solomon Gursky
Was Here,* added a stash of cross-dresser women's clothing to the
contents of Franklin's ships. What accounts for such appropriation?
Is it that we identify with well-meaning non-geniuses who get tragically messed up by bad weather and evil food suppliers? Perhaps. Or
perhaps it's because—as they say in china shops—if you break it, you
own it. Canada's north broke Franklin, a fact that appears to have
conferred an ownership title of sorts.

It's a pleasure to welcome *Frozen in Time* back to the bookshelves
in this revised and enlarged edition. I hesitate to call it a groundbreaking book, as a pun might be suspected, but groundbreaking
it has been. It has contributed greatly to our knowledge of a signal

event in the history of northern journeying. It also stands as a tribute to the enduring pull of the story—a story that has passed through all the forms a story may take. The Franklin saga has been mystery, surmise, rumour, legend, heroic adventure, and national iconography; and here, in *Frozen in Time,* it becomes a detective story, all the more gripping for being true.

From Eve to Dawn

>>><<<

(2004)

From Eve to Dawn is Marilyn French's enormous three-volume, sixteen-hundred-page history of women. It runs from pre-history until the present, and is global in scope: the first volume alone covers Peru, Egypt, Sumer, China, India, Mexico, Greece, and Rome, as well as religions from Judaism to Christianity and Islam. It examines not only actions and laws, but also the thinking behind them. It's sometimes annoying, in the same way that Fielding's *Amelia* is annoying—enough suffering!—and it's sometimes maddeningly reductionist; but it can't be dismissed. As a reference work it's invaluable: the bibliographies alone are worth the price. And as a warning about the appalling extremes of human behaviour and male weirdness, it's indispensable.

Especially now. There was a moment in the early 1990s when, it was believed, history was over and utopia had arrived, looking very much like a shopping mall, and "feminist issues" were supposed dead. But that moment was brief. Islamic and American right-wing fundamentalisms are on the rise, and one of the first aims of both is the suppression of women—their bodies, their minds, the results of their labours—women, it appears, do most of the work around this planet—and, last but not least, their wardrobes.

From Eve to Dawn has a point of view, one that will be familiar to the readers of French's best-selling 1977 novel, *The Women's Room*. "The people who oppressed women were men," French claims. "Not all men oppressed women, but most benefited (or thought they benefited) from this domination, and most contributed to it, if only by doing nothing to stop or ease it."

Women who read this book will do so with horror and growing anger: *From Eve to Dawn* is to Simone de Beauvoir's *The Second Sex* as wolf is to poodle. Men who read it may be put off by
the depiction of the collective male as brutal psychopath, or puzzled
by French's idea that men should "take responsibility for what their
sex has done." (How responsible can you be for Sumerian monarchs,
Egyptian pharaohs, or Napoleon Bonaparte?) However, no one will
be able to avoid the relentless piling up of detail and event—the
bizarre customs, the woman-hating legal structures, the gynecologi-
cal absurdities, the child abuse, the sanctioned violence, the sexual
outrages—millennium after millennium. How to explain them? Are
all men twisted? Are all women doomed? Is there hope? French is
ambivalent about the twisted part, but—being a peculiarly American kind of activist—she insists on the hope.

Her project started out as a sweeping television series. It would
have made riveting viewing. Think of the visuals—witch-burnings,
rapes, stonings-to-death, Jack the Ripper clones, bedizened courtesans, and martyrs from Joan of Arc to Rebecca Nurse. The television
series fell off the rails, but French kept on, writing and researching
with ferocious dedication, consulting hundreds of sources and dozens of specialists and scholars, although she was interrupted by a
battle with cancer that almost killed her. The whole thing took her
twenty years.

Her intention was to put together a narrative answer to a question
that had bothered her for a long time: How had men ended up with
all the power—specifically, with all the power over women? Had it
always been like that? If not, how was such power grasped and then
enforced? Nothing she had read had addressed this issue directly. In
most conventional histories, women simply aren't there. Or they're
there as footnotes. Their absence is like the shadowy corner in a
painting where there's something going on that you can't quite see.

French aimed to throw some light into that corner. Her first
volume—*Origins*—is the shortest. It starts with speculations about
the kind of egalitarian hunter-gatherer societies also described by
Jared Diamond in his classic *Guns, Germs, and Steel.* No society,
says French, has ever been a matriarchy—that is, a society in which
women are all-powerful and do dastardly things to men. But socie-

ties were once matrilineal: that is, children were thought to descend from the mother, not the father. Many have wondered why that state of affairs changed, but change it did; and as agriculture took over, and patriarchy set in, women and children came to be viewed as property—men's property, to be bought, sold, traded, stolen, or killed.

As psychologists have told us, the more you mistreat people, the more pressing your need to explain why your victims deserve their fate. A great deal has been written about the "natural" inferiority of women, much of it by the philosophers and religion-makers whose ideas underpin Western society. Much of this thinking was grounded in what French calls, with wondrous understatement, "men's insistent concern with female reproduction." Male self-esteem, it seemed, depended on men not being women. All the more necessary that women should be forced to be as "female" as possible, even when—especially when—the male-created definition of "female" included the power to pollute, seduce, and weaken men.

With the advent of larger kingdoms and complex and structured religions, the costumes and interior decoration got better, but things got worse for women. Priests—having arguably displaced priestesses—came up with decrees from the gods who had arguably replaced goddesses, and kings obliged with legal codes and penalties. There were conflicts between spiritual and temporal power brokers, but the main tendency of both was the same: men good, women bad, by definition. Some of French's information boggles the mind: the "horse sacrifice" of ancient India, for instance, during which the priests forced the raja's wife to copulate with a dead horse. The account of the creation of Islam is particularly fascinating: like Christianity, it was woman-friendly at the start, and supported and spread by women. But not for long.

The Masculine Mystique (Volume Two) is no more cheerful. Two kinds of feudalism are briskly dealt with: the European and the Japanese. Then it's on to the appropriations by Europeans of Africa, of Latin America, of North America, and thence to the American enslavement of Black people, with women at the bottom of the heap in all cases. You'd think the Enlightenment would have loosened things up, at least theoretically, but at the salons run by educated and intelligent women the philosophes were still debating—while hoovering up the refreshments—whether or not women had souls, or were just a kind of more advanced animal. In the eighteenth century, however, women were beginning to find their voices. Also they took to writing, a habit they have not yet given up.

Then came the French Revolution. At first, women as a caste were crushed by the Jacobins despite the key role they'd played in the aristocracy-toppling action. As far as the male revolutionaries were concerned, "Revolution was possible only if women were utterly excluded from power."

Liberty, equality, and fraternity did not include sorority. When Napoleon got control, "he reversed every right women had won." Yet after this point, says French, "women were never again silent." Having participated in the overthrow of the old order, they wanted a few rights of their own.

Infernos and Paradises is the third and longest volume. It takes us through the growing movement for the emancipation of women in the nineteenth and twentieth centuries, with the gains and reverses, the triumphs and the backlashes, played out against a background of imperialism, capitalism, and world wars. The Russian Revolution is particularly gripping—women were essential to its success—and particularly dispiriting as to the results. "Sexual freedom meant liberty for men and maternity for women," says French. "Wanting sex without responsibility, men charged women who rejected them with 'bourgeois prudery.' . . . To treat women as men's equals without reference to women's reproduction . . . is to place women in the impossible situation of being expected to do everything men do, and to reproduce society and maintain it, all at the same time and alone."

It's in the final three chapters that French comes into her home territory, the realm of her most personal knowledge and her deepest enthusiasms. "The History of Feminism," "The Political Is Personal, The Personal Is Political," and "The Future of Feminism" make up the promised "dawn" of the general title. These sections are thorough and thoughtful. In them, French covers the contemporary ground, including the views of anti-feminist and conservative women—who, she argues, see the world much as feminists do—one half of humanity acting as predators on the other half—but differ in the degree of their idealism or hope. (If gender differences are "natural," nothing to be done but to manipulate the morally inferior male with your feminine wiles, if any.) But almost all women, she believes—feminist or not—are "moving in the same direction along different paths."

Whether you share this optimism or not will depend on whether you believe the Earth *Titanic* is already sinking. A fair chance and a fun time on the dance floor for all would be nice, in theory. In practice, it may be a scramble for the lifeboats. But whatever you think of French's conclusions, the issues she raises cannot be ignored. Women, it seems, are not a footnote after all: they are the necessary centre around which the wheel of power revolves; or, seen another way, they are the broad base of the triangle that sustains a few oligarchs at the top. No history you will read, post-French, will ever look the same again.

Polonia

>>><<<

(2005)

What advice would I give the young? I have trouble answering this question. Here's why.

Just before Christmas I was in a cheese store, purchasing some cheese, when a very young man of—oh, say, between forty and fifty—entered, manifesting bewilderment. His wife had sent him out to get something called "meringue sugar," with strict instructions to buy no other kind, and he didn't know what the stuff was and couldn't find it, and nobody in any of the shops he'd so far wandered into had any idea either.

He didn't say this to me. He said it to the cheese shop person. She too appeared to be without a clue as to the meringue sugar mystery.

None of this was any concern of mine. I could have—should have—simply pursued my own personal goal of cheese acquisition. Instead, I found myself saying: "Don't buy icing sugar, that isn't what your wife wants. What she probably wants is something like fruit sugar or berry sugar, which is sometimes called powdered sugar but it isn't really powdered, it's a finer grind than ordinary white sugar, though you'll have a hard time finding it at this time of year. But really, ordinary white sugar works just fine for meringues as long as you beat it in very slowly, I use it all the time myself, and it helps if you add just a tiny bit of cream of tartar and maybe a half teaspoon of white vinegar, and . . ."

At this point my daughter—who'd succeeded in identifying the required cheese—got me in a hammerlock and dragged me over to the cash register, where a lineup was building. "The white vinegar, not the brown," I called in closing. But I was already appalled at myself. Why had I spewed out all this unasked-for advice to a complete stranger, albeit a helpless and confused one?

It's an age thing. There's a hormone in the brain that kicks in when you see a younger person in a state of shell shock over meringue sugar, or how to get the lids off jars or the beet stains out of tablecloths, or the right way of dumping the bad boyfriend who should be disposed of immediately because as anyone with half a wit can see the man is a psychopath, or which candidate is the best bet in the local election, or any number of other things on which you appear to yourself to have an overflowing fund of useful knowledge that may vanish from the planet unless you dish it out right and left, on the spot, to those in need. This hormone automatically takes over—like the hormone in a mother robin that forces her to cram worms and grubs down the gaping maws of plaintively cheeping nestlings—and reams of helpful hints unscroll out of your mouth like a runaway roll of toilet paper falling down the stairs. You have no way of stopping this process. It just happens.

It's been happening for centuries; no, for millennia. Ever since we developed what is loosely called human culture, the young have been on the receiving end of instruction from their elders whether they liked it or not. Where are the best roots and berries? How do you make an arrowhead? What fish are plentiful, where and when? Which mushrooms are poisonous? The instruction must have taken pleasant forms ("Great arrowhead! Now try it this way!") or unpleasant ones ("You idiot! That's no way to skin a mastodon! Do it like this!"). Since we've still got the same hardware as Cro-Magnon man, or so we're told, it's merely the details that have changed, not the process. (Hands up, everyone who's ever taped laundry instructions to the washer-dryer for the benefit of their teenage kids.)

There are mountains of self-help books testifying to the fact that the young—and not only the young—are fond of securing advice on every possible subject, from how to get rid of pimples, to the suave way of manoeuvring some youth with commitment issues into marriage, to the management of colic in infants, to the making of the perfect waffle, to the negotiation of an improved salary, to the purchase of a rewarding retirement property, to the planning of a really knockout funeral. The cookbook is one of the earliest forms of self-help book. Mrs. Beeton's enormous nineteenth-century tome, *The Book of Household Management,* expands the tradition, and includes not only recipes but advice on everything, from how to tell a real fainting fit from a sham one, to the proper colour choices for blondes and brunettes, to which topics of conversation are safe for afternoon visits. (Stay away from religious controversy. The weather is always acceptable.) Martha Stewart, Ann Landers, and Miss Manners are Mrs. Beeton's great-granddaughters, as is Mrs. Rombauer Becker of *Joy of Cooking* fame and every home handywoman, interior decorator, and sex expert you've ever watched on television. Look at the shows and read the books and authors quickly, in sequence, and you'll feel the need of some cotton wool to stuff in your ears as a defence against the endless stream of what would sound like relentless finger-waving, hectoring, and nagging if you hadn't chosen to let these folks in the door yourself.

With how-to books and self-help shows, you can absorb the advice if and when you want it, but relatives or friends or acquaintances or mothers cannot be so easily opened and then closed and put back on the shelf. Over the centuries, novels and plays have given us a stock character: the older female, or male—both versions exist—who's a voluble interfering busybody, deluging the young folk with unasked-for tips on how to conduct their lives, coupled with sharp-tongued criticisms when the advice is not heeded. Mrs. Rachel Lynde in *Anne of Green Gables* is a case in point. Sometimes this type of person will have a good heart—Mrs. Lynde does—although, just as often, he or she will be a sinister control freak like the Queen of the Night in Mozart's *The Magic Flute.* But good or bad, the meddlesome busybody is seldom entirely sympathetic. Why? Because we like other people—well-meaning or not—to mind their own business, not ours. Even helpful advice can be indistinguishable from bossiness when you're on the receiving end.

My own mother was of the non-interference school unless it was a matter of life and death. If we children were doing something truly dangerous and she knew about it, she would stop us. Otherwise she let us learn by experience. Less work for her, come to think about it, though there was of course the work of self-restraint. She later said that she had to leave the kitchen when I was making my first pie crust, the sight was so painful to her. I've come to appreciate these silences of my mother's, though she could always produce a condensed pill of sensible advice when asked for it. All the more puzzling, then, that I have taken to blurting out instructions to strangers in cheese stores. Perhaps I take after my father, who was relentlessly informative, though he always tempered the force of his utterances by beginning, "As I'm sure you know . . ."

I went to high school at a time when students were required to learn things off by heart. This work formed part of the exam: you were expected not only to recite the set pieces out loud but to regurgitate them onto the page, with marks off for faults in spelling. One standard item was the speech made in *Hamlet* by the old court counsellor, Polonius, to his son, Laertes, who is departing for a trip to France. Here's the speech, in case you may have forgotten it, as I found I had when I tried for total recall:

Yet here, Laertes! Aboard, aboard, for shame!
The wind sits in the shoulder of your sail,
And you are stay'd for. There—my blessing with thee!
And these few precepts in thy memory
Look thou character. Give thy thoughts no tongue,
Nor any unproportion'd thought his act.
Be thou familiar, but by no means vulgar:
Those friends thou hast, and their adoption tried,
Grapple them unto thy soul with hoops of steel;
But do not dull thy palm with entertainment
Of each new-hatch'd, unfledg'd comrade. Beware
Of entrance to a quarrel; but being in,
Bear't that the opposed may beware of thee.
Give every man thine ear, but few thy voice;
Take each man's censure, but reserve thy judgment.
Costly thy habit as thy purse can buy,
But not express'd in fancy; rich, not gaudy;
For the apparel oft proclaims the man,
And they in France of the best rank and station
Are most select and generous chief in that.

Neither a borrower nor a lender be;
For loan oft loses both itself and friend,
And borrowing dulls the edge of husbandry.
This above all—to thine own self be true,
And it must follow, as the night the day,
Thou canst not then be false to any man.
Farewell: my blessing season this in thee!

The method is aggressive—Polonius scolds Laertes because he isn't on the ship yet, then holds him back with a long list of dos and don'ts—but it's all very good advice. A rational person can't disagree with any of it. Yet in every performance of *Hamlet* I've ever seen, Polonius is played as a comical but tedious old pedant and Laertes listens to him with barely concealed impatience, although he himself has just dished out a heaping plateful of his own advice to his younger sister, Ophelia. Looked at objectively, Polonius can't really have been the boring idiot we're usually shown: he's chief adviser to Claudius, who's a villain but no fool. Claudius wouldn't have kept Polonius around if the latter had really been several bricks short of a load. Why then is the scene always played this way?

One reason is that it would be boring if done straight because advice you haven't asked for is always boring, and it's especially boring if the person giving the advice is old and you yourself are young. It's like the cartoon with the caption "What people say, what cats hear": over the head of the cat is a voice balloon with nothing in it. The advice to the cat may be perfectly good—"Don't mess with that big tomcat down the street"—but the cat isn't receptive. It will follow its own counsel because that's what cats do. And that's what young people do as well, unless there's something specific they want you to tell them.

Which is my way of ducking the question. What advice would I give the young? None, unless they asked for it. Or that's what would happen in an ideal world. In the world I actually inhabit, I break this virtuous rule daily, since at the slightest excuse I find myself blathering on about all kinds of things, due to the mother-robin hormone I've already mentioned. Thus:

As I'm sure you know, the most eco-friendly toilet is the Caroma.

You can state your position and stick to your guns without being rude. Awnings cut down on summer heat through your windows by 70 per cent or more. If you want to be a novelist, do back exercises daily—you'll need them later. Don't phone him, let him phone you. Think globally, act locally. After having a baby, you lose your brain and some of your hair, but they both grow back. A stitch in time saves nine. There's a new kind of crampon you can strap onto your boots, handy on icy sidewalks. Don't stick a fork into a wall socket. If you don't clean the lint trap on the dryer, it may burst into flames. If the hair on your arms stands up in a thunderstorm, jump. Don't step into a canoe when it's pulled up on the beach. Never let anyone pour you a drink in a bar. Sometimes the only way out is through. In the northern forest, hang your food from a tree some distance from your sleeping area and don't wear perfume. This above all, to thine own self be true. Eyebrow tweezers are handy for getting big wads of glop out of bathroom sink drains. Every household should contain a wind-up flashlight. And don't forget about the little touch of vinegar, for the meringues. That's the white vinegar, not the brown.

However, here's the best piece of advice of all: *Sometimes young people don't want advice from their elders.* They don't wish you to turn into Polonia, not as such. They can do without the main body of the speech—the long checklist of instructions. But they welcome the part at the end, which is a kind of benediction:

Farewell: my blessing season this in thee.

They want you to see them off on their voyage, which is—after all—a voyage they have to make on their own. Maybe it will be a dangerous voyage, maybe you'd be able to handle the danger better than they will, but you can't do it for them. You've got to stay behind, waving encouragingly, anxiously, a little plaintively: *Farewell! Fare well!*

But they do want the goodwill from you. They want the blessing.

Somebody's Daughter

>>><<<

(2005)

Few remember that to learn to read and write is one of the
great victories in life.

—BRYHER, *THE HEART TO ARTEMIS*

Akluniq ajuqsarniqangilaq: In times of scarcity, there is much
opportunity for innovative thinking.

—INUIT SAYING, FROM NUNAVUT, CANADA

Life has never been easy for the people of the Far North. For many
centuries they lived in one of the most unforgiving climates on earth:
no trees, no agriculture, extreme cold and darkness for many months
of the year. Using tools made of stone and bone, wearing clothing
made of skins, relying largely on fish and on the meat of seal, caribou,
polar bear, walrus, and whales, they had a culture finely tuned to their
environment. In this culture, men and women were interdependent:
hunters provided most of the food, but their clothing was made by
the women, and unless it was made very well the hunter could die: a
leaky *kamik* could mean a frozen foot. Each set of skills was known
to be necessary to the survival of all, and each was respected.

Then came the Europeans, and the gathering of a nomadic people
into settlements, and exposure to many of the more negative aspects
of "white" culture, including excessive drinking and violence toward
women; there was a break with traditional ways, and a sharp increase
in suicides. Children were forced into residential schools in an effort
to wrench them into the twentieth century, and two generations
have undergone extreme culture shock. One of the worst effects of

this has been the fracturing of families. In the old culture, sons were taught their hunting skills by fathers and uncles, daughters their sewing skills by mothers and aunts, but now many younger people are cultural orphans. There are still a number of elders—living treasures who remember the old ways.

Somebody's Daughter, a two-week camp that takes place in Nunavut in the Canadian Arctic, aims at a reconnection of the generations. It is run by Bernadette Dean, the social development coordinator for her district of Nunavut. Bernadette's Inuit name, Miqqusaaq—mica, or sparkling rock—describes her well: scintillating and clear but tough underneath. Like many who confront similar social problems, Bernadette knows that to improve the overall health of a community and its families you must improve the well-being and confidence of the women.

Somebody's Daughter is for women in their twenties, thirties, and forties who never had a chance to learn traditional Inuit sewing. Most of them have experienced tragedy, violence, or separation from their families. Bernadette explained the program's name to me: "Not everyone is a wife, not everyone is a mother, not everyone is a grandmother; but every woman is somebody's daughter." Immediately the participants are given a sense of belonging.

The "daughters" go out on the land with a group of elders and teachers. They live in tents, and make an article of clothing the old way, scraping, stretching, and softening the animal skin first, then cutting the pattern with a woman's curved knife or *ulu,* and sewing it with sinew—the best thread, as it expands in water and makes a garment watertight. It's hard to describe the joy that learning this skill can give.

But an improvement in literacy is also part of the plan because Nunavut exists in the same twenty-first century we all do. Computers and office jobs are now common, and for these and the money they can bring, literacy is needed. That is why two writers were invited to join the group: myself and children's writer Sheree Fitch, who had been there the two previous summers. We both felt very lucky to be involved.

But how to teach writing to women whose experience of it at school may well have been negative? Sheree told me that it could prove very difficult to get these women to set pen to paper: they might be shy, or afraid of writing; or they might not see the use of doing it at all.

The campsite this year was on the shore of Southampton Island, which is situated at the top of Hudson Bay and is as large as the land mass of Switzerland. It has one settlement, Coral Harbour, with less than a thousand people. It also has two hundred thousand caribou and a lively population of polar bears. We travelled from Coral Harbour to the site on a thirty-foot-long liner—a trip of sixty miles that took over five hours because of the high waves.

We set up our tents at a spectacular location—austere and beautiful, with the sea on one side and the land rising up behind us in a series of earlier shores. On the top ridge were some Dorset Culture dwellings many centuries old—rocks set into the ground in a circle, with a tunnel entrance and some fox traps and graves nearby. The ground at our site was smooth white limestone rocks, so our tents could not be pegged; instead their ropes were tied to boulders, a good plan in view of the eighty-mile-an-hour winds we soon experienced.

We had three expert hunters with us, to help with the site, to provide food, and to defend our camp. They immediately bagged a caribou, which was skinned and cut up; some of it became caribou stew, some was soon to be turned into mittens and kamiks; nothing would be wasted. We weren't the only hungry ones around, however: through the twilight came a healthy male polar bear, intent on dinner. The hunters chased it off on their Honda ATVs, then took turns standing guard all night—just as well because the bear came back four times. "Next time it's dinner," said one hunter. The bear must have heard him. "The elders tell us to be alert at all times," we were instructed.

The next day the women met with the elders and teachers in a round communal tent, where they received the skins they would work on. "What do you want to make?" they were asked by the elders, in Inuktitut. Then, "Who is it for?" (Sizes vary according to age, patterns according to gender.) This question—"Who is it for?"—gave Sheree and me a thread to follow. During our first writing session, we said that writing, like sewing, took one thing and made it into another; and that writing, like sewing, was always *for* someone, even if that someone was yourself in a future form. It was a way of putting your voice on paper and sending it—to someone you might know, or else to someone you might never meet, but who would be able to hear you anyway.

Then I explained that I was going to write a piece about the trip. Somebody's Daughter, I said, was part of a much larger movement—a movement to improve the lives of women all over the world. Some of these women—unlike themselves—might not even be able to write their own names yet. So for their first writing assignment, I would ask them to send a message to these other women. I would be their post-person. I said: I would deliver their message.

Every single woman wrote a message. Every message was positive and encouraging. Here is a sampling:

Whoever you are. I am a woman. I am proud of being me. You can be proud of who you are and be proud of yourself.

Don't ever think that we're nothing. But we the women are the most pretty inside and out because we are always helpful to our families and other people. Just think of yourself that you can do everything.

This message is coming from the North. To the women all over the world, take good care of yourself because you are the most needed in a family, you are a home to them so take good care of yourself. We women are all the same and we are as one.

Remember, everyone is created equally and that means if he cannot handle abuse neither should you, but please remember that we have to help and love our neighbours.

I'd love to teach when I learn more.

A message to the ladies in the world. Remember that you are loved very much and that you are not alone.

Please let your life be good and don't forget you're strong and a helper.

To all the women in the world from someone in the north—no matter what you look like you are very special. Always keep this in your mind.

And finally:

Learning begins when the learner feels safe and comfortable; provide an atmosphere of safety and comfort. And keep trying!

Writing messages of encouragement was in itself encouraging to the writers. The big round tent became a place of safety and comfort and healing for the women in it, and their writing also became—for most, I think—a place of safety and comfort and healing. In the tent, and also in the writing, the women laughed and joked and told stories, and also grieved: in this culture, grieving should be done—it is said—out loud, and with other people. Grieving in this way leads to healing, it is said.

Each of the women, with the help of her individual elder or teacher, completed the sewing project she had set out to do. Each continued to write—to expand her handling of the written word through daily journals, letters, and small poems. Confidence came through identity and achievement, and on the final day, at the suggestion of one of the women, the "daughters" wrote a communal poem, each of them contributing a line.

I'll use the last line of this poem to show how the sewing, the writing, and the healing all came together through this inspired program:

After I finished sewing the hard part of the kamik I feel like an eagle, so free and fly wherever I may go.

Five Visits to the Word-Hoard

>>><<<

(2005)

The title of my talk is in tribute to Robert Bringhurst's amazing book of his translations of the Haida poet Skaay—*Nine Visits to the Mythworld*—and also in tribute to the Anglo-Saxon poets far back in our literary tradition. The "word-hoard" was what they called their well of inspiration, which overlapped with the language itself; and "hoard" signified "treasure." A treasure is kept in a secret, guarded place, and words were seen as a mysterious treasure: they were to be valued. And so I hold them to be.

More simply, I'm talking about acts of writing—my own acts of writing, which are the only kind I can speak about—and how I've approached them over the years. This is an area I usually duck on chat shows. When people say, "How do you write?" I say, "With a pencil," or something equally terse. When they say, "*Why* do you write?" I say, "Why does the sun shine?" or, if I'm feeling crabby, I say, "People never ask dentists why they fool around inside other people's mouths."

Let me explain why I'm so evasive.

No, let me not explain why. Instead, I'll tell you a true story. As the creative writing teachers are always saying, "Show, don't state."

Here's the story: I have a friend who is a magician. He began in magic as a teenager, and did magic shows onstage, and from there went into radio, and then into television, and made a lot of money. But at heart he remains a magician, and he has invented many tricks and has contributed greatly to the literature of magic. Every year there's a magicians' congress in Toronto that revolves around him. Magicians come from far and near, and after the public part of the congress there's a party for the magicians. Sometimes non-magicians are there too. At this party you can hear the magicians talking to one another.

Among the magicians, things are the same as they are among the birdwatchers, or among the poets, or among the jazz musicians, or among the writers at a writers' festival, or among the members of any group of people who value an art, a craft, or a skill: that is to say, the usual social hierarchy—based on wealth or ancestry or company position or such—all of that dissolves, and individuals are valued by their peers according to their levels of accomplishment.

What are the magicians saying to one another? They're talking shop. Sometimes they'll split into pairs and trade secrets, one on one. The secrets they trade are trade secrets: they exchange tricks.

You've seen those TV programs in which magicians tell you How It Is Done. Those are immoral, as far as I'm concerned, because people go to magic shows to be dazzled and fooled and amazed— just as they read novels to enter into another world, and to be convinced that everything in that novel is real, at least within the covers of the book. People don't want to know How It Is Done about magic because that spoils the illusion. There's sometimes a smart kid in the audience who says, "I know how you did that!" And maybe, when we think about it, we do know. (Though not often, in my case.) But here's the point: even if we know, or think we know, *we can't do it ourselves.*

There's knowing what and there's knowing how, and the how comes from years of practice, and failure, and dropping the egg that was supposed to come out of the hat, and crumpling up Chapter One for the twentieth time and throwing it into the wastepaper basket. Robert Louis Stevenson burned three finished novels before he magically produced *Treasure Island.* Those incinerated novels were the three eggs he dropped. But the three broken eggs did not go to waste, for by dropping them he learned how to make the next egg appear out of what seemed like thin air.

Sometimes that never happens, of course. There's nothing inevitable about it. You can work away for years, but—alas, and to return to the metaphor of the magician—either you've got the hands or you don't, and if you don't have the hands you'll never rise above the level of the merely competent. Sometimes it's just one uncooked omelette after another.

But also: you may have the hands—the talent—but not the motivation. In that case, you'll abandon your art quite soon because you won't be prepared to put in the work—the work of the craft. I was once given a wonderful breakfast at a small Irish inn. When complimented, the man who ran the place said he'd worked as a chef, at a restaurant that had now gone downhill. By coincidence, we'd eaten supper there the night before. I said that the meal had been very good.

"Ah yes," he said. "Anyone can cook a good meal . . . once."

We've all encountered those first novels that shine with the freshness of dew, and the second novels that wilt, and even the third novels that cause their author to rise from the grave. Then there's the fourth novel, and the fifth, and the sixth—these are the ones that separate the sprinters from the marathoners. But art is cruel, and there's nothing necessarily more virtuous about a wondrous sixth novel—more virtuous, that is, than a wondrous first novel. It may demonstrate character and perseverance in the practitioner—his or her ability to look in the mirror and say, "Why am I doing this?" and to keep on writing anyway—but that's all it demonstrates. As with magic, an unforgettable performance is an unforgettable performance, whether or not it's ever followed by another.

Dylan Thomas has a poem that begins, "In my craft or sullen art." He names both art and craft: art, which requires some talent to begin with, which is why I will never be, and could never have been, an opera singer; and craft, which requires that the talent be honed and polished by focused discipline, which is why some people with marvellous voices will never become opera singers either.

Here is Robertson Davies, in his novel *Fifth Business*. The character is a young boy who's enamoured of magic—the conjuring kind—and longs to be able to do it. But he is clumsy, whereas Paul, the much smaller boy watching him practise his tricks, is not.

I cannot guess now how many weeks I worked on the sleight-of-hand pass called The Spider. . . . [J]ust try to do it! Try it with red, knuckly Scots hands, stiffened by grass-cutting and snow-shovelling, and see what skill you develop! Of course Paul wanted to know what I was doing, and, being a teacher at heart, I told him.

"Like this?" he asked, taking the coin from me and performing the pass perfectly.

I was stunned and humiliated, but, looking back on it now, I think I behaved pretty well.

"Yes, like that," I said. . . . He could do anything with his hands. . . .

There was no sense in envying him; he had the hands and I had not, and although there were times when I considered killing him, just to rid the world of a precocious nuisance, I could not overlook that fact.

It's much the same for any art—you need the hands. But you need more than the hands too. Here is Alice Munro, in a short story called "Cortes Island":

—it seemed that I had to be a writer as well as a reader. I bought a school notebook and tried to write—did write, pages that started off authoritatively and then went dry, so that I had to tear them out and twist them up in hard punishment and put them in the garbage can. I did this over and over again until I had only the notebook cover left. Then I bought another notebook and started the whole process once more. The same cycle—excitement and despair, excitement and despair. It was like having a secret pregnancy and miscarriage every week.

Not entirely secret, either. Chess knew that I read a lot and that I was trying to write. He didn't discourage it at all. He thought that it was something reasonable that I might quite possibly learn to do. It would take hard practice but could be mastered, like bridge or tennis. This generous faith I did not thank him for. It just added to the farce of my disasters.

The narrator and her husband, Chess, are both right: you can work at a thing, and you can learn it. But only up to a point. Beyond that comes the talent, which is a given. It's there or it isn't there, in varying quantities, and it can't be predicted or demanded, and it is not reasonable and predictable, and it can be with you at one point in your life and then vanish. Practising a craft can awaken a dormant talent. Conversely, too much practising can kill it. Such matters are incalculable, and much depends on coincidence and luck.

Much also depends on teachers, for all writers have teachers. Sometimes they are living people—writers or not—and sometimes—more often—they are dead writers, or writers known to the aspiring young person only through their books. Often, when they think back over their lives, writers can remember the exact book they were reading—the exact moment—when their talent was first called into life. Quite often this happens in youth. But not always, because every life is different, every book is different, and every future is unpredictable.

So what can I tell you that will be of any use to you, if you want to write or are already doing so? Read a lot. Write a lot. Watch and listen and work and wait.

Apart from that, I can't tell you what to do. I can only tell you a little about what I myself have done. So now I'm going to describe to you five of my visits to the word-hoard. I won't tell you too much about the dropped eggs. You'll have to trust me on this: sometimes there was egg from wall to wall.

My first novel to be published was not the first to be written. That one has never seen the light of day, which is just as well. It was quite a dark book, not to say a lugubrious one, and it ended with the heroine wondering whether or not to push the male protagonist off a roof. I was twenty-three when I wrote it, and living in a rooming house—the room cost about seventy dollars a month—and cooking my dinners on a one-ring hotplate. They had plastic packages that you could boil, then, and that is what I did. The rest of the food I kept in a bureau drawer. The bathroom was shared with others, and it was there also that you had to wash the dishes, which gave rise to the odd frozen pea or noodle in the bathtub. I had a day job—that was how I paid for the room in the rooming house. I had a typewriter at the day job, and I could do the job itself in half the time I was at work, so after I'd finished what was required of me I would just roll my novel into the typewriter and type away at it. This gave me a pleasingly industrious look.

When I had finished this novel I sent it out to publishers, such as they were in Canada in those times. Several of them expressed interest. One publisher indeed took me out for a drink, at the top of the Hotel Vancouver. He suggested that maybe I might change the ending to something a bit more cheerful. I said no, I didn't think I could do that. He leaned across the table and patted my hand. "Is there anything we can *do*?" he said, as if I had some kind of lingering disease.

That was Visit One. Here comes Visit Two.

My day job while I was writing the first, unsuccessful novel was with a market-research company of considerable eccentricity, and it was this material—material, just as in sewing, is anything you use to make the thing you are making—it was this market-research office material that got into the next novel. By this time I had a different job: I was in British Columbia, filling a university teaching job on the lowest rung of the ladder. I taught a survey course—from Chaucer to T.S. Eliot in tiny bite-sized chunks—and I also taught grammar to engineering students at 8:30 in the morning in a Quonset hut left over from the Second World War. The baby boom was hitting the universities then—it was 1964–1965—and there was a shortage of space. I made the engineers do writing exercises based on Kafka's short parables, which was good for them, I felt, since I was sure it would be of use in their future careers.

Meanwhile, I continued with my secret life, which was the life of a writer. Like vampires, I had to pursue this life at night. I had a real sink of my own now in which to put the dishes. Like many young people, I would use every dish until they were all dirty and the first ones to be put into the sink were sprouting mould. (Vancouver is a damp place.) Then I would wash them all at once, in a burst of energy and desperation. There's not much about Kraft Dinner with hot dogs cut up into it that I don't know. The rest of the time I ate at Smitty's Pancake Houses, especially on mornings when I did not have to be in the Quonset hut with the engineers. Sometimes, in a spurt of reckless hedonism, I went skiing.

I began my second novel in the spring of 1965. I wrote each chapter in handwriting, in empty exam booklets left over from my teaching duties. These booklets were a convenient size—a sort of chapter size. I sat at a card table to do this writing, beside a window that looked out over the harbour and the mountains—it isn't always a good thing for a writer to have a lovely view, it can be distracting. If the writing came to a halt or I couldn't get started, I might go to the movies. Luckily I had no television set—indeed I had hardly any furniture at all. I didn't see the point of it in those days—furniture was a thing parents had—and anyway I couldn't afford it.

I wrote on the right-hand pages, and on the left-hand pages I drew little pictures, when I wanted to visualize more completely what one of the characters was wearing. Or I would make notes there. Then I would type the handwritten pages, an act complicated by the fact that I couldn't really type. (I used a typist for the final versions of novels until the personal computer became available. The last book I wrote in the old way was *The Handmaid's Tale,* in 1985.)

Using these imperfect methods, I cranked out my novel in roughly six months. A helpful hint: It's easier to go without sleep when you're younger. Then I sent off the typist's version to a publisher that had shown interest in the earlier one. (We didn't have agents in Canada then; now you'd have to go through an agent, no doubt, as there are a great many more people writing, and the publishers use the agents as a kind of sieve.) The publisher accepted the book, somewhat to my surprise. But then I didn't hear anything more about it for quite a few months.

By then I was back at Harvard studying for my Ph.D. orals. (I knew I would have to support my writing somehow, financially, and university teachers were in short supply then. I thought it would be better than waitressing, which I'd already tried, and also better than the few other things I might have been able to do. Note that I'd been turned down by the Bell Telephone Company, and also by both of the publishers who subsequently became mine. All were quite right to reject me: I wasn't cut out for the jobs they were offering.)

Once I'd passed my orals, I went in search of my vanished novel. Turned out the publishers had misplaced it. But they found it again, and I did a revision in yet another location: Montreal, in 1967–1968, while teaching both day and evening classes in Victorian and American Romantic literature there. It was published, in the fall of 1969—just in time for some, though not for others, to hail it as a product of the newly forged women's movement. It wasn't, of course. Its composition predated the en masse advent of this movement by four years. But it did sort of fit in, since it ends with . . . but then, you should never tell the ending.

By this time I'd moved again, to a place where the women's movement had not even been heard of—Edmonton, Alberta. It was there that I did my first-ever book signing, in the men's sock and underwear department of the Hudson's Bay Company. I sat at a table near the escalator with my little pile of books, with a sign proclaiming the title: *The Edible Woman.* This title frightened a lot of men—ranchers and oil tycoons, I like to think they were—who had wandered in at noon hour to buy their jockey shorts. They fled in droves. I sold two copies.

This was not my vision of the writing life. Proust never had to flog his books in a women's lingerie department, I reflected. I did wonder whether or not I had taken a wrong turn on my career path. Perhaps it was not too late to go into insurance, or real estate, or almost anything other than writing. But then, as Samuel Beckett said when he was asked why he'd become a writer, "Not good for anything else."

The third novel-writing experience I'll describe is somewhat more complex. We are now in the year 1994, and I have become a grown-up, at least to outward appearances. In spring, while on a book tour in Europe, in Zurich, city of Jung, and while staying in a hotel with a view out over the water—always so conducive to controlled hallucinations, I have found—I began writing the first chapter of a book. I hadn't intended to start a book right then, but the choice of starting time never seems to be under a writer's control. Another helpful hint: If you keep waiting for the perfect circumstances before you begin, you'll probably never begin.

As often before, I'd been trying to write another, quite different book just before this. But I found myself in the book that was eventually to become the 1996 novel, *Alias Grace.* By this time, I had evolved the following working method: I would write by hand for ten or fifteen pages. Then I would spend half the day typing up those pages, while continuing to advance, in handwriting, at what you could think of as the front lines of the book. It was a sort of rolling barrage technique. That way I could keep in mind where I had just been, while covering more new ground at the same time.

When I was about a hundred pages into the book—our family was spending some writing time in France, in the fall—I realized that I had started it wrong. This happened on the train to Paris, where I was going to do some promotion for an earlier book. I was keeping a journal at the time, and here is what I wrote:

> I had a sort of electrical storm in my brain—it came to me on the train that the novel was not working—but after two days of (here there is a drawing of clouds and lightning) I think I have the solution—it means throwing out some characters and stuff and rearranging, but it's the only way, I think—the problem is and always has been—what is the connection between A and B?

Looking at these notes now, I can't remember exactly what A and B were. I think I was trying one of those in-the-present, in-the-past structures—and I threw out the present timeline and got right into the past, which was a lot more interesting and peculiar, since *Alias Grace* is based on a real-life double murder that took place in 1843. (How I came to know about this murder is another story.) I also changed the person in which the book was written from the third to the first, and here is another helpful hint: If you're blocked, try changing the tense or the person. Frequently this will work. Also: If you have a really bad headache, go to sleep. Often you will have an answer in the morning.

By April 4, 1995, I had 177 pages of *Alias Grace*. By September 1995, I had 395 pages. You can see I was chugging along, rewriting as I went. I submitted the book to the publishers in January 1996, at which point I went to Ireland and became ill. This often happens when you finish an intense stretch of work of any kind: the body has wanted a rest for some time, and you haven't given it one, so it waits patiently until there's some breathing space, and then it takes revenge.

Back to methods. As a rule I start out writing slowly, feeling my way into the cave, if you like. Then I gather speed and increase the hours until by the end I'm writing for eight hours a day and can barely walk without bending over, and can no longer see straight. I don't recommend any of this. I think everyone should instead take up championship swimming, or speed skating, or ballroom dancing. It's much better for your health than writing is. The last thing I ever wanted was to be a role model, so don't take anything I've said about my own methods as an example to be followed.

The fourth book I'll talk about is *The Blind Assassin,* which was published in the year 2000. I set out with a sort of vision, induced probably by the family photograph albums—I was intending to write about my grandmother and my mother—both of their generations, which together would span the twentieth century—but my actual grandmother and mother were far too nice to be put into a book by me. So I started writing about a more problematic old lady who was dead, and who'd had a secret second life that was being discovered by a still-living character through some letters found in a hatbox. That didn't work, so I threw out the hatbox and the letters but kept the secret life.

Next I was writing about the same old lady, but now she was still alive. She was being discovered by two other characters—nosy people, they were—and there was a container in this book too: it was a suitcase, and inside it there was a photograph album. But this didn't work either—the two other characters started having an affair, and the man was married and had just had twins, so you can see that the affair was going to take over the book and eclipse the old lady, who was the one I really wanted to write about. So into a drawer went the adulterous pair, and away went the suitcase—though I kept one of the photos.

At last the old lady began to speak for herself, and then the book could go forward. This third version had a container in it as well—it was a steamer trunk, and inside it were all the things you will find inside it to this very day, in the chapter called "The Steamer Trunk."

I'm aware that the way I told this story makes it sound a lot like "Goldilocks and the Three Bears," but there's something to that. You have to keep trying one chair after another until you find the just-right chair—the one that fits—and hope that not too many bears will come out of the woods while you're doing it.

The fifth visit to the word-hoard took place in the summer of 2005, resulting in a book that is part of the Myths series, which has a dozen writers and thirty-four publishers around the world involved in it. The idea was to take a myth—any myth—and retell it in a peppy, relevant book of a hundred pages or so. This is a darn sight harder to do than you think, as I soon found out.

I did give it a try. I tried it this way and that, with no results. I couldn't seem to get the kite to fly. As every writer knows, a plot is only a plot, and a plot as such is two-dimensional unless it can be made to come alive, and it can only come alive through the characters in it; and in order to make the characters live, there must be some blood in the mix. I won't sadden myself by detailing my failed attempts. Let's just say there were so many of them that I was on the point of giving the thing up altogether.

Desperation being the mother of invention, I eventually started writing *The Penelopiad.* Don't ask me why because I don't know. Let's just say that the hanging of the twelve "maids"—slaves, really—at the end of *The Odyssey* seemed to me unfair at first reading, and seems so still. They were all hanged from the same rope, how frugal; as *The Odyssey* says, their feet twitched a little, but not for long. So although Penelope herself, wife of Odysseus, is the main narrator of *The Penelopiad,* the second narrator is the Maids. They keep interrupting: like the chorus in a Greek tragedy, they comment on the main action, and act as a counterpoint to it. Sometimes they do this in popular song. I'm afraid I have called them The Chorus Line.

Now I've said enough about the way I write. Or about the way I've written so far. It can all change. It can all stop. The blank page is always pure potential, for everyone, me included. Every time you begin, it's just as frightening, and just as much of a risk.

I'll close by telling you another true story. I was in a café the other day, getting some takeout coffee. Quite a few people now recognize me, especially since I let myself be talked into impersonating a goalie on the comedian Rick Mercer's show, and a man working in the café did too. He was from the Philippines, he told me. "You're the author," he said. "Is it a talent?" "Yes," I said. "But then you have to work very hard."

"And you must have the passion, as well," he said.

"Yes," I said. "You must have the passion. You must have all three things: the talent, the hard work, and the passion. If you have only two, you won't do so well."

"I think it's like that with everything," he said.

"Yes," I said. "I think it is."

"Good luck," he said.

"Good luck to you too," I said.

And now that I think of it, that's the other thing we all need. We need luck.

The Echo Maker

>>><<<

(2006)

The Echo Maker is Richard Powers's ninth novel. His first, the
acclaimed *Three Farmers on Their Way to a Dance,* came out in
1985. In the twenty-one years since then, Powers has been a vol-
cano of activity, producing works as varied as *Prisoner's Dilemma,
Galatea 2.2, The Gold Bug Variations, Plowing the Dark, Gain,* and
The Time of Our Singing. He's been nominated three times for the
National Book Critics Circle Award, and has received both of the
"Genius" prizes—a MacArthur Fellowship and a Lannan Liter-
ary Award. As I am writing this, he has just been nominated for a
National Book Award, for the very book I am now reviewing.

That sort of thing puts a critic on notice, and indeed Powers has
gathered critical comments that most writers would kill their gran-
nies for. "Powers is a writer of blistering intellect," said the *Los Angeles Times Book Review.* "He only has to think of a subject and the
paint curls off. He is a novelist of ideas and a novelist of witness, and
in that respect he has few American peers." There's more in that vein,
and more, and more.

So, if he's so good, why isn't he better known? Let me put it
another way—why haven't his books won more medals? It's as
if juries have recognized the prodigious talent, the impressive
achievement, and have put him onto short lists, but then have
drawn back, as if they've suddenly felt that maybe they might be
giving an award to somebody not quite human—to Mr. Spock of
Star Trek, for instance. He's got a Vulcan mind-meld on the critics, all right, but could it be that he's just not cozy enough at the

core—that he's too challenging, or daunting, or—dread word—too bleak?*

On the other hand, there are books you read once and there are other books you read more than once because they are so flavourful, and then there are yet other books that you *have* to read more than once. Powers is in the third category: the second time through is necessary to pick up all the hidden treasure-hunt clues you might have missed on your first gallop through the plot. You do gallop, because Powers can plot. Of some books you don't ask, *How will it all turn out?* since that isn't the point. It's certainly part of the point with Powers. Only part, however.

If Powers were an American writer of the nineteenth century, which writer would he be? He'd probably be the Herman Melville of *Moby-Dick.* His picture is that big. *Moby-Dick* sank like a stone when it first came out: it had to wait almost a century before its true importance was recognized. Given Powers's previous interest in devices like time capsules, I'd hazard that he has the long view in mind: open him up in a hundred years and there, laid out before you in novel after novel, will be the preoccupations and obsessions and speech patterns and jokes and gruesome mistakes and eating habits and illusions and stupidities and loves and hates and guilts of his own time. All novels are time capsules, but Powers's novels are larger and more inclusive time capsules than most.

I doubt that Richard Powers will have to wait a hundred years, however. American literature students will be into him with their picks and shovels before long. He's the stuff of a thousand Ph.D. theses, or I'll be the Wizard of Oz.

But more of the Wizard of Oz later.

The Echo Maker is probably the best Powers novel so far. I say "probably" because it's not possible for Powers to write an uninteresting book, and after that it's a matter of taste. Trying to describe it is a bit like four blind men trying to describe an elephant—which end do you start at, with something so large and multi-limbed?

---

*Although he did win the Pulitzer Prize for Fiction in 2019 for his twelfth novel, *The Overstory.*

Of his 2000 novel, *Plowing the Dark,* Powers—when asked to sum up its subject—said, "It's about a disillusioned woman artist conscripted to work on a virtual reality project, an American hostage held in solitary confinement in Lebanon for four years, and the empty white room where they meet. It's about whether the imagination is powerful enough to save ourselves from its power." Disillusion, virtual reality, solitude, imagination, power—all keys to the world of Powers. Also typical is the way Powers jams wildly disparate elements together in a kind of atomic-bomb manner—what he wants is fission, then fusion, and a big bang at the end.

The wildly disparate elements in *The Echo Maker* are the endangered sandhill cranes—known to Indigenous people as "the echo makers" because of their sonorous calls—and their migratory stopover on the Platte River in flat, flat, flat Nebraska; and Mark Schluter, a sweet do-nuthin' of a young man who's had a spectacular and mysterious skid-and-flip accident while driving at night through this same bird-haunted territory, and who's incurred a brain trauma that's given him a case of Capgras syndrome. The illness makes the sufferer think that his nearest and dearest have been spirited away and replaced with cunning facsimiles of themselves. Mark thus becomes a sort of echo maker. He thinks, for instance, that his house, "The HomeStar," and his dog, Blacky, have been taken somewhere else, and that a fake HomeStar and a fake Blacky exist in their places, exact in every detail but fake nonetheless. (It's hard on the dog.)

Add to this the three sets of tire tracks at the scene of the accident—who else was there, what made Mark brake and crash?—and a note on Mark's hospital bedside table that no one will admit to having written, and that reads:

I am No One
but Tonight on North Line Road
GOD led me to you
so You could Live
and bring back someone else.

The five lines of this note provide the titles for the five sections of the book.

Everything and everyone else in the novel is tied to this set of factors. Karin Schluter, Mark's loving sister and his only next of kin—their two child-walloping, religious-fanatic parents having died—arrives to take care of Mark and is promptly denounced by him as an imposter. Dr. Weber, an Oliver Sacks–like neuroscientist and famous author of popular brain-oddity books, is lured to Mark's bedside by Karin in the desperate hope that he can work some sort of neuromancy and bring Mark back to her. There he encounters Barbara, a hospital aide who's been attending to Mark. She is a stranger to the grungy town of Kearney, Nebraska, who appears to be working below her level of competence. She is the one person Mark unequivocally trusts, although he calls her "Barbie Doll," thus adding her to the growing roster of replicants.

Then there's Mark's perky girlfriend, Bonnie, whose day job is impersonating a pioneer woman, in pretend costume and all. "Nobody's quite what they say they are," Mark muses about Bonnie, "and he's just supposed to laugh and play along." Mark's observation about Bonnie—about the disjunction between the front she presents and the hard-to-grasp reality behind it—is true on some level about everyone else in the novel.

As for the sandhill cranes, they're the hub of another spiral nebula of plot. Both of Karin's former boyfriends are connected with them. The ascetic Daniel, a boyhood friend of Mark's, is a conservation worker dedicated to preserving the cranes' traditional habitat. Robert Karsh is a sexy developer and con man who wants to exploit them by putting up an expensive facility for crane tourists—in reality, a covert land grab that will lead to the cranes' destruction.

Karin has hauled her way up and out of Kearney by her fingernails, job by job, and has now been sucked back into its deadening orbit through no fault of her own, only to find that the love with which she hopes to save her brother from Capgras is ineffective. In despair, she teams up again with both men, cheating on the meek, worthy, but wet-blanket Daniel as she has in the past, disporting herself during illicit trysts with the charming but polygamous Robert, whose appeal is—or appears to be—that he offers no illusions. (Daniel has angered her by ogling a waitress, then denying it. "Love was not the antidote to Capgras," she reflects. "Love was a form of it, making and denying others, at random.") The reader cannot judge her too harshly for her two-timing, though she beats herself up about it quite a bit: the poor girl is sorely in need of comfort, and it's any dork in a storm.

Who left the mysterious note, which Mark views as both a curse and a set of instructions? Why has his life been saved, who is he supposed to "bring back"? Who was driving the other two cars, the ones that left those tire tracks? What white object—bird, ghost, human being—did Mark see that night on the road, causing him to swerve to avoid hitting it and thus total his truck? Will Mark ever get his true self back?

On another level: What do we mean by "his true self"? Dr. Weber can (and does) provide some thinking on that subject—none of it very reassuring because who wants to be reduced to a set of electro-chemical connections in a lump of corrugated grey tissue? In the face of his bombardment of expertise, you do feel a little like Dr. Johnson, who claimed he could refute Berkeley's arguments about the non-existence of phenomena by kicking a stone. It doesn't perk us up to be told, as a gloss on the phantom limb phenomenon, "Even the intact body was itself phantom, rigged up by neurons as a ready scaffold. The body was the only home we had, and even it was more a postcard than a place."

Even apart from his discouraging knowledge, Dr. Weber's not much of a crutch because he's having a spot of trouble with his own true self, and especially with his made-up alter ego, "Famous Gerald," the version of himself who shills his books. His latest opus, *The Country of Surprise,* is being pasted by reviewers. They're accusing Weber of shallowness, of coldness toward his subjects, of invasion of privacy, and—worst of all—of outdated methodology; of being, in other words, a fraud. These accusations resonate with his dwindling sense of self-worth, and as a result he's beginning to experience an identity meltdown, right there in the Kearney MotoRest, where everything seems like an imitation of itself—even the apples on the reception desk, "real or decoration, he couldn't tell until he sank a fingernail into one." In this mansion of facsimiles, even the sandhill cranes appear only as pictures on tourist brochures. No wonder he starts yearning for Barbara, the unfathomable health worker, as his rock-of-ages marriage turns to Jell-O in his mind.

What is solid, what is dependable, what is authentic? Is it love that makes things "real," as in Margery Williams's *The Velveteen Rabbit: Or How Toys Become Real*? Possibly, but only for the lover. And then, where does "love" come from? From that same unreliable lump of crinkly grey goo inside our skulls? If not from there, where else?

But *The Echo Maker* may be read on yet another level: What is wrong with the "self" of America? Has the true America been taken away, has a fake America replaced it? Are the characters—and by extension the reader—situated in a sort of Stepford America? Are we "living in the age of mass hypnotism," as Weber's wife says of corporate America and its Enron-like smoke-and-mirrors economic shams? Is "America" now a phantom limb, like the ones discussed by Weber—long gone, but still hurting? What are the essential ingredients that give a place or a country its identity, and that make a person a true version of him- or herself?

Here I would like to speculate about *The Wonderful Wizard of Oz* and its possible connection with *The Echo Maker*.

This speculation does not come out of nowhere. Structuring a novel on the floor plan of another novel (or story, or work of art) is the kind of thing Richard Powers likes to do. (Consider, for instance, *Prisoner's Dilemma*, built on a fantasy about Walt Disney, and *The Gold Bug Variations*—theme first, variations second. Musical structures interest Powers.) There are in fact some clues to Powers's intentions sprinkled lightly onto the text: at one point, Weber's wife, Sylvie, says, "Yo, Man—I'm home! . . . No place like it!" And five pages later, Weber reflects: "The utter estrangement of it: *I've a feeling we're not in New York anymore.*" The originals of these snippets are well known: the first recalls Dorothy's refrain in the Land of Oz, the second echoes what she says to her little dog, Toto, to explain the strangeness of what they are both encountering.

The Wonderful Wizard of Oz is usually billed as the first real American fairy tale. It's one of those books that have endured because they say more than they know. It was written in 1900, at a time when the rise of feminism and the advent of Darwinism—hence those power-packed witches and winged monkeys—were troubling the sleep of many.

Dorothy, its little-girl heroine, is an orphan who lives with her grey, unsmiling Auntie Em and Uncle Henry in flat, flat, flat, grey Kansas. She is swept off to the Land of Oz by a tornado, and when she gets there she meets three companions: a straw man with no brain, a tin man with no heart, and a lion with no courage. (Political pundits have a saying that a great leader needs three things: brains, heart, and guts, or its modern variant, balls. Churchill, for example, had all three. Now start doing your own sums: FDR surely had all three; Nixon had brains and guts, but not much heart. Reagan had a good facsimile of a heart, but not much of a brain. And so forth.)

The Land of Oz, we are told, has a great wizard in it, and also some witches, good and bad. The four friends set off for the Emerald City of Oz to have their wishes fulfilled by the Wizard. The three male companions want their missing parts, and Dorothy wants to go home because there's no place like it.

When encountered, Oz the Great and Terrible does a pretty good imitation of God, manifesting himself as a ball of fire, a fierce beast, a lovely lady, a giant head—all of these have Biblical or theological precedents—and finally as a disembodied voice that announces, "I am everywhere." But then he's revealed as an imposter—he's just a ventriloquist and sideshow performer from Omaha, Nebraska, who was blown over the deserts that encircle Oz in an off-course balloon. Even the colour of the Emerald City is an illusion, produced by the green glasses everyone in it wears. So the Wizard has no real magic powers; but the witches do, and the Wizard has put on his God show to frighten them off.

Deficient males, powerful females, in a land of imitations, in the heart of the heartland of America. In the 1939 film version, the Land of Oz—the Land of Awes, surely—is inside Dorothy's head. Dorothy has been knocked unconscious during the tornado, and has been dreaming. Oz, like the "country of surprise" in Dr. Weber's book, is a land of brain episodes. The Kingdom of Oz—like Christ's Kingdom of God, like Milton's inner Paradise, and like Weber's reality-as-we-experience-it and body-as-place-as-postcard—is within.

If *The Wonderful Wizard of Oz* is the underlying sketch for *The Echo Maker*—if the former is the theme on which the latter builds its variations—then Mark's sister, Karin, is an ironic Dorothy figure. She's not "home" because she wants to be there—on the contrary, she tried very hard to get away from Kearney. Her difficulty is not that "there's no place like home" in the old sense, but that there's no place available to her that even remotely resembles the idea of the home. "There's no place like home" has taken on a modern, ominous meaning; there is, literally, no trustworthy home.

Mark would correspond to the scarecrow figure, the brain-deficient one; wispy-bearded, vegetarian Daniel (the non-lion in the lions' den) is the one lacking in balls; and Robert Karsh, the developer, is the flashy tin man without a heart. (The winged monkeys—destructive or helpful, depending on the situation—may possibly be represented by Mark's two primitive-minded video-gaming pals, fellow travellers to yet another realm of virtual reality.)

Dr. Weber is of course the wizard as fraud; he too comes and goes through the air, though he uses an airplane, not a balloon. Like the Wizard, he too finds an unsuspected strength hidden beneath his own fakery. Barbara—who seems to have magic powers of some kind—might be a blend of Glinda the Good Witch and the Wicked Witch of the West.

What shared void brings Weber and Barbara together? What are they doing lying entwined on the ground with all those sand-hill cranes around them, in that cold field, in the dead of night? Is Glinda the Good really Glinda the Bad? Why is kindly Barbie Doll so empty and depressed, and how did she get that way? Was it a surfeit of world news, or something more personal? Both, as it turns out, because in Powers's novels the mini-story always connects with the bigger picture.

We're not in Kansas anymore. We're not even in Oz. We're in Nebraska, the ruined heart of the heartland of America, and things are looking grim. As an answer to the hypothetical question "What has happened to America?," *The Echo Maker* does not initially offer much solace. But it does at length offer some. There's grace of a sort to be had, in the country of surprise. There's forgiveness to be at least tried out. There are amends to be made.

The amends to be made have, in the end, something to do with the cranes because Powers has paid attention to Chekhov's observation that if there's a pistol on the table in the first act, it has to go off in the third. There are cranes on the first page of the book, and at the beginning of each of the next four sections, so we know that something will therefore—most likely—be made of these cranes at the end of the book. They are dependent on the wide Platte River, but it is shrinking, due to the water-guzzling depredations of men like Robert.

It's always difficult to meld the world of nature and the human world in novels. Unless you introduce talking bunnies or their equivalent—tame beavers, perhaps—it's hard to paper over the fact that nature's wild denizens don't really care about people very much unless they can eat them, or unless they're being hunted by them. And people—including readers—care mostly about other people, just as termites care mostly about other termites. Such things as sandhill cranes may inspire awe, and wonder, and joy, and curiosity, and transcendent delight, but they don't inspire fuzzy huggy feelings. Quite the opposite.

Powers doesn't paper this part over. Instead, he emphasizes it. "The outcome of owls will orchestrate the night," he says, "millions of years after people work their own end. Nothing will miss us." But the wild cranes in the heart of the heartland are threatened because people do not recognize them for the essential spiritual lifeblood that they are. Mankind may do itself in, but it will do in a lot of other creatures first.

The book's preoccupation with the destruction of nature may seem very modern—trendy, even—but it is in fact a very old strain in American literature. James Fenimore Cooper's *The Leatherstocking Tales*—a series that was arguably the first major stab at using the novel as a method of exploring the American reality and psyche—began with the 1823 novel *The Pioneers*. In it, Natty Bumppo, the forest-dweller and companion of Indians, is a ludicrous and victimized elderly man. Cooper took a lot from Walter Scott and the Waverley novels, and the *Pioneers* version of Natty is the equivalent of the wild but droll, savage but noble, comic but tragic dialect-speaking Highlanders in Scott's novels. In subsequent Leatherstocking books, Natty was to grow younger and younger as he receded farther and farther into the pristine, unspoiled wilderness of an earlier time. He was to accumulate a batch of more heroic-sounding titles—Pathfinder, Deerslayer, Hawkeye—as if Cooper wished he hadn't initially stuck the poor man with such a boobyish name as "Bumppo."

It's in *The Pioneers,* however, that Natty takes his first, eloquent stand against the greed that is threatening to destroy the abundance of nature. God made both man and the other creatures, Natty asserts. God allows man to kill and eat his other creatures—just as they kill and eat one another—but such killing and eating should be done only to satisfy hunger and supply immediate needs, and should be treated as a gift. The incoming settlers, however, are indulging in wholesale slaughter—killing not because they must but because they can. They are grasping gluttons, intent on turning a profit. They have no respect for God's creation, and the end of their wastefulness will be famine.

Cooper's Natty was concerned with the obliteration of fish and game. The passenger pigeon had not yet been wiped from the face of the planet, so it did not occur to him that the same forces that were depleting the woods of deer might later deplete the world of entire species. Disgusted by the incursions of the mass killers and money-grubbers, Natty finally fades away into the wilderness, where he feels more at home. Daniel's contemplation of the vanishing sandhill crane is not far in spirit from Natty Bumppo, and at the novel's end he takes a similar course of action, moving farther north, farther away from the blight of Kearney and, by extension, of America. "Doesn't want to be around, when we finally wreck the place," as Mark puts it.

The cranes are most likely doomed by man; they're living fossils, but so very possibly are we. Why then should people like Daniel devote their lives to saving them? Perhaps because birds have always represented the human soul, to our imaginations: the epigraph of *The Echo Maker* is "To find the soul it is necessary to lose it." This is a book about lost souls, but it is also about souls that are found again. The lines of the creepy anonymous note that has so bedevilled Mark turn out to have a sort of truth to them: in order to find your own lost soul, you have to "bring back someone else." The solution to Mark's frightening doubled world may be found in the doctor's bag of chemical gizmos, but it also lies in another realm entirely.

That neuroscience would consider "the soul" to be just some brain-event illusion is beside the point: in its terms, everything is a brain-event illusion, including the body, so if we think we have "souls," it's the same as actually having them. The old self-help truism—you can change the world by the way you think about it—may be accurate, after all. We must live as if the replica were the original—as if it were worth saving and improving—because there's no other option available to us. As Mark is finally able to say, "Just as good . . . I mean, us. You. Me. Here . . . Whatever you call all this. Just as good as the real thing."

The Echo Maker is a grand novel—grand in its reach, grand in its themes, grand in its patterning. That it might sometimes stray over the line into the grandiose is perhaps unavoidable: Powers is not a painter of miniatures. Of the two extremes of American mannerist style, the minimalist or Shaker chair (Dickinson, Hemingway, Carver) and the maximalist or Gilded Age (Whitman, James, Jonathan Safran Foer), Powers inclines toward the latter. He gets his effects by repetition, by a Goldberg Variations–like elaboration of motifs, by cranking up the volume and pulling out all the stops.

It all adds up to one enormous oratorio-like brain episode. You stagger out of Powers's novel happy to find yourself, like Scrooge the morning after, grasping your own bedpost, saying, "There's no place like home," and hoping you still have a chance to set things right. As a slice of virtual reality, *The Echo Maker* is just as good as the real thing—or, as Mark Schluter says, "In some ways, even better."

Wetlands

>>><<<

(2006)

It's a real pleasure to be here with you this evening, at the Charles Sauriol Environmental Dinner. The proceeds from this dinner will be used by the Oak Ridges Moraine Land Trust and the Conservation Foundation of Greater Toronto. Together, these two organizations have protected thousands of acres of land; they are part of a growing movement—growing in awareness, growing in effectiveness, growing in advocacy power—propelled forward by people who realize that big oak trees grow from little acorns, and cannot grow without little acorns; and that all trees and indeed all life on dry land—which would include us language-wielding bipeds—needs soil and water, and clean air, and careful and informed consideration. Countless hours of thought and volunteer work have gone into these organizations. Everyone here applauds this work, and is proud to have been a part of it.

If organizations like this succeed in their work, you'll breathe easier, in so many more ways than one. You'll feel you've done something to help in a much larger struggle—the struggle against global warming and the huge amount of devastation it will bring, and is already bringing. You'll sleep better at night, partly—let's hope—because you won't be coughing so much.

I'm not a politician, so you may wonder what I'm doing making a speech on what has already become a political hot potato. Hot in so many ways: according to those who measure such things, including NASA, Earth is hotter now than it's been for millennia. If it gets very much hotter, we'll soon be beyond the point of no return.

"Oh well, that Margaret," they sometimes say. "She's just a fiction writer." Yes, I am a fiction writer, and that gives me a big advantage in the truth-or-fiction arena: unlike some politicians, I do know the difference between the two. Here's a bit from a piece I wrote for *Granta* last year—non-fiction this time. The subject was the melting Arctic ice, a situation I've seen for myself.

"You could write a science fiction novel about it," I said, "except that it wouldn't be science fiction. You could call it *Icemelt*. Suddenly there are no more small organisms, thus no fish up there, thus no seals. That wouldn't affect the average urban condo-dweller much. The rising water levels from—say—the melting of the Greenland and Antarctic ice caps would get attention—no more Long Island or Florida, no more Bangladesh, and quite a few islands would disappear—but people could just migrate, couldn't they? Still no huge cause for alarm unless you own a lot of shorefront real estate.

"But wait: there's ice under the earth, as well as on top of the sea. It's the permafrost, under the tundra. There's a lot of it, and a lot of tundra as well. Once the permafrost starts to melt, the peat on the tundra—thousands of years of organic matter—will start to break down, releasing huge quantities of methane gas. Up goes the air temperature, down goes the oxygen ratio. Then how long will it take before we all choke and boil to death?"

People sometimes tell me I can be a little harsh. "Now, Margaret," they say. "Isn't that a little harsh?" As if, by saying that the bare-naked emperor has in fact got no clothes on, I'd trampled a kitten or something.

So harsh, to wake sleepwalkers from their trance. Everyone would much rather be told that things are fine, the world is safe, we're all nice people, and nothing is anyone's fault—above all, that we can keep on doing exactly whatever we like, without taking any thought or changing our so-called lifestyle in the least, and there will be no bad consequences. I'd like to be told that too. Trouble is, it's not true. So maybe it's time to be a little harsh. The situation we find ourselves in cannot be dealt with through anything less than plain speaking.

For a long time now I've had a habit of clipping things out of newspapers and magazines, or downloading them from the Internet. When I was writing my 2003 novel, *Oryx and Crake,* set in the not-so-distant future, when global warming has raised sea levels so that New York is under water and there isn't any red-leaved autumn in New England because the climate there is semi-tropical, I built up a little stash of articles to corroborate such details, in case anyone might accuse me of hallucinating. Back then—just a few years ago—I was getting these pieces from science-oriented magazines, or from the science pages of newspapers. You had to search for this stuff.

But in the past year I haven't been able to keep up. There's been a deluge. The bad news has moved from the science pages to the covers of magazines like *Newsweek,* which in October carried a full spread on global warming. "Last Chance for Fish," proclaimed one insert; another piece was on frogs, another on coral, another on rainforest damage. In the first presidential campaign that George Bush sort of maybe won, his opponent Al Gore was derided for his green views. Not anymore.

Along with the bad news, there's some good news—reclamation projects that have succeeded, new technologies that will help us live greener lives. It's all happening very, very fast. For instance, we know the albatross is in trouble, due to human fishing methods. We even know how to save it. It wouldn't even cost that much. We just need the money.

The trouble with raising money for conservation, including birds and animals, is that people have trouble seeing the connection between human beings and the rest of the world. If you grow up behind plate-glass windows, if all your food comes from the supermarket, if you think water is generated by the faucet, you're going to have some trouble putting two and two together—until, that is, New Orleans floods or your own lights go out or you die because of contaminated spinach or the *E. coli* in your town water supply.

Of all charitable giving, only about 3 per cent goes to animal-related causes, and of that 3 per cent, half of it goes to human pets such as dogs and cats. We prefer to give to poor people, or to hospitals with heart and kidney foundations. But as you all know, degrade the environment—degrade it worldwide, as is now happening—and you'll get more poor people than you can possibly ever deal with. We're there already, come to think of it—because all human wealth is, in the end, based on the earth. As someone recently quipped, "The economy is a wholly owned subsidiary of the environment." Wreck the earth and you're wrecking yourself, and then it won't matter how much money you've given to hearts and kidneys because nobody will have hearts and kidneys anyway.

I myself didn't grow up behind plate-glass windows. As a child, I led the kind of double existence that used to be more typical of Canadians—part-time in the boreal forest, part-time in cities. In the forest we always had a garden because that was the only way we could get fresh greens—by growing them. And we got fresh fish by catching them. So I was pretty conscious about where food came from.

Because of my belief that we're living in decisive times and that small choices do make a difference, I recently started writing a set of green protocols to be used in my own home and my own office. In order to do that, I had to take stock—yet once more—of how I was in fact living. It's amazing where such an examination will lead you.

In our house, we'd already done quite a few things—the low-energy car, the list of permissible fish we carry around with us and haul out in restaurants and at the fish store, the elimination of air conditioning from our home, the installation of a couple of solar panels, the discarding of evil cleaning products, the low-energy, low-water washing machine, the recycling and reusing, the supporting of Forest Stewardship paper for our books—but as we took stock, we realized there was so much more to be done.

Conscious Green Living is as exacting as some relentless religious program—there's a sort of catechism that goes along with it, and an exhaustive list of sins. Just try avoiding paper towels in washrooms, or those hopelessly wasteful hot-air hand dryers that don't work anyway. It can be done—you carry a handkerchief, you use that, you discover it weeks later balled up in a mildewy corner in your purse—but it's hard. You do get the hang of it after a while, though. Like almost everything else, it's habit.

Trouble is, people who are making this difficult attempt feel they're going it alone. They aren't getting much official help, certainly not from our federal government. Private gains are being cancelled out by public losses.

If an asteroid were sweeping toward Earth, threatening a massive impact, with huge climate-altering clouds of dust, fires, floods, and the whole terrifying ball of cataclysmic wax, and if we knew how to stop it, and had the power to stop it, you'd think we'd take the necessary steps. But what's coming toward us now is going to have many of the same dismal effects. What exactly will it take to get a little real action out of our so-called leaders, who are behaving increasingly like the proverbial ostriches with their proverbial heads in the tar sands? When is Mr. Harper going to realize that people no longer want to listen to him tut-tutting about previous Liberal hypocrisy and inaction on environmental issues—and that we're not quite so stupid as he thinks, and we therefore know that his tut-tutting is in fact not going to cover up his own hypocrisy and inaction? Things are speeding up, Mr. Harper. Then is not now, and the difference is that now it's you in power, not the Liberals. The nothing that is being done is *your* nothing.

It's unfair to say you're doing nothing. There's the Clean Air Act— that's at least something, though not a really big something. However, if you wave it around enough, it might buy you some time.

You're keeping one of your promises, at any rate—your promise to build a firewall around Alberta. But people in Alberta are not so stupid either. They're beginning to realize that a hotter planet is going to mean droughts and water shortages, even for them. A lot of frizzled-up cattle. A big imbalance between the water that people need and the supply of water available to them. What happens when the place burns from the *inside* of the firewall, not from the outside? How now, brown cow?

Canada has long been thought of as a fairly green place. But we've been resting on our laurels, unfortunately, because Canada is not meeting its Greenhouse Gases Control goals set under the Kyoto Accord. It's promising to come up with some better form of legislation, sometime, but it's not reassuring that the present government doesn't seem to grasp the connection between air quality and climate change. The Clean Air Act will be useless if the atmosphere continues to heat up. What part of Hotter Planet Means Worse Air Means More Air Conditioning Means Hotter Planet Means Worse Air don't they get?

It's a message that voters—increasingly—do get. But there's the message, and then there's how people react to the message. If it's all doom and gloom, with no hope in sight, folks turn off because they feel there's nothing they can do. Or else they get cynical and greedy—if we're all going down the plughole, they reason, why not grab what you can and enjoy yourself in the meantime?

It's instructive to read about the Black Death—during its first murderous onslaughts, when people thought the world was coming to an end. Reactions varied. Some ran for safety—leaving cities where the plague was raging, fleeing for the countryside or for other cities, not realizing they were in fact bearing the plague along with them and infecting others. Some took to blaming—the plague was a result of witches or lepers or Jews poisoning the wells, or it was sent by God as a punishment for men's sins. That impulse is still with us, as witness some of the right-wing reaction to the onset of AIDS, and to the flooding in New Orleans. Man's sinfulness and God's retribution were pinned onto both, like a well-used tail to a shopworn donkey.

During the Black Death, some took to flagellating themselves. Some stayed in place and tried to care for the victims, with usually fatal results to themselves. Some went on the rampage, looting and raping and rioting, as civil order broke down. Some sequestered themselves in castles, hoping the plague would not come in. Some carried on with their ordinary lives as best they could. But nobody said, "It's not happening." Nobody will be able to say that about global warming and environmental catastrophe soon either. Hardly anyone is saying it now.

There's an upside to everything, by the way. After the plague had killed a third of Europe's population, workers' wages rose. Also, the neglected fields grew up into forests, ushering in—some say—the Little Ice Age, since bare fields reflect more heat back into the atmosphere than forests do. The Black Death—like the neutral zone between North and South Korea—was great for wildlife. Look on the bright side.

Another side effect was the fallout in the world of art. The Black Death ushered in those skull-and-hourglass tombstones with the MEMENTO MORI inscriptions, and the paintings of the Dance of Death, in which citizens of all social levels were shown being led in the dance by Death himself. In a world of mass epidemic or catastrophe, having lots of money and a private medical plan is not going to do you any good.

The difference between us and the plague sufferers is that we have at least some idea of how to avoid the approaching fate. It's not lack of knowledge, on our part. It's lack of political will.

It's all very well to say that individual consumer choices are what will make the difference—that government should stay out of it. If you want to buy a polluting leaf blower, if you want to drive a honking big-city tank, that's up to you. And if, on the other hand, you're conscientious, and you make the right environmental choices, and you pay more for them—as you often will—that's your choice too.

But that's penalizing those who do make the right environmental choices, and letting the others off the hook.

The air, the earth, and the water are a common good, and should be commonly protected. All will benefit if they are, all will suffer if they're not. Legislation is needed to level this particular playing field. We're waiting for it, Mr. Harper. If we wait too long, it will be too late. End of story.

This is about where I can expect to hear the word *alarmist*. But alarmist is good when the building's on fire. You sound the alarm, then hope that someone will help to put it out. In that sense, everyone in this room is alarmist. We've all seen the flames.

I'll end with an old story. King Midas was granted a wish, but he didn't think it through. He wished merely for wealth as it was then measured—he wished that everything he touched might turn to gold. And everything did turn to gold, including any food he tried to eat and any water he tried to drink. He starved to death.

There are more kinds of wealth than money. Instead of turning everything on Earth into gold, we have the chance to turn gold back into those old Four Elements—the things that are needed for life. Good water, fine air, healthy soil, clean energy. I hope we will all avail ourselves of that chance, while we still can.

Trees of Life, Trees of Death

>>><<<

(2007)

I'm very pleased to be delivering this tribute in honour of the Department of Forestry's centennial. I'll divide my talk into three parts, and I'll even tell you what they are, just so you know what's coming.

Part One is about my own background in relation to trees and forests. Part Two is about the mythological and symbolic significance of trees and forests. Part Three is about our present situation, in a world with dwindling forests. How much trouble are we in, really? And what should we do?

I have a long association with the Department of Forestry, and indeed with forests, which wasn't really of my own choosing. For instance: This March I happened to be in Okinawa. As we were driving north toward the forest of Yanbaru—home of the very rare Okinawa rail, which we failed to spot—I saw a long stretch of conifers that looked to be in trouble: dying or dead.

"You have an infestation," I said to our Japanese friend. "Is it an insect?"

Yes, it was an infestation, and yes, it was an insect—a beetle, in fact. (As J.B.S. Haldane so famously remarked, God seems to have had an inordinate fondness for beetles, having created so many of them; and, as he did not add, many of them eat trees.) But our friend was astonished that I would have noticed this infestation. "How did you know?" he asked.

Well, if there's one thing I can usually spot, it's an infestation. My father, Dr. Carl Atwood, was a research entomologist in the 1930s and the early 1940s with what was then called the Department of Lands and Forests. We'd be driving along the road during our numerous trips in the north, and suddenly we would pull over to the side. "An infestation!" we would cry. Out would come the tarpaulin and the axe. The tarpaulin would be spread out under an infested tree, my father would hit the trunk with the butt of the axe, and things—usually caterpillars—would cascade down from the branches. Then we kids would help collect them, and then we could resume our journey, until the next tempting infestation would cause us to screech to a halt.

Other families stopped for ice-cream cones. Ours stopped for infestations.

My father's specialties at that time were spruce budworm and sawfly, with a glance at forest tent caterpillars. He was in the habit of gathering the tent caterpillar webbing nests on their branches, as another person might pick roses, and putting the stems of these caterpillar bouquets into jars of water. But then he might forget to add fresh leaves, at which point the caterpillars would sally forth in search of fodder, making their way up walls and across ceilings, then plummeting into the soup. This was exciting for us kids, especially if company was present.

My father went up to what was then a remote area of northern Quebec way back in 1937. The nearest town was Timiskaming, which already had a sawmill, though this operation had not yet become Tembec. There was no road—access was by a small-gauge railroad. On the shores of a large lake, he set up a little insect lab—built out of logs, by himself and helpers. Due to his own background—he grew up in the backwoods of Nova Scotia, where his father ran a tiny sawmill—he was an expert with the axe.

This was not an untouched wilderness. Logging went on there, in the old way: the loggers and their horses worked in the winter, chopping down selected trees and dragging them onto the ice. When the ice melted in the spring, the logs were collected into a boom and towed by tugboat to a river entrance, then shot downstream to the sawmill on the Ottawa River. These loggers didn't practise clearcutting: it wouldn't have been worth their effort to cut down everything. I'm old enough to have seen this form of logging in operation, as a child. We would sometimes come across logs that had escaped, which could be made into very good rafts.

I first went to this remote Quebec location in the spring of 1940, five months or so after I was born. My mode of transport was by packsack. From then on, I spent a lot of time in forests. Although we lived in cities during the winters, insects being dormant in those months, we were up in the woods from April on, before the ice went out—and staying sometimes as late as November, by which time there would already be a lot of snow.

My father ran the Quebec lab until 1944, at which point he went over to Sault Ste. Marie to set up the insect lab there. After that—in 1946—he began teaching forestry at the University of Toronto. I spent some of my youthful hours—during the winters of the late 1940s—in the old zoology building, admiring the bottled eyeballs and the deadly white African cockroaches that were features of the place in those days. It was no accident that my first novel—written at age seven—was about an ant. I can't say this work is very gripping—not much conflict can be got out of the larval and pupal stages—but it has a happy ending, involving the capture, the biting, the finishing off, and the dragging to the communal ant nest of an especially delicious bug. I wish I could get the novels of my later period to end so optimistically.

My father was an early environmentalist—a very early one. For instance, he had his doubts about the wisdom of widespread spraying for infestations at a time when to have such doubts was to label yourself a lunatic; but as with many things, time has proven him right.

A week ago I received a letter from Orie Loucks, who was a graduate student of my father's in the early 1950s. He enclosed a reprint of his master's thesis work: "a study of shoreline reservations of pine left in the Quetico boundary waters at the time of a 1942–43 logging."

Forty-nine years after his first study, in 2002, Orie Loucks went back to Quetico-Superior to see how the project had done. The 200-foot shoreline reservation strip—as it turns out—has been instrumental in creating "a new pine forest 60–70 feet tall." In his journal of the trip, he comments on intergenerational influences—from my father, to him, and now to his students. By that time, my father had been dead for almost ten years. In many areas of life, it's not always possible to see how the choices we make will play out over time. This is particularly true of forestry, and of forestry in Canada, because most trees in the deciduous, mixed, and coniferous zones of this country grow very slowly in relation to us.

Here I'll quote the words of someone who ought to know, namely Treebeard the Ent, from *The Lord of the Rings*—a character who is either a tree-like hominid or a hominid-like tree. He is speaking about Old Entish, the language of the talking tree-folk. "It is a lovely language," he says, "but it takes a very long time to say anything in it, because we do not say anything in it, unless it is worth taking a long time to say, and to listen to."

On the mythological level, you might say that forestry is the study of Old Entish. It's the study of trees, but also of what trees tell us by how and where they grow, and of what changes they may bring about in the rest of the world by growing how and where they do. "I can see and hear (*and* smell *and* feel) a great deal from this, from this, *a-lalla-lalla-rumba-kamanda-lind-or-burúmë*," says Treebeard, using an Old Entish word. "Excuse me: that is a part of my name for it; I do not know what the word is in the outside languages: you know, the thing we are on, where I stand and look out on fine mornings, and think about the Sun, and the grass beyond the wood, and the horses, and the clouds, and the unfolding of the world." The word for all of this in the outside languages is probably the *environment,* or some such. But I prefer "the unfolding of the world."

As you have probably guessed, we are now in Part Two of my talk—the part about mythology and symbolism—having arrived there by labyrinthine ways—being lost in the forest being the original labyrinthine experience, as anyone will know who has ever found him- or herself walking around in circles in the woods. Just remember, water always flows downhill. One thing I learned as a child was how to mark a trail—you should do it on both sides of a tree trunk, so that when you look back at any point you will always know where you've just been.

The relationship of *Homo sapiens* to trees and forests is a very old one, and one that has always involved mixed emotions. One scientific origin story has our ancestors coming down from the trees, and some of our distant relatives still make nightly nests in them—up in the branches, where they are safer from nocturnal predators than they might be on the ground. Why do so many people have a so-called irrational fear of snakes, cats, and spiders? One theory is that those animals were the only ones that might be able to get at you if you were a primate nesting in a tree. A recent theory supposes that we left the forests because they were inhabited by a giant cat— *Dinofelis,* or "false sabre-tooth," a genus about the size of a large leopard that appears to have lurked in dense forests and specialized in eating our Australopithecine relatives.

Another version of our origin story has the forest dwindling due to climate change, to be replaced by a more open savannah, with hominids thus forced to adapt to a very different environment. Trees would still have been important for shade, and—after fire was domesticated—for fuel, but our ancestors may have developed an aversion to being completely surrounded by them because they provide such good cover for predators.

The countryside, with its tilled fields and meadows and copses, is a far cry from the deep forest. Few peoples in recent times have chosen to live inside deep forests—the jungle-dwelling pygmies are an exception. Indigenous North Americans settled by shores, and used waterways for transport as much as they could. They had networks of trails through the woods, but you went that way when there was no alternative. Indigenous New Zealanders similarly kept to the shorelines. Our feelings about the deep forest—as expressed in stories old and new—are dominated by uneasiness and fear.

In the oldest written poem we know about, *The Epic of Gilgamesh,* one of the big heroic battles is Gilgamesh and his friend Enkidu versus a forest-dwelling monster called Humbaba. Humbaba is the guardian of the cedar forest. Gilgamesh takes his axe to this forest, and Humbaba, although infuriated, loses the resulting fight and is then ruthlessly murdered. (What makes this murder even worse is that Gilgamesh and Enkidu commit it after they have been invited as guests into Humbaba's home—in most cultures it is strictly against the code to murder your host.) The plunder Gilgamesh brings back to the city of Uruk consists of the cedar trees he has cut down— a valuable commodity for a city built on a treeless plain. The god Shamash is pleased with this result, but the god Enlil is furious, and curses Gilgamesh. That conflict about tree-cutting has been played out ever since.

In ancient stories, to cut down a forest or a grove of trees is often to violate a taboo. Some groves are sacred—but sacred to which god? To cut or not to cut—either way, you're usually going to be in trouble with someone. Jehovah wants groves cut down; Ashtoreth, the moon goddess, wants them left standing. In Greek mythology, the moon goddess Artemis is also the goddess of forests and mistress of the animals. To demolish the forest is to strike a blow against the wild creatures, in favour—often—of pastoralists, who want grazing pastures, or agriculturalists, who want tilled fields. But anger the mistress of the animals too much and you'll be sorry, for she is also She-Who-Sends-Plagues. Does that remind you of anything you may have heard about species-jumping diseases such as Ebola, Marburg, and AIDS, and how they move to seek fresh hosts—such as us—as the old hosts disappear due to habitat destruction?

The Greeks told a story about Erysichthon, who, despite warnings, cut down a sacred grove. When his axe struck the first tree, blood gushed out—it was the blood of the Hamadryad who lived in the tree. His crime was punished by Demeter, goddess of vegetable fertility and harvests, who inflicted famine upon him. There is indeed a complex relationship between trees and soil fertility. Denude a landscape of its trees—especially a hilly landscape—and floods and soil erosion by wind or water will follow, with famine as the result—something the Greeks had already learned several thousand years ago.

The columns of Greek temples were imitation trees; so were the branched ribs of Norman cathedrals. And most mythologies include a World Tree or a Tree of Life, which upholds all life on Earth. In the Christian religion, the Tree of Life grows in the Garden of Eden—it's the one with the apples Adam didn't eat, having munched on the fruit of the Tree of Knowledge instead—which is why we're smart but not immortal, in case you were wondering.

But for every positive symbol, there's a negative counterpart. There's a Tree of Death as well as a Tree of Life. Poetic versions of the wasteland usually have dead trees in them, or no trees at all; or the trees have been destroyed and replaced by stone or metal pillars. In the Christian religion, the Tree of Death is represented by the cross, a dead tree upon which death is inflicted. The tree-herding Ents in

The Lord of the Rings are on the good side of things, and punish the tree-cutting wizard, Saruman; but in Tolkien's invented world there are wild trees and bad trees, as well as good trees—the bad ones have bad hearts; and there are also entire forests that have gone bad: their trees will grab hold of you or imprison you within themselves. Dorothy in *The Wonderful Wizard of Oz* encounters this bad kind of tree—there's a forest of fighting trees on the road to Oz that won't let her pass, and the problem is solved only by the decisive Tin Woodsman, who takes his axe to the brutes and clears a path. The powerful and destructive Whomping Willow in the Harry Potter series has a very respectable line of ancestors.

Dante's *Divine Comedy* begins with a labyrinth metaphor:

In the middle of the journey of our life
I came to my senses in a dark forest,
for I had lost the straight path.

Oh, how hard it is to tell
what a dense, wild, and tangled wood this was,
the thought of which renews my fear!

We are led to infer that this forest represents error and sin—a departure from the true path. It's a place where you stray, where you get lost. In olden days, being lost in the forest usually meant death by starvation, exposure, or wild beast, as indeed it still does. If you go down to the woods today, you might want to *see* the Teddy Bears' Picnic, but you'd surely prefer not to *be* the Teddy Bears' Picnic; as you may well be, if you overstay your visit.

Shakespeare's forests are less fearsome than Dante's, but they aren't exactly light and cheerful. Sometimes they're places of enchantment and illusion, inhabited by creatures not entirely human, like the forest in *A Midsummer Night's Dream,* and sometimes they're places of enhanced freedom. The Forest of Arden in *As You Like It* shelters exiles in flight from a tyrannical king—just as Sherwood Forest shelters Robin Hood. To that extent, the forest represents communion with nature, and freedom from the injustices of civilization—as it does, much later, in Fenimore Cooper's *The Leatherstocking Tales.*

But outlaws can just as easily be robbers and murderers, and many of these are met with in literature, and especially in folk tales. For the forest is the realm of predators—we can't seem entirely to forget that. It's when Red Riding Hood goes off the path into the dark forest that she encounters the wolf.

The quintessential dark-forest experience is graphically described in that classic children's tale, Kenneth Grahame's *The Wind in the Willows.* The Wild Wood is a dangerous place, and little Mole ought to have heeded the warnings he was given about it.

> Everything was very still now. The dusk advanced on him steadily, rapidly, gathering in behind and before; and the light seemed to be draining away like flood-water. . . . [Eventually, as Mole] lay there panting and trembling, and listened to the whistlings and the patterings outside, he knew it at last, in all its fullness, that dread thing which other little dwellers in field and hedgerow had encountered here, and known as their darkest moment—that thing which the Rat had vainly tried to shield him from—the Terror of the Wild Wood!

Those who live in the open—on plains, or far north, above the treeline—are gazers rather than listeners because anything that's going to get you will be seen before it's heard. But those who dwell in forests are listeners, because anything that's going to get you will be heard before it's seen. That's why the whistlings and the patterings are so very frightening to Mole.

The fact is that—no matter how many ecological reports we read about the importance of maintaining forests—we're secretly afraid of them. And we're also in awe of them, a fact of our nature that keeps throwing up fictional versions like the wood where all names are lost, in *Alice Through the Looking-Glass,* and the elf-ruled golden forest of Lothlórien in *The Lord of the Rings,* where you may become "entangled," and the wood where Merlin lies in an enchanted sleep, in Arthurian lore. Stay in such forests too long and you'll forget who you are. The forest may be alluring, but you enter it at your peril.

E.O. Wilson, in his disconcerting book *The Future of Life,* sets out our relationship to forests in an interesting way. What kind of location do human beings prefer? He suggests we look at what rich people do: those who can afford anything choose to build on a height of land overlooking an open landscape in which there's a river or a lake, with some trees in the distance but not too close and thick. This would be in fact an ideal spot for hunter-gatherers: water to drink and to attract game, forest to shelter animals but not too close, a good view all around. This may account for the huge amount of forest burning done by the Australian Aboriginals before contact: they liked a clear understory and a wide view. This same kind of view—or even a picture of it on the wall—has been found to reduce by a factor of six the time it takes people to heal in the recovery rooms of hospitals. It seems we find this prospect soothing. Do we therefore have an innate bias in favour of cutting down trees? Wilson thinks we may have.

If we give in to it completely, it will be the worse for us because if we cut down all the trees in the world, we'll be doomed. An old proverb from India says, "Forests precede civilization; deserts follow." This formula has played itself out many times over our history already: the story of Easter Island, where the destruction of all the trees led to soil erosion and famine and cannibalism, is only one of many. We've been told many times about the importance of the Amazon forests—the lungs of the planet, they've been called—to the maintenance of Earth's climate, yet those forests continue to be felled. The forests of Borneo are going fast. The axe of Gilgamesh is busily at work, and some of the gods are pleased—the gods of money, for instance, and those who promote the idea of something for nothing, and the delusion that you can take from nature endlessly without giving back. But the mistress of the animals is getting very annoyed with us; and one of her maxims may well be "There is no free lunch."

Canada contains the largest boreal forest in the world. It has a long association with trees and tree-cutting: the early settlers cut down everything they could, for fear of forest fires and to clear pasture, and to make charcoal, and to export to Europe. We're still cutting away, often quite stupidly and indiscriminately. We're still indulging ourselves in fantasies of endlessness. We're still telling ourselves that anything produced by nature is ours by right, and also free. Why are we still saying that clear-cutting is a natural thing to do because forest fires are natural too, and they burn large areas, so isn't it the same thing? Why are we turning priceless old-growth forest into toilet paper? Part of this is just laziness and greed, but part of it comes from our ancient ambivalence toward forests—our fear of them. How long do we go on this way before we destroy our enormous natural carbon sink, reduce the fragile North with its thin soil covers to a rocky wasteland, and in the process wipe out a large number of species, before we scorch ourselves to death? How soon before we start paying people *not* to cut down trees, just as farmers have been paid for not planting potatoes?

Because I'm a cheerful person, I like to introduce a ray of hope. There are many counter-movements already set in motion. World Wildlife has long known the importance of habitat to species protection, and has bought up large tracts of forest all over the world. Nature Conservancy is very active in Canada and in the United States, and has been successful in acquiring smaller but very significant pieces. The old form of logging is coming back—selective logging, with minimal damage to the forest. It may interest you to know for instance that a group of Buddhists is carrying on single-tree logging, with horses, in Nova Scotia right now.

One of the reasons people are afraid of forests is that—especially if they've grown up in cities—they aren't familiar with them. The value of early education is being increasingly recognized, as witness the growth of "outdoor classrooms" in Britain, where it's been found that children actually learn better when they're not in a closed-classroom environment. Young children have a natural interest in nature, if they aren't discouraged by adults. (How many outdoor classrooms do we have in Canada? None, at the moment. Though we do have summer camps.)

The Japanese have an expression: *forest bathing*—to immerse yourself in the forest for purposes of cleansing and relaxation. For a person who feels comfortable in the forest—and not afraid of it, like Mole—this does actually work. C.W. Nicol—the only Japanese ex-Canadian ex-Welsh karate seventh-degree black belt in the world, and an ardent environmentalist—has a small forest trust in Japan called the Afan Woodland Trust. This is a managed forest that produces some woods for local traditional crafts, and various precious medicinal fungi, and what the Japanese call "mountain vegetables." The vision is similar to managed rainforest and shade coffee plantations—serving human needs in concert with restoration and maintenance.

At the Afan Woodland Trust, they've also been doing several kinds of studies concerning people-forest interactions. One measures the ability of a stay in a forest to normalize blood pressure: low pressure increases, high pressure decreases. Another has involved work with abused and damaged children, which has proven amazingly successful: the forest can contribute to a healing of the psyche, as well as to a healing of the body.

The name "Woodland Trust" is suggestive. That's what we need: woodland trust. We need to trust the woodland, instead of feeling alienated from it and afraid of it. If we can do that, we may cease our indiscriminate destruction, and recognize our forests for what they are: ancient homelands, purifiers of air, shelters of species, protectors from sun, coolers of climate, healers of hearts, soothers of souls, unfolders of the world.

I'll end by quoting again from Treebeard the Ent—a few words we might well take as a motto. "There are wastes of stump and bramble where once there were singing groves," he says. "I have been idle. I have let things slip. It must stop!"

Ryszard Kapuściński

>>><<<

(2007)

When I heard that Ryszard Kapuściński had died, I felt I'd lost a friend. No, more than that: an essential person in my life. A person— one of the few, surely—who could be trusted to tell the truth about complex and difficult events, not in abstract terms but in their concrete details—their colour, smell, feel, touch; their weather. Yet I didn't know Ryszard Kapuściński very well at all. It was a rare quality of his, this befriending of people at a distance.

I first met Kapuściński in 1984. I was living with my family— Graeme Gibson, our seven-year-old daughter—in West Berlin, which was at that time still surrounded by the famous Berlin Wall. It was there that I began *The Handmaid's Tale*. The tone for a novel about a modern totalitarianism was readily available: East German fighter planes broke the sound barrier every Sunday, reminding us by their sonic booms that they could swoop down at any moment. The Soviet bloc stretched out to the east, and seemed as solid as a rock. We travelled to East Germany, with its surly border guards and its nail-polish ice cream and its *Smiley's People*–era chocolate, and to Czechoslovakia, where to say anything real we had to go out into the middles of parks, so afraid were our Czech friends of being bugged.

Finally we went to Poland, which was another story altogether. Poland had always been viewed by its neighbours as recklessly brave, or as bravely reckless. The well-known anecdote about the Polish cavalry charging the German tanks on horseback may or may not have been true, but it was emblematic; and that recklessness or defiance was still there in Warsaw in 1984. Taxi drivers wouldn't drive you anywhere unless you had hard currency; writers offered you armfuls of samizdat—unofficial publications—which they kept stored right on the premises of the supposedly Communist writers' organization. While we were there a priest had been found murdered, presumably by the secret police. There was a Catholic parade, and as we watched the flinty-eyed nuns and the angry, determined priests and their crowds of followers, we thought: *This regime is in trouble.*

And then we met the man who helped to bring it down.

Kapuściński wrote *The Emperor: Downfall of an Autocrat* in 1978. On the surface it's about Haile Selassie of Ethiopia and the collapse of his corrupt and absolutist regime, and, read simply as that, it's a terrific book. Kapuściński, the journalist with the Polish recklessness that took him through twenty-seven coups and revolutions—streams of refugees heading one way, away from trouble; Kapuściński heading the other way, into the middle of it—gets himself to Addis Ababa and sneaks around at night, interviewing former courtiers who are now in hiding, and setting down anecdotes about the emperor that range from the unintentionally comic—his cushion provider had to slide exactly the right size of cushion under his feet for every chair he sat on, at the risk of leaving his short legs dangling—to the horrifying: beggars gobble scraps from palace feasts, eyeballs squirt from sockets.

But *The Emperor* had another level of meaning for the Poles, who, throughout the Nazi occupation and then under the Soviets, had become used to speaking in coded language. As Kapuściński himself says of those times in *Travels with Herodotus,* "Nothing was ever plain, literal, unambiguous—from behind every gesture and word peered some referential sign, gazed a meaningfully winking eye." Thus, because one corrupt, autocratic regime is likely to have many things in common with another, *The Emperor* could be read as a critique of the moribund Polish Communist government. The book quickly made it on to the stage, in one dramatization after another, and contributed greatly to the popular unrest that finally toppled those in power. The brilliance of *The Emperor* as a tactic was that the Communists could hardly object to it, for wasn't it about the badness of monarchy—a form of government to which they were devotedly opposed?

The Emperor was translated into English in 1983, just in time for us to read it and then to meet Kapuściński in Warsaw in 1984, and to shake his hand. He was a member of the same extraordinary generation that included Tadeusz Kantor, the outstanding director and playwright, and the novelist Tadeusz Konwicki—men who had lived through the Second World War as children only to reach adulthood within a one-party Communist system, but had nevertheless managed to produce astonishing works of art. Although Kapuściński's settings were many and his material varied, his underlying themes remained constant—fear and oppression and how people cope with or transcend it, meagre circumstances and how they can both warp and ennoble, the stifling drawn-out torture of political monocultures, and the abiding desire of human beings to possess their own souls. Such themes are entirely understandable in view of Kapuściński's own constrained youth.

Kapuściński seemed to me shy and charming and diffident; Graeme said that might be so, but underneath all of that he was hard as nails. I suppose he would have to have been both: the shyness and charm and diffidence kept him from being shot at roadblocks in the midst of chaotic civil wars, and the nail-like hardness propelled him toward those roadblocks in the first place.

There was always something surreal about encounters with genuine writers inside the Soviet bloc in those days, and maybe Kapuściński's diffidence was caused in part by that surrealism. At polite official occasions there was what was said, and then there was what was not said but was supposed to be understood. "Why do you have so many beautifully illustrated children's picture books in Poland?" I asked another writer at a book fair. "Think about it," she replied, by which she must have meant that there was no problematic political content in kids' picture books.

In January 1986, Kapuściński was in Toronto for the English publication of his 1982 book, *Shah of Shahs,* about the spectacular overthrow of the shah of Iran and his brutal regime, which featured Savak, his hideous, torturing secret police. This book bears rereading now, so prescient is it about the patterns that continue to unfold in the Muslim world. Kapuściński was going to appear at the Harbourfront international writers' series, and he was nervous: he didn't think his English was good enough for a public reading. Would I be his English voice, and do the readings from his books for him? I said I would be honoured, but at the same time I was thinking, *Wait a minute! Ryszard Kapuściński is nervous? About reading in English? In safe, unthreatening Toronto, where everyone will love him even if he manages to blurt out only one word? What about the murderous turmoil in the Congo, the bombs falling in Honduras, and the life-risking riots in revolutionary Tehran?*

Kapuściński's nervousness on that Toronto occasion was endearing. It was also sort of like Mary, Queen of Scots, worrying about whether her cap was on straight while on her way to the scaffold. But then, there is no predicting other people's spheres of nervousness.

Because he was a foreign correspondent—for many years, Poland's only foreign correspondent—Kapuściński seemed ubiquitous, at least when it came to rotten political structures in their moments of crumbling or catastrophe or dire bloodshed. Where there was chaos, there he would be. In *Imperium,* which describes his journeys through the Soviet Union in 1989–1991, just as it was coming unglued, there is a characteristic passage:

> . . . the news exploded that a large city of a million inhabitants . . . had been poisoned severely, dangerously, mortally.
>
> "A new Chernobyl," commented a friend who relayed the news to me.
>
> "I'm going there," I replied. "If I can get a seat, I'm flying tomorrow."

All his life Kapuściński longed to travel, and he longed to travel to precisely those places that the ordinary pleasure-seeking tourist would take pains to avoid. It's therefore more than appropriate that in his last book, *Travels with Herodotus,* he invoked the first famous travel writer of this kind: Herodotus, "the father of history." What Kapuściński wanted more than anything as a young man was "to cross the border"—at first the border of Poland, but then, increasingly, every possible border. What drove him on was his endless curiosity about humanity, in all its forms. Like Herodotus, he listened and recorded but did not blame. All his life he was on a quest—a quest rather than a mission. What was it he wanted to find? Exotic detail, certainly; cultural differences; the rich patchwork that had been so absent in postwar Poland. But beyond that—even in the midst of the most extreme bloodshed and sadistic revenge and degradation—our common human goodness. In what lies our hope? Perhaps it was dignity—that simple dignity that is everywhere the target of oppressors, but that can never be entirely eradicated. The dignity that says no.

Surely no other writer has had greater grounds for pessimism, considering all he saw, but this is not an emotion Kapuściński expressed often. More frequent was the note of wonder: wonder that such things—both splendid and squalid—can exist on earth. Near the end of *Travels with Herodotus*, there's a single line. It describes merely a scene inside a Turkish museum, but it has the ring of an epitaph for this modest man who was a superlative witness to our times, and so I will place it as one:

"We stand in darkness, surrounded by light."

Anne of Green Gables

>>><<<

(2008)

Lucy Maud Montgomery's famous novel *Anne of Green Gables* is a hundred years old this April, and the Annery is in full swing. Already there's a "prequel," Budge Wilson's *Before Green Gables,* which chronicles the life of spunky, strange, but endearing Anne Shirley *before* she hit Prince Edward Island's Green Gables farmhouse in a splatter of exclamation marks, apple blossoms, freckles, and embarrassing faux pas. And there's yet another mutton-sleeved, button-booted, Gibson-girl-hairdo'ed television show in the offing—*Anne of Green Gables: A New Beginning*—due in 2009, following the 1919 silent film, the 1934 talkie, the 1956 television version, the 1979 Japanese animé, the 1985 Green Gables series, the 1990–1996 *Road to Avonlea,* and the PBS animated series of 2000; not to mention the various parodies—*Anne of Green Gut, Fran of the Fundy,* and its brethren—that have appeared over the years.

On top of all that, a fresh edition of the first Anne book is available from the New Canadian Library, complete with the original illustrations. These are unsettling, as everyone in them has a very small head—Marilla in particular is not only pinheaded but practically bald—leading us to wonder about the degree of inbreeding that was going on around Avonlea. There's a curiously shaped Anne—more like a sort of Mary Poppins puppet than a girl—who turns into a pretty Dresden china figurine by book's end. But Anne's original image defects have been corrected over and over in the course of the century. In the many subsequent pictorial renditions of her, Anne's head returns to normal size—sometimes it gets a little too big—and the hair becomes much more prominent.

Nor is this process at an end: from the Anne of Green Gables Licensing Authority that gives the nod to all collateral products, expect more Anne boxed sets, Anne notepaper and Anne pencils, Anne coffee mugs and Anne aprons, Anne candies and Anne straw hats, and Anne—well, what else? Anne lace-edged pantaloon under-clothing? Anne cookbooks—oops, we already have those. Talking Anne dolls that say, "You mean, hateful boy! How dare you!" fol-lowed by the sharp crack of a slate being broken over a thick skull, or else, "I hate you—I hate you—I hate you! You are a rude, unfeeling woman!" I always liked those parts.

For those of you who did not read this book as a child—Are there any? Yes, and they are most likely male—*Anne* is the story of an orphaned, red-headed, freckled, eleven-year-old girl who's been sent to the Green Gables farm in Avonlea by mistake. Marilla and Matthew Cuthbert, the elderly brother and sister who own the place, wanted a boy orphan to help with the chores, but eager, imagina-tive, drama-queen Anne makes such an impression on shy old bach-elor Matthew—shown in the original illustrations as a dubious cross between Santa Claus and a tramp—that he wants her to stay, and tart, stern Marilla comes around to his way of thinking.

Anne's subsequent adventures, awkward scrapes, aesthetic hyper-ventilations, and temper tantrums are both touching and amusing, as she grows from ugly-duckling waif to talented and beautiful swan, having dyed her hair temporarily green in the meantime. Ultimately she wins the admiration and affection not only of Marilla but of just about everyone in Avonlea, except the girl we love to hate, whose name is Josie Pye. Finally, there's a bittersweet ending, wherein the wonderful Matthew dies—killed by a heart attack brought on by the shock of a failing bank that wipes out all his savings, thus giving us An Anne for Our Times—and scholarship-winning Anne renounces her larger college ambitions, at least for a while. She stays at Green Gables to help Marilla, who's at risk of going blind and would have to sell the place otherwise. This is the part where you really cry a lot.

The book was an instant success when it first appeared—Anne "is the dearest and most loveable child in fiction since the immor-tal Alice," growled crusty, cynical Mark Twain—and it's been going strong ever since. Anne has inspired many imitations: her more genuine literary descendants surely include Pippi Longstocking, not to mention Sailor Moon—girls who kick over the traces, but not too much. Montgomery herself wrote a string of sequels—*Anne of Avonlea, Anne of the Island, Anne's House of Dreams,* and more; but the grown-up Anne is not the same, and neither is Avonlea after the outbreak of the First World War. As a child reader, I felt about these later books much as I felt about Wendy growing up at the end of *Peter Pan:* I didn't want to know.

Anne of Green Gables was first published in 1908, a year before my mother was born, so when I first grinned and snivelled my way through it at the age of eight, it was a youthful forty. I revisited it through the eyes of my own child in the 1980s, when it was approaching eighty. Then our family actually went to Prince Edward Island, and stayed in Charlottetown, and saw the sprightly, upbeat *Anne of Green Gables* musical that's been running there continuously since 1965. I enjoyed it a lot, but watching a show about an eleven-year-old girl with some real eleven-year-old girls casts a different light on things: some of that enjoyment was vicarious.

We didn't buy any Anne dolls or cookbooks, nor did we visit the Green Gables facsimile farmhouse, which—judging from online accounts of it—is as complete as Sherlock Holmes's digs on Baker Street, containing everything from the slate Anne broke over Gilbert Blythe's head to her wardrobe of puffed-sleeve dresses to the brooch she was accused, wrongly, of losing. There's even a pretend Matthew who gives you drives around the property, though he's not described as running to hide out in the barn at the approach of lady visitors, as the real Matthew would have done. Now I wish I'd taken in more of these sights while I had the chance, though somewhere along the way we did check out the early twentieth-century one-room schoolhouse where the high double desks were just like the ones Anne would have known.

From the point of view of the Annery, we were unsatisfactory consumers, though the many Japanese tourists who'd come a very long way to see the musical were snapping up the dolls, straw hats, books, and aprons with encouraging briskness. I worried about these tourists during the musical itself—wouldn't the egg-and-spoon race present an insuperable cultural barrier?—but I needn't have. When a Japanese person takes up a hobby, that hobby is studied with extreme thoroughness, and I suspect that every Japanese visitor knew a great deal more about egg-and-spoon races than I did myself.

Anne's popularity in Japan (and she's been extremely popular) used to be a mystery to me. Then I went to Japan, and was able to ask a Japanese audience to explain Anne's fascination for them. There were thirty-two answers, all duly recorded by a nice lady who wrote them down, typed them out, and sent them to me. Here are some of them:

Anne of Green Gables was first translated by a Japanese author who was very well known and well loved already. Anne was an orphan and there were a lot of orphans in Japan right after the Second World War, so many readers identified with her. Anne has a passion for apple blossoms and cherry blossoms—the latter are especially dear to the hearts of the Japanese—so her brand of aesthetic sensibility was very sympathetic. Anne had red hair, which—before the past twenty years or so, when even middle-aged Japanese ladies may sometimes be spotted with blue, green, red, or orange hair—was thought to be extremely exotic. Anne is not only an orphan, but a poor girl orphan—the lowest of the low on the traditional Japanese social ladder. Yet she wins over that most formidable of Japanese dragons, the bossy older matron. (In fact, she wins over two of them, since she adds overbearing, opinionated, but good-at-heart Mrs. Rachel Lynde to her collection basket.)

Anne has no fear of hard work: she's forgetful because she's dreamy, but she's not a shirker. She displays a proper attitude when she puts others before herself, and even more praiseworthy is the fact that these others are elders. She has an appreciation of poetry, and although she shows signs of materialism—her longing for puffed sleeves is legendary—in her deepest essence, she's spiritual. And, high on the list, Anne breaks the Japanese taboo that forbade outbursts of temper on the part of young people. She acts out spectacularly, stamping her feet and hurling insults back at those who insult her, and even resorting to physical violence, most notably in the slate-over-the-head episode. This must have afforded much vicarious pleasure to young Japanese readers; indeed, to all Anne's young readers of yesteryear, so much more repressed than the children of today. Had they thrown scenes like the ones Anne throws, they would have got what my mother referred to as What For, or, if things were particularly bad, Hail Columbia. (I myself did not get What For or Hail Columbia, but they were a feature of my mother's stories about her own upbringing in rural Nova Scotia, which—as far as the schoolhouse and the churchgoing and the attitudes toward children went—was remarkably similar to Anne's.)

Those are all the Japanese reasons for Anne's popularity that I can remember, though there were more.

"God's in his heaven, all's right with the world," Anne whispers in the very last lines of *Anne of Green Gables*. She's fond of Victorian poetry, so it's appropriate that she ends her story by quoting from a song sung by the optimistic heroine of Robert Browning's dramatic poem "Pippa Passes"; doubly appropriate, since Anne Shirley herself acts a kind of Pippa throughout the book. Pippa is a poor Italian orphan girl who slaves away in a silk-spinning mill, yet manages to preserve a pure imagination and a love of nature despite her lowly status. Like Pippa, Anne is an unselfconscious innocent, who, unbeknownst to herself, brings joy, imagination, and the occasional epiphany to the citizenry of Avonlea, who are inclined to be practical but dreary.

It's unlikely that Anne Shirley would have been allowed to read all of "Pippa Passes." Pippa's fellow characters are far from wholesome, and their doings are so sordid and explicitly sexual as to have caused moral outrage when the poem was first published: one of them is a mistress, and another has plans to debauch Pippa and lure her into a life of white slavery. Browning's view is the more realistic: in actual life, an orphaned girl like Anne would have had few prospects. "What a starved, unloved life she had had—a life of drudgery and poverty and neglect," thinks Marilla; and it's this starved, unloved life that Budge Wilson has explored in her "prequel." Judging from what we know about the lives of orphans at that time, including the many "London street Arabs," as Marilla calls them, who were being sent to Canada by the Barnardo Homes, a statistically accurate Anne would have continued to be poor and neglected. However, through luck and her own merits, Anne is rescued by the Cuthbert siblings, thus joining a long line of redeemed fictional Victorian orphans, from Jane Eyre to Oliver Twist to little Tom the chimney sweep in Charles Kingsley's *The Water-Babies*. Fairy-tale endings, we call these; for, in mythology and folklore, orphans were not merely downtrodden outsiders: they might be heroes-in-training, like King Arthur, or under the special protection of the gods or fairies. (There is certainly something uncanny about Anne—a "witch," she's often called—and a few centuries earlier she might well have been burnt at the stake.)

Outside of fiction, however, orphans weren't only exploited, they were feared and despised as fruits of sin: children with no identifiable fathers, resentful and even criminal Bad Seeds who'd do things like setting fire to people's houses "on purpose," as Rachel Lynde informs Marilla. This is why Montgomery goes to such lengths to provide Anne with two educated, respectable parents who were married to each other. But a real-life Anne would have led a Dickensian life of grinding child labour and virtual bondage as an unpaid mother's help—Anne has performed this function earlier in her life, once in a bare-bones backwoods household that sports three sets of twins. At worst, she'd have been raped by the men in such households. Then, when found to be pregnant, she'd have been shipped back to the orphan asylum in disgrace, where she would have produced yet another orphan, for how could a girl like her—without money or family, and with her reputation in ruins—ever have supported a child? And after that, what?

In my sourer moments, I confess to having imagined yet another *Anne* sequel, to be called *Anne Goes on the Town*. This would be a grim, Zolaesque epic that would chronicle the poor girl's enticement by means of puffed sleeves, then her sexual downfall and her subsequent brutal treatment at the hands of harsh male clients. Then would follow the pilfering of her ill-got though hard-earned gains by an evil madam, her dull despair self-medicated by alcohol and opium-smoking, and her sufferings from the ravages of an incurable STD. The final chapter would contain some *Traviata*-like coughing, her early and ugly death, and her burial in a nameless grave, with nothing to mark the passing of this waif with a heart of gold but a volley of coarse jokes from her former customers. However, the presiding genius of *Anne* is not the gritty grey Angel of Realism, but the rainbow-coloured, dove-winged Godlet of the Heart's Desire. As Samuel Johnson said about second marriages, *Anne* is the triumph of hope over experience: it tells us not the truth about life, but the truth about wish fulfillment. And the main truth about wish fulfillment is that most people vastly prefer it to the alternative.

This is one of the reasons *Anne of Green Gables* has had such an ongoing life, but this in itself would hardly be enough: if *Anne* were nothing but a soufflé of happy thoughts and outcomes, the Annery would have collapsed long ago. The thing that distinguishes *Anne* from so many "girls' books" of the first half of the twentieth century is its dark underside: this is what gives *Anne* its frenetic, sometimes quasi-hallucinatory energy, and what makes its heroine's idealism and indignation so poignantly convincing.

The dark side comes from the hidden life of Anne's author, L.M. Montgomery. Some of Montgomery's journals have been published, and several biographies have appeared, as well as a haunting 1975 television docudrama called *The Road to Green Gables*. There's a new biography due in October from Mary Henley Rubio—*Lucy Maud Montgomery: The Gift of Wings*—and doubtless in it we will learn even more about that hidden life, though what we know already is disheartening enough. Montgomery was a semi-orphan: her mother died when she was under two, and her father packed her off to be brought up by her strict Presbyterian grandparents in Cavendish, P.E.I. The description of the chilly bedroom where Marilla puts Anne on her first night at Green Gables—a bedroom "of a rigidity not to be described in words, but which sent a shiver to the very marrow of Anne's bones"—is doubtless a metaphor for this household. Anne's plaintive cry, "You don't want me! . . . Nobody ever did want me," is a child's outraged protest against the unfairness of the universe that seems to come straight from the heart. Montgomery was an orphan sent to live with two old people, but unlike Anne, she never did win them over. Marilla and Matthew are what Montgomery wished for, not what she got.

Anne's experiences minding other people's babies are bad enough—Marilla, "shrewd enough to read between the lines," pities her—but Montgomery's own experiences were if anything worse.

The father she'd idealized from a distance moved out west and remarried, and Montgomery was sent for; but the joyful family reunion she must have anticipated didn't happen. Instead, she found herself kept out of school so she could tend to the baby of her uncongenial new stepmother. Her father was seldom there.

Anne's precocious reading tastes and romantic imagination are similar to what we know of Montgomery's, but Montgomery did not star in a post-girlhood series of sequels in which she marries Gilbert Blythe. Instead, she went through two serious relationships: an engagement to a man she did not love, and a non-engagement to a man whom she loved passionately but couldn't bring herself to marry because he was an uneducated farmer. The farmer died, after which she renounced her romantic dreams and stayed home to look after her unpleasant grandmother. When she finally did marry, four months after the grandmother's death, she had premonitions of disaster—it's not a good omen to sit at your wedding breakfast feeling that it's your own funeral. Indeed, things did not work out very well. Her husband, Ewen Macdonald, was a minister, and Montgomery had to perform the many tedious duties of a minister's wife, for which she was by no means as well suited as the beloved Mrs. Allan of Avonlea. But Ewen began to suffer bouts of something then called "religious melancholia," which today might be classified as clinical depression or even bipolar disorder, and Montgomery had to devote more and more time to his care. Later in her life, she herself suffered from nervous collapses, and no wonder. "Nobody ever did want me" was a burden imposed on her by her own childhood, and it proved a hard one to overcome. The many fictional worlds she created through her writing were both an escape from and a way of coming to terms with a deep underlying sadness.

There's another way of reading *Anne of Green Gables,* and that's to assume that the true central character is not Anne but Marilla Cuthbert. Anne herself doesn't really change throughout the book. She grows taller; her hair turns from "carrots" to "a handsome auburn"; her clothes get much prettier, due to the spirit of clothes competition she awakens in Marilla; she talks less, though more thoughtfully, but that's about it. As she herself says, she's still the same girl inside.

Similarly, Matthew remains Matthew, and Anne's best chum Diana is equally static. Only Marilla unfolds into something unimaginable to us at the beginning of the book. Her growing love for Anne, and her growing ability to express that love—not Anne's duckling-to-swan act—is the real magic transformation. Anne is the catalyst who allows the crisp, rigid Marilla to finally express her long-buried softer human emotions. At the beginning of the book, it's Anne who does all the crying; by the end of it, much of this task has been transferred to Marilla. As Mrs. Rachel Lynde says, "Marilla Cuthbert has got *mellow*. That's what."

"I was wishing you could have stayed a little girl, even with all your queer ways," says Marilla in one of her weepy passages toward the end of the book. Marilla has finally allowed herself to make a wish, and now it's been granted: over the past hundred years, Anne *has* stayed the same. Good luck to her for the second hundred.

Alice Munro: An Appreciation

>>><<<

(2008)

Alice Munro is among the major writers of English fiction of our time. She's been accorded armfuls of super-superlatives by critics in both North America and the United Kingdom, she's won many awards, and she has a devoted international readership. Among writers themselves, her name is spoken in hushed tones. Most recently she's been used as a stick to flog the enemy with, in various inter-writerly combats. "You call this writing?" the floggers say, in effect. "Alice Munro! Now *that's* writing!" She's the kind of writer about whom it is often said—no matter how well known she becomes— that she ought to be better known.

None of this happened overnight. Alice Munro has been writing since the 1960s, and her first collection—*Dance of the Happy Shades*—appeared in 1968. To date—and including her latest, the rapturously received *Runaway* (2004)—she has published ten collections, averaging nine or ten stories each. Though her fiction has been a regular feature of *The New Yorker* since the 1970s, her recent elevation to international literary sainthood took as long as it did partly because of the form in which she writes. She is a writer of stories—"short stories," as they used to be called, or "short fiction," which is now more common. Though many American and British and Canadian writers of the first rank have practised this form, there is still a widespread but false tendency to equate length with importance.

Thus, Alice Munro has been among those writers subject to periodic rediscovery, at least outside Canada. It's as if she jumps out of a cake—*Surprise!*—and then has to jump out of it again, and then again. Readers don't see her name in lights on every billboard. They come across her as if by accident or fate, and are drawn in, and then there is an outbreak of wonder and excitement, and incredulity— *Where did Alice Munro come from? Why didn't anybody tell me? How can such excellence have sprung from nowhere?*

But Alice Munro did not spring from nowhere. She sprang—though it's a verb her characters would find overly sprightly, and indeed pretentious—from Huron County, in southwestern Ontario.

Ontario is the large province of Canada that stretches from the Ottawa River to the western end of Lake Superior. This is a huge and varied space, but southwestern Ontario is a distinct part of it. It was named Sowesto by the painter Greg Curnoe, a name that has stuck. Curnoe's view was that Sowesto was an area of considerable interest, but also of considerable psychic darkness and oddity, a view shared by many. Robertson Davies, also from Sowesto, used to say, "I know the dark folkways of my people," and Alice Munro knows them too. You are likely to run into quite a few signs in Sowesto wheat fields telling you to be prepared to meet your God, or else your doom—felt to be much the same thing.

Lake Huron lies at the western edge of Sowesto, Lake Erie to the south. The country is mostly flat farmland, cut by several wide, winding rivers prone to flooding, and on the rivers—because of the available boat transport, and the power provided by water-driven mills—a number of smaller and larger towns grew up in the nineteenth century. Each has its red-brick town hall (usually with a tower), each its post office building and its handful of churches of various denominations, each its main street and its residential section of gracious homes, and its other residential section on the wrong side of the tracks. Each has its families with long memories and stashes of bones in the closets.

Sowesto contains the site of the famous Donnelly Massacre of the nineteenth century, when a large family was slaughtered and their home burnt as a result of political resentments carried over from Ireland. Lush nature, repressed emotions, respectable fronts, hidden sexual excesses, outbreaks of violence, lurid crimes, long-held grudges, strange rumours—none are ever far away in Munro's Sowesto, partly because all have been provided by the real life of the region itself.

Oddly enough, a number of writers have come from Sowesto. Oddly because when Alice Munro was growing up in the 1930s and 1940s, the idea of a person from Canada—but especially one from small-town southwestern Ontario—thinking they could be a writer to be taken seriously in the world at large was laughable. Even by the 1950s and 1960s, there were very few publishers in Canada, and even they were mostly textbook publishers who imported whatever so-called literature was to be had from England and the United States. There might be some amateur theatre—high-school performances, Little Theatre groups. There was, however, the radio, and in the 1960s Alice Munro got her start through a CBC program called *Anthology*, produced by Robert Weaver.

But very few Canadian writers of any sort were known to an international readership, and it was taken for granted that if you had hankerings of that kind—hankerings about which you would of course feel defensive and ashamed, because art was not something a grown-up morally credible person would fool around with—it would be best for you if you left the country. Everyone knew that writing was not a thing you could ever expect to make your living at.

It might be marginally acceptable to dabble around the edges of watercolour painting or poetry if you were a certain kind of man, described by Munro in "The Turkey Season": "There were homosex-uals in town, and we knew who they were: an elegant, light-voiced, wavy-haired paperhanger who called himself an interior decorator; the minister's widow's fat, spoiled only son, who went so far as to enter baking contests and had crocheted a tablecloth; a hypochondriacal church organist and music teacher who kept the choir and his pupils in line with screaming tantrums." Or you could do art as a hobby, if you were a woman with time on your hands, or you could scrape out a living at some poorly paid quasi-artistic job. Munro's stories are sprinkled with women like this. They go in for piano-playing, or write chatty newspaper columns. Or—more tragically—they have a real though small talent, like Almeda Roth in "Meneseteung," but there is no context for them. Almeda produces one volume of minor verse, published in 1873, called *Offerings:*

> The local paper, the *Vidette,* referred to her as "our poetess."
> There seems to be a mixture of respect and contempt, both
> for her calling and for her sex—or for their predictable
> conjuncture.

At the beginning of the story, Almeda is a maiden lady whose family has died. She lives alone, preserves her good name, and does charitable works. But by the end, the dammed-up river of art has overflowed—helped on by hefty doses of laudanum-laced painkiller—and sweeps her rational self away:

> Poems, even. Yes, again, poems. Or one poem. Isn't that the
> idea—one very great poem that will contain everything and,
> oh, that will make all the other poems, the poems she has
> written, inconsequential, mere trial and error, mere rags? . . .
> The name of the poem is the name of the river. No, in fact it
> is the river, the Meneseteung. . . . Almeda looks deep, deep into
> the river of her mind and into the tablecloth, and she sees the
> crocheted roses floating.

This seemed to be the fate of an artist—of necessity, a minor artist—in the small Sowesto towns of yore: silence enforced by the need for respectability, or else an eccentricity verging on madness.

If you moved to a larger Canadian city, you might at least find a few others of your ilk, but in the small towns of Sowesto you'd be on your own. Nevertheless, John Kenneth Galbraith, Robertson Davies, Marian Engel, Graeme Gibson, and James Reaney all came out of Sowesto; and Alice Munro herself—after a spell on the West Coast— moved back there, and lives at present not far from Wingham, the prototype of the various Jubilees and Walleys and Dalglieshes and Hanrattys in her stories.

Through Munro's fiction, Sowesto's Huron County has joined Faulkner's Yoknapatawpha County as a slice of land made legendary by the excellence of the writer who has celebrated it, though in both cases *celebrated* is not quite the right word. *Anatomized* might be closer to what goes on in the work of Munro, though even that term is too clinical. What should we call the combination of obsessive scrutiny, archaeological unearthing, precise and detailed recollection, the wallowing in the seamier and meaner and more vengeful undersides of human nature, the telling of erotic secrets, the nostalgia for vanished miseries, and rejoicing in the fullness and variety of life, stirred all together?

At the end of Munro's *Lives of Girls and Women* (1971), her only novel and a *Bildungsroman*—a novel of development, in this case a portrait of the artist as a young girl—there's a telling passage. Del Jordan of Jubilee, who has by now—true to her last name—crossed over into the promised land of womanhood and also of writerhood, says of her adolescence:

> It did not occur to me then that one day I would be so greedy for Jubilee. Voracious and misguided as Uncle Craig out at Jenkin's Bend, writing his history, I would want to write things down.
>
> I would try to make lists. A list of all the stores and businesses going up and down the main street and who owned them, a list of family names, names on the tombstones in the Cemetery and any inscriptions underneath. . . .
>
> The hope of accuracy we bring to such tasks is crazy, heartbreaking.
>
> And no list could hold what I wanted, for what I wanted was every last thing, every layer of speech and thought, stroke of light on bark or walls, every smell, pothole, pain, crack, delusion, held still and held together—radiant, everlasting.

As a program for a life's work, this is daunting. Nevertheless it's a program Alice Munro was to follow over the next thirty-five years with remarkable fidelity.

Alice Munro was born Alice Laidlaw in 1931, which means that she was a small child during the Depression. She was eight in

1939, the year Canada entered the Second World War, and she attended university—the University of Western Ontario, in London, Ontario—in the postwar years. She was twenty-five and a young mother when Elvis Presley first became famous, and thirty-eight at the time of the flower-child revolution and the advent of the women's movement in 1968–1969, a moment in time that saw the publication of her first book. In 1981, she was fifty. Her stories are set mainly over these years—the 1930s to the 1980s—or even before then, in the time of ancestral memory.

Her own ancestry was partly Scottish Presbyterian: she can trace her family back to James Hogg, the Ettrick Shepherd, friend of Robert Burns and the Edinburgh literati of the late eighteenth century and author of *The Private Memoirs and Confessions of a Justified Sinner,* which could itself be a Munro title. On the other side of the family there were Anglicans, for whom the worst sin is said to consist of using the wrong fork at dinner. Munro's acute consciousness of social class, and of the minutiae and sneers separating one level from the next, is honestly come by, as is—from the Presbyterians—her characters' habit of rigorously examining their own deeds, emotions, motives, and consciences, and finding them wanting. In a traditional Protestant culture, such as that of small-town Sowesto, forgiveness is not easily come by, punishments are frequent and harsh, potential humiliation and shame lurk around every corner, and nobody gets away with much.

But this tradition also contains the doctrine of justification by faith alone: grace descends upon us without any action on our part. In Munro's work, grace abounds, but it is strangely disguised: Nothing can be predicted. Emotions erupt. Preconceptions crumble. Astonishments leap out. Malicious acts can have positive consequences. Salvation arrives when least expected, and in peculiar forms.

But as soon as you make such a pronouncement about Munro's writing—or any other such analysis, inference, or generalization about it—you're aware of that mocking commentator so often present in a Munro story—the one who says, in essence, *Who do you think you are? What gives you the right to think you know anything about me, or about anyone else for that matter?* Or, to quote from

Lives of Girls and Women again, "People's lives . . . were dull, simple, amazing and unfathomable—deep caves paved with kitchen linoleum." The key word here is *unfathomable*.

The first two stories in this selection, "Royal Beatings" and "The Beggar Maid," are from a book with three different titles. In Canada it was called—after a term of peevish accusation used to let the air out of somebody else's puffed-up head—*Who Do You Think You Are?* In England it was called, plainly and simply, *Rose and Flo,* and in the United States it was called, romantically, *The Beggar Maid.* The stories in this enigmatically titled book have a common protagonist, Rose, who grows up in a poorer section of a town called Hanratty with her father and her stepmother, Flo, then goes to university on scholarship, marries a man from a social level far above hers and later runs away from him, and then, later still, becomes an actress—a cardinal sin and cause for shame in the Hanratty still inhabited by Flo. *Who Do You Think You Are?* is thus another *Bildungsroman*—an account of the formation of its heroine—and another portrait of the artist.

What is fakery, what is authenticity? Which emotions and modes of behaviour and speech are honest and true, which pretended or pretentious? Or can they be separated? Munro's characters think frequently about such matters.

As in art, so in life. Hanratty society is divided in two by the river that flows through the town:

> In Hanratty the social structure ran from doctors and dentists and lawyers down to factory workers and draymen; in West Hanratty it ran from factory workers and foundry workers down to large improvident families of casual bootleggers and prostitutes and unsuccessful thieves.

Each half of the town claims jeering rights against the other. Flo goes across to Hanratty, the better part of town, to shop, but also "to see people, and listen to them. Among the people she listened to were Mrs. Lawyer Davies, Mrs. Anglican Rector Henley-Smith, and Mrs. Horse-Doctor McKay. She came home and imitated their flibberty voices. Monsters, she made them seem, of foolishness, and showiness, and self-approbation."

But when Rose goes to college and boards with a lady professor and becomes engaged to Patrick, son of a West Coast department store tycoon, and gets a look at upper-middle-class surroundings, Flo in turn becomes monstrous in Rose's eyes, and Rose is divided against herself. Patrick's visit to Rose's home town is a disaster for Rose:

> She felt ashamed on more levels than she could count. She was ashamed of the food and the swan and the plastic tablecloth; ashamed for Patrick, the gloomy snob, who made a startled grimace when Flo passed him the toothpick-holder; ashamed for Flo with her timidity and hypocrisy and pretensions; most of all ashamed for herself. She didn't even have any way that she could talk, and sound natural.

Yet as soon as Patrick begins to criticize her town and family, Rose feels "a layer of loyalty and protectiveness . . . hardening around every memory she had . . ."

This state of divided allegiance applies to Munro's vocation as well as to considerations of social status. Her fictional world is peopled with secondary characters who despise art and artifice, and any kind of pretentiousness or showing off. It's against these attitudes and the self-mistrust they inspire that her central characters must struggle in order to free themselves enough to create anything at all.

Yet at the same time her protagonists share this scorn of the artificial side of art, and the distrust of it. What should be written about? How should one write? How much of art is genuine, how much just a bag of cheap tricks—imitating people, manipulating their emotions, making faces? How can one affirm anything about another person—even a made-up person—without presumption? Above all, how should a story end? (Munro often provides one ending, then questions or revises it. Or else she simply distrusts it, as in the final paragraph of "Meneseteung," where the narrator says, "I may have got it wrong.") Isn't the very act of writing an act of arrogance, isn't the pen a broken reed? A number of stories—"Friend of My Youth,"

"Carried Away," "Wilderness Station," "Hateship, Friendship, Courtship, Loveship, Marriage"—contain letters that display the vanity or falsity or even the malice of their writers. If the writing of letters can be so devious, what about writing itself?

This tension has remained with her: as in "The Moons of Jupiter," Munro's artistic characters are punished for not succeeding, but they are punished also for success. The woman writer, thinking about her father, says:

> I could hear him saying, Well, I didn't see anything about you in *Maclean's*. And if he had read something about me he would say, Well, I didn't think too much of that writeup. His tone would be humorous and indulgent but would produce in me a familiar dreariness of spirit. The message I got from him was simple: Fame must be striven for, then apologized for. Getting or not getting it, you will be to blame.

"Dreariness of spirit" is one of the great Munro enemies. Her characters do battle with it in every way they can, fighting against stifling mores and other people's deadening expectations and imposed rules of behaviour, and every possible kind of muffling and spiritual smothering. Given a choice between being a person who does good works but has inauthentic feelings and is numb at heart and one who behaves badly but is true to what she really feels and is thus alive to herself, a Munro woman is likely to choose the latter; or, if she chooses the former, she will then comment on her own slipperiness, guile, wiliness, slyness, and perversity. Honesty, in Munro's work, is not the best policy: it is not a policy at all, but an essential element, like air. The characters must get hold of at least some of it, by means fair or foul, or—they feel—they will go under.

The battle for authenticity is waged most significantly in the field of sex. The Munro social world—like most societies in which silence and secrecy are the norm in sexual matters—carries a high erotic charge, and this charge extends like a neon penumbra around each character, illuminating landscapes, rooms, and objects. A rumpled bed says more, in the hands of Munro, than any graphic in-out, in-out depiction of genitalia ever could. Even if a story is not primarily about a love affair or sexual encounter, men and women are always aware of one another as men and women, positively or negatively, recognizing sexual attraction and curiosity or else sexual revulsion. Women are immediately attuned to the sexual power of other women, and are wary of it, or envious. Men show off and preen and flirt and seduce and compete.

Munro's characters are as alert as dogs in a perfume store to the sexual chemistry in a gathering—the chemistry among others, as well as their own visceral responses. Falling in love, falling in lust, sneaking around on spouses and enjoying it, telling sexual lies, doing shameful things they feel compelled to do out of irresistible desire, making sexual calculations based on social desperation—few writers have explored such processes more thoroughly, and more ruthlessly. Pushing the sexual boundaries is distinctly thrilling for many a Munro woman; but in order to trespass you have to know exactly where the fence is, and Munro's universe is criss-crossed with meticulously defined boundaries. Hands, chairs, glances—all are part of an intricate inner map strewn with barbed wire and booby traps, and secret paths through the shrubbery.

For women of Munro's generation, sexual expression was a liberation and a way out. But out of what? Out of the denial and limiting scorn she describes so well in "The Turkey Season":

> Lily said she never let her husband come near her if he had
> been drinking. Marjorie said since the time she nearly died
> with a hemorrhage she never let her husband come near
> her, period. Lily said quickly that it was only when he'd been
> drinking that he tried anything. I could see that it was a matter
> of pride not to let your husband come near you, but I couldn't
> quite believe that "come near" meant "have sex."

For older women like Lily and Marjorie, to enjoy sex would have been a humiliating defeat. For women like Rose, in "The Beggar Maid," it's a matter for pride and celebration, a victory. For later generations of women—post–sexual revolution—enjoying sex was to become simply a duty, the perfect orgasm yet another thing to add to their list of required accomplishments; and when enjoyment becomes a duty, we're back in the land of "dreariness of spirit." But for a Munro character in the throes of sexual exploration, the spirit may be confused and ashamed and tormented, even cruel and sadistic—some of the couples in her stories get pleasure out of torturing each other emotionally, just like some real people—but it is never dreary.

In some of the later stories, sex can be less impetuous, more calculated: for Grant, in "The Bear Came Over the Mountain," it's the decisive element in an astonishing feat of emotional commodities-trading. His beloved wife, Fiona, has dementia, and has become attached to a similarly afflicted man in her care facility. When this man is taken home by his hard-bitten, practical wife, Marian, Fiona pines and stops eating. Grant wants to persuade Marian to put her husband back in the institution. Marian refuses: it would cost too much. But Grant detects that Marian is lonely and sexually available. She has a wrinkled-up face, but her body is still attractive. Like an adroit salesman, Grant moves in to close the deal. Munro knows full well that sex can be a glory and a torment, but it can also be a bargaining chip.

The society Munro writes about is a Christian one. This Christianity is not often overt; it's merely the general background. Flo in "The Beggar Maid" decorates the walls with "a number of admonitions, pious and cheerful and mildly bawdy":

> THE LORD IS MY SHEPHERD
> BELIEVE IN THE LORD JESUS CHRIST AND THOU SHALT
> BE SAVED

Why did Flo have those, when she wasn't even religious? They were what people had, common as calendars.

Christianity is "what people had"—and in Canada, church and state were never separated along the lines laid down in the United States. Prayers and Bible readings were daily fare in publicly funded schools. This cultural Christianity has provided ample material for

Munro, but it is also connected with one of the most distinctive patterns in her image-making and storytelling.

The central Christian tenet is that two disparate and mutually exclusive elements—divinity and humanity—got jammed together in Christ, neither annihilating the other. The result was not a demigod, or a god in disguise: God became totally a human being while remaining at the same time totally divine. To believe that Christ was only a man or to believe he was simply God were both declared heretical by the early Christian Church. Christianity thus depends on a denial of either/or classifying logic and an acceptance of both-at-once mystery. Logic says that A cannot be both itself and non-A at the same time, Christianity says it can. The formulation "A but also non-A" is indispensable to it.

Many of Munro's stories resolve themselves—or fail to resolve themselves—in precisely this way. The example that first came to mind—though there are many—is from *Lives of Girls and Women,* in which the teacher who'd staged the high school's airy and joyful operettas drowns herself in the river.

> Miss Farris in her velvet skating costume . . . Miss Farris *con brio* . . . Miss Farris floating face down, unprotesting, in the Wawanash River, six days before she was found. Though there is no plausible way of hanging those pictures together—if the last one is true then might it not alter all the others?—they are going to have to stay together now.

For Munro, a thing can be true, but not true, but true nonetheless. "It is real and dishonest," thinks Georgia of her remorse in "Differently." "How hard it is for me to believe that I made that up," says the narrator of "The Progress of Love." "It seems so much the truth it is the truth; it's what I believe about them. I haven't stopped believing it." The world is profane *and* sacred. It must be swallowed whole. There's always more to be known about it than you can ever know.

In a story called "Something I've Been Meaning to Tell You," jealous Et describes her sister's former lover—a promiscuous ladies' man—

and the look he gives to every woman, a look "that made him seem to be a deep-sea diver diving down, down through all the emptiness and cold and wreckage to discover the one thing he had set his heart on, something small and precious, hard to locate, as a ruby maybe on the ocean floor."

Munro's stories abound in such questionable seekers and well-fingered ploys. But they abound also in such insights: within any story, within any human being, there may be a dangerous treasure, a priceless ruby. A heart's desire.

Ancient Balances

>>><<<

(2008)

Canadian nature writer Ernest Thompson Seton had an odd bill presented to him on his twenty-first birthday. It was a record kept by his father of all the expenses connected with young Ernest's childhood and youth, including the fee charged by the doctor for delivering him. Even more oddly, Ernest is said to have paid it. I used to think that Mr. Seton Senior was a jerk, but now I'm wondering, What if he was—in principle—right? Are we in debt to anyone or anything for the bare fact of our existence? If so, what do we owe, and to whom or to what? And how should we pay?

When I was asked to give the 2008 Massey Lectures, I decided to use them to explore a subject I know little about, but which for this reason intrigues me. That subject is debt.

Not debt management, or sleep debt, or the national debt, or about managing your monthly budget, or about how debt is actually a good thing because you can borrow money and then make it grow, or about shopaholics and how to figure out that you are one: bookstores and the Internet abound in such materials.

Nor the more lurid forms of debt: gambling debts and Mafia revenges, karmic justice whereby bad deeds trigger reincarnation as a beetle, or melodramas in which moustache-twirling creditors use non-payment of the rent to force unwanted sex on beautiful women, though it may touch on these. Instead, it's about debt as a human construct—thus an imaginative construct—and how this construct mirrors and magnifies both voracious human desire and ferocious human fear.

Writers write about what worries them, says Alistair MacLeod. Also about what puzzles them, I'd add. This subject is one of the most worrisome and puzzling things I know: that peculiar nexus where money, narrative or story, and religious belief intersect, often with explosive force.

The things that puzzle us as adults begin by puzzling us as children, or this has certainly been the case for me. In the late 1940s society in which I grew up, there were three things you were never supposed to ask questions about. One of them was money, especially how much of it anyone made. The second was religion: to begin a conversation on that subject would lead directly to the Spanish Inquisition, or worse. The third was sex. I lived among biologists, and sex—at least as practised by insects—was something I could look up in the textbooks that were lying around the house: the ovipositor was no stranger to me. So the burning curiosity children experience vis-à-vis the forbidden was focused, for me, on the two other taboo areas: the financial and the devotional.

At first these appeared to be distinct categories. There were the things of God, which were unseen. Then there were the things of Caesar, which were all too material. They took the form of golden calves, of which we didn't have many in Toronto at that time, and also the form of money, the love of which was the root of all evil. But on the other hand stood the comic-book character Scrooge McDuck—much read about by me—who was a hot-tempered, tight-fisted, and often devious billionaire named after Charles Dickens's famous redeemed miser, Ebenezer Scrooge. The plutocratic McDuck had a large money bin full of gold coins, in which he and his three adopted nephews splashed around as if in a swimming pool. Money, for Uncle Scrooge and the young duck triplets, was not the root of all evil but a pleasurable plaything. Which of these views was correct?

We kids of the 1940s did usually have some pocket money, and although we weren't supposed to talk about it or have an undue love of it, we were expected to learn to manage it at an early age. When I was eight years old, I had my first paying job. I was already acquainted with money in a more limited way—I got five cents a week as an allowance, which bought a lot more tooth decay then than it does now. The pennies not spent on candy I kept in a tin box that had once held Lipton tea. It had a brightly coloured Indian design, complete with elephant, opulent veiled lady, men in turbans, temples and domes, palm trees, and a sky so blue it never was. The pennies had leaves on one side and king's heads on the other, and were desirable to me according to their rarity and beauty: King George VI, the reigning monarch, was common currency and thus low-ranking on my snobby little scale, and also he had no beard or moustache; but there were still some hairier George Vs in circulation, and, if you were lucky, a really fur-faced Edward VII or two.

I understood that these pennies could be traded for goods such as ice-cream cones, but I did not think them superior to the other units of currency used by my fellow children: cigarette-package airplane cards, milk-bottle tops, comic books, and glass marbles of many kinds. Within each of these categories, the principle was the same: rarity and beauty increased value. The rate of exchange was set by the children themselves, though a good deal of haggling took place.

All of that changed when I got a job. The job paid twenty-five cents an hour—a fortune!—and consisted of wheeling a baby around in the snow. As long as I brought the baby back, alive and not too frozen, I got the twenty-five cents. It was at this time in my life that each penny came to be worth the same as every other penny, despite whose head was on it, thus teaching me an important lesson: in high finance, aesthetic considerations soon drop by the wayside, worse luck.

Since I was making so much money, I was told I needed a bank account, so I graduated from the Lipton tea tin and acquired a red bank book. Now the difference between the pennies with heads on them and the marbles, milk-bottle tops, comic books, and airplane cards became clear because you could not put the marbles into the bank. But you were urged to put your money in there, in order to keep it safe. When I'd accumulated a dangerous amount of the stuff—say, a dollar—I would deposit it at the bank, where the sum was recorded in pen and ink by an intimidating bank teller. The last number in the series was called "the balance"—not a term I understood, as I had yet to see a two-armed weighing scales.

Every once in a while an extra sum would appear in my red bank book—one I hadn't deposited. This, I was told, was called "interest," and I had "earned" it by having kept my money in the bank. I didn't understand this either. It was certainly interesting to me that I had some extra money—that must be why it was called "interest"—but I knew I hadn't actually earned it: no babies from the bank had been wheeled around in the snow by me. Where then had these mysterious sums come from? Surely from the same imaginary place that spawned the nickels left by the Tooth Fairy in exchange for your shucked-off teeth: some realm of pious invention that couldn't be located anywhere exactly, but that we all had to pretend to believe in or the tooth-for-a-nickel gambit would no longer work.

However, the nickels under the pillow were real enough. So was the bank interest because you could cash it in and turn it back into pennies, and thence into candy and ice-cream cones. But how could a fiction generate real objects? I knew from fairy tales such as *Peter Pan* that if you ceased to believe in fairies they would drop dead: if I stopped believing in banks, would they too expire? The adult view was that fairies were unreal and banks were real. But was that true?

Thus began my financial puzzlements. Nor are they over yet.

During the past half-century I've spent much time riding around on public transport. I always read the ads. In the 1950s, there were a lot of girdle and brassiere ads, and ads for deodorants and mouthwashes. Today these have vanished, to be replaced by ads for diseases—heart problems, arthritis, diabetes, and more; ads to help you stop smoking; ads for television series that always feature a goddess-like woman or two, though these are sometimes ads for hair dye and skin cream; and ads for agencies you can call if you have a gambling addiction. And ads for debt services—there are a lot of this kind.

One of them shows a gleefully smiling woman with a young child. The caption says, "Now I'm in charge ... and the collection calls have stopped." "Like hell money doesn't buy happiness—debt is manageable," says another. "There *is* Life after Debt!" punningly chirps a third. "There *can* be a happily ever after part!" trills a fourth, catering to the same belief in fairy tales that inspired you to shove the bills under the rug and then make believe they'd been paid. "Is someone on your tail?" queries a fifth ad, more ominously, from the back end of a bus. These services promise not to make your burdensome debts vanish in a puff of smoke but to help you to consolidate them and pay them down in bits and pieces, while learning to avoid the free-spending behaviour that got you so deeply into the red in the first place.

Why are there so many of these ads? Is it because there are unprecedented numbers of people in debt? Very possibly.

In the 1950s, the age of girdles and deodorants, the adsters evidently felt that the most anxiety-making thing imaginable was to have your body lolloping about unconfined, and stinking up the place into the bargain. It was the body that might get away from you, so it was the body that had to be brought under control; if not, that body might get out and do things that would bring a shame upon you so deep and sexual that it could never be mentioned on public transport. Now things are very different. Sexual antics are a part of the entertainment industry, and thus no longer a matter for censure and guilt, so your body is not the main focus of anxiety unless it gets one of the much-advertised diseases. Instead, the worrisome thing is the debit side of your ledger.

There's good reason for this. The first credit card was introduced in 1950. In 1955, the average Canadian household debt-to-income ratio was 55 per cent; in 2003, it was 105.2 per cent. The ratio has gone up since then. In the United States, the ratio was 114 per cent in 2004. In other words, a great many people are spending more than they're earning. So are a great many national governments.

On the microeconomic level, a friend tells me of an epidemic of debt among over-eighteens, especially college students: credit card companies target them, and the students rush out and spend the maximum without stopping to calculate the consequences and are then stuck with debts they can't pay off, at very high interest rates. Since neurologists are now telling us that the adolescent brain is quite different from the adult one, and not really capable of doing the long-term buy-now, pay-later math, this ought to be considered child exploitation.

At the other end of the scale, the financial world has recently been shaken as a result of the collapse of a debt pyramid involving something called "sub-prime mortgages"—a pyramid scheme that most people don't grasp very well but that boils down to the fact that some large financial institutions peddled mortgages to people who could not possibly pay the monthly rates and then put this snake-oil debt into cardboard boxes with impressive labels on them and sold them to institutions and hedge funds that thought they were worth something. It's like the teenage credit card ploy, but at a much greater level of magnitude.

A friend of mine from the United States writes: "I used to have three banks and a mortgage company. Bank One bought the other two and is now trying hard to buy the mortgage company, which is bankrupt, only it was revealed this morning that the last bank standing is also in serious trouble. Now they are trying to renegotiate with the mortgage company. Question One: If your company is going broke, why would you want to buy a company whose insolvency is front-page news? Question Two: If all the lenders go broke, will the borrowers get off the hook? You can't imagine the chagrin of the credit-loving American. I gather that whole neighborhoods in the Midwest look like neighborhoods in my hometown, empty houses with knee-high grass and vines growing over them and no one willing to admit they actually own the place. Down we go, about to reap what we sow."

Which has a nice Biblical ring to it, but still we scratch our heads. How and why did this happen? The answer I hear quite often— "greed"—may be accurate enough, but it doesn't go very far toward unveiling the deeper mysteries of the process. What is this "debt" by which we're so bedevilled? Like air, it's all around us, but we never think about it unless something goes wrong with the supply. Certainly it's a thing we've come to feel is indispensable to our collective buoyancy. In good times we float around on it as if on a helium-filled balloon; we rise higher and higher, and the balloon gets bigger and bigger, until—*poof!*—some killjoy sticks a pin into it and we sink. But what is the nature of that pin? Another friend of mine used to maintain that airplanes stayed up in the air only because people believed—against reason—that they could fly: without that collective delusion sustaining them, they would instantly plummet to earth. Is "debt" similar?

In other words, perhaps debt exists because we imagine it. It is the

forms this imagining has taken—and their impact on lived reality—
that I would like to explore.

Our present attitudes toward debt are deeply embedded in our entire
culture—culture being, as primatologist Frans de Waal has said, "an
extremely powerful modifier—affecting everything we do and are,
penetrating to the core of human existence." But perhaps there are
some even more basic patterns being modified.

Let's assume that all of the things human beings do—the good,
the bad, and the ugly—can be located on a smorgasbord of behaviours with a sign on it reading *Homo sapiens sapiens*. These things
aren't on the smorgasbord labelled *Spiders,* which is why we don't
spend a lot of time eating bluebottle flies, nor are they on the smorgasbord labelled *Dogs,* which is why we don't go around marking fire
hydrants with our glandular scents or shoving our noses into bags
of old garbage. Part of our human smorgasbord has actual food on
it, for, like all species, we are driven by appetite and hunger. The rest
of the dishes on the table contain less concrete fears and desires—
things such as "I'd like to fly," "I'd like to have sexual intercourse with
you," "War is unifying to the tribe," "I'm afraid of snakes," and "What
happens to me when I die?"

But there's nothing on the table that isn't based on or linked to our
rudimentary human patterns—what we want, what we don't want,
what we admire, what we despise, what we love, and what we hate
and fear. Some geneticists even go so far as to speak of our "modules,"
as if we were electronic systems with chunks of functional circuitry
that can be switched on and off. Whether such discrete modules
actually exist as part of our genetically determined neural wiring is
at present still a matter for experiment and debate. But in any case,
I'm assuming that the older a recognizable pattern of behaviour is—
the longer it's demonstrably been with us—the more integral it must
be to our human-ness and the more cultural variations on it will be
in evidence.

I'm not proposing a stamped-in-tin immutable "human nature"
here—epigeneticists point out that genes can be expressed, or
"switched on," and also suppressed in various ways, depending on
the environment in which they find themselves. I'm merely saying

that without gene-linked configurations—certain building blocks or foundation stones, if you like—the many variations of basic human behaviours that we see around us would never occur at all. An online video game such as *Everquest,* in which you have to work your way up from rabbit-skinner to castle-owning knight by selling and trading, co-operating with fellow players on group missions, and launching raids on other castles, would be unthinkable if we were not both a social species and one aware of hierarchies.

What corresponding ancient inner foundation stone underlies the elaborate fretwork of debt that surrounds us on every side? Why are we so open to offers of present-time advantage in exchange for future though onerous repayment? Is it simply that we're programmed to snatch the low-hanging fruit and gobble down as much of it as we can, without thinking ahead to the fruitless days that may then lie ahead of us? Well, partly: seventy-two hours without fluids or two weeks without food and you're most likely dead, so if you don't eat some of that low-hanging fruit right now you aren't going to be around six months later to congratulate yourself on your capacity for self-restraint and delayed gratification. In that respect, credit cards are almost guaranteed to make money for the lender, since "grab it now" may be a variant of a behaviour selected for in hunter-gatherer days, long before anyone ever thought about saving up for their retirement. A bird in the hand really was worth two in the bush then, and a bird crammed into your mouth was worth even more. But is it just a case of short-term gain followed by long-term pain? Is debt created from our own greed or even—more charitably—from our own need?

I postulate that there's another ancient inner foundation stone without which debt and credit structures could not exist: our sense of fairness. Viewed in the best light, this is an admirable human characteristic. Without our sense of fairness, the bright side of which is "one good turn deserves another," we wouldn't recognize the fairness of paying back what we've borrowed, and thus no one would ever be stupid enough to lend anything to anyone else with an expectation of return. Spiders don't share out the bluebottles among other adult spiders: only social animals indulge in sharing out. The dark side of the sense of fairness is the sense of unfairness, which results in gloating when you've got away with being unfair, or else guilt; and in rage and vengeance, when the unfairness has been visited upon you.

Children start saying, "That's not fair!" at the age of four or so, long before they're interested in sophisticated investment vehicles or have any sense of the value of coins and bills. They are also filled with satisfaction when the villain in a bedtime story gets an unambiguous comeuppance, and made uneasy when such retribution doesn't happen. Forgiveness and mercy, like olives and anchovies, seem to be acquired later, or—if the culture is unfavourable to them—not. But for young children, putting a bad person into a barrel studded with nails and rolling him or her into the sea restores the cosmic balance and removes the malevolent force from view, and the little ones sleep easier at night.

The interest in fairness elaborates with age. After seven, there's a legalistic phase in which the fairness—or, usually, the unfairness—of any rule imposed by adults is argued relentlessly. At this age, too, the sense of fairness can take curious forms. For instance, in the 1980s there was a strange ritual among nine-year-old children that went like this: during car rides, you stared out the window until you spotted a Volkswagen Beetle. Then you hit your child companion on the arm, shouting, "Punch-buggy, no punch-backs!" Seeing the Volkswagen Beetle first meant that you had the right to punch the other child, and adding a codicil—"No punch-backs!"—meant that he or she had been done out of the right to punch you in return. If, however, the other child managed to shout "Punch-backs!" before you could yell out your protective charm, then a retaliatory punch was in order. Money was not a factor here: you couldn't buy your way out of being punched. What was at issue was the principle of reciprocity: one punch deserved another, and would certainly get it unless an Out clause was inserted with the speed of lightning.

Those who fail to discern in the Punch-buggy ritual the essential *lex talionis* form of the almost four-thousand-year-old Code of Hammurabi—reformulated as the Biblical eye-for-an-eye and tooth-for-a-tooth law—are blind indeed. *Lex talionis* means, roughly, "the law of retribution in kind or suitability." Under the Punch-buggy rules, punches cancel each other out unless you can whip your magical protection into place first. This kind of protection can be found throughout the world of contracts and legal documents, in clauses that begin with phrases such as "Notwithstanding any of the foregoing."

We'd all like the right to a free punch, or a free lunch, or a free anything. We all suspect that the likeliness of our getting such a right is scant unless we can jump in there with some serious abracadabra. But how do we know that one punch is likely to incur another? Is it early socialization—the kind you get while squabbling over the Play-Doh at preschool and then saying, "Melanie bit me"—or is it a template hot-wired into the human brain?

Let's examine the case for the latter. In order for a mental construct such as "debt" to exist—you owe me something that will balance the books once it is transferred to me—there are some preconditions. One of them, as I've said, is the notion of fairness. Attached to that is the notion of equivalent values: What does it take to make both sides of the mental score sheet or grudge tally or double-entry bookkeeping program we're all constantly running add up to the same thing? If Johnny has three apples and Suzie has a pencil, is one apple for one pencil an acceptable exchange, or will there be an apple or a pencil remaining to be paid? That all depends on what values Johnny and Suzie place on their respective trading items, which in turn depend on how hungry and/or in need of communication devices they may be. In a trade perceived as fair, each side balances the other, and nothing is thought to be owing.

Even inorganic nature strives toward balances, otherwise known as static states. As a child, you may have done that elementary experiment in which you put salty water on one side of a permeable membrane and fresh water on the other side and measure how long it takes for the sodium chloride to make its way into the H_2O until both sides are equally salty. Or, as an adult, you may simply have noticed that if you put your cold feet on your partner's warm leg, your feet will get warmer while your partner's leg will get colder. (If you try this at home, please don't say I told you to do it.)

Many animals are able to tell "bigger than" apart from "smaller than." Hunting animals have to be able to do this, as it could be fatal to them to literally bite off more than they can chew. Eagles on the

Pacific coast can be dragged to a watery grave by salmon that are too heavy for them, since, once having pounced, they can't unhook their claws unless they're on a firm surface. If you've ever taken small children to the big-cat enclosure at the zoo, you may have noticed that a medium-sized feline such as the cheetah won't pay much attention to you but will eye the kids with avid speculation, because the youngsters are meal-sized for them and you are not.

The ability to size up an enemy or a prey is a common feature of the animal kingdom, but among the primates, the making of fine bigger-than and better-than distinctions when the edible goodies are being divided up verges on the unnerving. In 2003, *Nature* magazine published an account of experiments conducted by Frans de Waal, of Emory University's Yerkes National Primate Center, and anthropologist Sarah F. Brosnan. To begin with, they taught capuchin monkeys to trade pebbles for slices of cucumber. Then they gave one of the monkeys a grape—viewed by the monkeys as more valuable—for the very same pebble. "You can do it twenty-five times in a row, and they are perfectly happy getting cucumber slices," said de Waal. But if a grape was substituted—thus unfairly giving one monkey a better pay packet for work of equal value—the cucumber-receivers got upset, began throwing pebbles out of the cage, and eventually refused to co-operate. And the majority of the monkeys got so angry if one of them was given a grape for no reason that some of them stopped eating. It was a monkey picket line: they might as well have been carrying signs that read *Management Grape Dispensing Unfair!* The trading was taught, as was the pebble/cucumber rate of exchange, but the outrage appeared to be spontaneous.

Keith Chen, a researcher at the Yale School of Management, also worked with capuchin monkeys. He found he could train them to use coin-like metal disks as currency, coins being the pebble idea, only shiny. "My underlying goal is to determine what aspects of our economic behaviour are innate, deep in the brain, and conserved over time," said Chen. But why stop at obviously economic behaviour such as trading? Among social animals that need to co-operate in order to achieve common goals such as—for capuchins—killing and eating squirrels, and—for chimpanzees—killing and eating bush babies, there has to be a sharing-out of the results of group effort that is recognized as fair by the sharers. Fair is not the same as equal: for instance, would it be fair for the plate of a ninety-pound ten-year-old to contain exactly the same amount of food as that of a two-hundred-pound six-foot-sixer? Among the hunting chimpanzees, the one strongest in personality or physique typically gets more, but all who have joined in the hunt receive at least something, which is pretty much the same principle used by Genghis Khan for doling out the results of his conquering, slaughtering, and looting activities among his allies and troops. Those who express surprise at winning political parties for their pork-barrelling and favouritism might keep this in mind: if you don't share out, those folks won't be there when you need them. At the very least, you have to give them some cucumber slices, and avoid giving grapes to their rivals.

If fairness is completely lacking, the members of the chimpanzee group will rebel; at the very least, they're unlikely to join in a group hunt next time. To the extent that they're social animals interacting in complex communities in which status is important, primates are highly conscious of what's fitting for each member and what, on the other hand, constitutes uppity counter-jumping. The snobbish top-of-the-pecking-order Lady Catherine de Bourgh of Jane Austen's novel *Pride and Prejudice,* with her exquisitely calibrated sense of rank, has nothing on capuchin monkeys and chimpanzees.

Chimpanzees don't limit their trading to food; they regularly engage in mutually beneficial favour-trading, or reciprocal altruism. Chimp A helps Chimp B to gang up on Chimp C and expects to be helped in turn. If Chimp B then doesn't come through at the time of Chimp A's need, Chimp A is enraged and throws a screaming temper tantrum. There seems to be a kind of inner ledger involved: Chimp A senses perfectly well what Chimp B owes him, and Chimp B senses it too. Debts of honour exist among chimpanzees, it appears. It's the same mechanism that's at work in Francis Ford Coppola's film *The Godfather:* a man whose daughter has been disfigured comes to the Mafia boss for help and gets it, but it's understood that this favour will need to be repaid later in some unsavoury way.

As Robert Wright says in his 1994 book, *The Moral Animal: Why We Are the Way We Are:*

Reciprocal altruism has presumably shaped the texture not just of human emotion, but of human cognition. Leda Cosmides has shown that people are good at solving otherwise baffling logical puzzles when the puzzles are cast in the form of social exchange—in particular, when the object of the game is to figure out if someone is cheating. This suggests to Cosmides that a "cheater-detection" module is among the mental organs governing reciprocal altruism. No doubt others remain to be discovered.

We do want our trades and exchanges to be fair and above-board, at least on the other person's side. A "cheater-detection" module assumes a parallel module, one that evaluates non-cheating. Small children used to chant, "Cheaters never prosper!" in the schoolyard. That's true—we judge cheaters harshly, which affects their future prosperity—but it's also true, alas, that they receive this judgment from us only when they get caught.

In *The Moral Animal*, Wright gives an account of a computer simulation program that won a 1970s contest proposed by Robert Axelrod, an American political scientist. The contest was designed to test what sort of behaviour patterns would prove to be the fittest by surviving the longest in a series of encounters with other programs. When one program first "met" another, it had to decide whether to co-operate, whether to respond with aggression or cheating, or whether to refuse to play. "The context for the competition," says Wright, "nicely mirrored the social context of human, and pre-human evolution. There was a fairly small society—several dozen regularly interacting individuals. Each program could 'remember' whether each other program had cooperated on previous encounters, and adjust its own behaviour accordingly."

The winner of the contest was called Tit for Tat—an expression that descends from "Tip for Tap," both words having once meant a hit, push, or blow—thus, "You hit me and I'll hit you back." The computer program Tit for Tat played by a very simple set of rules: "On the first encounter with any program, it would co-operate. Thereafter, it would do whatever the other program had done on a previous encounter. One good turn deserves another, as does one bad turn." This program won out over time because it was never repeatedly victimized—if an opponent cheated on it, it withheld co-operation next time—and, unlike consistent cheaters and exploiters, it didn't alienate a lot of others and then find itself shut out of play, nor did it get involved in escalating aggression. It played by a recognizable eye-for-an-eye rule: Do unto others as they do unto you. (Which is not the same as the "golden rule"—Do unto others as you would have them do unto you. That one is much more difficult to follow.)

In the computer program contest won by Tit for Tat, it was a given that each player had equal resources at its disposal. Treating a first approach with friendliness and then replying to subsequent ones in kind—returning good for good and evil for evil—can be the winning stratagem only if the playing field is level. None of the competing programs were permitted to have superior weapons systems: had one of the entrants been allowed an advantage such as the chariot, the double-recurved bow of Genghis Khan, or the atomic bomb, Tit for Tat would have failed because the player with the technological advantage could have obliterated its opponents, enslaved them, or forced them to trade on disadvantageous terms. This is in fact what has happened over the long course of our history: those who won the wars wrote the laws, and the laws they wrote enshrined inequality by justifying hierarchical social formations with themselves at the top.

Scrooge

>>><<<

AN INTRODUCTION

(2009)

Charles Dickens wrote *A Christmas Carol* in 1843. He was already very famous, having made his name with *The Pickwick Papers* and then enhanced it with *Oliver Twist, Nicholas Nickleby, The Old Curiosity Shop,* and *Barnaby Rudge*—and all this before he was thirty. This pace was prodigious. No writer alive has written at such a pace and produced such high-quality work at such a young age.

Dickens is said to have written *A Christmas Carol* in six weeks, to pay off a debt—perhaps that was why grasping money-lenders were much on his mind—and he presented this novella as a light-hearted jeu d'esprit—a Christmas fairy tale or ghost tale, intended to entertain, and to put his readers in good humour. The story has the traditional three-part structure of a fairy tale—three Spirits of Christmas, three ages of Scrooge (past, present, future)—and it has also a fairy-tale ending, in which light triumphs over darkness, goodness and harmony reign, and an innocent life in peril—Tiny Tim's—is saved, not to mention the gnarly old soul of Scrooge.

Dickens's more covert intention—signalled by the work's one-time working title, "The Sledgehammer"—was to strike a few more blows for the social justice he was so keen on by contrasting avarice and poverty, then proposing his usual antidote: an outflowing of private benevolence. For, as George Orwell has commented, though Dickens burned with anger at social injustices, he never went so far as to urge a whole-scale political revolution.

But none of this would account for the overwhelming longevity and popularity of the *Carol*'s protagonist—Ebenezer Scrooge. Scrooge is one of those characters—like Hamlet—who has become detached from the story in which he had his birth, and has become instantly recognizable, even by those who may never have read the book.

Why should that be? Let me consult my own model of that favourite Dickensian repository of infallible knowledge, "The Human Heart." When did I first meet the immortal Scrooge, and why did I become so fond of him? I seem always to have been aware of him. Did I hear *A Christmas Carol* read on the radio during my 1940s childhood? It's likely—those were radio days. Or did I encounter him the way I encountered so much else—peering out with sly and narrow but nonetheless twinkling eyes from the colourful ads in magazines? In this respect, Scrooge was a sort of anti–Santa Claus— Santa Claus's dark twin. The one, fat and jolly and round and red, dispensing largesse; the other, skinny and pinched and dour, withholding it. Yet at the end of the *Carol,* the new, redeemed, turkey-purchasing, Bob Cratchit–salary–raising Scrooge has become a sort of Santa; which raises the chilling possibility that Santa might one day shrivel and wizen, and morph into Scrooge at his worst—that crabby geezer in the opening chapter of the book. Consider those punitive Santean lumps of coal—not much mentioned these days, but kept, you can bet, in Santa's worst-case reserve arsenal of dirty tricks. Coal in your stocking would be just what the mean version of Scrooge would have liked.

Whatever the case, by the time my seven-year-old self discovered Disney's Scrooge McDuck, I knew quite well what the name "Scrooge" was supposed to signify. It included the fact that within McDuck's ancient, scheming husk there flickered a kindly and generous impulse. It was a good sign that the Duck triplets adored their Uncle Scrooge—he was a lot of fun because in recreational moments he often behaved just as childishly as they did themselves.

This is one key to the original Ebenezer Scrooge: he's a child at heart. But, when we first meet him in *A Christmas Carol,* he's a wounded child, albeit an elderly one. In writing Scrooge, Dickens delved deep within, and put a good measure of his own hidden pain into his creation. He had never forgotten the most hopeless period of his life, when his feckless father had been locked into debtors' prison, and young Charles had been wrenched from school and set to work in a blacking factory to help support the destitute Dickens family. This period did not last forever, but for a child the present moment is forever: the young Dickens could see no possibility of rescue from the unfamiliar hell into which his father's financial mishaps had thrust him.

The most poignant moment in *A Christmas Carol* is not the death of Tiny Tim, weep-making though that is; nor is it the plangent picture of Scrooge's own possible future corpse, "plundered and bereft, unwatched, unwept, uncared for." (The objective mind might comment that it doesn't much matter to a corpse what sort of outfit it's wearing or who is standing around it, though it mattered a lot to Dickens.) No, the most sniffle-making scene is the first picture the Spirit of Christmas Past shows to Scrooge: his young boy self, "a solitary child, abandoned by his friends" at a cheerless, run-down boarding school, while everyone else has gone home for Christmas. Luckily this child Scrooge does have some friends, but they are imaginary ones—they exist only in books. However, by the next picture—several years later—even these friends have gone, and despair has taken their place.

To be alone—to be a helpless child, neglected and forgotten, in a dreary place—such is the Dickensian nightmare acted out by Scrooge. It's this, not the arrival of Scrooge's sister, Fan, to take him home from school, nor the happy dancing and capering that goes on during Scrooge's apprentice years at Mr. Fezziwig's, that sets the miserly part of Scrooge on the road it has followed into old age. Scrooge's famous cry of "Bah! Humbug!" means "I won't even admit the possibility of human sharing and happiness because they were denied to me in the most important period of my life." The idea that Christmas open-heartedness and brotherly love are frauds had ample proofs in the childhood of Scrooge, and even to some extent in that of Dickens. For "sordid school," read "blacking factory." For "uncaring father neglecting his son," read "imprisoned father whose lack of money caused the son's ordeal." Scrooge's heart withered on the vine because Dickens's almost did.

Due to the blacking factory episode, Dickens seems to have been torn throughout his life between two impulses—the fear of going bankrupt, which drove him to work himself into a frenzy in order to make more money; and the desire to exercise, himself, the generosity that would have saved his child self from the blacking factory, had anyone turned up with some of it then. In many of his fictions, Dickens is fond of arranging characters in pairs. The look-alikes Charles Darnay and Sydney Carton of *A Tale of Two Cities* are the most obvious examples: the virtuous idealist versus the cynic and wastrel. We find such arrangements melodramatic: heroes and villains no longer convince us. However, in Ebenezer Scrooge, Dickens melds the two opposites into one. Being neither hero nor villain, Scrooge is both, and also an individual whose conflicts we can understand. Perhaps this is a clue to Scrooge's long life, and to the popularity he still enjoys: with Scrooge, we don't have to choose. Not only that, the two halves of Scrooge correspond to our own two money-related impulses: rake in the cash and keep it all for yourself, or share with others. With Scrooge, we can—vicariously—do both.

There's yet another of those young-Dickens hapless-child avatars in *A Christmas Carol*: Tiny Tim. Some people find wee Tim far too cloying to take straight: he's so infernally good. But when the Victorians said, "He's too good for this world"—which they often did—the kind of goodness they intended was a passivity due to illness: such children usually died early. Having already written the death of Little Nell in *The Old Curiosity Shop*—to international mass wailing, and, according to Dickens, with the tears coursing down his cheeks as he polished her off—Dickens was well up to the pathos needed for the shorter and more indirect dispatch of Tim. But Tim is a boy who can be rescued, as Scrooge was not—or not until it was rather too late—and Scrooge himself can do the rescuing. He can perform for Tim the act of generosity that would once have saved his child self; he can become "a second father"—the benevolent, competent, and financially sound father figure Dickens himself never had, and that he so frequently invented.

At the end of *A Christmas Carol*, when all three Spirits have come and gone, and Scrooge has had a good repentant cry—always a positive sign in the Dickensian world—and Christmas morning has dawned, and all the bells are ringing, and Scrooge has discovered he isn't dead after all, he declares that he is not only as happy as an angel, he's also as merry as a schoolboy. Now which schoolboy might that be? Certainly not the one Scrooge himself was, left alone and abandoned and despairing in the chilly, dank school of his youth. Rather the merry schoolboy he ought to have been, and that he can now be vicariously through Tim.

Our age is one that avoids mention of the salvation of souls, preferring to speak instead of Delayed Mastery and the Healing Process, and perhaps this is how we can best make sense of Scrooge. But whatever the terms of our interpretations, Scrooge has passed the only real test for a literary character: he remains fresh and vital. *Scrooge Lives!* we might write on our T-shirts. Yes, he does, and we rejoice with him.

A Writing Life

(2009)

Ah yes. Writing. Life. When? Where? How? That's the problem. You can have a life or you can do some writing, but not both at once, because although life may be the subject of writing, it is also the enemy. For instance:

MONDAY: My daughter drives us back to Toronto from the small house in the snowy woods acquired, in part, for writing. But we hadn't done any writing. Instead, we'd coloured in the white spots on the walls left by the previous owner's pictures, using aquarelle crayons. We'd filled the bird feeders, then watched the winter birds—chickadees, nuthatches, hairy woodpeckers, goldfinches—a soporific activity that causes you to drool if you overindulge. We'd gone for a snowshoe, she striding along, me puffing. I did write a dozen long-overdue snail-mail notes. I'd also obsessed about: (1) the editing of the novel that will come out in the fall; (2) my piece on birdwatching; (3) other procrastinations. Obsession is the better part of valour.

TUESDAY: In the early morning, aided by my friend Coleen, we formed a line—along the hall, out the front door, and down to the car—along which we passed the bags of food-bank food collected at our annual maple-syrup baked-bean drop-in—an event that removes three days annually from the writing life. I couldn't get the new Cuisinart to work—the former one broke last year, causing a dearth of carrot salad. However, that's backtracking. The obsession of this Tuesday: What happened to my small metal recipe box? Had someone pinched it and sold it on eBay? It's full of "writing," illegible, mine: wheat-germ muffins and the like. *Good luck reading it, recipe-box pilferer,* I thought. Questioned everyone who might know. Blanks all round.

Started 2009 Journal, a mere two weeks late. Drew nice picture at the beginning, however. Glued in a movie ticket: *Frost/Nixon.* Or vice versa.

WEDNESDAY: Did do some writing today, on a speech to be delivered at another writer's birthday party on Saturday. A delicate matter, as this relationship dated from the late 1960s and early 1970s, when I was not the Pillar of Society I am today and we were all somewhat more tempestuous. Speech to be five minutes or so. Wrote it. Showed to Life Partner, who advised me to take out the snider parts. Obsessed more about the recipe box. Phoned daughter: Had she seen it? She said, "You already asked me that." Decided that recipe-box loss was causing major writer's block. Started reading a fine book by Joan Acocella, who said that writer's block was a twentieth-century American concoction. Decided not to have it anymore. This decision did not help.

THURSDAY: Went for bloodletting but standard medical tests. As usual, felt I had failed the test of peeing in the jar. Went to bank. Rewrote birthday party speech. Slightly funnier, less dire. Began to make notes on another deadline project: "Five Predictions," meant to raise money for a deserving cause—a Canadian magazine called *The Walrus.* Why *The Walrus*? Not sure, except that the walrus spirit is supposed to be the strongest one. Stronger than the clam, for instance. Not only that, but you can make a stellar dogsled-team whip out of a walrus penis. Doubt the editors knew that when choosing the name.

But *The Walrus* does good investigative articles, and I'm all for it. The predictions conceit is that I am clairvoyant (untrue but supported by the eerie timing of my *Payback* lectures about debt, which appeared in October of 2008, just as the economy was melting down). The predictions are to be rolled up into a scroll, stuffed into a crystal vase, and auctioned off at a dinner that is now a week away. Today's obsession: What to predict? This enterprise was not helped by the fact that a Toronto magazine has published a creepy photo of me in yellow TV makeup and purple lipstick that looks—said one mean newspaper commentator—like Edward Scissorhands. Too true.

Failed again to find recipe box. Used this as an excuse for not working on overdue bird piece.

FRIDAY: Snow poured down. Went for usual morning walk despite that. Bought things, including bathmats for small house in snowy woods that is supposed to be for "writing." Rewrote other writer's birthday speech again. Made Life Partner read it. He said it was okay. Had my doubts. Answered a lot of emails. Thought about how much writing I could get done if it weren't for the emails.

SATURDAY: Having rewritten speech yet again, waded through snow to writer's birthday party. In cloakroom was the familiar Canadian winter scene of boots being removed and indoor shoes stuck on. Many other writers there—we are all looking a bit like Edward Scissorhands, except a few who are looking—in their winter coats—like characters in *War and Peace*. Life becomes increasingly valedictory. Delivered speech. Not too bad. Conferred with editor of novel—who was at party—about when she might be ready with final comments. Said I was in no rush (a lie). Waded home through snow. Looked on pedometer to see how many steps I'd taken—a new obsession. Still no recipe box. Wondered if the inheriting of my mother's recipe box (larger, neater, wooden) had caused my own to vaporize. Thought: *That way madness lies.*

SUNDAY: Life Partner drove us up to small house in snowy woods, through appalling sleet and slush. Glad that car has anti-skid mechanism. Got to house just in time to refill the empty bird feeders. Set up table so I could actually write something, somewhere. Failed to access email, a blessing in disguise. The woods are lovely, dark, and deep. Why write?

MONDAY: No water pressure. Fooled with pump, uselessly. Life Partner entered tool room to find steaming hot water gushing from ceiling.

He turned off the taps, but we feared frozen and burst pipe. Expert arrived to say, Not frozen—simply a bad soldering job. Pipes fixed.

So pleased by this narrow escape that I actually wrote the predictions, all five pages of them. Worried that they wouldn't fit into crystal bottle. Went for walk along white-blue snowy road as pink-yellow sun was setting. Very Arthur Lismer (Canadian painter). Looked for deer tracks. None.

TUESDAY: Sister visited with news of where the deer actually were, bringing wheat-germ-muffin articles made from the recipe in missing box. Sister said box was an Heirloom, and understood the significance of its loss.

Returned to city. Printed the predictions in 11 point with big margins, cut off the margins, rolled pages up in orange rice paper, sealed them with sealing wax, added string so they could be got out of bottle without smashing it, stuffed them in. Checked this item off the list.

Looked again for recipe box, discovered it fallen down behind a drawer, along with an elderly Annie's Organic Oat Bar and some tinned gingko nuts. Very happy to recover this box—I am not yet going mad! Got an email suggesting I write about the Writing Life; and, blockage released by the recipe-box rescue, I sat right down, and here it is: 1,208 words, 120 minutes. Now I can write the bird piece. Maybe.

PART II

>><<

2010 TO 2013

ART IS OUR NATURE

The Writer as Political Agent? Really?

>>><<<

(2010)

Formal Invocation to the Reader:

Dear (Mysterious) Reader, Whoever You May Be:

Whether near or far, whether in the present or the future or even—in your spirit form—in the past,

Whether old or young, or in the middle of your life,

Whether male or female, or located somewhere along the continuum that joins these two supposed polarities,

Of whatever religion, or none; of whatever political opinion, or nothing much definite;

Whether tall or short, whether luxuriously haired or balding; whether well or ill; whether a golfer or a canoeist, or a soccer fan, or the player or devotee of any number of other sports and pastimes;

Whether a writer yourself, or a lover of reading, or a student forced into reluctant readership by the necessities of the educational system;

Whether reading on paper or electronically, in the bathtub, on a train, in a library, school, or prison, under a beach umbrella, in a café, on a rooftop garden, under the covers with a flashlight, or in a myriad other manners and possible locations;

It is you whom we writers address, always, in your unknown singularity.

O Reader, live forever! (You—the individual reader—won't live forever, but it's fun to say, and it sounds good.)

We writers cannot imagine you; yet we must,

For without you, the activity of writing is surely meaningless and without destination,

And therefore it is by its very nature an act of hope, since writing implies a future in which the freedom to read will exist:

We conjure and invoke you, Mysterious Reader; and Lo: You exist! The proof of your existence is that you have just read about that existence of yours, right here.

There. That's what we're talking about: the fact that I could write these words, on July 10, 2010, and that you, via the go-between of paper or screen, can read them.

Which is by no means a foregone conclusion: for this is the very process that all governments and many other groups—religious, political, pressure lobbies of all shades and varieties, you name it— would like to harness, control, censor, bowdlerize, twist to their own purposes, exile, or extirpate. The extent to which they can implement this desire is one of the measures on the graduated line that extends from liberal democracy to locked-down dictatorship.

The publication of this special commemorative issue of *Index on Censorship* is a noteworthy occasion—and it is an important one, for often PEN International and Index on Censorship have been the chief witnesses and recording angels of the erasures of books, as well as other acts against our shared writing-and-reading activity—the murders of journalists, the closings-down of newspapers and publishing houses, the trials of novelists.

Neither organization wields any power apart from the power

of the word: what is sometimes called "moral suasion." Thus, both organizations can exist only in societies that allow a fairly free circulation of words. I say "fairly free," for there has never been a society that sets no limit at all on what can legally be made public, or "published." A country in which anyone could say anything he or she chose would be one without any legal recourse for the slandered or traduced. "Bearing false witness" is probably at least as old as language, and no doubt so are the prohibitions against it.

But a brief history of censorship would by no means be brief. Cast your mind over the various laws, past and present, here and there, against hate speech, child pornography, blasphemy, obscenity, treason, and so forth, all of which come with the best of justifications— preserving public order, protecting the innocent, enhancing religious toleration and/or orthodoxy, and so forth, and you'll see there's been no end of effort. It's the balance between Forbidden and Permitted, however, that is one of the litmus tests of an open democracy in progress. Like the coloured water in a tube barometer, this balance is in constant flux.

I've been asked to write some words about "the writer as political agent." This is a little difficult for me to do because I don't believe that writers necessarily are political agents. Political footballs, yes; but political agent implies a deliberately chosen act that is primarily political in nature, and this is not how all writers work. Instead, many writers stand in relation to politics as the small child does to the Emperor with No Clothes: they remark on the man's nakedness not to be bratty or disruptive but because they just can't see any clothes. Then they wonder why people are yelling at them. It can be a dangerous kind of naiveté, but it's common. No one was more surprised than Salman Rushdie by the fatwa issued against him for *The Satanic Verses:* here he thought he was putting immigrant Muslims on the literary map!

There are of course many different kinds of writers. Journalists and non-fiction writers often write deliberately as political agents— that is, they want to further a specific end, often by making known facts that are inconvenient to those with power. It's frequently these kinds of writers who are gunned down in the street, like so many Mexican journalists, or assassinated on their doorsteps like the crusading Russian journalist Anna Politkovskaya, or have air-to-surface missiles lobbed at them, like the Al Jazeera broadcasters during the American invasion of Baghdad. Such deaths are intended to shut down dissent, both by silencing individuals and by sending a message to any others who might feel the temptation to get mouthy.

Government crackdowns on the media have now been circumvented to some extent by the Internet. You can take the guts out of the investigative journalists, both figuratively and literally, but so far no one has been able to completely suppress the human urge that's at least as old as the Book of Job: the need to tell. Catastrophes strike Job's family members, one after the other; but each of them produces its messenger, who says: "I only am escaped alone to tell thee." The urge to tell is balanced by the urge to know. We want the story, we want the true story, we want the whole story. We want to know how bad things are, and whether they might affect us; but also we want to make up our own minds. For if we don't know the truth of a matter, how can we have any valid opinions about it?

True or *not true:* these are the primary categories that we apply to reporting journalism and political non-fiction. But I am primarily a fiction writer and a poet, so it's the suppression of these two kinds of writing that concerns me the most. What we expect from journalists is accuracy, but the "truths" of fiction and poetry are other. Let's just say that if you can't make a novel plausible in its detail, engaging in its language, and/or compelling in the story it is telling, you will lose the Mysterious Reader.

Novelists, poets, and playwrights have had varying stated intentions over the years: the re-enactment of a society's core myths, the flattering of the aristocracy, the holding of a mirror up to Nature so that we might see our own natures in it. During and after the Romantic era, it became a truism that the "duty" of a writer was to write in opposition to whoever was in power, as such incumbents were assumed to be corrupt and oppressive; or to expose abuses, as in Dickens's take on the kill-a-boy Dotheboys Hall schools of his time; or to tell the stories of the oppressed and marginalized, as in *Les Misérables,* an approach that has subsequently launched millions of novelistic ships; or to champion a cause, as *Uncle Tom's Cabin* did for abolition.

But this is very far from saying that novelists and poets *have* to write with such intentions. To judge novels on the justness of their causes or the "rightness" of their "politics" is to fall into the very same kind of thinking that leads to censorship.

Many is the revolution that has ended by eating its writerly young, as their once-acceptable productions are pronounced heretical by the victors in the inevitable power struggles. As a red-diaper friend of mine said recently of her parents' Communist group, "They were always so hard on the writers."

For revolutionaries, reactionaries, the religiously orthodox, or simply the passionate adherents of any cause whatsoever, the writing of fiction and poetry is not only suspect but secondary—writing is a tool to be employed in the service of the cause, and if either the work or its author doesn't toe the line of the moment or, worse, goes directly against it, the author must be denounced as a parasite, ostracized, or disposed of as Lorca was by the Fascists—shot without trial, then dumped into an unmarked grave.

But for the fiction and poetry writer, the writing itself—the craft and the art—is primary, whatever other impulses or influences may be in play. The mark of a society approaching freedom is the space allowed to the far-ranging human imagination and to the unfettered human voice. There's no shortage of folks standing ready to tell the writer how and what to write. Many are those who feel impelled to sit on panels and discuss the "role of the writer" or the "duty of the writer," as if writing itself is a frivolous pursuit, of no value apart from whatever external roles and duties can be cooked up for it: extolling the Fatherland, fostering world peace, improving the position of women, and so forth.

That writing *may* involve itself in such issues is self-evident, but to say that it *must* is sinister. *Must* breaks the bond between the writer, such as me, and you yourself, Mysterious Reader: For in whom can you place your readerly trust if not in me, the voice speaking to you from the page or screen, right now? And if I allow this voice to be turned into the dutiful, role-fulfilling sock puppet of some group, even a worthy one, how can you place any faith in it whatsoever?

Both Index on Censorship and PEN International defend the word *may* in this connection, and oppose the word *must*. They defend the open space in which writers may use their own voices freely, and readers may then read freely. Thus I was happy to write something for them; though it may not be exactly what they had in mind.

Literature and the Environment

>>><<<

(2010)

I am truly honoured to have been invited to speak today at the PEN Congress here in Tokyo.

There is nothing that repressive governments desire more than imposed silence. The inability to speak encourages the unspeakable, and secrecy is an important tool not only of power but of atrocity. That is why writers of all kinds, including many journalists, have been shot, imprisoned, exiled, and—to use a fairly new word—*disappeared,* and why so many newspapers and publishing houses have been closed down. New media are also being targeted: last year, for the first time, PEN America honoured an Internet writer—Nay Phone Latt, a blogger imprisoned in Burma for reporting too accurately on conditions there.

We like to think that all evil deeds will eventually come to light and that all stories about them will sooner or later be told, but in many cases this is simply not true. There are countless unknown victims. As the torturer O'Brien tells the hapless Winston Smith in George Orwell's novel of the future, *Nineteen Eighty-Four,* posterity will not vindicate him because posterity will never even hear about him. PEN supports those writers everywhere who have come under fire—often literally—because they have sought to give a human voice—fictional or not—to those whose voices have been silenced. I am proud to be a member of PEN, as I am sure all of you are as well.

Possibly you are expecting that I will now deliver a sermon about your duties as writers. It's an odd thing, but people are always lining up to preach to writers about their duties—what they ought to be writing, or what they should not have written; and they are very ready to tell the writer what a bad person he or she is because he or she has not produced the sort of book or essay that the preacher feels he or she ought to have produced. In fact, there's a strong tendency to speak to and about writers as if they are the government; as if they actually possess that kind of physical-world power, and therefore ought to use it for the betterment of society, as they surely would do if they were not filled to the brim with laziness, cowardice, or immorality. If by some chance the preacher realizes that the writer does not in fact possess that kind of power, he or she is likely to be dismissed as a frill, an irrelevance, a self-indulgent narcissist, a mere entertainer, a parasite, and so forth.

Doesn't the writer have a responsibility? these preachers ask. And shouldn't the writer exercise that responsibility by doing the good and worthy thing that the preacher will now proceed to spell out? Kurt Vonnegut used to have a rubber stamp he'd use on students' question-filled letters to him; it said, "Write your own essay." I do feel I might have quite a lot of success with a T-shirt—to be worn only by writers—that would say "Write your *own* book." Or, even better, "Write your own *worthy* book."

The list of good and worthy things has recently expanded to include something often called "the environment." We have recently been made very conscious of the many threats to "the environment"—threats that may range from melting glaciers and sea ice, to rising global temperatures and the more extreme weather that results from these temperatures, to pollution of the air and water, to the chemicals we are unwittingly putting into our children's mouths through industrial food, to the extinction of many plant and animal species, to the failing harvests on land and the dwindling fish stocks in the ocean—and even to the higher risk of plagues and illnesses that such environmental changes will almost certainly precipitate. All of these subjects can be placed into the basket called "the environment," and I suppose that anything written about them might be termed "literature." In that sense, a great many writers are concentrating on these problems already. You can hardly open a newspaper without hearing of some new oil spill or food contamination or forest fire or threatened extinction or mutated microbe or heat wave or flood.

But I take it that by "literature" you might have expected me to talk about fiction—about storytelling. And yes, every human communication involves storytelling of a sort: we live in time, and time is one event after another, and unless we have lost both our short-term and our long-term memories, we describe ourselves and others in narrative form. But today I would like to confine myself to the kinds of stories or narratives told by *fiction* writers. How do such stories interact with that nebulous something we call "the environment"? How ought they to interact with it? What is the connection between them?

The short answer is that if we didn't have "the environment"—the air we breathe, the water we drink, the food we eat—there wouldn't be any literature at all because we ourselves would not exist. Three days without water and a human being is usually dead. The oxygen we breathe was not always such a large part of Earth's atmosphere as it is now: it was created by green plants, which continue to create it, so if we do away with all plants, we'd be gone. If Earth's temperature rises much higher, our planet will become uninhabitable—not by all life, perhaps—a few deep-ocean forms will surely survive, unless the ocean boils away—but certainly by us.

In that sense, the preservation of an environment similar to the one we have is a precondition of literature. Unless we can preserve such an environment, your writing and my writing and everyone else's writing will become simply irrelevant, as there will be nobody left to read it.

One of the recurring themes in science fiction is the discovery of planets that have been inhabited once but have changed so much that the intelligent life that once lived on them has become extinct. Typically, the space explorers in such stories find a time capsule or record that tells the tale of the vanished civilization, and that the space travellers—how convenient!—can invariably translate. This form of tale—in the Western tradition at any rate—may ultimately descend from Plato's fable of the lost civilization of Atlantis, a civilization that was very advanced but doomed by an act of the gods, or of nature. The ancient "lost civilization" story was then fuelled by the discovery, in the nineteenth century, of many real lost civilizations—from the vine-covered Mayan ruins in Central America to the once-mythical city of Troy, to the mysterious Easter Island in the Pacific, with its huge enigmatic stone statues.

Will we ourselves soon be a lost civilization? Will our own books and stories ultimately become time capsules for some future archaeologist or space explorer? Looking down the pathways that lie before us—and I say *pathways* rather than *path* because the future is not *the* future but an infinite number of possible futures—it's hard not to indulge in fantasies of this kind. Should we all put our novels into lead-lined boxes and bury them in a hole in the backyard? It would be considerate of us—then the future explorers from outer space would have something to dig up. It would also be considerate of us to request in our wills that some of our favourite daily objects be placed in our coffins. I myself hope to be buried with a few twenty-first-century artifacts—my toaster, perhaps, or my laptop computer—to give those future space explorers something to write academic papers about. Perhaps they will think that these products of our industrial and technological era are the cult objects of a strange religion. As indeed, in some sense, they are.

Let us leave these sombre reflections about the possible demise of our own civilization, and look in the other direction—at the past. Why do we have such a thing as "literature" at all? Where did it come from, what purposes did it once serve, and does it still serve the same purposes today? And what do such questions have to do with "the environment"? Isn't literature part of that division we call "art," whereas "the environment" is that other part we call "nature"? Are not these two divisions polar opposites—art over here, man-made and symbolic, and nature over there, a blob of raw material useful to us only insofar as we can make things out of it—whether bricks and trucks and houses, or paintings, books, and films?

But I don't think that art and nature are so widely separated. It is my premise that art was originally intertwined with nature and came out of it in the first place, and that literary art in particular was once an essential aid to our survival as a species. I would like to consider this matter under two headings: on the one hand, storytelling—whether oral or written—and on the other, writing itself as a method for recording and transmitting stories.

First: storytelling, or the narrative act. Travel with me back in time—before cities, before villages, before agriculture.

Language and symbolic thinking—both of which are required for storytelling—are ancient. We've recently been informed that the Neanderthals undoubtedly had languages, just as they most likely had funerals and music and body decoration. We've also been told that we ourselves share some of their genetic material—contrary to earlier opinion, which held that the Neanderthals were separate from us—a different species—and that they became extinct once we hit the scene. But if they and we could interbreed and have fertile offspring that carried genes from both, we were in fact subsets of the same species. Thus, our common ancestors must have had language and symbolic thinking, or the patterns enabling them, before the Neanderthals split off as a subset.

Very, very old, then—language and symbolic thinking. Ontogeny repeats phylogeny, goes the biological mantra—the development of the individual recapitulates the developmental history of the species, which—they say—is why we have gills and tails in the early stages of our embryonic life. Leaving the gills and tails aside—for whatever else embryos may do, they do not make art—consider the behaviour of small children under the age of five. They learn language effortlessly, as long as they are surrounded by people who speak to them; they sing and dance; they make visual images, and they have an astonishingly early capacity to listen to and tell stories. In other words, they do everything that artists do, the only difference being that most of them do not carry on with these activities professionally as adults, though virtually all continue to participate in music, in visual art, and in storytelling in some way. Every religion we know anything about contains these elements. The arts are not something separate from us, to be taken up and discarded at will: they seem to be built-in. We're hard-wired for them, you might say. As others have observed, art is not opposed to nature; for human beings, art *is* our nature. It is woven into our very being.

But why? Lots of other living creatures get along perfectly well without it. So far as we know, there are no epics or pop stars or paintings among the horses. Those who speculate about the genetic component of human art consider it to be an evolved adaptation that was selected for and developed during the very long period of time we spent in the Pleistocene, in hunting-and-gathering cultures. It must have been an aid to survival in those times—otherwise, it would have been dropped in the course of our evolution. You can see how the ability to create or transmit a narrative—to use language to tell a story—would have given any group that possessed it a great advantage. Older members could tell younger members not only stories of disaster—how the crocodile ate Uncle George—but also stories of success—how Cousin Arnold hunted and killed an antelope—so that each generation of young people did not have to learn these things from scratch. Which plants were edible, which poisonous—this was essential knowledge, and those with no teachers wouldn't have lived long.

Hearing second-hand how to avoid being eaten by a crocodile would have been very useful in an environment that abounded in crocodiles, and—because someone else told me this—I can now tell you one of the secrets, in case you ever need it: crocodiles can run very fast over a short course, but they can't turn corners quickly. Therefore, don't run away in a straight line—choose a zigzag.

And don't go jogging in cougar country. They might mistake you for prey. What I've told you is a fact, and you might well forget it immediately because you don't need it right now: there are no cougars in this room. But if I told you a story about a young woman called Ann, who was riding her bicycle in British Columbia one day when a cougar jumped on her from behind, and if I described how it sank its teeth into her shoulder, and how she tried to fight it off, and how her friend Jane—also on a bicycle—turned around and saw the struggle, and came riding back, and hit the cougar on its nose so that it let go—you see, I prefer happy endings—and if I put in the hot breath of the cougar and its green eyes, and Ann's blood coming out, and Jane's fear; and, even better, if I dressed up as a cougar and two others dressed up as Ann and Jane and we acted all of this out, with perhaps some musical instruments and singing and dancing—well, you would be much less likely to forget that. And, in fact, the brain scientists tell us that people assimilate things much better through stories than through recitals of mere facts. Stories quickly create neural pathways—they "inscribe" us. Which may be why so many people consider them important: what kinds of stories—for instance—our children are taught in school, or what kinds of stories you can tell about a real person without facing a libel action.

Once, our narrative abilities were necessitated by our environment—everything not-us that surrounded us—which was huge and demanding and intricate and often harsh, but was also the source of our life. In those times, the space between the story and the subject of the story was almost non-existent. There were no books, there were no cozy armchairs in which you could curl up safely to read about wars and murders and monsters that would come in the night to eat you up. The story was told in—let's say—a small circle of light, safe perhaps for the moment, but only for the moment. The danger that was in the story was also in the world, right next to you: just outside the circle of firelight, just outside the mouth of the cave.

Such stories were potent things. No wonder that they came to include built-in protection—some supernatural beings, let's say, who, if treated right and respected, might reward you with a favourable hunt, or at least not eat you. I shouldn't even say "supernatural," which would imply that such beings were apart from nature. No: at first they were very much *in* and *of* nature. Every being in the environment—even rocks and trees—might be credited with what we would now call a soul, and each of these souls—if mistreated—could turn against you and create a lethal amount of bad luck. One theory has it that the earliest form of story is the story of a journey between this reality—the here-and-now reality in which the storyteller and listeners both exist—and another realm, which might be the past or the world of the ancestors or the world of the dead. Those who enacted such journeys were once called "shamans," and it was their task to enter a trance, and journey in spirit from this world to another one, to commune there with other spirits—of ancestors, of animals, of plants, of numinous beings—and then to bring back some knowledge or power that would be of use to the community. Such journeys were typically undertaken at times of need, we're told—when famine threatened, for instance, or when there was a plague. That is one function of stories: to tell us about our choices, about the actions we might take.

We know of many cultures that once contained variations on such themes, and that have also preserved instructions about how to treat natural entities properly so that they will grant prosperity to you. In one Greenlandic community that has gone back to hunting in the traditional way, the proper way to treat narwhal is to let the first ones pass, and not to kill too many. If you don't respect this custom, the narwhal will resent your contemptuous treatment of them, and they won't come back.

We told such stories for a very long time before we began to write them down, and then to create other stories—new ones, stories we like to think of as "original"—right on the page. It's arguable that the more involved we became with the technologies for preserving and generating stories in set form, the further away we moved from the environment that gave rise to stories in the first place.

Even those story-recording technologies, however, came out of nature. Before we could write, we had to have alphabets—systems of symbols that might mean sounds that could be strung together into words, or else that might themselves be words, or stand for objects. Many scripts derived from pictures—the ancient Egyptian, the Chinese. Some would say all—even the ABCs of English—are based on shapes found in nature.

Although we seem to pick up spoken languages very easily as children, the same is not true of reading and writing. Both of these require a lot of study: like playing the piano, they are affiliated with capabilities we already have, but they are not in themselves "natural": they must come through practice. Those who study the brain now seem to think that reading is based on the same neural program as the one used for tracking, in the sense of animal tracking. An experienced tracker can read the marks left by an animal as one reads a story: as a series of events and actions centring around a cast of characters. The tracks and marks tell the history of the fox walking, the fox lying in wait, the death of the rabbit.

There's an odd but suggestive fact: reading and writing are not located in the same parts of the brain, and you can have a rare kind of stroke that allows you to write but renders you incapable of reading what you yourself have just written. If reading is based on the neural program used for tracking, what is writing based on?

Many animals use visual signals and signs to communicate with one another. Could it be something like that? I don't know. But recent discoveries suggest that the foundations of writing go back much farther than was once thought.

However, we were storytelling for a long time before we developed the tool we call writing, and when we did develop it, in every instance that we know about it was used first not for poetry and narrative—people were doing that anyway—but to keep track of the proliferation and trading of material objects. In other words, it was used for accountancy. And as agriculture took over as the main method of food production, populations increased, hierarchies developed, and this tool became almost indispensable. It was soon used for the writing down of laws—such as the ancient Babylonian Code of Hammurabi. In ancient Chinese "shell bone writing," characters were scratched on turtle shells or bones and used for divination, or the magical prediction of the future.

These two functions—record-keeping and magic—still inhere in the act of writing. Setting something down—as opposed to memorizing it and transmitting it orally—freezes it, in a way; causes it to stand still in time. And you would think that this setting down and freezing would also limit the meaning of what is recorded—which is a good thing to have in a legal system, I suppose. But also, it creates a text subject to ambiguity—to many interpretations, many "readings." In times in which hardly anyone could read, the physical writing—on a scroll or tablet—and the ability to read it—to transform it back into a voice, and also to interpret its meaning—were deeply respected and much feared, and those who had this ability wielded considerable authority, and were sometimes credited with supernatural power—even a demonic form of power. Writers can still be credited with those kinds of powers, though in much-diminished form. Book-burnings reflect both the respect and the fear: no one would feel impelled to burn an innocuous book.

This is what we've inherited from the deep past, Dear Fellow Writers—the innate ability to tell and understand stories, which came from our interactions with a demanding natural environment; and the neural programs that enable us to read and write, which also came from that environment. The time when we lived embedded in nature is—generationally speaking—not far away from us at all. Yet here we are—everyone in this room, and most people on the planet—in an increasingly man-made environment, in which we treat animals not as fellow beings with souls but as machines. Almost everything that happens to us, and almost everything we do—including this event, so dependent on electricity—would not exist at all without a great deal of technology that we ourselves have made. But the ability of these technologies to supply power, and thus food and water, is not keeping pace with our rapid modernization and burgeoning populations.

Worse than that, it's these very same extremely efficient technologies—technologies built for the exploitation of nature—that are now depleting the larger biological world on which we depend.

What shall we do? We can't go back to a time before our technologies and live in unmediated nature. A few days without clothing, cutting tools, or fire, and we'd all be dead ducks.

What kinds of stories can we writers tell about our increasingly desperate situation? What kinds might be of any help to the human community of which we are a part?

I can't tell you that because I don't know. But I do know that as long as we have hope—and we still do have hope—we will be telling stories, and—if we have the time and the materials—we'll be setting them down; because the telling of stories, and the wish to listen to them, transmit them, and derive meaning from them, is built into us as human beings. As for "the environment," and all the threats to it that we've mentioned—will we writers set out to deal with that, and if so, how? Through didactic warnings of a too-preachy kind, through exemplary narratives that act out our choices, or just as background to a story with a more conventional foreground?

Already there's a trend: stories about survival in extreme conditions—we've always been fond of those, but we're becoming fonder of them as the extreme conditions loom closer. Disaster stories, in which the disasters are not wars or invasions of vampires or Martians, but such things as droughts and floods. On the more positive side, stories about people adapting, or trying to live less wasteful lives.

Though perhaps we will not tackle these themes directly or deliberately. Perhaps we may think we are telling a story about love, or war, or growing old—about our ancient, constant themes, human desires and human fears. But we will weave "the environment" into our stories whether we intend to or not because storytellers have always been attached to their world—both physical and social—and their stories have changed as the world has changed, and our own world is changing very quickly.

So our stories will inevitably reflect those changes; and once in a while we may even be able to slip into a modern version of the shaman's trance, and journey in spirit to another realm, and bring back something from the Otherworld. It won't be a book of instructions— there isn't one. Perhaps it will be a talisman, to protect us, even a little. Perhaps it will be a list of dangers. Perhaps it will be a charm, to alter the way in which we see. Perhaps we will once more talk with animals, and be instructed by plants. Who knows what forms our metaphors will take?

Alice Munro

>>><<<

(2010)

There's a chunk of public statuary in honour of Alice Munro in the centre of Wingham, Ontario, her birthplace. It shows a young bronze girl lying on a bronze lawn reading a bronze book. "It's really pretty good," comment the two not-young, non-bronze women observing it, one of whom happens to be Alice Munro, the other myself. "It's very nice." Their tone is that of two women checking out—for instance—curtain material: cautious, evaluating, understated.

This statue is in a town that once sent Alice Munro her first vicious hate mail. "What was the hate mail about?" I ask.

"People thought I'd put them into my books," she says.

"And did you?"

She shoots me a look. "People always think that."

How did it come to this—bronze statues? (*Spending good money,* Munro's own characters mutter. *Useless!*) And the Alice Munro Literary Garden? And a tour of "Alice Munro's Wingham," which may be arranged through the town museum? And the stories published in *The New Yorker,* and the many volumes in hardcover and paper, and the prizes—three Governor General's Awards and two Giller Prizes among them. And now the Man Booker International Award for her entire body of work! Who would have thought Alice would even have a "body of work," at the beginning?

It's been a long journey. Alice Munro grew up in the southwestern Ontario of the Depression 1930s and the wartime 1940s, which were not boom-time years for the arts in Canada. She first honed her special talents through one of the few encouraging outlets then: the *Anthology* program on CBC Radio, which encouraged poetry and short stories as opposed to the novel, and taught you to pay attention to the value and force of the spoken word. How people talk is important, not only what they maliciously say; what they wear and how shamefacedly they wear it; not only what they furtively do. Like the characters of William Trevor—and it's no surprise that Alice Munro admires him—her characters live intensely within narrow boundaries, springing as they do from a time when you made what you had from what others might consider to be very meagre materials.

Yet those narrow boundaries can't hold: reality shimmers, perceptions dissolve. Uneasiness inhabits Munro's stories; jittery moments abound, and the giddy, queasy sensation of walking on a cliff's edge. The characters are faced with their own double motives: you value the creation of art, but sneer at yourself for doing so. You escape from the strictures of place to grow into your true self, only to find you've left that self behind you. You stay rooted in your "authentic" locale, only to be crushed and stunted by it. You remember each detail of the past, each violence and cruelty and feud, while seeing the landscape once intimate as your own skin transformed to distance and neutrality by time. Yet that transformation may reverse: years peel off like old wallpaper, revealing a fresh and startling pattern beneath.

Alice Munro has often been compared to Chekhov, but perhaps she's more like Cézanne. You paint an apple, you paint an apple over again, until this utterly familiar object becomes strange and luminous and mysterious; yet it remains only an apple. Isn't she, after all, something of a mystic? "Thou art in small things great, not small in any," said George Herbert. And so it is with Alice Munro.

("Oh for heaven's sakes," says the voice of Alice. "Restrain yourself! Herbert was talking about God! Wasn't that statue enough for one day? Anyway, are you sure it's bronze?")

The Gift

>>><<<

Gifts pass from hand to hand: they endure through such transmission, as every time a gift is given it is enlivened and regenerated through the new spiritual life it engenders both in the giver and in the receiver.

And so it is with Lewis Hyde's classic study of gift-giving and its relationship to art. *The Gift* has never been out of print. It moves like an underground current among artists of all kinds, through word of mouth and bestowal. It is the one book I recommend without fail to aspiring writers and painters and musicians, for it is not a how-to book—there are many of these—but a book about the core nature of what it is that artists do, and also about the relation of these activities to our overwhelmingly commercial society. If you want to write, paint, sing, compose, act, or make films, read *The Gift*. It will help to keep you sane.

I doubt that Lewis Hyde knew while he was writing this book that he was composing such an essential work. Perhaps he felt he was merely exploring a subject of interest to him—in its short form, why poets in our society are seldom rich—and enjoying the many tributaries he was uncovering through this exploration without realizing that he had hit on a wellspring. When asked by his original editor who his presumed audience was, he couldn't really pinpoint it, but settled for "poets." "That's not what most editors want to hear," as he says in his foreword to the 2006 edition. "Many prefer 'dog owners seeking news of the dead.'" As he then tells us, "the happy fact is that *The Gift* has managed to find an audience beyond the community of poets." Which is an understatement of some vastness.

I first encountered both Lewis Hyde and *The Gift* in the summer of 1984. I was in the midst of writing *The Handmaid's Tale,* begun in the spring in that combination of besieged city and consumer showcase that was West Berlin at the time, and where the twentieth-century clash between communitarianism gone wrong and Mammon-worship gone wild was most starkly in evidence. But now it was July, and I was in Port Townsend, Washington, at a summer school for writers of the kind that were then multiplying. In that secluded area, all was bucolic.

Lewis Hyde was also teaching at the summer school. He was a genial young poet whose hobby was lepidoptery, and he shyly presented me with a copy of *The Gift.* In it he wrote: "For Margaret. Who has given all of us many things." I like the slipperiness and ambiguity of this—"many things" could include anything from the poems and novels I hope he had in mind to "a case of herpes" and "the heebie-jeebies"—for the word *gift* is itself slippery and ambiguous. Think of "Greeks bearing gifts," a reference to the fatal Trojan horse, and the poisoned apple given to Snow White, not to mention that other apple given to Adam, and the wedding gifts that burn Medea's rival to the bone. The double-handedness of gifts is in part what Lewis Hyde's book is about.

The Gift was first published in 1983, when it was originally subtitled *Imagination and the Erotic Life of Property.* On the cover of my Vintage paperback is a Shaker painting of a basket of apples— a choice explained in a note by Hyde:

> The Shakers believed that they received their arts as gifts from
> the spiritual world. Persons who strove to become receptive
> of songs, dances, paintings, and so forth were said to be
> "labouring for a gift," and the works that they created circulated
> as gifts within the community. Shaker artists were known
> as "instruments"; we know only a few of their names, for in
> general it was forbidden that they be known to any but the
> church elders.

This note is followed by a copyright line that, in view of the origins of *Basket of Apples,* reads ironically: "*Basket of Apples* is reprinted through the courtesy of The Shaker Community Inc." So the community of gift-givers has now become incorporated, and its gifts have been transformed to property by the commodity market that now surrounds us on all sides. One of the questions Hyde asks is whether a work of art is changed by the way it is treated—as gift or as commodity for sale. In the case of *Basket of Apples* I would say not: the word *courtesy* implies that no money changed hands. But it could have, whereas under the Shaker rules such a thing would have been impossible. Hyde's point is taken.

The painting itself is instructive. The basket of apples is not depicted realistically. The basket is transparent, as if made of glass, and the apples float within it as if levitating. They are not red apples but golden ones, and if you look at them closely they morph from flat design to 3-D, with something like molten gold leaf glowing within them. Thus the picture shows a gift—the glowing energy—within a gift—the apples—within another gift, the entire basket. Each apple most likely represented a single Shaker, warmed and glimmering with an inner gift, but not thereby standing out from the community, for all the apples are the same size. My guess is that the container that holds them all together—the transparent basket—would have meant, to its original viewers, Divine Grace. Hyde chose his cover with care.

Both the original cover image and its note have fallen by the wayside. More recent editions of *The Gift* have different images on their covers, and the note is therefore absent. Yet together, *Basket of Apples* and its commentary encapsulate the large questions Hyde is posing. What is the nature of "art"? Is a work of art a commodity with a money value, to be bought and sold like a potato, or is it a gift on which no real price can be placed, to be freely exchanged?

And if works of art are gifts and nothing but, how are their creators to live in the physical world, in which food will sooner or later be needed by them? Should they be sustained by reciprocal gifts made by the public—the equivalent of the gifts placed in the Zen monk's begging bowl? Should they exist in quasi-Shaker communities of the like-minded, of which creative writing departments may be a secular version? Present copyright law takes a stab at this problem.

If a creation or a version of it is traded in the marketplace, a creator is entitled to control who may reproduce the work and is entitled to a portion of the sale price. And this right may be inherited. But that entitlement ends a certain number of years following the creator's death, after which the work passes into the creative commons and is freely available to all, to do with as they will. Hence *Pride and Prejudice and Zombies* and *Mona Lisa* postcards with moustaches on them. Gifts are not always treated in a way that respects their original spirit.

This and many other questions are tackled by Hyde through a mixture of economic theory, anthropological works about tribal gift-giving customs, folk tales about the use and misuse of gifts, snippets from etiquette guides, accounts of archaic funeral rites, marketing stratagems for such things as children's underwear, organ donation practices, religious observances, the history of usury, the cost-benefit analyses made by Henry Ford when deciding whether to recall a model with a potentially lethal flaw, and much more.

Then Hyde follows up with two case studies of writers, both of whom gave much thought to the knot between art and money: Walt Whitman, so generous that he risked obliterating the boundary between self and universe—how much of yourself can you give away without evaporating?—and Ezra Pound, so obsessed with the unfair and distorting effects money can have on artists that he became a supporter of the Fascists in Italy, as they seemed to give credence to some of his wackier theories about what money should be and how it could be made to grow, if not exactly on trees, then like trees. This chapter is called "Ezra Pound and the Theory of Vegetable Money," and it is one of the few things I've ever read that explains how Pound might have come by his corrosive anti-Semitism. The account of Allen Ginsberg's generous and redemptive visit to Pound at the end of his life is intensely moving, and is—again—an illustration of Hyde's theories in practice.

The Gift was first published over three decades ago, when personal computers were in their infancy, when there were no e-readers or e-books, and no social media on the Internet. Now all these things have come to pass, and Hyde's examination of the relationship between gift-giving and the creation and reinforcement of the communities that form around it is more pertinent than ever.

Many have scratched their heads over the monetization of social sites—how are these things to be paid for, and how shall they make money?—and over the tendency of the Internet to demand that everything on it be somehow "free," despite the salaries that must be paid to those pulling the e-strings and making those intangible e-objects appear and disappear. But as Hyde expounds, gift exchange demands reciprocity and is fed by it: thus one retweet deserves another, shared enthusiasms are exchanged with the enthusiasms of others, and those who offer advice for nothing may expect to receive it for nothing when in need. But gifts create bonds and obligations, and not everyone wants these or understands them. There is, in fact, no totally free lunch.

If you've lifted a song or a film off the Internet without paying—if you've got something out of it, as we say—if you've treated it as a gift, which by its nature has spiritual worth but no monetary value, what do you owe its creator, who has been the instrument through which it has arrived in your hands? Your gratitude, via a word of thanks? Your serious attention? The price of a latte deposited in a beggar's-bowl e-tip jar?

The answer is never "nothing." Much digital ink has been spilled over these issues, with copyright wars taking centre space. Surely part of the solution is the education of the new e-audience in the ways of gifts. A gift is a gift when the giver exercises his or her choice; if something is taken against an owner's will or without his or her knowledge, that's called "theft." But that line can get blurry: as Hyde points out, it's not for nothing that in the ancient Greek world the messenger god, Hermes, was in charge of movement of all kinds: buying and selling, travel, communications, tricks, lies and jokes, the opening of doors and the revealing of secrets and stealing— something the web is particularly good at. But Hermes sets no moral value on how a thing changes location: he just facilitates that change. Whether those using the information highways and byways know it or not, the presiding god of the Internet is Hermes.

Every reader of *The Gift* I've ever spoken to has come away from it with new insights, not only into his or her artistic practices, but also into questions that are so much part of daily life that we don't look at them too closely. If someone opens the door for you, do you owe that person a thank-you? Should you spend Christmas with your family if you're trying to solidify an identity of your own? If your sibling asks you to donate your kidney to her, do you immediately say you'll give it to her or do you charge her a couple of thousand dollars? Why shouldn't you accept a gift from the Mafia if you don't want to find yourself on the receiving end of a request that you perform a criminal act? What about that case of wine from a lobbyist, if you're a politician? Are diamonds a girl's best friend, or should you prefer a sentimental kiss on the hand that you will never be able to turn into cash?

One guarantee: you won't come out of *The Gift* unaltered. This is a mark of its own status as a gift; for gifts transform the soul in ways that simple commodities cannot.

Bring Up the Bodies

>>><<<

(2012)

Oh, those Tudors! We can't get enough of them. Whole bookshelves have been filled with them, acres of film consecrated to their antics. How badly behaved they were. What Machiavellian plottings and betrayals. Will we never tire of the imprisonments, torturings, entrail-windings, and burnings at the stake?

Philippa Gregory has very successfully tackled the Boleyn girls, Mary the Mistress, and Anne the Aggravating. Then there's *The Tudors,* the TV series, in which Church geopolitics are ably dealt with, though some of the underwear is anachronistic and Henry VIII is a dark, brooding romantic who never gets fat. This is stretching it, but makes for much better sex than if he were to wheeze and grunt and ooze from his decaying leg all over the bedsheets, as in real life.

I have a weakness for the Tudors, so I inhaled Hilary Mantel's terrific Booker-winning *Wolf Hall*—the first in her series about Thomas Cromwell the Calculating and Ruthless—in almost one sitting. Now comes the aptly titled *Bring Up the Bodies,* which picks up the body parts where *Wolf Hall* left off.

As the book opens, it's summer. Henry and his court are staying at Wolf Hall, home of the Seymours, where Henry has his piggy eye on stiff, prudish little Jane, destined to be his next queen. Thomas Cromwell is flying his hawks, named after his dead daughters. "His children are falling from the sky," Mantel begins. "He watches from horseback, acres of England stretching behind him; they drop, gilt-winged, each with a blood-filled gaze. . . . All summer has been like this, a riot of dismemberment." And we're off, into the deep, dark, labyrinthine, but strangely objective mind of Thomas Cromwell.

The historical Cromwell is an opaque figure, which is most likely why Mantel is interested in him: the less is truly known, the more room for a novelist. Cromwell rose from obscure and violent origins through a life abroad—sometime soldier, sometime merchant—to become England's top go-to man, the prime maker-and-breaker of fortunes and spines, secretly hated and despised, especially by aristocrats. He played Beria to Henry VIII's tyrannical Stalin: he did the dirty work and attended the beheadings, while Henry went hunting.

Cromwell elevated reform-minded Anne Boleyn, and sided with her until she stupidly thought she could get rid of him. Then he joined with her enemies to overthrow her, which we see him doing with steely finesse in *Bring Up the Bodies.* He was very feared and very smart, with a capacious memory for facts and also for slights, none of which he left unavenged.

While Cromwell has always had a bad press, Henry has generated mixed reviews. His early life was golden—Renaissance prince, sportsman, composer of poems, sprightly dancer, the glass of fashion and the mould of form, and so on—but he became increasingly despotic, bloodthirsty, rapacious, and possibly crazy. Charles Dickens, in his quirky *A Child's History of England,* has no use for him, calling him "a most intolerable ruffian, a disgrace to human nature, and a blot of blood and grease upon the History of England." In his later years, says Dickens, Henry was "a swollen, hideous spectacle, with a great hole in his leg, and so odious to every sense that it was dreadful to approach him." It's a twenty-first-century sport for doctors to weigh in on what exactly was wrong with Henry: It used to be thought he had syphilis, but diabetes now appears to be winning out. That, and possibly a brain injury from his jousting accident—an accident that causes Cromwell to lose his cool, since if Henry dies without an heir there will be civil war. Whatever else the Tudors did, they brought peace to England, and peace is what Cromwell works for. That, for Mantel, is one of the more praiseworthy motives for all the bloodletting that Cromwell engineers.

Peace rests on a stable king, and in that respect Cromwell has his work cut out. Already by the book's beginning Henry is beginning to fade, swell, and drool; his paranoia is growing, and the Plantagenets are plotting in the shrubbery. Cromwell sees this with precision and clarity, as he sees everything. He's a very self-aware narrator, and does not spare himself his own unwavering view, as when he appraises the portrait Hans Holbein has painted of him, "his dark purposes wrapped in wool and fur, his hand clenched around a document as if he were throttling it." His own son tells him he looks like a murderer, and other portraitists achieve a similar effect: "Wherever they begin, the final impact is the same: if he had a grievance against you, you wouldn't like to meet him at the dark of the moon."

But he also has corners of tenderness, and sees these in others: he's deep, not merely dark. And through him we experience the texture of how it feels to be sliding into a perilous dictatorship, where power is arbitrary, spies are everywhere, and one wrong word can mean your death. It's a reflection, perhaps, of our times, when democracies appear to be slipping back into the dungeon-filled shadowland of arbitrary power.

Cromwell's main opponent, Anne Boleyn, is as wilful and flirtatious as she usually is in fiction, but by the time of her death she has shrivelled to "a tiny figure, a bundle of bones." Is she more to be pitied than blamed? Not by Cromwell: "She does not look like a powerful enemy of England, but looks can deceive. . . . If her sway had continued, the child Mary might have stood here; and he himself . . . waiting for the coarse English axe." Anne knew the rules of the power game but she hasn't played well enough, and she has lost. And, for the time being, Cromwell has won.

The ambiguous Cromwell is a character who fits Mantel's particular strengths. She's never gone for the sweet people, and is no stranger to dark purposes. Beginning with smaller canvases—novels set in present-day England—she moved to widescreen historical fiction with the masterful *A Place of Greater Safety* (1992), featuring the major actors of the French Revolution as well as a large supporting cast and its twisted interactions. She relies on the same talent for intricacy in *Wolf Hall* and *Bring Up the Bodies*. There are a lot of people lurking around in Henry's court, all of them on the make or trying to sidestep the axe, and helping the reader keep track of them is a special craft.

Historical fiction has many pitfalls, multiple characters and plausible underwear being only two of them. How should people talk?

Sixteenth-century diction would be intolerable, but so would modern slang; Mantel opts for standard English, with the occasional dirty joke, and for present-tense narration much of the time, which keeps us right there with Cromwell as his plots and Mantel's unfold. How much detail—clothes, furnishings, appliances—to supply without clogging up the page and slowing down the story? Enough to allow the reader to picture the scene, with lush fabrics and textures highlighted, as they were at the time. Mantel generally answers the same kinds of questions that interest readers in court reports of murder trials or coverage of royal weddings. What was the dress like? How did she look? Who really went to bed with whom? Mantel sometimes overshares, but literary invention does not fail her: she's as deft and verbally adroit as ever.

We read historical fiction for the same reason we keep watching *Hamlet:* it's not what, it's how. And although we know the plot, the characters themselves do not. Mantel leaves Cromwell at a moment that would appear secure: four of his ill-wishing enemies, in addition to Anne, have just been beheaded, and many more have been neutralized. England will have peace, though it's "the peace of the hen coop when the fox has run home." But really Cromwell is balancing on a tightrope, with his enemies gathering and muttering offstage. The book ends as it begins, with an image of blood-soaked feathers.

But its end is not an end. "There are no endings," says Mantel. "If you think so you are deceived as to their nature. They are all beginnings. This is one." Which will lead us to the final instalment, and to the next batch of Henry's wives and Cromwell's machinations. How much intricate spadework will it take to "dig out" Cromwell, that "sleek, plump, and densely inaccessible" enigma? Reader, wait and see.

Rachel Carson Anniversary

>>><<<

(2012)

In my 2009 novel, *The Year of the Flood*—set in that always-available patch of real estate, The Near Future—Rachel Carson is a saint.

Of course many people think she's a saint anyway, but in this book it's official. The God's Gardeners—members of a fictional cult that reveres both Nature and scripture—needed some saints. The Gardeners would choose them for their devotion to the divine natural world, and their saintly deeds could range from the writing of creature-friendly poetry—like that of Saint Robert Burns of Mice—to the saving of a species, like the efforts of Saint Dian Fossey of Gorillas.

But my first choice was Rachel Carson. She fully deserved beatification, and now she has it: in the God's Gardeners hagiography, she is Saint Rachel of All Birds.

This year marks the fiftieth anniversary of the publication of Rachel Carson's momentous book, *Silent Spring*, considered by many the most important environmental book of the twentieth century. Its subject was the human poisoning of the biosphere through the wholesale deployment of a myriad of new twentieth-century chemicals aimed at pest and disease control. Rachel Carson was already the most respected nature writer in the United States, and a pioneer in that field. She knew how to explain science to ordinary readers in a way that they could understand; she knew also that if you don't love a thing you won't save it, and her love for the natural world shines through everything she wrote. For *Silent Spring*—which she already knew would be her last tilt at the windmill—she polished all her rhetorical weapons, and synthesized a wide range of research. She was able to combine a simple and dramatic presentation with a formidable array of backup statistics, and to forge a call to specific action. The impact was enormous—many groups, pieces of legislation, and government agencies were inspired by it—and its main insights remain central today.

The book also met with furious resistance, chiefly from the big chemical companies and the scientists in their employ. Multiple attempts were made to destroy not only Carson's scientific credibility but also her personal reputation: she was a fanatic, she was a "bunny hugger," she was a dangerous reactionary who would drag modern society backwards into a new Middle Ages filled with pests, vermin, crop destruction, and lethal diseases. Yet *Silent Spring* never advocated an outright ban on pesticides: only careful testing and informed use, in contrast to the scorched-earth policies that had been pursued, with disastrous outcomes.

Many of the personal attacks on Carson were gender-specific, shaped by mid-century perceptions about women: their feeble mental capacities, their bleeding-heart sentimentality, their tendency toward "hysteria." One puzzling accusation came from the former U.S. Secretary of Agriculture, Ezra Taft Benson, who wrote in a private letter that because Carson was unmarried despite being attractive, she was "probably a Communist." (What did this mean? That Communists indulged in free love, or that they spurned sex?)

Through it all, Rachel Carson persevered, countering the vilification with grace, dignity, and courage. Just how much courage soon became apparent, for she was suffering from cancer, and died in early 1964. *Silent Spring* thus acquired the added force of a deathbed testament.

Silent Spring made a splash worldwide, but it also made one in our family. My father was an entomologist who studied insect infestations that destroyed forests, especially the coniferous forests that cover most of Canada's north. He had been working as a forest entomologist throughout the 1930s, and had seen the advent of the insecticide revolution. It must at first have seemed like a miracle: no insects had yet developed resistance, and the first results looked like a clean sweep. The chemical solution to insect-caused problems was pushed hard by the manufacturers: not only for forest insects, but for crops of all kinds—apples, cotton, corn—and disease-carrying bugs, and irritating mosquitoes, and roadside wildflowers, and, well, anything that crawled, or simply grew where you didn't want it to. Spraying was cheap and effective, and safe for human beings, so why wouldn't you do it?

The general public believed the pitch: the stuff was safe for people, unless you drank it. One of the delights of our 1940s childhood was to be allowed to wield the Flit gun—a spray pump with a barrel containing a DDT preparation that did indeed slay any insect you sprayed with it. We kids breathed in clouds of it as we stalked around assassinating houseflies and squirting each other for a joke.

Such carefree attitudes toward the new chemicals were common throughout the next decade. When I worked as a camp counsellor in the late 1950s, the premises were routinely fogged for mosquitoes, as were campgrounds and whole towns in many parts of the world. After the fogging, rabbits would appear, running around in circles, jerking spasmodically, then falling over. Might it be the pesticides? Surely not. We had not yet read the studies—already in progress—of liver damage and neurological damage, not to mention cancer. But Carson was reading them.

Toward the end of the 1950s, my father became an opponent of widespread spraying. His reasons were the same as those detailed in *Silent Spring*. First, that kind of widespread blanket spraying killed not only the target insect but the parasitic foes of the target; and not only insects, but many other life forms as well; and not only those life forms, but everything dependent on them for food. The result of intensive spraying was a dead forest.

Second, some insects would survive and pass on their resistant genes, and soon you'd have a whole generation of hardier descendants that would far outmunch their ancestors, and against whom newer and ever more toxic insecticides would then have to be deployed, until—as Carson puts it—the chemicals would become so deadly that they would kill absolutely everything, us included.

My father took a gloomy pleasure in saying that the insects would inherit the earth because they would quickly adapt to any controls we could throw at them. (He didn't yet know about superbugs in hospitals, and about species-jumping microbes such as Ebola and Marburg, and about the many invasive species that were already complicating our lives, but they would have fitted right in.) In the future, my father would proclaim, there would be nothing left but cockroaches and grass. And ants. And maybe dandelions.

This was not very cheerful fare for young and impressionable minds such as those of my brother and my teenage self. On the other hand, it was bracing. So when *Silent Spring* appeared in 1962, we were ready for it.

But most people were not. It's hard to imagine the shock it caused. It was like being told that orange juice—then being proclaimed as the sunshine key to ultra-health—was actually poisoning you.

Those were less cynical times: people still trusted large corporations. Cigarette brands were still cozy household names, sponsoring such beloved figures as radio's Jack Benny; Coca-Cola was still a synonym for wholesomeness, with white-gloved maidens sipping it from their pure lips. Chemical companies were thought to be making life better every day, in every way, all over the world, which—to be fair—in some ways they were. Scientists in their white coats were presented as crusaders against the forces of ignorance and superstition, leading us forward under the banner of discovery. Every modern scientific innovation was "progress" or "development," and progress and development were always desirable, and would march inevitably onward and upward: to question that belief was to question goodness, beauty, and truth.

But now Rachel Carson was blowing the lid off. Had we been lied to, not only about pesticides, but about progress, and development, and discovery, and the whole ball of wax?

So one of the core lessons of *Silent Spring* was that things labelled progress weren't necessarily good. Another was that the perceived split between man and nature isn't real: the inside of your body is connected to the world around you, and your body too has its ecology, and what goes into it—whether eaten or breathed or drunk or absorbed through your skin—has a profound impact on you. We're so used to thinking this way now that it's hard to imagine a time when general assumptions were different. But before Carson, they were.

In those years, Nature was an "it," an impersonal and unconscious force; or, worse, malignant: a Nature red in tooth and claw bent on afflicting humanity with all the weapons at its disposal. Against brute Nature stood "we," with our consciousness and intelligence. We were a higher order of being, and thus we had a mandate to tame Nature as if it were a horse, subdue it as if it were an enemy, and "develop" it as if it were a female bustline or a male set of Charles Atlas biceps—how awful to be underdeveloped! We could then exploit Nature's resources, which were thought of as inexhaustible.

Three streams of thinking fed into this civilization/savagery construct. The first was Biblical dominionism: in Genesis, God proclaims that man has dominion over the animals, and this was construed by some as permission to annihilate them. The second was informed by the machine metaphors that colonized linguistic space after the invention of the clock, and that spread across the West during the eighteenth-century Enlightenment: the universe was an unfeeling machine, and life forms too were machines, without souls or consciousness or even feeling. Therefore they could be abused at will because they weren't really suffering. Man alone had a soul, situated inside the machine of his body (possibly, thought some, in the pituitary gland). In the twentieth century, scientists threw out the soul but kept the machine: for a strangely long time, they held that to ascribe anything like human emotions to animals was anthropocentrism. Ironically, this was a direct contradiction of the granddaddy of modern biology, Charles Darwin, who had always maintained the interconnectedness of life, and—like any dog owner or farmer or hunter—was well aware of animal emotions.

The third line of thinking came—again ironically—from social Darwinism. Man was "fitter" than the animals, by virtue of his intelligence and his uniquely human emotions; thus in the struggle for existence man deserved to triumph, and Nature would have to give way eventually to a fully "humanized" environment.

But Rachel Carson questioned this dualism. Whatever airs we might give ourselves, "we" were not distinct from "it": we were part of it, and could live only inside it. To think otherwise was self-destructive:

> The "control of nature" is a phrase conceived in arrogance, born of the Neanderthal age of biology and philosophy, when it was supposed that nature exists for the convenience of man. The concepts and practices of applied entomology for the most part date from that Stone Age of science. It is our alarming misfortune that so primitive a science has armed itself with the most modern and terrible weapons, and that in turning them against the insects it has also turned them against the earth.

One can quibble with the metaphor—"Stone Age" people were much more in tune with the wholeness of the fabric of life than were the twentieth-century pundits Carson was up against—but the conclusion stands. If the only tool you have is a hammer, you see every problem as a nail. In the later sections of her book, Carson was exploring other tools, and other ways of solving problems. The world is catching up with her.

The groundwork for a wholistic view of nature already existed: the Romantics challenged the clockwork model; in the United States, worry about the misuse of nature went back as far as Fenimore Cooper and Thoreau. Teddy Roosevelt was an early conservationist. The Sierra Club was founded in 1892, and by Carson's time was a large grassroots organization.

Thus one reason *Silent Spring* became such a major story was the already widespread popularity of nature-related activities—in particular, of birdwatching as a hobby. Birdwatching had been given a huge boost by the 1934 publication of the Roger Tory Peterson *Field Guide*. A pursuit that had once required arcane knowledge was now within reach of any enthusiastic amateur. For decades, birders had been scanning backyards and fields and forests, forming networks. collecting data, and sharing their discoveries.

Many of these amateur naturalists had noticed a decline in bird numbers, especially among raptors such as eagles, falcons, and ospreys. Now there was an explanation: DDT accumulated in the bodies of alpha predators, since they fed at the top of the food chain. In the case of raptors it thinned their eggshells, so new generations were not hatching. This was only part of the story that Carson told in *Silent Spring*, but it was a part that ordinary observers could verify. Where were the American eagles that had once filled the skies all over the continent? And from eagles, it was a short jump to the rest of the story: If a chemical was exterminating birds, how good was it for people? And what about the other chemicals that were being poured into the environment in such vast amounts? It was Carson's book that began this public debate in earnest. Many of the results of that debate have been positive. No informed person now would seriously advocate deploying pesticides or herbicides or any other chemical agent in the wholesale manner of the 1940s and 1950s.

It's tempting to wonder what Carson would have done next had she remained alive. Would she have warned us that the human race was skirting the brink during the Vietnam War, when the fearsomely toxic herbicide Agent Orange was being shipped across the Pacific Ocean in huge vats to kill Vietnamese jungles? These jungles have not yet recovered; and the poisonous effect on both military and civilians is now known. But Carson might have alerted us to a greater danger. Imagine the consequences of a large Agent Orange spill. The death of the blue-green algae in the sea would have been a global disaster, since this algae makes 50 to 80 per cent of the oxygen in our atmosphere.

And what would Carson have said about the spraying of dispersants during the Gulf of Mexico oil spill? "Don't do it," no doubt. Many experts said this, but the powers that be did it anyway. What would she have said about the rapidly melting Arctic ice, or about the plans to shove a pipeline through the Great Bear rainforest to the Pacific shore?

She would have seen many signs of hope—thanks to her, people are at least aware of some of the problems. But how can anyone keep track of them all? Our high-tech civilization is leaking, and it's leaking into us. The more inventive we become, the longer grows the list of chemical compounds we may be breathing, eating, and rubbing onto our skin. PCBs, chlorofluorocarbon refrigerants, and dioxins have been identified and somewhat controlled, but many harmful chemicals are still at large, and are joined every year by new ones we know little about.

But as long as they don't fall over, most people don't spend much time worrying about invisible toxicity. We're a short-view species; for most of our history we've had to be: we stuffed ourselves while we had the chance, like most hunters and foragers. However, unless we stop fouling our own nest, the Earth, we may be a short-term species as well, and my father's gloomy prognostications about the cockroaches inheriting the planet will come true. Demonizing environmentalists—as happened with Carson, and as continues to happen today—will do nothing to change this.

On the positive front, awareness has grown. Although the percentage of giving to nature-related organizations is still pitifully small, there are now many organizations devoted to answering our biggest question: How can we live on our planet? Large groups such as Greenpeace, World Wildlife, and BirdLife International rest on a pyramid of other organizations, from the national to the local. Thanks to their members we know much more about the details of life on Earth than we did in Carson's time. We know where the sea currents flow, and how forests replenish their nutrients, and how seabird colonies enrich marine life. We know that although we have destroyed 90 per cent of fish stocks since the 1940s, the establishment of marine parks allows regeneration. We know where the bird species nest, and what hazards they must navigate while migrating, and the importance of habitat preservation in our well-mapped Important Bird Areas.

But though our knowledge is immense, our collective political will is not strong. The energy for change—and thus our preservation— will have to come from grassroots networks, which is where it's most often come from.

One of Rachel Carson's recent indirect descendants may seem unlikely: Bug A Salt, a toy rifle filled with table salt and used to shoot flies. A crowd-sourcing campaign just raised half a million dollars for its inventor: seems like a lot of folks want to shoot bugs, just as we 1940s kids wanted to shoot the Flit gun.

Bug A Salt has two green selling points: it needs no batteries, and it uses no pesticides. I'm not sure it's the answer to widespread forest infestations covering hundreds of square miles: that would take a lot of table salt. But still, Saint Rachel would applaud its core values: no bird is ever likely to be silenced by Bug A Salt.

The Futures Market

>>><<<

STORIES WE TELL ABOUT TIMES TO COME

(2013)

The future—not the afterlife but the real here-on-Earth future—was once very beckoning and bright. When was that? Maybe in the nineteenth century, when so many utopias predicting a shining future were written that it would take days to list them all. Maybe it was in the 1930s, when not only science fiction magazines but ordinary magazines and also the Chicago World's Fair of 1933–1934—subtitled "A Century of Progress"—were filled with the promise of all things streamlined, toasters included. We fondly believed we would soon be wearing Flash Gordon skin-tight outfits, using ray guns, and zipping around in our own teeny jet-propelled air vehicles.

Similar promises are appearing today, though they tend to focus on bioengineering. Soon we will have the ability to choose our children's genes, much as you'd choose a wardrobe, and we ourselves will be able to live, if not forever, at least for a much longer time than people live now. Then there are those who think it would be a good idea to get your brain changed into data, uploaded and shot into outer space, where you will dwell forever and ever in a simulacrum, minus your body. But hey! You will not notice the difference, until some other simulacrum pulls the plug on your server. Other than those sorts of cheerful fantasies, we are finding the future more than a little foreboding these days. What with Hurricane Sandy, climate change, a new rash of mutated diseases for which antibiotics no longer work, biosphere depletion, rising sea levels, and levels of methane in the atmosphere, we no longer imagine the future as a stroll in the park. It looks more like a slog in the swamp.

Then there is the Zombie Apocalypse, another item situated in the future. This coming event seems to be much on people's minds, at least in the world of popular culture. Like the genetic engineering and the prolonged life and the uploading of your brain, this cluster of memes concerns our relationship with our bodies and thus with mortality—something that's always preoccupied us as a self-conscious species—only the other way around. Instead of overcoming mortality as zombies and also as zombie victims, we will be possessed by it or overcome by it. The human being running away from the zombie figures forth a hunt in which your own death is pursuing you.

I became interested in zombies because I initially failed to grasp their charm, though others seemed to have grasped it. So an investigation was in order: What was I missing? Part of my investigation turned into a two-hander serial zombie novel, *The Happy Zombie Sunrise Home,* written with zombie expert Naomi Alderman and residing on the Wattpad.com story-sharing site. I have to say that this story, although reasonably entertaining, has attracted perhaps a disproportionate amount of attention. I just hope that this particular title is not what is going to be carved on my tombstone, supposing I stay put once underground. Possibilities abound.

There are other monstrous things you can turn into, in the world of literature and other plot-driven human modes of communication, such as films; and these other forms of monstrosity provide at least some benefits to those so transformed. You acquire superpowers of various kinds, whereas with zombies you get subpowers. In order to plumb the depths of the zombie apocalypse, to dig, as it were, deeper into its subtext, we need to do a tear and compare. So I will attempt to give some perspective on, (a) literary monsters in general, with various types—most of which are ancient, or at least old—itemized, and (b) plagues of zombies in particular, which are a recent phenomenon and pertain to the future.

Before talking about zombies, their form and function, I offer the following observations on the future. We might subtitle this part of my remarks, with a nod to Raymond Carver, as "What we talk about when we talk about the future." The short answer is "the present," since that's all we have to go on. Surprise piece of information: The future doesn't really exist. Therefore, it is up for grabs because unlike the past nobody can fact-check the future. If you are a novelist, that's a good thing. If you're a stock promoter, it's also a good thing. In fact, it's probably to everyone's advantage that we cannot predict in every single detail what is really about to happen. It would deprive us of our sense that we have a free will, which, whether it is an illusion or not, is in my opinion absolutely necessary to being able to haul yourself out of bed in the morning.

Earlier this fall I watched a movie on a plane, as I often do. That's how I saw *Kung Fu Panda,* which I recommend. On another flight, compelled by the need to do some serious research about the future, I chose *Men in Black 3.* Here is the description: "Agent Jay travels back in time to 1969 [needless to say, from the future], where he teams up with a younger version of Agent Kay to stop an evil alien from destroying the future." On the way to being allowed to view my movie selection (parental supervision recommended), I was treated to some delightful advertisements. I always watch the ads, having come of drinking age not two blocks from Marshall McLuhan, who began his career with *The Mechanical Bride,* a psycho-social-literary reading of some popular ads of the late 1940s. My favourite of these is probably "Deep Consolation." The title is a Joycean play on words, the hidden subject being corpse burial. The 1940s liked those Joycean plays on words. In the picture, a young woman is looking out the window at the rain with a serene expression that signals, "I don't care if it's raining because I have done the right thing." What is being sold? The Clark Metal Grave Vault, a coffin container in which you could place your dead loved one so that he would not get wet in the rain. It must have been that quite a few people were buying this item, or enough so that the company could afford the magazine ads.

McLuhan's sidebars read, "How dry I am," "I cried until they told me it was watertight," and "More stiffs are turning to the watertight brand." His message was that people would sell anything and people would also buy anything, in that Mad Men ad-ruled age. McLuhan expected us to find it mildly hilarious that anyone would think their loved one could be kept "safe" inside such a contraption. Did they have any idea of what was going on in there, from a microbiological perspective? But that was the point—to evade and obscure such exact knowledge by making death a fuzzy cosmetic affair only, and by enforcing the fairy tale that your loved one was in some sense still alive and would be very appreciative of your watertight efforts on behalf of his embalmed remains. At least his suit would not get wet, with rain in any case.

However, with my new-found zombie knowledge and having seen *Night of the Living Dead* back in 1970 (who knew that it would have such an influence?), I discern a more sinister subtext to this pricey, coffin-shaped tin can. Perhaps the Clark Metal Grave Vault was not to keep the loved one safe from the elements outside. Perhaps it was to keep the loved one in, so he could not dig his way out and go wandering around as a zombie. This makes more sense. I'd pay for that.

The pre-movie ad on my plane, however, was perkily future-oriented, as it was hoping to get me to use that company for my share purchases. It told me that I needed to be part of the possible because the present didn't really count. It is the "next" that counts, the future. *Now* is only the prologue, it said, morphing Shakespeare, who said more accurately, "what's past is prologue." Of course, if now is only the prologue, then the future, when we get there, will be now, and thus merely a prologue, which won't count, since only the *next* next will count, and so on, ad infinitum. Thus, buying shares—when you consider it—is an investment of something that never actually exists.

For the Christmas of 2011, I received a charming calendar put out by *Cabinet* magazine, dedicated to predictions of the end of the world. The end of the world has been predicted with amazing frequency, though never so far accurately. Here is the pitch for the marvellous calendar:

> When the current cycle of the Maya Long Count calendar
> concludes on 21 December 2012, the world will end. Of course,
> this is hardly the first time the planet's demise has been
> prophesied. And so *Cabinet* offers you, doomed reader, a guide
> to the brief time that remains. This oversized wall calendar,

featuring artworks by Bigert & Bergström illustrating twelve methods of divination, ignores the familiar holidays in favour of more than sixty significant dates in the history of apocalyptic prophecy. Starring comets, aliens, floods, returning messiahs, and more, *The Last Calendar* will be with you for all the days of the coming year, and ends—as will you—on 21 December 2012.

Among the methods of divination, some are familiar—animal entrails, for instance—and some not. Divination by coffee grounds? We know about tea leaves, but . . . coffee? Then I came to "potatomancy," which is divination by potatoes. *Mancy* is from a Greek word for *prophecy*. The term also gives us *manic* and *maniac,* as earlier prophets went into raving trances about the future, unlike *Forbes* magazine. The potatomancy photo showed some very twisted potatoes, with little sticks stuck into them for legs.

They made this up, I thought. Well, yes and no. Turning to the Internet, that modern-day equivalent of consulting the oracle, I did find two entries on potatomancy. The first is from an Abracadabra forum, which told me how to do potatomancy: "Select a blue potato and move your knife around until the point of insertion feels right. Cut the potato in two. Gaze into the potato slice until you see a pattern and dip it into dye if this helps. Interpret the pattern according to inspiration." I do not intend to try this at home, but you may wish to. Maybe it would be a good cure for writer's block: after days of gazing at a potato slice, returning to our discouraging manuscript might look attractive.

The second is from a Wikia [now Fandom] scratchpad:

Masters of Potato Energy are known as Potatomancers . . . [they] are said to draw power from an object known as "The Black Potato." One presumably exists at the core of every planet, and in time of need when the whole race is threatened, a potatomancer may call upon the powers of every potatomancer to raise the charred potato from the center of the planet, and hurl it at an opponent. The superheated potato is unstoppable and explodes on contact.

The world being what it is, I expect that in the future workshops devoted to the teaching of potatomancy will arise, and perhaps a cult. This cult will be funded by Frito-Lay, or possibly the more purist Kettle Chips, on the theory that anything that raises potato status is good for their business. There is a franchise opportunity here. Remember that the present is prologue: it's the Next that's important and then the NEXT next, and the next.

Methods of divination that counted for something in the past have been many and varied. Kings of olden days employed prophets, with whom they had a love-hate relationship. On the one hand, the kings did not want bad news: they wanted good news. On the other hand, they did not want false good news. Either way, they certainly did not want prophets who denounced the wicked ways of kings. That is a problem in today's world as well, except the kings are called by other names, such as corporate presidents. The bad news that they do not want has to do with things such as climate change drying up the Midwest, and toxic leakages destroying the ocean . . . little details like that.

But prophets were not the only vectors of news about the future. Other ancient methods included flights of birds; meteors and signs in the heavens; books of divination, such as the *I Ching;* and cards and horoscopes—these last still doing a brisk business in daily newspapers. Greek oracles, of course, had a reputation for speaking ambiguously. For the most part they seem to have told people more or less what they wanted to hear, with a slippery-worded out-clause just in case. All of which gives us an idea of how undependable predictions about the future can be.

Now, as promised, here come the zombies. Zombies were originally associated with Haitian voodoo: they were living people who'd had will and memory removed, courtesy of some sort of mixture containing, possibly, a neurotoxin from pufferfish. After undergoing a mock interment, they became mindless slaves. You couldn't remember a thing, including who you were; and certainly you had no worries about what was going to happen tomorrow.

But in their most modern iteration, dating roughly from the first *Night of the Living Dead* film in 1968, zombies are quite different.

The condition is caused by a plague of uncertain origin, which is spread, like rabies or vampirism, by bites. One crosses the life-death threshold by dying, then one crosses it the other way by coming to a sort of life again, only to snack upon the living—the result of which snacking is to spread the plague.

As is the way with folk motifs, the imagery for this recent kind of zombie has cannibalized a number of other folk motifs. Some of them are from the art inspired by the original Black Death, or the Great Mortality of the Fourteenth Century, including crowds of the living dead as in the Dance of Death motif, gruesome colours, such as blue and greenish flesh, bad teeth, skeletons with rags of flesh falling off of them, tattered clothes, and so on. It's what you might see if the Clark Metal Grave Vault were to be opened after the loved one had been inside it for a while. One point that the Dance of Death images were making is that Death was the great equalizer and leveller. Princes were forced to partake, as well as rich townspeople, soldiers, and paupers. The zombie apocalypse makes a similar point: when it comes to zombiehood, there are no social hierarchies and wealth means nothing.

But surely some of the sources of imagery for the zombie apocalypse are more recent. This event is increasingly imagined as a mass phenomenon that will cause widespread social collapse and physical infrastructure destruction, as in the 2002 film *Twenty-Eight Days Later*. The infected in this film are not exactly from *The Walking Dead*, but apart from that, the social-collapse scenario and the scenes of wreckage and corpses are very similar.

Why do we have such imagery at our fingertips? Maybe we were drenched in it throughout the twentieth century. Listen to the following description: ". . . this is all that can be seen. . . . Corpses, rats, old tins, old weapons, rifles, bombs, legs, boots, skulls, cartridges, bits of wood & tin & iron & stone, parts of rotting bodies and festering heads lie scattered all about." This is not a film-set description of a zombie apocalypse. It is the poet John Masefield's description of a First World War battlefield. Whoever lived through the last nine-tenths of the twentieth century was and is familiar with such imagery. Anyone who lived through the middle of that century and the Second World War got another dose of it, via photography, and especially the images of the death camps when the almost-dead were liberated from them. Just as the Black Death gave rise to Black Death art, and then to a spate of tombstones featuring skeletons and hourglasses—that last a symbol of time running out—so, surely, the twentieth century's two big horrors underlie the popular zombie apocalypse imagery of today.

This package of images has been combined with a plot that is essentially that of Albert Camus's 1947 novel, *The Plague,* as well as of various other widespread-disaster novels and films in which mass infections take place and a small, beleaguered saving-remnant group holds out. One thinks of Ionesco's play *Rhinoceros* and of the Portuguese writer Saramago's novel *Blindness,* as well as, on a less literary level, of the 1956 film *Invasion of the Body Snatchers* and the 1953 film *Invaders from Mars.* In some interpretations, these constructions, especially those that date from the 1950s, are metaphors of a political kind: awful ideologies such as Nazism and Communism are spreading like germs, taking over people's minds, and only a few holdouts remain either to combat them or to survive the bad patch.

Zombie stories are always told from within the small, beleaguered not-yet-infected group. As is emphatically not the case with other kinds of monsters, the infections are always mass. It is not a case of a single vampire having his way with nightgown-clad lovelies by night, nor of a single werewolf cavorting in the woods and taking chunks out of passers-by. The danger is in the hordes. Zombies, unlike vampires and werewolves, are not strong and quick; they are weak and slow. But there are a lot of them, and even though they shamble around in a feeble and witless manner, they can corner you. Note that in some recent iterations, such as *The Walking Dead,* they've become smarter—necessary if one is to keep the plot going—and in the film *Warm Bodies,* zombies have even done the impossible: they have become sexy. Only by becoming human again, mind you. There are limits.

But back to basics. Here is a good description of zombie hordes, from what may perhaps be an unexpected source.

> *Under the brown fog of a winter dawn,*
> *A crowd flowed over London Bridge, so many,*

I had not thought death had undone so many.
Sighs, short and infrequent, were exhaled,
And each man fixed his eyes before his feet,
Flowed up the hill and down King William Street
To where Saint Mary Woolnoth kept the hours
With a dead sound on the final stroke of nine.
There I saw one I knew, and stopped him, crying: "Stetson!
"You who were with me in the ships at Mylae!
"That corpse you planted last year in your garden,
"Has it begun to sprout? Will it bloom this year?
"Or has the sudden frost disturbed its bed?
"Oh keep the Dog far hence, that's friend to men,
"Or with his nails he'll dig it up again!"

This is from T.S. Eliot's 1922 poem, *The Waste Land*—from the section entitled "The Burial of the Dead." There are the undead shuffling across a bridge in hordes, complete with a quote from Dante about death having undone so many. There is the mindlessness and the crowdedness. There is the corpse coming to life again, sprouting up through the soil, and there is the war reference: Mylae was a battle and Stetson was a fellow soldier, but now he is one of the living dead.

But why are zombies so popular right now? Why do kids want to impersonate zombies, go on mass zombie walks, and so forth? Why Colson Whitehead's *Zone One*, why Naomi Alderman's popular exercise-aid game, *Zombies Run*? If zombies are not a mere passing fad like Hula-Hoops, what do they mean? All such monsters, being man-made, are entirely metaphorical. A giant squid has a being of its own outside the human imagination, but a vampire or a zombie does not. Therefore, zombies mean what we think they mean. But what *do* we think they mean?

First, what's on offer? On the surface of it, zombies have nil to add to the life of anyone who turns into one. Consider the perks, significations, and downsides for various competing types of monsters. I will list some of these in their order of appearance. Grendel, originally in *Beowulf*, is a cannibalistic wild creature who does not say much—though in John Gardner's wonderful update novel, *Grendel*, he is possessed of an inquiring mind and is the maker of many jokes.

A perk of being Grendel: he is very strong. The downside is that his arm is detachable. Since he is accursed, the afflicted part of him is his soul—he is an offspring of Cain, the result of the Fall, and Original Sin and so on. He is Fallen Nature incarnate.

Dr. Frankenstein's failed attempt at creating a perfect man, in Mary Shelley's novel *Frankenstein,* is a talkative monster, a narrator of his own story, and a great reader. He is not to be confused with the film version Frankenstein monsters, who are dim and malevolent from the get-go. The perk is that this man-made creature is excessively strong, a vigorous climber, and impervious to cold. The downside is that nobody likes him. He is not allowed to have a girlfriend, so he is very lonely. The part of him that is afflicted is his heart: his feelings have been fatally wounded.

He does not embody Fallen Nature, but rather Modern Man. His operative principle is electricity, which vivifies the nervous system, through that tangle of scientific apparatus we are familiar with from the films. He was created by Man, not God, though there is some suggestion that the monster is to Dr. Frankenstein as Adam is to God. Metaphysical probings are on offer, therefore. Who am I? Who made me? Why has my maker deserted me? The meaning of this monster is connected to the nineteenth century's crisis of faith, especially in the face of science and its unsettling discoveries. Neither Grendel nor the Frankenstein monster can communicate a disease, nor can they reproduce themselves. Each is a menace but not a plague. Neither of them is a human being transformed—your boyfriend will never turn into either one—and neither of them will destroy civilization.

Now for three kinds of monsters that are created through transformation, human into monster, and that can spread their condition through contagion:

1. Werewolves: Animal transformation has an extremely long lineage. Originally a transformation to an animal form would have occurred during a shamanistic trance, its purpose being to allow the shaman to communicate with the world of animal spirits in order to acquire game for the tribe. As agriculture replaced hunting, such practices were shunted to the sidelines

and demonized. Belief in shape-changing has been very widespread. The animal forms in question have included bears, wolves, seals, snakes, deer, geese, swans, and snails.

Werewolves as such, in European and North American folklore, have taken various forms. In Quebec, the Loup Garou was a man who had not taken Easter communion three years in a row, thus taking on a religious significance. There is some suggestion that, once killed by a silver bullet that may or may not have been made from a melted crucifix, the werewolf regains human form, with an implication that the demonic part may have departed and the soul may have been redeemed. Robert Louis Stevenson's *Dr. Jekyll and Mr. Hyde* is a werewolf story of modern times, with the transformative element being not trance or magic, but chemistry. The disease most closely comparable to werewolf episodes, if any, is rabies, but there is some possibility that the werewolf state in its modern manifestations, hairiness and out-of-control behaviour, may just be a characteristic of the onset of male adolescence, though women are increasingly moving in to claim some of that free-and-howling territory.

Perks for werewolves include wild freedom, increased strength, more acute senses, and getting away with vandalism. Werewolves are cunning. In their human shape, they are entirely capable of narration and have frequently, in recent times, related their own stories. Werewolves can spread their condition, and sometimes travel in packs and mate, but they are not a mass phenomenon.

2. Vampires: The perk is immortal life, under certain conditions. Vampires can mesmerize people and are sexually seductive toward prone, drowsy women, who often welcome the penetration of fangs. They reproduce by exchanging blood with victims, thus creating more vampires. The downside is that they are not good with daylight. In the original *Dracula,* the vampire has really bad breath—and a damned soul, which can, however, be released by a stake through the heart.

The disease that may be suggestive is tuberculosis, with its bad breath, blood in the mouth, weight loss and thinness, pallor, hectic flushes, and languor, and—in nineteenth-century belief—

heightened sexual sensations. Some have discerned in the nineteenth-century outbreak of vampires—as in certain kinds of ghost stories, such as Henry James's *The Turn of the Screw*— a repressed sexuality, or at least the impossibility of publishing material that was overtly sexual in upmarket books of the time.

Vampires are viewed in *Dracula* as capable of instituting a small-scale plague, though it is less like a plague as such than a kind of vampire takeover of certain residential districts. Let's note that vampires are talkative, as in the sagas by Anne Rice; they are also very cunning and usually rich, due to their long lives, during which they've accumulated much pelf. The religious implication is that vampires, being semi-satanic, can be deterred by crucifixes. They can, however, be redeemed, if their bodily form has a stake pounded through its heart, a treatment once meted out also to suicides.

3. Zombies: What a sorry figure zombies cut by comparison! They're disgusting in appearance, weak, and shambling. They lack minds and language, uttering nothing much more than feeble moans. Werewolves and vampires have a religious dimension: the soul or spirit is supposed to be in there somewhere. But zombies seem to be only about the body. Perhaps in an age in which nobody much appears to have a soul anyway, zombies do not have souls either. Or perhaps they cannot have souls because they do not have a self, an I. They can never be the narrators of their own stories because they cannot remember or record. What, therefore, is the point of them?

Here are a few speculations.

Point One: The four previous monsters are of the past. Werewolves originate in hunter-gatherer societies, Grendel lurks on the border between paganism and Christianity, vampires are aristocrats and landowners with fancy outfits and capes, and the Frankenstein monster is a creature of the Enlightenment, what with the scientific apparatus and all. But the zombie apocalypse, although its visual imagery may be borrowed from earlier gruesome events, is not of the past but of the future. An *apocalypse,* a word we have appropriated from the Bible and morphed, is now taken to mean something that is to come, not something that has already happened. So part of the appeal of the zombie apocalypse is that, no matter how bad you think things are now, they could get a lot worse. This makes the present look quite good by comparison.

Point Two: Similarly, you think you're ugly? Well, think how much uglier you'd be should you become a zombie. All that dental work has gone to waste, not to mention hair care. The very thought makes one feel like a thing of beauty and a joy forever.

Point Three: If zombies are a metaphor for a disease, then zombies are to X as vampires are to tuberculosis. What disease might it be? It might be Alzheimer's or dementia perhaps. At no time in history has a society included such a large percentage of people who are no longer themselves due to impaired memories, and who—given free rein—would wander aimlessly to and fro. In this reading, zombies have been thrown up by the collective unconscious in reaction to the energy-sucking presence of a great many mindless old people, a number set to increase. Some have postulated that dementia is being augmented by junk food, which gives you diabetes of the brain. Aha! The real plague vector!

Point Four: But most members of the zombie apocalypse are young rather than old. Could the zombie hordes be the reverse side of the kind of mass youth protest that has produced the Egyptian Spring, Occupy Wall Street, the recent London riots and the Black Block smash-a-store-window-and-disrupt-political-events movement? Active form: We have no future and no ownership stake in this society, and we object. Passive form: We have no future and no ownership stake in this society; we opt out and amble and attack in slow-motion swarms.

Naomi Alderman, in a November 2011 *Granta* piece called "The Meaning of Zombies," says:

> While vampires tend to be more popular in times of economic
> prosperity—think of *Interview with the Vampire*'s lush heyday
> in the 1980s and early 1990s—zombies, the shuffling mass
> dressed in rags, tend to come to the fore in more austere times.
> George Romero's *Dawn of the Dead* comes to us from the

depression of the 1970s and of course zombies are having a massive renaissance—as it were—now.

The zombie apocalypse is the death of civilization, the moment when all that becomes important is the answer to the questions: Do you have food? Do you have guns? We want to practise this in fantasy, to imagine it all the way through, especially in times of economic crisis. We live in cities now, far from sources of food, not knowing our neighbours. Zombies are the horrifying crowd of the urban poor, the grasping hands reaching out for something, which, if you gave it to them, would destroy you. They're the interchangeable anonymous people we encounter on our daily commute, those whose humanity we cannot acknowledge.

There is a plus side to the mindlessness as well. The other transformational types have a self, a memory, a language, and therefore they know what they have lost. But zombies exist in the eternal now because they lack memories and foresight, as well as the worry, doubt, anxiety, and suffering that may come along with these. They have no goals and no responsibilities; they're strangely carefree, as in the old song "The Zombie Jamboree": "Back to back, belly to belly, we don't give a damn and we don't give a helly . . ."

Zombies exist without past or future, and thus outside time. Although they themselves are symbols of death, they paradoxically live outside death, since time and death are interrelated. In some ways, zombies are oddly blessed—though, I do stress, oddly. So the zombie apocalypse may be an escape from a real future we quite rightly fear—due to the predictions of climate change and the societal collapse that haunt our times—into a fearsome future that is not at all real and is therefore consoling.

When I first started doing question-and-answer sessions with audiences back in the 1960s, people were asking, "When are you going to kill yourself?" I was a woman poet and in those Sylvia Plath–haunted times, suicide seemed required. In the early days of the women's movement, they were asking, "Do you hate men?" Then in the 1980s, people started asking about the writing process. After 1985, they wanted to talk about *The Handmaid's Tale,* as they do now:

it seems that in the state-control-of-women's-bodies department, I was a little too close to the mark.

But lately they've been asking, "Is there hope?" My answer is, "There's always hope." Hope is built-in. It's also catching: where there is hope, there will be more hope, because with hope, people make an effort. An effort is what, in the future, we will all have to make. Maybe that is the true meaning of zombies: they are ourselves, but without the hope.

I wish you hope.

Why I Wrote *MaddAddam*

>>><<<

(2013)

Why did you write *MaddAddam*? I'm sometimes asked. I'm tempted to quote alpine climber George Mallory, who, when asked in 1924 why he wanted to climb Mount Everest, said, "Because it is there." *MaddAddam* had to be there because the two books that came before it—*Oryx and Crake* (2003) and *The Year of the Flood* (2009)—both end on unfinished business. So *MaddAddam* had to come along and close those open endings, didn't it? Or close them at least in part.

The first two books follow different groups of people, but they both end at the same point in time, and in the same place, as those groups come together. *MaddAddam* carries on from that moment, and tells us what happens next. It also fills us in on the past of a character who isn't explored thoroughly in the first two books: Zeb, an authority on Urban Bloodshed Limitation and on the skinning and broiling of small animals, and, as we discover, an accomplished thief and hacker.

When it appears in Germany, this book will be called "The Story of Zeb"—since the word *MaddAddam* is impossible to translate into German—and it does indeed contain the story of Zeb; but it also contains, as they say on promotional flyers, "and more." We discover, for instance, whether the rumours about Zeb floating around in *The Year of the Flood* are true. Did he indeed once eat both a bear and his co-pilot? What was he doing with Lucerne, an obviously unsuitable woman? And what exactly is his relationship to Adam One, pacifist, theologian, and wearer of odd caftan-like garments that look as if they're sewn by gnomes?

I began writing the story of Adam and Zeb as part of *The Year of the Flood,* but there wasn't room for it in that book so it had to be in the next one. At the end of *In the Wake of the Flood,* the documentary film made by Ron Mann of sphinxproductions.com about the unconventional book tour I did for *The Year of the Flood*—a tour that combined a musical and dramatic presentation with bird conservation awareness—the camera catches me typing away at *MaddAddam. Zeb was lost,* I type. *He sat down under a tree.* And he does get lost, and he does sit down under a tree.

The word *MaddAddam* is a palindrome: it's a mirror word, the same word whether read forwards or backwards. (Why the double *D*s? Two reasons: The intellectual excuse is that there are mirror *D*s to go with the duplicated DNA used in gene-splicing. But I made that up after the fact. The simple reason is that someone already had the domain name for Madadam, and I didn't like the idea of my book title being used, possibly, for a porn site, as has been known to happen.)

In addition to this, MaddAddam is the name of a group of people performing acts of bio-resistance against the Corp-controlled regime that now holds extreme power. They in turn have taken their name from the code name of the GrandMaster who runs Extinctathon, an online game. "Adam named the living animals. MaddAddam names the dead ones. Do you want to play?" You can tell, both from the word itself and from its context, that the MaddAddam entity—whether singular or plural—is angry about something. Or possibly crazy, since *mad* can mean both of those things. Possibly angry enough to do crazy, risky things; which turns out to be accurate.

Extinctathon—in which the players challenge one another by guessing the names of recently extinct species, of which there are many now and many more in the future—is one of the violent and/or geeky games played in *Oryx and Crake* by Jimmy and Glenn, the two main characters, when they're in high school. They too use code names to play this game: Glenn is "Crake," and that's the name we know him by. It's as Crake that Glenn creates a bioengineered race of beings named after him, designed to avoid the planet-destroying mistakes made by old-style human beings (us). The Crakers are uniformly beautiful. They also have built-in sunblock and built-in insect repellent, so they will never invent clothing, the growing of cotton, the raising of sheep, toxic dyes, or the Industrial Revolution. They purr to self-heal. They are so vegetarian they can eat leaves, like rabbits; they find meat repulsive, so they will never start raising livestock or farming chickens. And they mate seasonally and in groups, so they never experience sexual jealousy or rejection. Warfare and aggression are unknown to them.

But they wouldn't stand a chance against old-style human beings, who would either kill them or exploit them, so Crake takes care of that problem by exterminating most of the old-style human race by means of a virus concealed in a sex-enhancement pill called Blyss-Pluss. The users of this pill do get the Blyss, but they also get the Pluss: once the virus has been deployed, it becomes contagious by touch, and spreads very rapidly.

But Jimmy has been chosen by Crake to survive the pandemic and become the guardian of the Crakers in the brave new depopulated world that awaits them after they leave the egg-shaped dome in which they were created. After the death of Crake and the woman both he and Jimmy love, a former child prostitute code-named Oryx, Jimmy renames himself Snowman—after the Abominable Snowman, which may or may not exist and which may or may not be human. This is how we first encounter him in *Oryx and Crake:* living in a tree, watching over the Crakers, and creating a mythology for them in which their Creator is Crake—true enough—helped by a goddess called Oryx, the authority in their interrelationships with the animals that surround them. These include several bioengineered species that have proliferated since the virus: glowing green rabbits; Mo'Hairs that grow human hair—originally for transplant; gentle rakunks, a blend of raccoon and skunk; and liobams, a cross between lions and lambs. Most importantly, the pigoons, experimental pigs that contain not only multiple human transplantable kidneys but human neocortex tissue as well. Pigs in general are smart, but these pigs are *very* smart.

Oryx and Crake ends as Jimmy is trying to decide whether or not he can trust the three human stragglers he has stumbled across. Perhaps they might be his friends; on the other hand, perhaps they will be fatal to the Crakers. What to do?

The Year of the Flood follows the path of Toby, rescued by Adam One and the God's Gardeners from a hideous life entangled with slum crime and SecretBurgers (nobody knows what's in them); and also of Ren, one-time underaged girlfriend of Jimmy. Each has survived the "Waterless Flood"—Gardener code name for the viral pandemic: Ren holed up in Scales and Tails, the upmarket sex club where she's been working, and Toby barricaded into the AnooYoo Spa in the Park, where she's been working under an assumed name after the Gardeners have been outlawed. *The Year of the Flood* brings Toby and Ren onto the scene just as Jimmy, addled by his infected foot, is trying to decide whether to shoot or not, and ends several hours after that. The moon is rising, the evil Painballers are roped to a tree, securely, we hope; the Crakers are approaching, the hostile pigoons roam the forest. What next? we wonder.

   MaddAddam tells us what next.

Those are the reasons within the books themselves; they have to do with story, and the unfairness of leaving stories unfinished unless you intend to tell more. I grew up reading Sherlock Holmes, and I always wanted just one more story about him; which is probably why people are still writing those stories, long after the original author died.

   But there are other reasons for writing books—ones that have to do with content rather than plot. We live in extraordinary times: on the one hand, technologies of all sorts—biological, robotic, digital— are being invented and perfected by the minute, and many feats that would once have been considered impossible or magical are being performed. On the other hand, we are destroying our biological home at breathtaking speed. On the third hand (for there's always a hidden hand), the democratic form of government we have extolled and promoted in the West for centuries is being undermined from within by super-surveillance technologies and the power of corporate money. When 1 per cent of the population controls over 80 per cent of the wealth, you have a top-heavy social pyramid that's inherently unstable.

This is the world we already live in. The MaddAddam trilogy builds it out a little further, and then explores it. We already have the tools to create the MaddAddam world. But will we use them?

Seven Gothic Tales

>>><<<

INTRODUCTION

(2013)

On the Danish fifty-krone banknote there's a portrait of Isak Dine-sen. It's signed *Karen Blixen,* which is how she is known in Den-mark. She's shown at the age of sixty or so, wearing a wide-brimmed hat and a fur collar and looking very glamorous indeed.

I first saw Isak Dinesen when I was ten, in a photo shoot in *Life* magazine. My experience then was similar to that of Sara Stam-baugh, one of her bio-critics: "I well remember my own excitement around 1950, when, leafing through a used copy of *Life* magazine, I stumbled across an article on the Danish Baroness Karen Blixen, her identity not simply revealed but celebrated in big, glossy black-and-white photographs. I still remember one in particular, show-ing her leaning dramatically from a window, striking, turbaned, and emaciated."

To my young eyes, this person in the pictures was like a magical creature from a fairy tale: an impossibly aged woman, a thousand years old at least. Her outfits were striking and the makeup of the era had been carefully applied, but the effect was carnivalesque—like a dressed-up Mexican skeleton. Her expression, however, was bright-eyed and ironic: she seemed to be enjoying the show-stopping if not grotesque impression she was making.

Could Isak Dinesen have been contemplating such a moment in *Seven Gothic Tales,* twenty-five years earlier? In the story "The Supper at Elsinore," the de Coninck siblings are described as living memento mori: ". . . as you got, from the face of the brother, the key of understanding to this particular type of family beauty, you would recognize it at once in the appearance of the sisters, even in the two youthful portraits on the wall. The most striking characteristic in the three heads was the generic resemblance to the skull."

Isak Dinesen was already ill at the time of the 1950 pictures. Nine years later she made a final triumphant visit to New York. She was lionized; famous writers paid homage to her, including E.E. Cummings and Arthur Miller; her public appearances were packed; and there were more photos. Less than three years later she was dead, as she must have known she would be. Her flamboyant self-presentation takes on, in retrospect, a new meaning: in her place, other doomed sufferers might have stayed in seclusion, concealing from the camera the wreckage of a once-striking beauty, but instead Dinesen chose the full public spotlight. Was she incarnating one of her own dominant literary motifs—the brave but futile gesture in the face of almost certain death? It's tempting to think so.

New York was a fitting choice for her swan song, since it was New York that had made her famous back in 1934 when *Seven Gothic Tales* took America by storm. Rejected by several publishers for the usual reasons—short stories didn't sell, the author was unknown, the stories themselves were odd and not attuned to the zeitgeist—the book was finally picked up by a smaller American publisher, Harrison Smith and Robert Haas. There were conditions: the well-known novelist Dorothy Canfield must write an introduction, and the author was to receive no advance. Karen Blixen gambled and took the offer. Then she won, for, much to the surprise of all, *Seven Gothic Tales* was chosen by the Book-of-the-Month Club, which was a guarantee of wide publicity and large sales.

Now it was time for Karen Blixen to make her own condition: she would publish under a nom de plume, Isak Dinesen. Dinesen was her maiden name, Isak was the Danish version of Isaac, "laughter," the name picked by the elderly Sarah in the Book of Genesis for her late and unexpected child. Blixen's American publisher tried to talk her out of using a pseudonym, but to no avail: she was determined to be multiple. (And, by the way, male, or at least genderless. Perhaps she did not wish to be thrust into the Lady Scribbler cage, suggestive of lesser merit.)

"Isak" was appropriate: Karen Blixen's emergence as a writer was indeed late and unexpected. She'd returned from Africa to Denmark in 1931, stony flat broke—her marriage was finished, her African coffee farm had failed, her romantic lover, big-game hunter Denys Finch Hatton, had died in a plane crash. Although she'd written much earlier—her first stories were published when she was barely twenty—she'd chosen marriage and Africa over writing; but that life was now finished. At forty-six, she must have been feeling both desolate and desperate; but also, evidently, boiling with creative energy.

The stories in *Seven Gothic Tales* were written at speed and under pressure. They were also written in English: one reason usually given was that she felt English would be more practical than Danish, since many more potential readers spoke it. But there were surely some deeper motives. Blixen herself was fluent in English; so what, we might ask, could she have been reading in English during her formative years? What, that is, might have led her to write "tales" rather than "stories"? Chaucer's *Canterbury Tales*? Old wives' tales? Fairy tales? *The Winter's Tale,* the Shakespeare play that lent its name to a later Dinesen collection?

The distinction between the two forms was well understood in Victorian times. In a "tale," a woman may change into a monkey before our very eyes, as one does in the Dinesen tale "The Monkey"; in a mainline short story, she cannot.

"Tales" have tellers and listeners within them, much more frequently than realistic stories do. The most famous tale-spinner of all is Scheherazade, narrating to stave off death, and that is the very first storytelling situation Dinesen offers us. In "The Deluge at Norderney," a courageous group of aristocrats who have chosen to exchange places with a small peasant family waits out the night while a flood rises around them, telling stories to encourage one another and pass the time. Perhaps a boat will arrive at dawn to rescue them; perhaps they will be swept away first. Dinesen ends her story thus:

> Between the boards a strip of fresh deep blue was showing, against which the little lamp seemed to make a red stain. The dawn was breaking.
>
> The old woman slowly drew her fingers out of the man's hand, and placed one upon her lips.

"*À ce moment de sa narration,*" she said, "*Scheherazade vit paraître le matin, et, discrète, se tut.*"

Seven Gothic Tales is filled with storytellers, and also with the kind of fractal exfoliation and multi-chambering structures so abundantly typical of more ancient tales, such as those in *The Thousand and One Nights* and Boccaccio's *Decameron.* There is a "frame"—a couple of men on a boat, for instance, whiling away the time by telling about their lives, as in "The Dreamers"; then one of those stories leads into another, told by yet another person within it, which opens up into another, which then links back to the first, and so on. As with Scheherazade, much of this tale-telling (and indeed much of the action in the tales recounted) takes place at night.

But *Seven Gothic Tales* also echoed a more recent period in which writers drew upon these older-time forms of tale-telling. Karen Blixen was born in 1885, three years after Robert Louis Stevenson published his first collection, *New Arabian Nights.* That moment ushered in a rich period of late Victorian and Edwardian tale-telling, in both short and long forms, that stretched to the outbreak of the First World War. Not only Stevenson, but Arthur Conan Doyle, M.R. James, the Henry James of *The Turn of the Screw* and "The Jolly Corner," the Oscar Wilde of *The Picture of Dorian Gray,* the early H.G. Wells of *The Time Machine* and *The Island of Doctor Moreau,* Bram Stoker of *Dracula,* the H. Rider Haggard of *She,* the George du Maurier of *Trilby,* and a host of other English-language tale-spinners engaged with ghosts and possession and the uncanny were energetically publishing in those years. Borges, Calvino, and Ray Bradbury, among others, drank from the same well.

Stevenson was possibly the most important of these for Dinesen. She kept a collected edition of his work in her library, and alludes to him overtly in the story "The Dreamers" by naming one of her characters, Olalla, after one of his. That particular story plays with many other motifs from the tale-telling tradition, not all of them English: the heroine of multiple identities, as in *The Tales of Hoffman;* the dark enchanter, a mirror reversal of the Svengali figure in *Trilby,* linked with an opera singer who has lost her voice.

Two motifs from Stevenson's early work are particularly dominant throughout *Seven Gothic Tales:* the courageous act or last throw of the dice in the face of impending doom, as in (to give only one instance) Stevenson's "The Pavilion on the Links"; and the controlling older person manipulating the sexual destinies of the young, as in his "The Sire de Maletroit's Door." In Stevenson's stories all turns out well, but in Dinesen's variants things do not go so smoothly. In "The Poet," the old arranger gets shot and bashed to death by the two young *innamorati* with whose fates he has been playing, and who will now face execution themselves; in "The Monkey," a marriage designed to cloak homosexuality is forced, not only by rape, but by a horrifying metempsychosis; in "The Roads Round Pisa," the old arranger is deceived into fighting an unnecessary duel, then dies of a heart attack from the stress. In "The Deluge at Norderney," the marriage arranged by the elderly Baroness is not only invalid—the officiating Cardinal being in fact another person entirely—but all the participants may soon perish. Dinesen affirms the Romantic through her insistence on the spiritual validity of honour, but she also subverts it. Not so fast with the happy endings, she seems to be telling us.

As with the stories in *New Arabian Nights,* and indeed as with modern "Romantic" conventions, many of Dinesen's tales are placed long ago and far away; but whereas with Stevenson the choice was primarily aesthetic, for Dinesen there is another layer of significance. For she was gazing back at that late Victorian and Edwardian golden age of tale-telling across a vast gulf: not only the years during which her own earlier life had ended up as wreckage, but also the First World War, which had smashed the social fabric of belief, status, and social convention that had held sway in the two centuries before it.

Dinesen can see that vanished country. She describes it in minute and loving detail, even the more unpleasant sides of it—the provincialism, the snobbery, the inturned, stifled lives—but she can't return to it except through storytelling. It's lost to all but words. There's a vein of stoic, clear-eyed nostalgia running through her work, and, despite the ironic distance she often assumes, the elegiac tone is never far away.

Nevertheless, what pleasure she must have felt in the process; and what pleasure she has provided for her many readers, over time.

Seven Gothic Tales is the opening act of a remarkable writing career, one that placed Isak Dinesen on the list of essential twentieth-century authors. As James Joyce invokes Daedalus the maze-maker at the end of *A Portrait of the Artist as a Young Man*—"Old father, old artificer"—so many readers and writers might invoke Isak Dinesen: "Old mother, old tale-spinner, stand me now and ever in good stead."

And from those *Life* magazine photographs, her enigmatic, ornamented skeleton self with the living eyes gallantly returns our gaze.

Doctor Sleep

>>><<<

(2013)

Doctor Sleep is Stephen King's latest novel, and it's a very good specimen of the quintessential King blend. According to Vladimir Nabokov, Salvador Dalí was "really Norman Rockwell's twin brother kidnapped by gypsies in babyhood." But actually there were triplets: the third one is Stephen King.

The Rockwell small-town rocking chair, the old-fashioned house with the welcome mat, the genial family doctor, the grandfather clock: there they are, depicted in all their lifelike, apparently cozy detail. Both Rockwell and King know such details intimately, right down to the brand names. But there's something very, very wrong. The rocking chair is coming to get you. The family doctor is greenish in hue and has been dead for some time. The house is haunted, and the welcome mat is alive with *things.* And, pace Dalí, the clock is melting.

Doctor Sleep picks up on the story of Danny, the little boy with psycho-intuitive powers in King's famous 1977 novel, *The Shining.* Danny survived both his evil-infested dad, Jack Torrance, and the ghouls that inhabited the grisly Overlook Hotel in Colorado, escaping by the hair of his chinny-chin-chin just before the clock struck midnight and the hotel's infernal boiler blew up, incinerating the forces of bad and leaving readers hiding under the bed but cross-eyed with relief.

In *Doctor Sleep,* Dan has grown up, but he retains his "shining" abilities. Having wrestled the Demon Drink to an uneasy standstill—his father had that problem too, as we recall—he's attending AA and working at a palliative care facility, where, with his mind-probing talents, he helps the dying to reconcile themselves to their often misspent lives. Thus his nickname, Doctor Sleep, which echoes his childhood nickname, "doc." (As in the "What's up?" of Bugs Bunny fame. What, indeed?)

Enter another magic child, Abra—as in "cadabra," as the text helpfully points out—who's even better at the shining stuff than Dan is. She alarmed her parents early on by predicting the 9/11 disaster while still in her crib, and has since caused dismay by sticking all the spoons to the ceiling during her birthday party.

The two shiners soon find themselves in spiritual communication, which is a lucky thing because young Abra is going to need big help. She is the target of a rackety, entertaining bunch called the True Knot, who lust to drink her spiritual mist, or "Steam." (This is a whole new twist on steampunk.) The Knot members have been alive for a Very Long Time—not usually a good sign, as those who know their *Dracula* and *She* can testify—and, disguised as vacationers roaming the countryside in RVs, they kidnap and torture their victims, then imbibe their essences. They also bottle these in case of shortages; for if they run out of Steam they evaporate, leaving their clothes behind them, like the Wicked Witch of the West when melted.

They're led by a beautiful woman named Rose the Hat, whose main lover is a gent known as Crow Daddy. (From *crawdaddy*, we assume. King loves wordplay and puns and mirror language: remember REDRUM, from *The Shining*? Who could forget?) The names of King's characters are frequently appropriate: Dan "Lions' Den" Anthony (the tempted saint) Torrance (it never rains but it pours) is a case in point. Rose is a sinister Rosa Mystica, a negative version of the Virgin Mary. (For starters, she ain't no virgin.)

As for the Overlook Hotel—on the site of which the True Knotters have pitched their main encampment—its name has at least three layers: the obvious one (it looks out over the landscape), the semi-obvious (the bad folks overlook something), and the deeply embedded, which I'm guessing has to do with the old song about the four-leafed clover and the somebody I adore; for King's good and evil arrangement is usually yin and yang, with a spot of darkness in every goodie and a tiny ray of sunshine in every baddie. Even the True Knotters are sweet with one another, though their status as human beings is dubious. As one new recruit says, "Am I still human?" And as Rose replies, "Do you care?"

Wild ectoplasmic partially decayed vampire horses would not tear from me the story of what happens next, but let me assure you King is a pro: by the end of this book your fingers will be mere stubs of their former selves, and you will be looking askance at every person in the supermarket lineup because if they turn around *they might have metallic eyes.*

King's inventiveness and skill show no signs of slacking: *Doctor Sleep* has all the virtues of his best work. What are those virtues? First, King is a well-trusted guide to the Underworld. His readers will follow him through any door marked DANGER, KEEP OUT (or in more literary terms, ABANDON HOPE ALL YE WHO ENTER HERE) because they know that the inferno they'll be touring will be thorough—no gore left unspilled, no shriek left unshrieked—but they also know that King will get them out alive. As the Sibyl of Cumae puts it to Aeneas, it's easy to go to Hell, but returning from it is the hard part. She can say that because she's been there; and, in a manner of speaking—our intuition tells us—so has King.

Second, King is right at the centre of an American literary tap-root that goes all the way down: to the Puritans and their belief in witches, to Hawthorne, to Poe, to Melville, to the Henry James of *The Turn of the Screw,* and then to later exemplars like Ray Bradbury. In the future, I predict, theses will be written on such subjects as "American Puritan Neo-Surrealism in *The Scarlet Letter* and *The Shining,*" and "Melville's *Pequod* and King's Overlook Hotel as Structures that Encapsulate American History."

Some may look askance at "horror" as a sub-literary genre, but in fact horror is one of the most literary of all forms. Its practitioners are widely read—King being a pre-eminent example—since horror stories are made from other horror stories: you can't find a real-life example of the Overlook Hotel. People do "see" some of the things King's characters see (for a companion volume, try Oliver Sacks's *Hallucinations*), but it is one of the functions of "horror" writing to question the reality of unreality and the unreality of reality: What exactly do we mean by "see"?

But dig down below the horror trappings, and *Doctor Sleep* is about families. The biological families of Dan and Abra, the "good" family of AA, to which *Doctor Sleep* is a kind of love song, and the "bad" family of the True Knot. High on the list of King sins are the maltreatment of children by male relatives, and the brutalizing of women, mothers in particular. Righteous anger and destructive anger both have their focus in the family. As Doctor Sleep himself says to young Abra, "There's nothing but family history": often the narrative glue that sticks a King novel together. The family dimension, too, is quintessentially American horror, all the way from "Young Goodman Brown" and "The Fall of the House of Usher" on up.

What will King do next? Perhaps Abra will grow up, and become a writer, and use her "shining" talent to divine the minds and souls of others. For that, of course, is yet another interpretation of King's eerie, luminescent metaphor.

Doris Lessing

>>><<<

(2013)

Wonderful Doris Lessing has died. You never expect such rock-solid features of the literary landscape to simply vanish. It's a shock.

I first encountered Lessing on a park bench in Paris in 1963. I was a student, living on baguettes, oranges, and cheese, as one did; and suffering from a stomach ailment, as one did; and therefore washroom-hopping, as one did. My pal Alison Cunningham and I had been barred from our hostel during the day, so Alison was soothing my prostrate self by reading from *The Golden Notebook*, which was all the rage among such as us. Who knew we were reading a book that was soon to become iconic?

Just as we were getting to a crucial moment in the life of Anna Wulf, along came a policeman who informed us that lying down on park benches was against the law, so we decamped for a bistro and another interesting washroom experience. (Footnote: This was before second-wave feminism. It was before widespread birth control. It was before miniskirts. So Anna Wulf was a considerable eye-opener: she was doing things and thinking things that had not been much discussed around the Toronto dinner tables of our adolescence, and therefore seemed pretty daring.)

The other woman we were sneakily reading in 1963 was Simone de Beauvoir, but the childhoods of little-girl colonials such as ourselves lacked starched petticoats and were not very French. We had more in common with a remote-places-of-the-Empire parvenue such as Doris Lessing: born in Iran in 1919, growing up on a bush farm in Rhodesia (now Zimbabwe); then, after two failed marriages, running away to England with scant prospects, which was where us colonials with scant prospects ran away to then.

Some of Lessing's energy may have come from her outland origins: when the wheel spins, it's on the edges that the sparks fly. Her upbringing also gave her an insight into the viewpoints and plights of people unlike herself. And if you know you will never really fit in—that you will always be "not really English"—you have less to lose. Doris did everything with all her heart, all her soul, and all her might. She was sometimes temporarily wrong, as in the matter of Stalinist Communism, but she never hedged her bets or pulled her punches. She went for broke.

If there were a Mount Rushmore of twentieth-century authors, Doris Lessing would most certainly be carved upon it. Like Adrienne Rich, she was pivotal, situated at the moment when the gates of the gender-disparity castle were giving way, and women were faced with increased freedoms and choices, as well as increased challenges.

She was political in the most basic sense, recognizing the manifestations of power in its many forms. She was spiritual as well, exploring the limits and pitfalls that came with being human, especially after she became an adherent of Sufism. As a writer she was inventive and brave, branching out into science fiction in her Canopus in Argos series at a time when it was a dodgy thing for a "mainline" novelist to do.

She was also very down-to-earth, famously remarking, "Oh Christ!" when informed in 2007 that she had won the Nobel Prize. She was only the eleventh woman to do so, and never expected it; a lack of expectation that was in itself a kind of artistic freedom, for if you don't think of yourself as an august personage, you don't have to behave yourself. You can still kick up your heels and push the limits, and that was what interested Doris Lessing, always. Her celebrated experiment with a pseudonym as a demonstration of the hurdles facing unknown writers being just one example. (Her "Jane Somers" novels were reviewed as pale imitations of Doris Lessing, which must have been a little daunting for her.)

I never met Simone de Beauvoir—that would have been, in my youth, a terrifying prospect—but I did meet Doris Lessing, several times. These meetings took place in literary contexts, and she was everything a younger female writer might hope for: kind, helpful, interested, and with a special understanding of the position of writers from elsewhere within England.

As we age, we face a choice of caricatures; for women writers vis-à-vis younger ones, it's Cruella de Vil versus Glinda the Good. I encountered my share of Cruellas along the way, but Doris Lessing was one of the Glindas. In that respect, she was an estimable model. And she was a model also for every writer coming from the back of beyond, demonstrating—as she so signally did—that you can be a nobody from nowhere, but, with talent, courage, perseverance through hard times, and a dollop of luck, you can scale the topmost storyheights.

How to Change the World?

>>><<<

(2013)

When I first saw the title of this conference, "How to Change the World?," it raised three questions for me. First, what is meant by "change"? Second, what is meant by "how"? And third, what is meant by "the world"?

Then, when I actually attended the conference as a member of the second panel discussion for that day, I found that the other panellists had varying answers to these three questions. Most defined "change" in terms of social change. They also assumed that any change they themselves would be postulating would be change for the better. Since the first panel discussion that day had been devoted to all the things that were wrong with the present state of affairs, the bias toward positive change was built in. Very few pundits or politicians would in any case ever confess to an intention to change the world for the worse. Even those great twentieth-century catastrophes—Hitler of the camps, Stalin of the gulag, and Mao of the terrible famines—first arrived on the scene bearing banners of utopian futures in which all would be changed for the infinitely better, once a few obstacles had been overcome and everyone they didn't like had been eliminated. That's always a problem when sweeping utopian changes are proposed: What do you do about those who don't agree with you? It's the shadow side of any plans for positive change, and has made some—such as myself—quite nervous about the casual use of the word *progress*. Progress for whom, or for what? Is it true—as Aunt Lydia in my novel *The Handmaid's Tale* says—that better for some always means worse for others? Or are there indeed some forms of positively intended change that make things better for everyone? We must hope so.

At the conference, the field of questioning was largely social, so the suggested "hows"—the various tools that would affect the proposed positive changes—were alterations to human institutions. As for "the world," this word was taken to mean the primarily urban, modern, Western, and human world where those speaking at the conference, and also those attending it, primarily live.

Much of the panel debates focused on the relative merits and demerits of political systems—socialisms, capitalisms, oligarchies. How should society be arranged, how directed? How should wealth be created, and how distributed? Associated questions arose: Are "our" value systems bankrupt? What sorts of belief systems are possible anymore? What to think of those once-sterling terms *freedom, the individual,* and *democracy* in a new age controlled and influenced by mega-corporations on the one hand, and by Internet-connected but relatively anonymous groupings of people on the other? Were "nations" a thing that could still be taken seriously? What does "morality" mean in our present context? Now that total surveillance seems within reach, via drones and mini-cams and satellites, is it desirable? In other words, would the ability to prevent all crimes by snooping on their moments of genesis turn out to be a sinister weapon that could lead to a Big Brother of gargantuan proportions, and stifle any dissent?

Such questions are of course well worth discussing. But there was a very large elephant in the room that nobody really wanted to mention. The most urgent problems facing us today have to do simply with the necessities of life, of biological life; with the supply of those elements essential to our physical being, our existence on this planet. They are physical problems, not ideological problems. Unless they are addressed, very soon and in a concrete and practical way, all discussions and disputes and dialectics will be beside the point, either because there will be no human beings left to do the discussing or because those who do survive will be fully occupied with the basic footwork of food and shelter, civilization as we know it having melted down.

Once upon a time, those voicing such concerns were regarded as fanatics, lunatics, nutty professors, and the like, and tremendous efforts were made by those profiting from current practices to discredit such messengers. When Rachel Carson published *Silent Spring* in 1962, the big pesticide-producing chemical companies spent much time, energy, and money trying to destroy both her professional reputation and her personal one. In the case of *Limits to Growth,* the M.I.T.–generated study produced by the Club of Rome in 1972 that predicted a collapse sometime in the twenty-first century if we continued along our present unchecked pathway, the attacks were more gradual; but their cumulative effect was to erode the credibility of the report by the 1990s.

Now, however, both Carson and the Club of Rome are being vindicated by actual events, though opposition to their ideas remains ferocious. As Ugo Bardi said in his 2008 *Oil Drum* article, "Cassandra's Curse":

> Prophets of doom, nowadays, are not stoned to death, at least not usually. Demolishing ideas that we don't like is done in a rather subtler manner. The success of the smear campaign against the LTG [Limits to Growth] ideas shows the power of propaganda and of urban legends in shaping the public perception of the world, exploiting our innate tendency of rejecting bad news. Because of these tendencies, the world has chosen to ignore the warning of impending collapse that came from the LTG study. In so doing, we have lost more than 30 years. Now, there are signs that we may be starting to heed the warning, but it may be too late and we may still be doing too little.

The latest warnings are not coming from lone scientific journalists like Rachel Carson, nor from groups of intellectuals like the Club of Rome. They are coming from the Pentagon, not noteworthily a collection of tree-hugging bunny-lovers, which warned in 2004—in a secret report to the Bush administration—that climate change posed a worse threat than terrorism, and that it could plunge the world into a state of anarchy. A similar position has been taken by the World

Bank—again, not known for its eco-freaky extremism—in its 2012 report, *Turn Down the Heat: Why a 4° Centigrade Warmer World Must be Avoided*. This report, painstakingly prepared by the Potsdam Institute for Climate Impact Research, concludes:

> With pressures increasing as warming progresses toward 4°C and combining with nonclimate-related social, economic, and population stresses, the risk of crossing critical social system thresholds will grow. At such thresholds existing institutions that would have supported adaptation actions would likely become much less effective or even collapse. One example is a risk that sea-level rise in atoll countries exceeds the capabilities of controlled, adaptive migration, resulting in the need for complete abandonment of an island or region. Similarly, stresses on human health, such as heat waves, malnutrition, and decreasing quality of drinking water due to seawater intrusion, have the potential to overburden health-care systems to a point where adaptation is no longer possible, and dislocation is forced.
>
> Thus, given that uncertainty remains about the full nature and scale of impacts, there is also no certainty that adaptation to a 4°C world is possible. A 4°C world is likely to be one in which communities, cities and countries would experience severe disruptions, damage, and dislocation, with many of these risks spread unequally. It is likely that the poor will suffer most and the global community could become more fractured, and unequal than today. The projected 4°C warming simply must not be allowed to occur—the heat must be turned down. Only early, cooperative, international actions can make that happen.

Both of these reports focus on the effects of a warming world on human beings, concentrating on such results as rising sea levels, extreme weather, and desertification. However, there are two other factors that do not loom large in these reports but that could prove decisive to our own fate as a species on this Earth.

The first is the release of methane into the atmosphere, from a variety of sources, including the decaying of permafrost vegetation as it thaws and the thawing of frozen methyl hydrates. As a global warmer, methane is twenty-five times more powerful than carbon dioxide. In Alaska alone, says Andrew Wong, writing in January's *Alternatives Journal,* "retreating glaciers and thawing permafrost are releasing 50 to 70 percent more methane than previously believed."

The second factor is the vital role that algae play in the creation of oxygen. Before the reign of the cyanobacteria, approximately 1.9 billion years ago, there was so little oxygen in Earth's atmosphere that iron didn't rust. Today, the various algae produce 50 to 80 per cent of the oxygen that we breathe. Kill the oceans, and we kill ourselves: quite simply, we will be unable to breathe.

In light of these problems—the problems concerning our rapidly altering physical context, a context that is the basis for any social arrangement whatsoever, since it is the basis for human life— I choose to define "change," "how," and "the world" in a fairly elemental way. "The world" I take to mean the total world: the physical space of gases, liquids, and solids in which we live, and which thus encloses all of our social spaces. "Change" I take to mean physical change: to the water, the air, the land, and to the weather. "How" I take to mean some combination of positive physical intervention and negative physical action that will affect our physical space. In order to preserve it and thus keep ourselves alive, we must do some new things; we must do some old things differently; and we must stop doing some of the things that we are presently doing.

When we ask "How to Change the World?" within these parameters, the topic appears to be more than a little outrageous. On the face of it, the question seems impossible, because changing the world in itself seems to be an impossible task. Surely we—we as tiny, puny individuals—do not overestimate our own capabilities to that extent. We don't feel that we, personally, have the power to change the world, and even if we did have such power, in our saner moments we know that we lack the wisdom. If each of us were to be given the magic wand that would fulfill our every command, would we choose those commands well? Or, as in most folk tales that involve wishes, would we choose disastrously?

On the other hand, the world has changed many times without our intervention. There have been warm periods and cold periods; continents have collided and drifted apart, all without us lifting a finger. (Not hard: we weren't there.) But the world has also *been* changed recently, by human beings. The agents of change in the world before our advent have been many, with solar activity being the main driver; but once life became established, it began its own rearrangements. We are not the only life form to have affected the conditions prevailing on Planet Earth. The algae began that process over 1.9 billion years ago, when they added oxygen to the air, and countless bioforms—from mosses and mushrooms to nematodes, ants, beavers, bees, and elephants—have altered their landscape to suit themselves. Once people came, they too began making dams, tunnelling, and erecting constructions. But, with the aid of the cheap energy provided by fossil carbon fuels, *Homo sapiens* is now conducting earthworks on an unprecedented scale, and with unforeseen consequences.

So yes, we can change the world. We have already changed it, we are continuing to change it, and unless we can now change some of it back, we are facing challenges unprecedented since we first began to record our history.

Unlike most of the other speakers at the conference, I do not come from the university realm, nor from that of business. I am a mere scribbler, and, as such, a synthesizer, a magpie who filches gems from others, and a ferreter into matters about which I don't know very much. I am primarily a writer of fiction, and sometimes of "science fiction" or "speculative fiction"—in any case, fictions set in the future, on this planet, and within the realm of possibility. My fictions of this type extrapolate from present facts and trends, project them into time, and postulate their consequences. If such fictions were called upon to justify their existence, they might indicate their efficacy as minor strategic tools. *This is where the road seems to be heading,* they might say. *This is its possible destination. Do you really want to go there? If not, change the road.*

A writer of fictions of this kind is constantly pondering changes. Changes for the better, changes for the worse; once-improbable changes that have nonetheless occurred, such as the advent of the Internet; plausible changes that once seemed about to happen but have never materialized, such as personalized mini-jet travel; possible catastrophic changes that are facing us but may yet be averted, such as global atomic warfare; and other catastrophic changes we are told are all but inevitable, such as climate change.

Of course, fiction writers specialize in made-up stories, but for those discussing a real-life subject such as "How to Change the World?"—a subject that necessarily situates itself in the future, which hasn't happened yet—perhaps it's not beside the point to ask first: What kind of story do we think we're in, "we" being the human race? Because the answer will, in part, determine the outcome. If it's a comedy—in the classic meaning of the word, which has to do with structure rather than jokes—"we" will face a series of obstacles, culminating in a moment of doom in which all seems lost; but through a combination of spirit, determination, cleverness, love, and possibly a *deus ex machina* or absurd piece of luck, we will overcome these obstacles and emerge triumphant, and have a wonderful feast at the end in which all the characters, or mostly all, may join. But if it's a tragedy, we will be so inflated with our sense of our own wisdom and importance that we will be blind to our own shortcomings, thus overlooking the obvious. We will then topple from a great height to an ignominious end, after which a being or beings unrelated to us will inherit the kingdom or world or planet we once thought was ours, and possibly do better at living on it, or with it.

If our story is a melodrama, we will experience a mixture of both: up and down like a roller coaster; which is probably more like real life.

Which of these three structures best describes the story we think we're in? Judging from the newspapers, the tragedy and the melodrama are favoured, with a few hardy souls betting on the comedy. These happy-ending folks almost invariably propose salvation through cleverness (or technology), which they see as our only way out of the hole we've dug ourselves into through cleverness (or technology). Almost nobody, anymore, is pinning all hopes on the *deus ex machina* or dumb-luck solution. Though some still hold out hope for benevolent extraterrestrials.

Once we've decided—or, more accurately, taken a stab at guessing—what sort of story we're in, we might narrow it down even further.

There is a venerable tradition of stories about changes to our world that transform it either into something much better than it is today—like the New Jerusalem, courtesy of the Book of Revelation, with its living city, streams of pure water, and excellent music—or else into something much worse, like the destruction of the universe, accompanied by four horsemen, rains of blood, whole-scale incineration, all-out war, and so forth; also courtesy of the Book of Revelation.

The first kind of story is usually called a "utopia," and it contrasts the current deplorable state of affairs with an If-only scenario in which the defects of the present are eliminated via various schemes and gizmos that the writer brings into play. The moral trajectory of this kind of story is upward—that is, humanity is moving toward the Heaven that was once thought to exist above the layer of Quintessence that encircled the globe, above the other four essences—earth, water, air, and fire. In a utopia, we are likely to find the kinds of things we are thought to like and appreciate: personal freedom, delicious and wholesome food, lovely natural surroundings, friendly animal life, beautiful people who are also kind, long life, jolly and risk-averse sex, attractive clothing, an absence of disease and famine, a strange lack of liars, cheaters, stealers, and murderers, and not a single war in sight.

The second kind of story is called a "dystopia." In dystopias, things have become a lot worse than we feel they are today. The moral trajectory of dystopias is downward, and in these worlds we find all the things we are thought to dislike, including totalitarianisms, torture, starvation, gruesome food, weapons of mass destruction in the hands of those who don't like us, horrible and usually coerced sex, bad smells, inferior decorative schemes, the destruction of nature, discordant sounds, and every other thing that we find repellent.

Sometimes when we fiction writers make pronouncements about the world that most people agree is the real one, we are accused of writing "science fiction." But perhaps science fiction is now writing us. Put another way: Do we invent the technologies—and thus the changes in the world that they cause—because we have imagined them first? The list of human desires and fears is very old, and fairly constant. Thus, we have wanted to fly like birds for a long time, and now we do fly; though not exactly like birds, nor do we like all of the consequences of our flights, which now include bombs and drones.

For each of our technologies is a two-edged sword. One edge slices the way we want it to, the other edge cuts our fingers. The world we've made would seem magical to the people of even five hundred years ago; yet we are less sorcerers than sorcerers' apprentices. We can release the genies from their bottles, but trying to cram them back in again seems at present to be well beyond us. We've created the juggernaut; we live within it; if it were to stop, the most horrible chaos and anarchy would result. Just imagine what would happen if the lights all went out and the trains and cars stopped running. In the cities—where most of us now live—the food would run out in a couple of days, and then what? We're inside the wondrous mechanism we ourselves have constructed, and we don't know how to get out; yet unless we make some radical improvements to it, it will end by digesting itself, and us along with it.

What are our remedies? What positive changes can we make? Here are some possibilities that I frequently hear being proposed.

First, science and technology. Surely, say some, our human intelligence will save the day. We're smart enough to foresee our possible demise, and to analyze our own role in it. Are we not also smart enough to devise gizmos that will mitigate or even reverse the dire trends we have been tracking? Possibly. And many are busily at work on that very thing. More efficient solar-power gatherers, some tube-shaped; batteries that allow solar power to be effective even at night; better wind turbines; lily-pad devices that float on water, generating power through wave motion; technologies that suck CO_2 out of the atmosphere; plans to shoot energy-deflecting particles into the air, producing a cooling effect; algae farms; cheap desalination and water-purification technologies; and much more. Will these be improved and deployed in sufficient quantities, and in time?

And what about the fact that, simply in order to build and transport them, yet more energy—oil, gas, or coal—will need to be consumed? And what about the massive fossil fuel lobby? Why would those industries welcome the advent of inventions that might interfere with their own power and influence, let alone your profit margins?

Thus, who is to fund all this new invention? There are only two possibilities: private corporations or governments. But the second is in thrall to the first. As scientists and entrepreneurs themselves will tell you, truly disinterested science is almost impossible now, and the first question asked about any new invention by possible funders is not whether it will save the planet but whether it will make lots of money.

Greener building standards, the re-cladding of energy-leaking buildings, a reduction in highway speeds for cars, and a return to rail travel: all are short-term energy-saving measures that might provide small fixes.

But such tinkerings with the existing system are up against a very large problem: the demographic time bomb. Yet another elephant in the room that no one wants to address is the burgeoning human population, and the understandable wish of each and every human being on the planet to improve its lot in life. The planet does not contain enough resources for everyone to live the average North American "lifestyle," as that is presently constituted. What if the richest were to reduce their rate of consumption in order to allow the poorest to raise theirs, and then if everyone were to cut the average in half? All very well with a stable population; but if the population doubles, the total amount of consumption and the total amount of energy expended remain the same.

Mention population control, however, and vociferous outrage will be directed at you. Religious leaders of many kinds will accuse you of sinfulness, others of racism or a wish to perpetrate genocide. As many as possible must be born, it seems. What happens afterwards—wars over dwindling resources, famines, diseases, and all the other results of overcrowding and undernourishing—do not appear to concern the megabirthers. Who is to have all these babies? One guess.

The education of women has been seen by many—including the Davos World Economic Forum—as key to an improved standard of living. Educated women have fewer children and invest more in those they do have, and contribute more to their societies. Yet the opposition to the education of girls and women is strongest in the very places that would benefit by it most. Some, it appears, would rather kill their women than allow them to help their own societies.

To the technological fixes and the educational fixes we might add a third: the political fixes. On the international level, attempts to come to some sort of agreement that would regulate carbon emissions have so far been a dismal failure. No one wants to go first. No one wants to sacrifice "economic growth" and risk the wrath of the populace. Most people seem willing to ignore the consequences of inaction as long as they cannot perceive an immediate threat to themselves. "Not here, not now, not me" is the prevailing mantra.

On the national level, a little more has been possible: some governments are attempting to become greener. On local levels, many cleanup and environmental restoration projects have been undertaken, with some success. But gains in one location can easily be defeated by losses in another. For those labouring on the ground, the attempt to preserve even a little of the bio-richness on which our survival ultimately rests often seems like the stone of Sisyphus: no sooner has the stone been rolled up the hill than it rolls back down again.

Perhaps our largest failure is a modern one: our severing ourselves from the universe, our failure to understand that everything really is connected to everything else. We are a part of Nature: we are not apart from it. Yet huge amounts of money continue to be directed toward such receding rainbows as cures for cancer, as if much of it was not caused by the industrial compounds and by-products we are dumping into our bodies; or quests for immortality and schemes to upload our brains into computers and shoot them into space. Meanwhile, a tiny speck of our wealth—less than 3 per cent of all charitable giving—is channelled into the increasingly desperate efforts to preserve a functioning biosphere.

By "functioning," I mean functioning in such a way that we ourselves can continue to exist. Does Nature—seen in overview—need us? No. We'll render the planet unfit for ourselves sooner than we can render it unfit for life as a whole. Despite our worse efforts, some insect or diatom or anaerobic microbe or deep-water squid is likely to wait us out. Do we need Nature? Yes, unless we can figure out some new way of breathing. Chemistry and physics don't negotiate, but they do balance their own books. Energy generated by increased heat must be discharged, in the form of more violent winds and higher waves; what goes up in increased evaporation will come down in the form of torrential rains and destructive blizzards. The new, less kindly, more unstable "Eaarth" written about by Bill McKibben in his 2010 book of that name is already here. We can adapt to it as best we may; we can attempt to scale back, and reverse or at least halt the relentless process we appear to have triggered; or we can attempt to deal with the nastiness that would ensue if our present society were to crumble.

I was talking recently to a Canadian Indigenous man who sells whitefish at a local farmers' market. I mentioned zebra mussels, an invader that was dumped into the water from the bilge of incoming freighters and is now a large and destructive presence in the Great Lakes, clogging pipes, littering beaches, and filtering up much of the food once available to native species, including fish fry. What did he think should be done about this problem? I asked the fisherman. Surely he was concerned: these mussels could affect his livelihood. But he only smiled. "Nature will take care of it," he said.

I took him to mean not that Nature would eliminate the zebra mussels but that some new balance or status quo would eventually emerge. If so, he was right, because it always does, with Nature. The result may not be one we might wish for, but Nature doesn't care about our human wishes. Physics and chemistry do not give second chances.

We care about our own human wishes, however. And we long for second chances: our religious stories and even our folk tales and films abound in them. We like to think that if we wish very hard for something, we can bring it into existence.

Maybe it's time for us to start wishing very hard for our own future survival. If we really want it, surely we can use our much-praised intelligence to bring it about.

PART III

>><<

2014 TO 2016

WHICH IS TO BE MASTER

In Translationland

(2014)

I'm delighted to have been invited to the University of East Anglia in Norwich to give this talk in honour of W.G. Sebald, a writer much admired and missed by all who followed his work.

W.G. Sebald must be accounted one of the essential writers of the twentieth century. Among other things, he disrupted the novel as a form, mixing fact with invention and going so far as to make up quotations. His approach is peripatetic, the forms that emerge having something to do with Menippean satire, something to do with what Northrop Frye called the anatomy, and something to do with the private meditation. As he to the novel, so I to the lecture: the namesake of this lecture entitles me—I feel—to emulate him, and to be just as peripatetic and serendipitous and diversionary and, well, odd as Sebald was himself.

Sebald was interested in that charming seventeenth-century Norwich writer and physician Sir Thomas Browne, an eloquent statue of whom broods pensively over the pulled pork and smoked haddock and tip-top sausages in the Norwich market; and here I will insert my first diversion. Browne's prescription to cure baldness involved rubbing roasted moles and honey onto your head. I offer this tip to Big Pharma, which in the past has had some success with the commercialization of erstwhile folk remedies. I ask for no remuneration.

I have always felt a kinship with Merlin of *The Sword in the Stone* not only because of the pet owl but because Merlin has some invisible spirit helpers who supply the objects he needs. When he says "Hat," a hat appears. It may not be the right hat, but it's a hat. There's a more high-falutin' literary way of describing this phenomenon—

I could invoke George Eliot's simile from *Middlemarch* about the candle held up to the mirror that causes the random scratches on the glass to arrange themselves in a pattern—but why not allow for both? Therefore, no sooner had I agreed to give the Sebald lecture on the subject of translation than some letters by W.G. Sebald himself miraculously dropped through the mail slot, contained in a literary journal called *Little Star*. And these letters were written to Sebald's own translator, Michael Hulse; and they were on the subject of . . . guess what! Translation! "Thank you, Invisible Magic Helpers and Candle/Mirror," I said. "Now I can put one of these letters into my Sebald lecture and impress the trousers off my auditors! Or the skirts. Anyway, some metonymous item of clothing."

So here is that very letter.

19.ix.97

Dear Michael:

Bill has asked me to send the last chapter directly to you so that you can deal with it before going to King's Lynn.

I feared that these pages would prove particularly difficult. You must have cursed me more than once when you grappled with them. Inevitably, I think, much of the finer grain in the "quoted" passages got lost in translation. Even yesterday evening I racked my brain for a better way of rendering "Wehwirtshaft" (p. 14), but not to much avail.

This morning I still made some changes to the list of moths on p. 3 because two of the ones in the original are (contrary to what the text says) rather inconspicuous. And I don't want to upset the British moth watchers, who are very numerous. In order to check my choices I rang up a carpenter in Beccles who has taken me out moth watching several times. But I could only get his wife on the phone because he, as she put it, had gassed himself in his car last month. Very strange, all this is, don't you think. If you have the time to come down to Norwich from the other end of Norfolk, I shall be around here until 2 October.

All good wishes Max

As you can gather, W.G. Sebald was living in Norfolk at that time.

Here comes another candle/mirror piece of serendipity: exactly thirty years ago, in 1983–1984, my family and I spent the good part of a year in Norfolk over the fall, winter, and spring. Thus, we were living in the territory so eloquently mused upon by Sebald in *The Rings of Saturn,* which is a meditation upon transience, as is so much of his writing. We were staying in Blakeney, once a large port, as testified by the imposing fifteenth-century church of Saint Nicholas, but now much smaller and fronted by tidal flats. The mists, the windy sea and the villages that have fallen into it, the twisting back roads, the once affluent estates now fading: we dwelt among these before reading about them in *The Rings of Saturn.* We also wandered around in the city of Norwich itself, so it's not a total coincidence that Julian of Norwich appears as the patron saint of the last chapter of my novel *The Year of the Flood:* I made her acquaintance, too, during the same time period.

We'd selected Blakeney because that coast was one of the best bird-watching spots in Britain: the gales from Siberia blew many a rare species over to the salt marshes and tidal flats along the coast. Our other project was to do some writing—we each had a novel in view—but I'm sorry to say this came to nothing. Neither of us produced a book.

In my case, the Norfolk failure might have had something to do with the spirit presences in our rented house. We were told by the locals that this building—in the thirteenth century, a leprosarium run by nuns—was haunted, not only by the nuns, said to prefer the sitting room, but also by a jolly cavalier—in the dining room, where he would be, since the liquor was kept there—and a headless woman, who was confined to the kitchen, as headless women so often are.

We questioned our landlord, a vicar who lived in London. He laughed heartily. "Hohoho, you've been listening to the locals," he said. Then, with a piercing look: "Have you seen them?" He dismissed the headless woman: she had been glimpsed only once, by an American in search of her roots and determined to uncover at least one headless woman no matter how many glasses of sherry it took. He was agnostic on the subject of the nuns, though clearly interested: his mother had seen at least one. We didn't go into the jolly cavalier, though we ran into him one evening. He turned out to be a stray reveller from the pub next door who'd wandered outside for the reasons that jolly cavaliers do, and had got confused on the way back.

So all this spirit life might have been interfering with my creational wavelengths, inducing the severe blockage that I found myself experiencing. Or it might have had other causes. During the days I was supposed to be writing in a cobblestone fisherman's cottage, using a manual typewriter on which the *l* got stuck every time it was hit. This leads to an avoidance of words with *l* in them, which can be inhibiting. Possibly I could give my sexy male lead a distinguished lisp? "I wuve you," he said wustfully, in his wow, wiwting tones. "I wong to kiss your awwuring, wuscious wips." No, it would not do.

The cottage was heated by a small fireplace, which I could never master, not having the knack of setting fire to large chunks of sopping wet wood. It had a stone floor, and thus I got my first chilblains, since I would go back to the nun-haunted sitting room of the main house and stick my frozen feet up by the blazing grate. I was thrilled with these chilblains, once I had identified them. "These must be . . . yes! Chilblains," I exclaimed. "At last! How Dickensian!"

I'm sure my blockage was enhanced by the array of distracting romantic novels about Mary, Queen of Scots, left by summer visitors. When your writing isn't going well, there's nothing like Mary, Queen of Scots, to cheer you up. "At least my wig won't come off when they decapitate me," you can murmur to yourself.

But most likely my productive failure was due to the fact that I didn't know Spanish. (You knew I was going to get around to the language issues, sooner or later.) You see, the novel I was trying to write was set in Mexico. Whatever put that into my head? Not only did I not know Spanish, but I also did not know Nahuatl, Maya, Zapotec, Mixtec, Otomi, Totonac, Tzotzil, Tzeltal, Mazahua, Mazatec, Huastec, Ch'ol, Chinantec, Purépecha, Mixe, Tlapanec, or Tarahumara—half of which have more native speakers today than London did at the time of Shakespeare. I did not need to master all of these languages in order to write my novel, but one or two might have been useful. Nowadays I could go online and take a course in them, but this was in the days before the Internet: courses in Mixtec were not easy to come by in Blakeney.

Blakeney was itself thick with translation pitfalls of a different kind. Children inhale new languages and accents, so it took our six-year-old daughter mere weeks to acquire a Norfolk accent indistinguishable from that of her schoolmates. Thereafter we, her parents, with our blatant Canadian accents, were a source of constant embarrassment to her. "Mummy, Daddy," she would say. "Don't say underpants! Say knickers!" It did not help that Graeme was the only male person to pick up a child from Brownies in the town of Blakeney, most likely ever. Oh, the shame of it: dozens of Norfolk mums in headsquares, and then a lone, tall, bearded, obviously deranged Canadian man . . .

But much is forgiven to foreigners, sometimes, and depending on what kind of foreigners they are. At least we weren't Americans! At least we weren't French! At least no one could tell where we were from, exactly—Canada, in the minds of its local imaginers if any, being a great big empty white space on the map. Better still, in the land of carefully calibrated accents, no one could tell what social class we were from; so we could talk in a friendly manner with everyone in the village without being rebuffed. Which we did.

But now to the serious business; though for a fiction writer it's all serious business. You can stand or fall by whether you allow a given character to say "underpants" or "knickers," since books are made of language and nothing but. "What do you read, my lord?" asks Polonius. To which Hamlet replies, accurately, "Words, words, words." That's all we poor labourers in the verbal salt mines have to work with—words. There's no sound track or visuals except the ones in the reader's head. Thus, words in all their rich variety are of primary importance to us. It's not only what you say—the plot, the descriptions, the characters—but how you say it. Voice and tone; the rank and culture of origin and generation of the speaker; who is talking to whom—in Japanese you can't even say "Delighted to meet you" without knowing whether the other one's position is higher than yours, at the same level, or lower. Then there are the options of slang or formal speech, with many gradations of each; and also the matter of the historical period.

All of which may be influenced by whether or not the character is (for instance) a Mohican, as in *The Last of the Mohicans;* or a rabbit, as in *Watership Down;* or a pig, as in *Charlotte's Web.* Or a Hobbit. Or an orc: these have poor grammar. Or an elf, a superior sort of person. Or a horse. Or a wolf. Or a vampire. Or, as in the case of *Last of the Curlews,* a curlew. There are so many possibilities.

The choices that bedevil the writer bedevil the translator ten times over, with, in addition, weighty responsibilities of many other kinds. Whether a reader in another language will grasp anything at all about an author's work is dependent on the translator alone. His or her task is to produce a text that is accurate, or accurate enough, but also one that is readable in the language of translation, and, in addition, is engaging, funny, heart-wrenching, and so forth, in all the right places. This kind of double-headed trapeze act is a lot to expect of any human brain. When a writer is having a bad day, he or she can murmur not only "At least I'm not Mary, Queen of Scots," but also "At least I don't have to translate my own freaking books!"

I am doubly grateful that I don't have to translate my own freaking books because I realize I'm sometimes a bit of a nightmare for my translators. I'll take out the *sometimes.* I am always a bit of a nightmare for my translators. I make puns (almost impossible to translate) and jokes (difficult) and also I create neologisms, especially in the realm of genetically engineered species and imagined consumer products. How much better for the translator if I would stick to a kind of stately standardized English, with an emphasis on murders. Plot-driven books are the easiest to translate, I'm told, though even in that realm there are hazards: the French translations of that quintessentially American writer, Raymond Chandler, make his Los Angeles sound oddly like the seedier parts of Paris inhabited by, for instance, Inspector Maigret, except that in the latter city it rains a lot.

But what is the alternative, for a translator? Do you want a seamless translation that makes the reader feel the book was written in its second language? The totally bilingual writer Mavis Gallant once said that you can tell a good translation by reading a passage in the first language and then switching to the second, and if you don't notice a difference, then it's excellent.

Or do you want to include some colourful phrases in the original language to signal that we are in fact in a very different culture and place? Does Chingachgook invite you into his wigwam, or into his pointed tent? Does he kill you with a tomahawk, or with a small hand-axe suitable for splitting kindling? Do you translate the Norwegian "gjetost" or "brunost" as "really stinky brown caramelized goat cheese," or simply as "brown cheese," or do you retain the original, for flavour? The Ojibwe word "orenda"—as in Joseph Boyden's novel of the same name—takes a paragraph in English to explain it. (Roughly, "spiritual/magical force believed to be present in all people and objects, but especially strong in shamans.") Do you translate this word within the body of the novel, or do you retain it as is and add a glossary at the back? Such questions keep translators awake at night.

I recently spent a couple of weeks at the Banff Centre during their annual Literary Translators' session. Translators are paired with the authors of the texts on which they are working. My twin was a very bright young man from Egypt, who was translating *The Penelopiad* into Arabic. He had a list of words for me. "Is this an old word, a new word, a slang word, a formal word, or did you make it up?" he would ask. It all mattered.

Why did I end up spending my life thinking about things like this, rather than—for instance—how to grow a human kidney inside a pig? Or, to broaden the scope: How do we get that way? By "we," I mean those who deal in words—thus, writers and translators both.

We're all born languageless, though we pick the stuff up very quickly. Once we get into the alphabet soup, we spend much of our childhood translating. "What does that mean? What about this? How about that over there?" Some of us acquire all the words we need quite early, and don't bother our heads too much about it after that. The word folk, however, keep on going.

Strait is the gate, many are the twisted roads, obscure the motivations, dire the dangers, fortunate the happenstances—though demanding the apprenticeships and numerous the crumpled holograph pages—that lead eventually to the fabled Kingdom of Paper Delicacies (or, these days, to the Land of Digital Delights, as well). Here follows my own tiny personal pathway.

I spent my early childhood—which coincided with the years of the Second World War—in a remote part of the northwest Quebec bush. We were there in the spring, summer, and fall, not in a village or town, but right out among the trees, bears, blackflies, and loons. Transport was by boat or trail. There was no electricity, running water, school, shop, theatre, cinema, or television. (There wasn't any television anyway.) Later on, there was a rudimentary radio, on which we could occasionally hear either very distant French—it being Quebec—or, over the short wave, oddly enough, Russian. In the winter we lived in the city of Ottawa, where there was better reception, and what we heard on the radio there was, among other things, this:

> *Weeoooeeeooo . . . Bong bong bong bong; bong bong bong bong.*
> *Bong. Bong. Bong. Bong. Bong. Bong. This is London calling Noth*
> *Ammedddica. Hyah is the BBC news.*

Child's unasked question: Why did they talk like that? Also: What was London? And, even harder to answer: What was the BBC?

But also coming over the radio were things like:

> *Mairzy doats and dozy doats and liddle lamzy divey*
> *A kiddley divey too, wooden shoe?*

Or else:

> *Chickery chick, cha-la, cha-la*
> *Check-a-la romey*
> *In a bananika*
> *Bollika, wollika, can't you see*
> *Chickery chick is me.*

What languages were *those* in?, the child listener well might wonder. Or the adult listener, as far as that goes. The first one was a puzzle, which could be deciphered; the second was nonsense. How early in life children grasp the fact that some words are just plain silly! That's why they appreciate Edward Lear—"He goes! He goes! The Dong with the Luminous Nose!" (Why did I love the Dong but hate Rudolph the Red-Nosed Reindeer with a passionate loathing that persists to this day? Note to self: Ponder more on this.)

Apart from the radio, and still in the realm of words without obvious meanings, there was of course the immortal *Alice.*

'Twas brillig, and the slithy toves
Did gyre and gimble in the wabe:
All mimsy were the borogoves,
And the mome raths outgrabe.

Helpfully, some translation was provided in the text, though the translator was an egg. He was, however, an egg with a translator's determination.

"When *I* use a word," Humpty Dumpty said, in rather a scornful tone, "it means just what I choose it to mean—neither more nor less."

"The question is," said Alice, "whether you *can* make words mean so many different things."

"The question is," said Humpty Dumpty, "which is to be master—that's all."

This reader took Humpty Dumpty's lesson to heart. Well may we ask! Which *is* to be master? Do you as a writer expand the meanings of words, or are you merely their tool? Is your own language programming you like a computer, or are you wielding it like Prospero's magic charms, and is there in fact a difference? Small children, when asked by Jean Piaget what part of their body they thought with, said, "My mouth." Is thought possible without words? Do words determine what we can think, and if so, can we think some thoughts in one language that are impossible to articulate in another? Could the promotional writing on artisanal salt packets from France ever be translated into English with the same lyrical effect? "As the rays of the health-giving sun peep rosily over the azure sea, the old salt gatherer plies his ancient calling on the wind-caressed beach, selecting each crystal of delicate salt, suffused with . . ." No, I think not.

Note to self: Ponder more on this, as well.

Back to the Quebec north woods. True, in our house, or rather our cabin, the language was English; but all around us, though at some distance, spread a penumbra of French. This was not French as the French understood it, but Québécois, which has its own accent and vocabulary, and includes joual, the extreme vernacular. The swearing in French French vs. Québécois French is quite different, that of Quebec containing many religious terms—drop something on your foot and you may say "Baptême!" for instance, whereas the French say "Merde." Our area was right on the Quebec/Ontario border, so in the nearby town—not nearby by English standards; let's say, in the last outpost before we hit the woods—many people made do with Franglais, a combo language understood by all, though somewhat limited. A catch-all word like *ma'chine* could mean almost any object of utility, though it could not mean a person.

There were also words that had originally come from English, such as *le scrinporch*—the screened porch, so necessary in the land of the blackfly and mosquito—and *le backouse,* the backhouse, so necessary if you didn't have plumbing. Such an exchange of words is fair enough, as many English words were originally French—William I being what he was. Someone remarked recently that the words for domesticated animals in English are usually from Anglo-Saxon— cow, pig, sheep—whereas those for the parts of the animal that get eaten are from French—boeuf/beef, porc/pork, mouton/mutton. Whereby you can make a good guess as to who was doing the farming and who was doing the feasting, and who conquered whom. But I digress. As I warned you I would.

Among the earliest things I read in this northern borderland were signs in French. Petite Vitesse, Gardez le Droit—on the narrow, precipitous roads; and, in the post office made of squared timbers, Défense de crâcher sur le plancher. And, wherever two or more might be gathered together, along with an icebox: Buvez Coca-Cola. Glacé. The backs of cereal boxes were also instructive, being bilingual, and I spent much time trying to transcribe the French. "Hé! Les enfants! Gagnez!" The prizes you could win by collecting the box tops were the same in both languages, but they sounded more glamorous in French. As things do. Such as artisanal salt.

What were the effects on me of this early non-immersion—*non* because there was no one to translate for me? It signalled to me that there was at least one other linguistic universe, in which things that were opaque to me were self-evident to others. One of the motives for writing is surely that the writer is in search of the answers to various mysteries that might perhaps be discovered through the act of writing. Without surprises for the writer, less joy for the reader. Or so I fondly believe, which is one of my reasons for not making outlines in advance, the other being mental disorganization.

I was an early reader, there being few other things to do when it was raining. Luckily there were a lot of books in our small abode, though not many of them were for children. However, the devil finds books for idle eyes to read, which is why I read all those Dell murder mysteries at far too tender an age. Helpful warning: Beware blondes in red nightdresses—either they have pistols in their evening bags or they'll attract murderers like flies, and you don't want to get caught in the line of fire.

But French cereal boxes and murder mysteries were not the only things requiring decipherment by me. There were also the funny papers, which were then at their height. The characters in them said "Waal" and "H'aint," if hillbillies, or "Vot's up?" if the Katzenjammer Kids, with Germanish accents; and various other strange things. Many of them swore in punctuation marks: you were supposed to add the actual swearing yourself. But ours was a non-swearing family; at the worst, my mother might say "Dad-ratted" or "She gave him Hail Columbia"—so I could see the swearing in the comics, right there on the page, but I couldn't hear it. A swearing vocabulary is now essential to a translator, there being so much of it in writing of the present age, but such was not the case then. (Though swearing was forbidden, gags we would now think of as racist and misogynist were thick upon the page, and nobody gave them a passing thought.)

Then there was sex. *Lady Chatterley's Lover* was not permitted in the United States until 1959; 1960 in Canada. People made love by means of asterisks until those watershed court decisions. "And then they were one, dot dot dot dot dot," the text would say. "She was strangled, but had not been interfered with," was an intriguing newspaper euphemism. "Mum, what does this mean?" "I'm busy, ask me later." When I first saw the term *child molester* in a newspaper, I thought it said *child mole-ster,* a job available to children, in which they would be paid for collecting moles. This isn't quite as stupid as it sounds: I'd seen people collecting worms.

Other sources of puzzling words were the science fiction magazines of the times. It was still the bug-eyed space-alien monster era, so these stories featured many languages containing high-value Scrabble letters such as *Q, X,* and *Y.* My older brother and I were thus fluent inventors of bizarre names for the space aliens we were fond of putting into our handmade books. Helpful hint: Don't go for a walk on Neptune. Everything there, animal or vegetable or combo, has a *Q,* an *X,* or a *Y* in it, and is lethal.

Thus already pre-loaded, as it were, with verbal scrambled eggs, and, not incidentally, well primed to be a coiner of neologisms later in life, I entered my adolescent years. We were not taught languages properly then. There were no language labs—it was all written work—and we had no access to the vocabularies of swearing or sex. Think how much more interesting French would have been with a few choice *Madame Bovary* excerpts, or Latin with a sampling of the more outrageous epigrams of Martial! But it was not to be. Caesar droned on about himself in the third person, conquering this, overthrowing that, while we drew arms on the Venus de Milo in the textbook; and in French class, the pen of my aunt rested inexorably on the desk, in the past, the past perfect, and the future perfect.

We were taught Latin by an Indian man from Trinidad, and French by a woman from Poland. (This was postwar.) German was taught at lunch hour by a flustered Bulgarian; we'd sit there munching our cheese sandwiches while the unfortunate woman waxed lyrical over the dative. Then it was on to university, where Anglo-Saxon and Middle English were added to the list of things that needed to be translated by me. What practical use were the languages I learned then? Some; although the first time I went to France, I found I could ask neither for a coffee nor for a bathroom, these not having been mentioned by Racine.

Shortly thereafter—shortly in geological time—books that I myself had written were being translated into other languages. One of the first to tackle the job was Grasset, in France, whereupon a fight broke out between the French end of things and the Quebec one. My book was set in those very Quebec north woods of which I have spoken, so local word choice was a matter of pride for the Québécois distributor. "This must not sound so French," he said. "Abitibi is not the Bois-de-Boulogne." But of the alternative phrases he suggested, the French said, "Mais—c'est pas français!" "But—this is not French!" Which is what my high-school Polish French teacher used to say about my compositions.

Many have been my adventures with my translators, over the years. "Is this funny, or is it not funny?" I have been asked. "Both" is hard to describe. "Ah. It is the Anglo-Saxon humour," they have been known to say; meaning *dark,* I do believe. "What is granola?" my first Chinese translator asked. "What is a Smile Button?" And if they did not know what granola was, what else might they not have known, without knowing that they did not know it?

It would be exciting to live in Ursula K. Le Guin's future world, where an ansible translates immediately for you as you roam from galaxy to galaxy, experiencing fresh languages and brand-new modes of experiencing reality. A language that's heavy on the nouns, like English, has trouble with languages that are slanted more toward gerunds. Do we live in a world of solid objects, or in one of process? What do you think? Or rather: How do you say?

But we're here, on this Earth. We don't have ansibles; instead we have translators. They're better; because, unlike machines, they can appreciate nuance, and they can create individual interpretations. It's been my privilege to work with some excellent translators over the years: seeing my work through their eyes and ears has given it other dimensions, even for me. To quote W.G. Sebald to his own translator: "I don't think it could have been done better & I am truly grateful to you for the long hours and the enormous effort you must have put into this."

So thank you, Dear Translators. As writers, we are in your hands. As readers, you open doors for us that would otherwise remain shut, and you allow us to hear voices that would otherwise remain silent. Like writing itself, your work rests on a belief in the possibility of human communication. That's no small hope.

In parting, let me say: Merci bien. Tak. A sheynem dank. Arigatou gozaimasu. Muchas gracias. Vielen Dank. Megwich. Grazie. And, from the Inuit: Naqurmiik.

On Beauty

>>><<<

(2014)

Little girls don't have to be very old before they get tangled up with Beauty: the idea of it ("Aren't you pretty!"), the entrancing objects that go along with it ("See, that's you in the mirror"), even its enticing taboos ("That's Mummy's lipstick, don't touch"). For a child, there's something magical about Beauty. It's pink. It's sparkly. It shimmers. You can put it on, and a lot of five-year-olds, given their first fairy-princess ballerina dress, refuse to take it off.

But Beauty can have some strange things about it, as kids learn early. In the Mother Goose rhyme about the milkmaid and the gentleman, he comments on her pleasing appearance, then questions her about her financial status. "My face is my fortune," she replies. "Then I can't marry you," he says. "Nobody asked you," she retorts, putting him in his place; but still, questions remain in the child's mind. What does it mean—that her face is her fortune? Is her face detachable, and if it comes off and is sold, what might be underneath it?

In my own childhood, the detachability of faces connected with the popular saying "Beauty is only skin-deep," quoted by grown-ups as a palliative when some other little girl had a more attractive party dress. The implication was that a beautiful soul was more to be admired than a beautiful exterior, as in *Beauty and the Beast,* where the Beast wins love through a mix of engaging conversation, sentimentality, and a stunning palace. However, we young girls noted that this combo worked only for males: the tale was not called "The Unfortunately Plain Though Well-Meaning and Affluent Girl and the Beast."

Nor was the notion of superior inner beauty consoling to us princesses-in-waiting. So what if beauty was only skin-deep? We little girls did not therefore despise it. No: we wanted beautiful exteriors ourselves, so that other little girls might envy us instead of the other way around. In addition to which, it was obvious to us that in order to be transformed from a grubby kitchen slave to a gasp-making fascinator, you'd need a supernatural godmother and a killer dress. Magic and fashion had a part to play, and they were joined at the hip.

Oh, and don't forget the shoes. The shoes were very important.

There were other female characters in such fairy tales—evil witches, false brides, malevolent sisters—and they were ugly every one; or at least—in the case of Snow White's wicked stepmother—not as radiant as the heroine. Did we ever pause to consider their point of view—how diminished they must have felt in view of the heroine's aggravating loveliness? A high rate of Barbie Doll disfiguring has taken place over the years, and attic trunks conceal many a hairless Barbie, tattooed with purple Magic Markers and minus her arms. Could it be that their one-time owners suspected themselves of not being up to the Cinderella standard and, in a ritual act of reverse sympathetic magic, were taking it out on their dolls? Could these angry girls have been restored to self-esteem by a weekend course in makeup, a session with a fashion consultant, and a really good manicure? Possibly. Though possibly not.

The positive side of Beauty, we child readers learned, was that with its aid you could rise in life. When we grew a little older and got stuck into Greek mythology, however, it became clear that there was a negative side to Beauty, as well: if you were too beautiful, you would attract the unwelcome attention of the gods, a sadistic and undisciplined lot. If the god was male, he would chase you around, and then you'd be either kidnapped and dragged off to the Underworld, like Persephone, or raped by Zeus in the form of a swan, like Leda, and have to give birth to an egg; or, to avoid such a fate, you'd be changed into a tree or a river. This was not how we wanted to spend our Saturday-night dates.

If the god was female, you might find your beautiful self held up as a prize in a beauty contest, like Helen of Troy, who was then doomed to fall in love with Paris, run off on her husband, and start the Trojan War. Or you might become an object of jealous rage, like Psyche, who annoyed Venus by being too attractive. This isn't a problem that generates a lot of sympathy—it's like being "too rich"— but it's instructive to know that some have had it. Envy can generate results in the real world, spite and malice being among them.

So how much Beauty was too much was a crucial question for growing girls in the 1950s, which was when I started pondering such matters. And, just as important to consider: What kind of beauty was best? For there was more than one variety on display. The beautiful women in the men's magazines, such as *Playboy,* were different from the beautiful women in the women's magazines, such as *Vogue;* nor has that changed, though the superficial details such as hairdos morph yearly.

Why do the two diverge? Men's magazines show images of women the way men would like them to be: large breasts and hips— signalling fertility—and inviting smiles, signalling compliance. As for makeup, it's excessive, signalling either Come Hither or Face-for-Sale. These are not people you would want as a fiancée: they're too generally available, either for money or as part of a willing sexual exchange. But, just like *Vogue* models, they're constructs. "It takes a lot of money to look this cheap," Dolly Parton once quipped, and she was right about that: the tarty look is as carefully lit for the photo shoot as its good-taste opposite.

Women's fashion magazines, by contrast, contain images of women the way they themselves wish to appear when outfacing rivals or discouraging unwanted suitors: slender figures decked out in elegant clothes and topped with blank expressions, hard-to-please pouts, artfully made-up faces, bored scowls, and even menacing frowns.

Could it be that the aloofness of these images has to do with self-defence? The aim of Cinderella is to be desired, but she herself must not place herself at a disadvantage by being too desiring in return. To want something you don't have is to be vulnerable, especially if that something is a love object: desire makes you too readily seducible, and readily seducible girls easily make fools of themselves, allowing others to jeer at them, or worse.

Thus, no ingratiating smiles. The blank-faced woman has a forbidding wall around her: you can look, but you can't touch. She doesn't need you, she doesn't care about you; she's sufficient unto herself, like all those Cruel Mistresses of courtly love poetry. The extravagant clothes and high-end makeup jobs send the same signal: *You can't buy me except at my own price, which is apt to be very high, because I already have what I want.*

That's the message for potential love partners. For other, competitive women, the message is: *I am what you aspire to. Envy me. Oh, and if I let you inside my charmed circle, that will be a privilege for which you should be grateful.*

The ancient Egyptians painted their faces as protection against malign forces, and the objects used to cast this spell—the beauty materials—were themselves potent. For the Greeks, extraordinary beauty was at the very least semi-divine. *Glamorous, charming, fascinating, entrancing, enchanting*—all these words trace their origins to the supernatural. Skin-deep or not, curse or blessing, disdainful or seductive, reality or constructed illusion—beauty retains its magic power, at least in our imaginations.

And that's why we continue to buy those countless little tubes of lip gloss: we still believe in fairies.

The Summer of the Stromatolites

>>><<<

(2014)

A summer! But which of the seventy-five summers I have spent? The summer of 1957, when I was a waitress at a boys' camp on an island in Lake Huron and first ate a rattlesnake? The summer of 1965, when I was writing *The Edible Woman* in exam booklets on a card table in Vancouver? Perhaps the summer of 1976, when we took our three-month-old to a log cabin in the Quebec north woods, with no electricity or running water, and gave her baths in the dishpan?

Or something more recent. Perhaps the summer of 2012, when we finally sailed east through the Northwest Passage in the Canadian Arctic, with the Adventure Canada group. One of our first stops was at a recently discovered field of stromatolites—the fossilized mounds of blue-green algae that first created atmospheric oxygen 1.9 billion years ago. *Stromatolite* means "stone mattress," and that's what these fossils look like: rounded pillows of stone—though in cross-section they look more like layered pastries.

Led by the on-boat geologist, making our way over the low-growing red, yellow, and orange foliage (for in those parts it was already autumn), protected by the bear-gun carriers who are always on hand in the Arctic in case of polar bears, and eyed by ravens, we shed our life jackets and clambered up the fossil ridges to explore the many stromatolites on view. Some had shattered into quarters, and it struck me that one of these heavy wedges would make a good murder weapon. It also struck me that if you snuck around the edge of the third ridge you'd be out of sight, not only of the gun carriers, but of everyone else.

The dinner-table conversation that night turned to murder, as it tends to do on boats. How could you murder someone here, without getting caught? Graeme Gibson, my partner of forty years, had the perfect plan. The murder would have to be committed onshore, since a corpse on the boat would be conspicuous; and you couldn't push your victim over the rail, considering the long hours of daylight and the hordes of bird-watchers cluttering up the place.

The victim would have to be travelling alone, and killed early in the trip, before he'd got to know anyone very well. Then the murderer would have to make it appear that his cabin was still inhabited. Graeme had yet more practical tips, and I made a mental note never to get on his really bad side.

"Stone Mattress" was such a suggestive phrase that I couldn't resist writing a story of that title. I began it on the boat itself, and read the first parts to my fellow passengers. They all wanted to know how it would come out, so I promised to finish it, and then publish it.

And I did finish it, and I did publish it: first in *The New Yorker,* and now in the collection called—not unsurprisingly—*Stone Mattress.*

The murder weapon is on my kitchen table.

Kafka

>>><<<

THREE ENCOUNTERS

(2014)

In 1959, when I was nineteen, I wrote an essay about the work of Franz Kafka. It was eleven pages long, with thirty-two lines per page and an average of thirteen words per line, which, by multiplying thirty-two by thirteen by eleven, gives a count of approximately four thousand five hundred words. (That's how we used to do word counts, back in the dark ages before our computers took over that task.) Every one of those words was typed by me using a manual typewriter, and, since I couldn't touch-type—evidence of which is everywhere on the somewhat grubby pages, in the form of scratchings-out and inky corrections and over-typings—I must have been very dedicated to Kafka. Which, as I recall, I was. But why?

I'm wondering that as I reread my essay now. As so often happens when folks attempt to tackle Kafka, or indeed any writer with more than one layer of possible meaning, my real subject was not the author of the books, but the author of the essay: me, a somewhat stern-minded and pedantic neophyte writer preoccupied with her own pressing artistic concerns. I start off on a bright note—"Franz Kafka was one of the foremost literary innovators of the twentieth century"—fair enough, though the century was little more than half over in 1959. The rest of that paragraph isn't too bad, as such things go: "His name has been linked with those of Joyce and Rilke, and is often mentioned when the progenitors of such modern experimentalists as Samuel Beckett and Albert Camus are being discussed. One has only to read . . ." Goodness, how formal, that "one"! Should I have used "we"? Perhaps. But I did not.

"One has only to read a page of his seemingly artless but strangely disturbing prose to realize why: the feeling conveyed is unmistakably direct, but an explanation of it, an effort to analyze it, often seems as futile and elusive as the Hunter Gracchus's journey into nowhere." Also fair enough, though you might suspect that my nineteen-year-old essay-writing self will shortly get tangled up in the futility and elusiveness, which is in fact what happens.

I launch into the futility and elusiveness with a brisk statement to the effect that Kafka the artist must be separated from Kafka the neurotic—a pet thing of mine then, as I was averse to linking artistic productions to their producers, and especially averse to being told that all good writers were crazy, or at least highly strung, like Keats, Shelley, and Poe, as was in fashion then. I myself felt sadly lacking in craziness—I kept waiting for the nervous collapse that others assumed would be the mark of my artistic seriousness, but it failed to materialize. Did that mean I was doomed to be a substandard writer? More than likely, I can recall thinking.

Having detached Kafka the writer from Kafka the person, I slog through what I supposed to be Kafka's main motifs, namely: (1) his relation to authority figures, including fathers, anyone official with a badge or uniform, and possibly God; (2) the sense of weakness, guilt, and helplessness his central characters experience in face of these authority-wielders. No news about Kafka there; and, in fact not much news from me in toto, even at the end of the essay, since I seem not to have known what to make of "The Writings of Franz Kafka," as I call them in the essay's title.

I watch my young self getting snarled up in the line of reasoning. Did the father-authoritarian motif mean I would have to reattach Kafka's writing to Kafka's personal history, after all, since he was known to be in lifelong conflict with his own forceful dad? I dodged that issue, as I dodged anything having to do with Kafka's historical period (before, during, and after the First World War; he died in 1924, just as Hitler had staged the Munich putsch), his geographic location and cultural milieu (Czechoslovakia, and Middle Europe generally), and his Jewishness, and—what must have been even more fragile and isolating as an identity—his German-Jewishness in the midst of the Czech-speaking city of Prague.

Nor did I say what I might have said, had I known more: that, as in the 2009 Michael Haneke film, *The White Ribbon*—about "the roots of evil," says its director—the authoritarian, sadistic, and repressive family structures mirrored by Kafka are so often mirrored by authoritarian, sadistic, and repressive state structures; or that Kafka might be linked to other Middle European Jewish writers of the time such as Joseph Roth (unknown to me in 1959) and Bruno Schultz (also unknown to me). I could have used the word *prescient* when citing the Kafka story "In the Penal Colony," as well as the bureaucratic totalitarian nightmares of *The Trial* and *The Castle,* prefiguring, as they do, the horrors of Nazism and Soviet state socialism that were about to unfold, but I missed that chance.

In my nineteen-year-old mind, Art with a capital A should ideally exist in a Platonic abstract world, floating above the Earth and free from any real-life connections. That way, I didn't have to admit to putting my ex-boyfriends into the somewhat darkish fictions I was already writing.

But I missed the boat on Kafka's takes on Art with a capital A, as well. Surely I ought to have seen that several of Kafka's most famous stories were really about capital-A Art and Artists? "Josephine the Mouse Singer," for instance, in which Josephine isn't very good and is mostly despised by her mouse audience, but keeps on trying; or "In the Penal Colony," in which the sentence being carried out on the hapless condemned man is, literally, a sentence, engraved on him with an enormous set of stabbing pens; and especially "The Hunger Artist," in which the artist is at first admired, but then is increasingly neglected as he becomes too familiar and fails to amuse. Meanwhile, he's starving to death because he cannot eat anything but the perfect food, which he never manages to identify. Even Kafka's most famous story, "Metamorphosis," in which Gregor Samsa wakens one morning to find that he has been transformed into an arthropod, could be interpreted as being about the artist's feelings of monstrosity, of non-human-ness, in face of bourgeois reality. (Some time was spent later, by myself and a fellow Kafka fan, in trying to identify the arthropod in question. It could not have been an insect, such as a beetle or a cockroach: it has too many legs, no carapace—Gregor's back is soft—and feeble waving antennae. We decided on a house centipede.)

Fast-forward to the year 1984. Twenty-five years have passed; I was now forty-four, living with my family in West Berlin. Happily we had a chance to visit Prague—city of Kafka—under the auspices of the Canadian Embassy there; we took it. At that time, Czechoslovakia was a tightly controlled Soviet satellite state. People were afraid to discuss the things that were bothering them—such as the lethal levels of air pollution from soft coal—inside any building, or even in a car: you had to assume such locations were bugged. Only the middle of a park was considered safe. In our hotel room, the bellboy gestured at the chandelier, then motioned us into an alcove—out of hearing of the hidden microphone—and asked us if we wanted to exchange some hard currency. (When one of the light bulbs blew, we stood under the chandelier and complained: the bulb was swiftly replaced.) We were at first surprised to note a number of well-dressed, attractive single women in the almost-empty bar, until we understood that they were operatives posing as call girls to pry secrets out of visiting businessmen. The ancient Charles Bridge was denuded of its baroque statues, as they referred to a past that the regime was trying to obliterate. The Old Town Square with its famous Astronomical Clock and Twelve Apostles was virtually empty.

Prague Castle loomed above the city, dark and forbidding, and I thought of Kafka's Castle. It wasn't just an abstract symbol; there was a real castle, after all. *The Castle* was unfinished when Kafka died, and critics have been pondering over its meaning ever since. Is the hero K., wandering in the frustrating labyrinths of the castle, in search of someone who's in charge and can help him? Is the book a commentary on the inhuman ways of bureaucracy? Is K. in search of God, who, Beckett-like, fails to manifest himself but is nevertheless somehow *there*? If I'd thought of it back in 1959, I would have mentioned some of the various literary castles that might have some bearing on Kafka's choice of venue, or at least set it in context: the brooding castles of German Romantic Gothicism; Edgar Allan Poe's setting for "Masque of the Red Death," though his edifice is technically a palace; Walter Scott's Torquilstone castle of evil repute, in *Ivanhoe,* where maidens are imprisoned and Jews tortured; and, of course, the ominous Castle Dracula, haunted by the Undead. As a general rule, castles were not usually the scene of lighthearted merriment in the nineteenth century, connected as they were with echoes of an overbearing and ruthless aristocratic power.

So the Castle that was the physical co-relative of Kafka's complex metaphor was still there; but Kafka himself had been all but erased from the city of Prague. When we asked about him, people shook their heads fearfully. No books by him were available. We were told privately that there was a young man who'd elected to read Kafka's works out loud on a street corner; that was considered a daring thing to do, although so far the man hadn't been arrested: he may have been considered a harmless lunatic. No residence where Kafka had lived was decorated with a commemorative plaque, as would have been the case in any city of the West that had produced such a world-renowned writer. My spouse, Graeme Gibson—who had once taught a course called "Justice and Punishment in Modern European Literature"—replete with Dostoevsky, Kafka's *Trial,* and Beckett, and dubbed by his students "Introduction to Despair"—nevertheless set out by night in search of Kafka's Prague. (I was babysitting, so I did not go.) He went to the first address he had. The door opened to reveal a long flight of stairs, at the top of which the members of a hiking club, dressed in short leather pants, were making merry. There was a concierge, so Graeme inquired of her. "Kafka?" he said. "No, no, no, no," she replied.

He snuck back later. Outside the building there was a scaffold, erected for repairs, and he climbed it cautiously. A blue light was shining from above. Reaching the level of the upper window, he peered in. Asleep on a sofa, and almost filling the small room, there was an enormous man. The light was coming from a flickering television, on which nothing at all was being shown. "Kafkaesque," we said about this experience. Kafka would have relished it, from many points of view.

The third encounter with Kafka was quite different. Fast-forward again, to the later 1990s. The Berlin Wall had come down, the former Soviet Union had crumbled, the Cold War was supposedly over, and shopping was the new sex. We were in Prague again, this time for a Western-style literary festival. The city was now crammed with tourists and a hotspot for bohemians of various kinds, and, as it turned out, for the Russian mafia, who were making the most of real-estate opportunities around the world. Prague—having survived many of the ravages of the Second World War, and having been spared destruction by Hitler because he thought it was so beautiful—was all lit up, and looked like a fairy-tale city. The statues on the Charles Bridge were back in place, the once-dreaded Castle was a tourist centre, and a big handicrafts fair was under way in the Old Town Square, complete with a band that was playing "Hi ho, hi ho, it's off to work we go," from the Disney film *Snow White and the Seven Dwarfs*. Throngs of happy handicraft buyers inspected the wares at the numerous booths.

This time we'd come armed with a map, on which we had marked all of Kafka's addresses that we knew about. We walked from one location to the next, trying to imagine what these streets and buildings had been like when Kafka was living there. There was not yet a Kafka statue—though there is one now—but the various tourist-trap shops had many Kafka wares on display: Kafka matchbooks, Kafka postcards, Kafka handkerchiefs, Kafka booklets, Kafka statuettes, and even Kafka playing cards.

What would Kafka himself have thought of these efforts to commemorate him and/or cash in on him? I expect he would have laughed a lot; for one of the more unexpected things I learned about him between the ages of nineteen and sixty was that he found a lot of his own work uproariously funny. *The Trial,* funny? "The Hunger Artist," funny? "In the Penal Colony," funny? Well, yes, from a certain point of view. But then, Kafka didn't know what Hitler was about to do in real life.

In any case, the assemblage of Kafka souvenirs struck us as somewhat grotesque. In fact, it struck us as Kafkaesque. But Kafka in a more hilarious, or at least a more lighthearted, vein. If I were writing my 1959 essay now, in the second decade of the twenty-first century, perhaps I would place more emphasis on this side of Kafka. Is that just because my eyes, my ancient, glittering eyes are gay? Maybe. Nonetheless, I might see fit to conclude with a very short Kafka piece from 1912 called "Excursion into the Mountains." After an initial complaint—"nobody comes . . . nobody helps me"—he continues:

. . . a pack of nobodies would be rather fine, on the other hand. I'd love to go on an excursion—why not?—with a pack of nobodies. Into the mountains, of course, where else? How these nobodies jostle each other, all these lifted arms linked together, these numberless feet treading so close! Of course they are all in dress suits. We go so gaily, the wind blows through us and the gaps in our company. Our throats swell and are free in the mountains! It's a wonder that we don't burst into song.

There he is, not the isolated, persecuted K., but nameless, part of an anonymous crowd, free and almost singing. But only almost. It's always only almost, with Kafka. In literature as in life, with women, he has commitment problems. You can't pin him down.

Future Library

>>><<<

(2015)

I was very pleased to have been invited to be the first author for the Future Library project. Katie Paterson's artwork is a meditation on the nature of time. It is also a tribute to the written word, the material basis for the transmission of words through time—in this case, paper—and a proposal of writing itself as a time capsule, since the author who marks the words down and the receiver of those words—the reader—are always separated by time.

There are some disadvantages to being the first author. One, I have not yet seen the actual forest in Norway, so I can't say anything about it. Nor will I be able to stand in the Future Library room and see the names of the other authors and the titles of the works they have contributed. Authors far along in time—Year 90, Year 95—will know that when their sealed box is opened and their work published, those reading it will be their contemporaries. But those who will read my work are a hundred years into the future. Their parents aren't yet born, nor, in all likelihood, are their grandparents. How to address these unknown readers? What will they be able to understand of my world, the world that is the ground for my own contribution? And how will the meanings of words have changed in that time? For language itself is subject to pressure and metamorphosis, just as the rock of Earth's crust is.

Science fiction has made art out of space travel—travel to places that the author has never seen, and that may not exist except in the human imagination. Time travel is similar. In the case of the Future Library, I am sending a manuscript into time. Will any human beings be waiting there to receive it? Will there be a "Norway"? Will there be a "forest"? Will there be a "library"? It's hopeful to believe that all of these elements—despite climate change, rising sea levels, forest insect infestations, global pandemics, and all of the other threats, real or not, that trouble our minds today—will still exist.

As a child, I was one of those who buried treasures in jars, with the idea that someone, someday, might come along and dig them up. I found similar things while digging in the various gardens I have made: rusty nails, old medicine bottles, fragments of china plates. Once, in the Canadian Arctic, I found a tiny doll carved of wood— rare wood, for no trees grow there and such a piece of wood must have been driftwood. That is what the Future Library is like, in part: it will contain fragments of lives that were once lived, and that are now the past. But all writing is a method of preserving and transmitting the human voice. The marks of the writing, made by ink, printer ink, brush, stylus, chisel—lie inert, like the marks on a musical score, until a reader arrives to bring the voice back to life.

How strange it is to think of my own voice—silent by then for a long time—suddenly being awakened, after a hundred years. What is the first thing that voice will say, as a not-yet-embodied hand draws it out of its container and opens it to the first page?

I picture this encounter—between my text and the so-far non-existent reader—as being a little like the red-painted handprint I once saw on the wall of a Mexican cave that had been sealed for over three centuries. Who now can decipher its exact meaning? But its general meaning was universal: any human being could read it.

It said: *Greetings. I was here.*

Reflections on *The Handmaid's Tale*

>>><<<

(2015)

This year is the thirtieth anniversary of *The Handmaid's Tale*'s publication, which is amazing to me—it doesn't seem that long ago. Over that thirty years, this book has been published in approximately forty countries, and translated into approximately thirty-five languages. I say "approximately" because new ones keep popping up.

But things were slower at the beginning. I'd say the first reviews, in the English-language countries at any rate, were so-so. *The Handmaid's Tale* is not a very cozy book. It's not the sort of book in which you fall in love with the sprightly, courageous, but conscientious heroine and approve of everything she does. *Pride and Prejudice* it isn't. In fact, it got dissed in the *New York Times,* and being dissed in the *Times* invariably causes your publishers to cross to the other side of the street when they see you and then run away very fast and hide under a rock. The reviewer was the eminent American novelist and essayist Mary McCarthy, and she was not amused. (She was not amused in general, so I was not alone in failing to amuse her.)

Her review was somewhat incoherent—the *Times* told me later that she had recently had a stroke, though they hadn't known that when they assigned the review. She did agree that we should be wary of our credit cards—they were rather new then, back in 1985, having been deployed en masse only in the 1970s—because such cards, if we came to rely on them and only on them, could so easily be used to control us. And this was even before the Internet! We didn't even know about digital signatures.

But apart from the credit card angle, Mary McCarthy found the tale implausible—surely such a retrograde thing could never happen, in the forward-looking United States—and she also found the language uninventive. Her review was somewhat of a blow to me, as I remembered reading her novel, *The Group,* back in 1962, in the bathtub, with considerable interest. But it wasn't the first time I'd had a bad review, and it would not be the last. What doesn't kill you makes you stronger, though it sometimes also makes you more peevish. As you have just seen.

But after that rocky start, other commentary on *The Handmaid's Tale* appeared. The general import was: In the United Kingdom, they thought it was a pretty good yarn. They weren't too bothered by the prospect of its scenario actually happening in the U.K., as they'd already done their religious civil war, back in the seventeenth century, and they weren't anticipating another one anytime soon. In Canada, they asked nervously, "Could it happen here?" It's the sort of question Canadians often ask, since they imagine their country as the Land of the Hobbits, where the little furry folk innocently drink beer and play hockey and smoke pipeweed and have jolly parties, thinking no harm, and where the evil Eye of Mordor has not yet located them and sent trolls and orcs and Nazgûls and whatnot to exterminate them.

But in the United States, they asked, "How long have we got?" The handwriting was evidently already on the wall, back in 1985. In fact, some of it appeared on an actual wall, the seawall of Venice, California, where an anonymous hand spray-painted "The Handmaid's Tale Is Already Here." The book then went on to win the Los Angeles Times Book Award and to be nominated for the Booker Prize in the U.K., and to win the Governor General's Award in Canada, among others. So someone must have appreciated its virtues, such as they were.

And since that time, the book has never stopped selling. I suppose it's because new generations keep appearing to be terrified by it. People put it onto high-school courses, and other people then try to get it removed from them, partly because it has sex in it, or because those people erroneously believe it is anti-Christian, which indicates what an odd view of Christianity they must have. But we'll deal more extensively with that subject later.

This book has since morphed into a film, an opera, a ballet, a number of theatrical productions, and—forthcoming—a graphic novel rendition, and a television series. But, the finest tribute of all: People dress up as Handmaids on Hallowe'en. And other people Know What They Are Supposed to Be! My lowly Handmaid in her strange red dress has taken her place among the Klingons, Minnie Mice, Hulks, and Wonder Women of the Hallowe'en costume world. How thrilling is that?

I'll now get down to the nitty-gritty. I've been asked to speak about this novel from various angles, and I will attempt to do that. I'll talk about its context—the time in which it was created—and about how and why I set about writing it, and about the literary and historical influences on it, and about some of the choices I made when I was constructing its world. And then I will attempt to place it in the present day—the time we find ourselves in, right here and now. Does this novel still have relevance? If so, what and why? Can novels be prophetic, and if not, why not?

All of that is a tall order for a short talk, so I'll roll up my sleeves, figuratively, and get down to work.

But first, I'll tell you a true story. Once upon a time, maybe twenty years ago, myself and my spouse, Graeme Gibson, were throwing a party for the Ontario chapter of the Writers' Union of Canada. Backstory information: "Ontario" is a province, the Canadian equivalent of a state. "Canada" is a country, the equivalent, in population, of Mexico City. The Writers' Union was founded by us in the early 1970s because Canada did not have any agents at that time, so writers were entirely at the mercy of publishers, who lied to them about such things as what other writers got by way of an advance. Things are different now, though it's still true that "professional writer" as a job description is a cross between gambler, start-up entrepreneur, and sleight-of-hand card trickster. You have to run very fast to stay where you are, and if you want a pension plan, don't be a writer. It's almost as hard as being a twenty-three-year-old country singer. Most have day jobs.

One of the writers at this party of ours was a young woman of thirty-five, who announced she was having a heart attack. As she had already had a heart attack, this was serious. We kicked everyone out of the living room and Graeme did deep breathing with her while I called 911. Soon, two strapping young male paramedics arrived with their paraphernalia, their muscles bulging. (They have to have bulging muscles so they can heave the bodies around.) They expelled us from the room and got to work, and the following conversation then took place:

FIRST PARAMEDIC: Do you know whose house this is?
SECOND PARAMEDIC: No, whose house is it?
FIRST PARAMEDIC: It's Margaret Atwood's house!
SECOND PARAMEDIC: Margaret Atwood! Is she still alive?

It turned out that the young woman wasn't having a heart attack after all. She was having, and I quote, "a ball of gas as big as a grapefruit." She was just so excited to be in my house.

But I tell this story to illustrate a well-known fact: any writer whose work you study in high school is dead By Definition. And since a lot of kids have studied *The Handmaid's Tale* in high school over the years, there are a lot of people who are surprised to discover that I am still alive. It's getting so I'm sometimes surprised by that myself. But such is the effect of fame, even a moderate amount of it. You can get a zucchini mould—usually advertised at the backs of comic books—which, if placed around a growing zucchini, produces a zucchini in the shape of Elvis Presley's head. It could work with an eggplant, as well. I have yet to reach that level of fame.

And I had not got even close to the zucchini mould level when I began writing *The Handmaid's Tale*. Since some of you were not born then, and since others among you were of tender age, let me take you back in time.

First, me. Born in November 1939, just after the beginning of the Second World War. That means I am of the generation that remembers Hitler and Stalin, and not just from the history books. In 1949 I was ten, and thus read George Orwell's *Nineteen Eighty-Four* when it came out in paperback. I was fifteen in 1955, when Elvis made his TV debut. I was twenty in 1960, thirty in 1970, and forty in 1980. I always make a chart like this for characters in my books: I want to know how old they were in relation to major world events because our personal histories interact with what's going on in the world outside us.

In 1984, we were in a mini-backlash phase against hippies, women's liberation, and suchlike modes of social behaviour. In music, I think it was Late Disco. Hippies had burst forth in approximately 1968, just after beatniks and existentialists and folk singers and the Beatles; they had been preceded by the birth control pill, the advent of pantyhose, and miniskirts. (Those three things are connected, especially the pantyhose and the miniskirts.) Women's Lib, as it was called at the time, got going in approximately 1969. I wasn't there: I was in Edmonton, Alberta, which was far, far away from New York City. There was not yet any Internet. I heard about these doings in the form of letters from friends. I was also too old to have been a hippie, though I did go through the existentialism, and the folk singing, and the black eyeliner. Let's not forget that!

Feminism then entered its second wave. The first wave was in the late nineteenth and early twentieth centuries, its proponents were called suffragettes, and their goal was female suffrage, or getting the vote for women. Then they got the vote, and then there was the Depression—back to the home, women, to make room for jobs for men, though Amelia Earhart was a model for adventurous tomboys, who featured in magazine fiction—and then came the war—into the factories, women, to make weapons, and to appear in Rosie the Riveter posters, flexing your cute little biceps. Then, after the war, back to the home, women, to make room for jobs for the men; you were supposed to have four kids, a washer-dryer, a suburban bungalow, and Total Fulfillment through having discarded your brain. Meanwhile, the men back from the war were restless; they missed their freedom and adrenalin hit from the near-death experiences they had undergone. Along came Hugh Hefner, playing his Peter Pan flute, and calling to them: Why are you stuck in that domestic rut? Bungalows are boring! Ditch the wife and kids and come away to play! And so they did, giving rise eventually to the TV series *Mad Men*.

And that's when Betty Friedan came in with her book *The Feminine Mystique*, which I was reading in Vancouver in 1964. Her book was a protest against the lack of brain proposed by the back-to-the-home spinners of the late 1940s and the 1950s. Here is a spoof of that kind of spin, from the spurious *Housekeeping Monthly* 1955, called "The Good Wife's Guide":

Never complain if he comes home late or goes out to dinner, or other places of entertainment without you. Instead, try to understand his world of strain and pressure. . . . Don't complain if he's late home for dinner or even if he stays out all night. Count this as minor compared to what he might have gone through that day. . . . Don't ask him questions about his actions or question his judgment or integrity. Remember, he is the master of the house and as such will always exercise his will with fairness and truthfulness. You have no right to question him. . . . A good wife always knows her place.

This could as well have been called "The Roman Slave's Guide" or "The Serf's Guide in the Year 1000."

Friedan's *Feminine Mystique* struck a chord with all those American university-educated women who'd been told their real degree was an M.R.S. But the "master of the house" style of brainwashing didn't make much of a dint on young Canadian women. We were living in a cultural backwater, and were still doing the Amelia Earhart flying tomboy thing. Plus, we had a women's magazine called *Chatelaine,* with an editor called Doris Anderson, who'd been raised in a rooming house run by her mother after her father had deserted them, so she wasn't having any of the "fairness and truthfulness" pitch. She dealt with many women's issues head-on long before the women's movement hit in 1969, and she had to fight male management of the magazine chain at every step. They were quite keen on the "fairness and truthfulness" pitch. Just like Roman aristocrats.

On with the 1970s. It was a time of turmoil in the land of feminism: women of colour protested that they were not represented, and so did lesbians; *Ms.* magazine with Gloria Steinem appeared, plus many other publications; and on it went. In Canada, younger female writers were so busy trying to make a space where writers of any gender could be published and remunerated at all—founding magazines and publishing companies, building out infrastructure such as author tours and festivals and writers-in-residence at universities and public lending rights in connection with libraries, fight, fight, fight on all those fronts—that we were likely to see our male colleagues as fellow combatants rather than enemies.

By the early 1980s, fatigue had set in among some of the 1970s battling feminists, and they were resting on their oars. Meanwhile, the religious right was mounting a counter-attack. They wanted to go back to the 1950s, at least to the "Good Wife's Guide" version of that decade—skip the rock 'n' roll—but this time they wanted it shored up with the puritanical religious dogma that had underlain it all along. "He for God only, she for God in him," as John Milton had spelled it out in *Paradise Lost*. And, as Saint Paul had it, women could redeem themselves only through childbirth. This was a lot too close for comfort to the *Kinder, Kirche, Küche*—children, church, kitchen—advocated for women by the Nazis.

Remember what I said about Hitler? I was a great reader of literature about the Second World War, and I knew that he'd announced his platform very early on, in his book, *Mein Kampf.* This book was a non-starter at the time—Germans, at first, thought Hitler was a nut—good call—so he downplayed his real agenda until he got himself elected. Then he laid waste to democracy, and set about doing what he originally said he wanted to do.

So I believed two things. (1) That if true believers say they'll do a thing, when they get the chance they'll do it. (2) Whoever says "It can't happen here" is wrong. Anything can happen anywhere, given the right conditions, as history has demonstrated time and time again. And to those two, I'll add (3): Power corrupts, and absolute power corrupts absolutely. Again, there are many demonstration cases.

Thus I set about writing *The Handmaid's Tale.* I began it in note form, but set about it in earnest in the spring of 1984. We were living in West Berlin. The Berlin Wall had not yet come down—that was to happen in 1989—and there was no clue that it would come down anytime soon. For the flavour of those Cold War spy-versus-spy days in West Germany, read John le Carré's *Tinker Tailor Soldier Spy* series, or see the Alec Guinness TV series version; and for the flavour of East Germany then, see the film *The Lives of Others.* That's what it felt like.

So it was a good place to begin writing *The Handmaid's Tale.* I finished it in the spring of 1985, in Tuscaloosa, Alabama, where I was an M.F.A. chair at the University of Alabama. That was a good place to finish, for very different reasons. Unfreedom was practised there too, but only for certain people, such as those with darker skin and, oddly, bicycle riders. ("Don't ride a bicycle here," I was told, "'cause they'll think you're a Communist and run you off the road.") Call those two locations the two sides of the coin.

The Handmaid's Tale set out to answer a couple of theoretical questions: (1) If the United States were to become a dictatorship or absolutist government, what sort of government would it call itself? (2) If women's place is in the home, and if women are now out of the home and running all over the place like squirrels, how do you stuff them back into the home and make them stay there?

The answer to (1), in the book, is: It would be a religious dictatorship, like Iran . . . which had become one of those right after I myself visited it in 1978. It would not be a Communist dictatorship, like Poland, Czechoslovakia, and East Germany, which I had also visited, later, in 1984. I thought at the time that an absolutist government in the name of liberal democracy would be a contradiction in terms, but I should have remembered McCarthyism; and now that we have digital surveillance, such an absolutism is well within our reach.

The answer to (2)—how to cram the women back into the homes—was simple: dial back history a hundred years—no, even less. Take away women's jobs and their access to money—the latter via their bank and credit cards. Oh, and their most recently won civil rights, such as the right to vote and the right to own property, and the right to their own children. To do that, you'd change the law. Some people are fond of invoking "the rule of law," but they should remember that there have been some very unjust laws. The Nuremburg Laws—directed against Jews—were laws. The Fugitive Slave Act was a law. The decree forbidding literacy for American slaves in the South was a law. The Roman grind-the-peasant tax laws were laws. I could go on for a very long time on that subject.

I made a rule for myself in the writing of this book: I would not include any detail that people had not already done, sometime, somewhere; or that they lacked the technology to do. In other words, I couldn't just make stuff up. A number of the historical precedents can be found in the Epilogue, which claims to be a lecture on the text given a few hundred years after the events described.

I set the novel in Cambridge, Massachusetts. Here is why.

I attended Harvard University in the years 1961 to 1963 and then 1965 to 1967, and while there I took some courses from Perry Miller, who, along with F.O. Matthiessen, was instrumental in establishing American literature and civilization as an academic discipline. What I first studied under his wing was the seventeenth century—that is, the Puritan century in New England. This was an eye-opener to me, as the only early American literature I had studied until then was from the nineteenth century—Poe, Melville, Emerson, Thoreau, Dickinson, Whitman, Henry James, and so forth. Miller was brilliant on the seventeenth century in New England, which was far from a liberal democracy at that time. Instead, it was a theocracy. It was in favour of religious freedom for itself, but against it for anyone else. It hanged—for instance—Quakers. As these Puritans were among my ancestors, I was of course transfixed by this history.

This society also—famously—went through the Salem witchcraft hysteria, and as one of those purported witches was also my ancestor, or so my grandmother would say on Mondays, I was even more interested. (On Wednesdays she denied the whole thing.) The Salem witch hunt has been a template for similar hysterias ever since, including McCarthyism—thus Arthur Miller's play *The Crucible*. So that is why *The Handmaid's Tale* is dedicated to both Perry Miller (who would have had a good laugh had he remained alive to read it) and also to Mary Webster, my possible ancestor. Mary was hanged, but the hanging didn't take—she was still alive the next morning. That's a good tough neck to inherit, if you're going to stick your neck out. As I have done.

As I've said, I didn't put anything into this book that hadn't already been done somewhere, or could be done given available technology. I drew on a wide variety of historical sources, including Romania under the Ceauşescu dictatorship, Hitler and his Polish baby-stealing and multi-wife policies for SS men, Argentina under the generals. I used the denial of literacy to American slaves, I used early Mormonism, I used group hangings in medieval times—if everyone pulls on the rope, the guilt is shared—and I used the Dionysian cult of ancient Greece, where sacrificial victims were torn apart by hand. Those are just a few.

For the clothing, I used the illustration on the Old Dutch Cleanser package of the 1940s that traumatized me as a child—the hidden face, the white hat, the billowing skirts. But I also used mid-nineteenth-century women's fashions, with the hide-a-face bonnets; and the sumptuary laws of medieval times, which dictated who could wear what. The colour-coding—blue for purity, red for sin and passion, and so on—is the same one employed by Christian painters of the Middle Ages and the Renaissance.

The social structure of Gilead is sometimes thought to be one in which all men have superior status and all women have low status, but that is not true. It's an absolutist or totalitarian scheme rather than one dictated strictly by gender divisions, so the spouses of high-status men have high status themselves, although lower status than their husbands. Low-status men have lower status than high-status women. That's how these things have worked historically. Only high-status men have more than one woman available for pro-creation; they alone have Handmaids. This too is pretty accurate, as such things go. First wife rules the roost; other, younger wives are under her thumb. The high-status man procreates with all of them, if he can manage it. Low-status men have to make do with Econo-wives, who have to perform all the functions that at higher levels would be carried out by several women: first wives for social occasions, mistresses and concubines or second wives for sex, servants for housekeeping. So it goes, in the world of *The Handmaid's Tale*, because so it has often gone in the real world.

The literary influences on *The Handmaid's Tale* were also numerous. The title comes from Chaucer, one of my faves. It's a "tale" rather than a history, as by the time it is given a name, several hundred years after the events take place, no one is able to establish very firmly what exactly went on and who exactly these people were. This is a problem historians frequently have: there are gaps in the record. And so it is with our Handmaid.

The second influence is, of course, the Bible. This is a very complex work, having not begun as a book at all but as a collection of scrolls. Only when the codex book arrived—the book form we have now, with the spine up one side and a series of pages that you turn—

did the "biblia," the little books, become one book; and only then did it take on the semblance of a unified work. As it was written down at different times—very different times—and by different people, it contains a lot of mixed messages. One of the messages is very favourable to widows, orphans, poor people, and the oppressed. But you can extract quite different messages from it, such as grinding your enemies to nothing and putting curses on them whereby they eat their own children, and many have favoured such messages.

In *The Handmaid's Tale,* so-called Biblical literalism is used to control women (and low-status men) for political reasons and to support a power elite. If you think that's the essence of Christianity, I would argue that you are sorely mistaken. In the text, you can find the Lord's Prayer as the Handmaid reinterprets it for her own circumstances. It therefore baffles me quite a lot when people decide that this book is "anti-Christian." Any religion has a positive node and a negative one—as my old friend Fanny Silberman, Auschwitz survivor, used to say, "There's good and bad of everyone"—and Gilead is the bad. That doesn't mean there isn't a good. Over to you on that one.

The other literary influences come from the world of utopias and dystopias, of the late nineteenth and early twentieth century. A "utopia" is a literary depiction of a society better than ours; the late nineteenth century was very fond of those, and wrote a great many of them—because so many advances had been made in such things as medicine and technology and the production and distribution of material goods that optimistic people didn't see why things couldn't just keep improving. Highlights of the utopia in English were William Morris's *News from Nowhere* and Edward Bellamy's *Looking Backward.* Unfortunately, along came the First World War, in which Europe tore itself apart, and then the Second World War, in which it tore itself apart some more, and, in the interim, Hitler's Germany, Mussolini's Italy, and Stalin's U.S.S.R.—all of which proposed themselves at first as utopias—everything would get better—and all of which turned into dystopias, or societies worse than ours. So the literary utopia became very hard to write plausibly, and literary dystopias gained ground. Highlights include Aldous Huxley's *Brave New World* and George Orwell's *Nineteen Eighty-Four.* If you'd like to know more about my take on all of that, there's a chapter in my SF book, *In Other Worlds,* that goes into it in tedious detail.

The Handmaid's Tale is a literary dystopia—a world worse than ours—and the influence on its form is thus the utopia/dystopia tradition itself. I was reading a lot of that kind of fiction as a teenager, and I later studied it as a graduate student, so sooner or later I was fated to take a crack at it, just to see if I could do it. And so I did. It was a slightly mad thing to do in the 1980s, as this kind of fiction was not in vogue then. In the present day, dystopias are thick on the ground, possibly because a lot of young writers are somewhat dismayed by the prospect before them.

Which brings us to the present day. People often ask me the following two questions:

1. Do you think *The Handmaid's Tale* is more relevant now than when you wrote it back in the mid-1980s?
2. And, another version of the same question: Do you think *The Handmaid's Tale* is prophetic?

Those are tantalizing questions. To the first I would answer: Whether the book actually is more relevant or is not more relevant is hardly for me to say; but it is clear that a lot of people—especially people in the United States—*think* it is more relevant now. During the last presidential election, the book's title became a social media meme, with posters saying things like "Someone tell the Republicans that *The Handmaid's Tale* is not a blueprint," or else "Here comes *The Handmaid's Tale*." Why was that? Because the Four Wise Republicans had opened their mouths and said what they really thought, and what they really thought was that women who were "really" raped would not get pregnant because their bodies had a way of preventing that; and that there was a difference between "real" rape and "not-real" rape, or rape that only looked and felt like rape but wasn't really. It was all reminiscent of witch trials, in which they tied you up and threw you into the water, and if you drowned you were innocent but if you floated you were guilty, so they could burn you. Dead either way, looks like.

As a generalization, let us say: absolutist governments have always taken an inordinate interest in the reproductive capabilities of women. In fact, human societies have taken such an interest. Who shall have babies, which babies shall be "legitimate," which shall be allowed to live, and which shall be killed (in ancient Rome it was up to the father, etc.), whether abortion shall be allowed or not, or up to what month; whether women should be forced to have babies they didn't want or couldn't support, and so forth. In general, hunter-gatherer societies spaced children and abandoned those they couldn't feed, but agricultural societies encouraged lots of childbirth, the better to work the farms and provide slave labour; and once mass armies got going, they *really* encouraged childbirth, since extra bodies were needed for what Napoleon called "cannon fodder." Hitler gave out medals to mothers who had lots of kids—there was a dearth of cannon fodder, due to the First World War—whereas Stalin allowed abortion as a means of birth control—they had more mouths than they could feed, thanks to the failure of the collectivization of farming.

So the real question to be asked about the inordinate interest taken by the powers that be in birth and who gives it, and child-snatching and who does the snatching, is the usual one in mystery stories: *Cui bono?* Who profits by it?

In the world of *The Handmaid's Tale*, babies are thin on the ground among the upper classes. So they are snatched from those who have them and distributed to the upper-echelon folks who want them. There are lots of historic examples to draw upon, some of them being the Argentine generals who snatched the babies of women suspected of being anti-government and then tortured and killed the mothers, and the nuns in Ireland who snatched the babies of unwed mothers, and sometimes just babies who had been left temporarily in their care, and sold them to rich, childless Americans. It was not unheard of in the 1940s and 1950s for such mothers in North America to be told that their babies had died at birth, when in truth they'd been sold.

And since *The Handmaid's Tale* leadership is a bunch that strip-mines the Bible to find stuff they can use to their own advantage, it's the woman's fault if no baby appears. There are a lot of historical precedents for that as well.

So, is this story more relevant now than when it was first published? I'd say that unfortunately it probably is, insofar as there are now much more concerted efforts to claim the bodies of women as state property. To a person of my age, such efforts are profoundly Stalinist, not to mention Hitlerian. But maybe that's just me. As a footnote, let us say that the institution of the draft similarly claims men's bodies as state property. Something to ponder.

The second question: Is the novel prophetic? No. No novel is prophetic except in retrospect. No one can predict the future really because there are too many variables and too many unknowns. The best-laid plans of mice and men too often go pear-shaped. You can make an educated guess, and a plausible attempt, but that's about all.

There. I have now told you lots of things about *The Handmaid's Tale*: its ancestry, its genesis, its past, and its present. As for its future, that will be in your hands—the hands of its readers—because that is where the future of any book always resides. The writer writes it, then relinquishes control over it and waves goodbye to it at the train station, and the book sets off on its travels to unknown lands and unknown minds. It will meet some people who like it and some people who dislike it. That happens to any book. That so many have liked it, over so many years, still astonishes me.

We Are Double-Plus Unfree

>>><<<

(2015)

"A Robin Red breast in a Cage, Puts all Heaven in a Rage," wrote William Blake. "Sufficient to have stood, though free to fall," wrote John Milton, channelling God's musings about humankind and free will in the third book of *Paradise Lost*. "Freedom, high-day, high-day, freedom . . . !" chants Caliban in *The Tempest*. Mind you, he is drunk at the time, and overly optimistic: the choice he is making is not freedom, but subjection to a tyrant.

We're always talking about it, this "freedom." But what do we mean by it? "There is more than one kind of freedom," Aunt Lydia lectures the captive Handmaids in *The Handmaid's Tale*. "Freedom to and freedom from. In the days of anarchy, it was freedom to. Now you are being given freedom from. Don't underrate it."

The robin redbreast is safer in the cage: It won't get eaten by cats or smash into windows. It will have lots to eat. But it will also not be able to fly wherever it likes. Presumably this is what troubles the inhabitants of Heaven: they object to the restriction placed on the flight options of a fellow winged being. The robin should live in nature, where it belongs: it should have "freedom to," the active mode, rather than "freedom from," the passive mode.

That's all very well for robins. Hooray for Blake!, we say. But what about us? The safe cage or the dangerous wild? Comfort, inertia, and boredom or activity, risk, and peril? Being human and therefore of mixed motives, we want both; though, as a rule, alternately. Sometimes the desire for risk leads to boundary-crossing and criminal activity, and sometimes the craving for safety leads to self-imprisonment.

Governments know our desire for safety all too well, and like to play on our fears. How often have we been told that this or that new rule or law or snooping activity on the part of officialdom is to keep us "safe"? We aren't safe, anyway: many of us die in weather events—tornados, floods, blizzards—but governments, in those cases, limit their roles to finger-pointing, blame-dodging, expressions of sympathy, or a dribble of emergency aid. Many more of us die in car accidents or from slipping in the bathtub than are likely to be done in by enemy agents, but those kinds of deaths are not easy to leverage into panic. Cars and bathtubs are so recent in evolutionary terms that we've developed no deep mythology about them. When coupled with human beings of ill intent they can be scary—being rammed in your car by a maniac or shot in your car by a mafioso carries a certain weight, and being slaughtered in the tub goes back to Agamemnon's fate in Homer, with a shower-murder update courtesy of Alfred Hitchcock in his film *Psycho.* But cars and tubs minus enraged wives or maniacs just sit there blankly.

It's the sudden, violent, unpredictable event we truly fear: the equivalent of an attack by a hungry tiger. Yesterday's frightful tigerish threat was Communists: in the 1950s, one lurked in every shrub, ran the message. Today, it's terrorists. To protect us from these, all sorts of precautions must, we are told, be taken. Nor is this view without merit: such threats are real, up to a point. Nonetheless we find ourselves asking whether the extreme remedies outweigh the disease. How much of our own freedom must we sacrifice in order to defend ourselves against the desire of others to limit that freedom by subjugating or killing us, one by one?

And is that sacrifice an effective defence? Minus our freedom, we may find ourselves no safer; indeed we may be double-plus unfree, having handed the keys to those who promised to be our defenders but who have become, perforce, our jailers. A prison might be defined as any place you've been put into against your will and can't get out of, and where you are entirely at the mercy of the authorities, whoever they may be. Are we turning our entire society into a prison? If so, who are the inmates and who are the guards? And who decides?

———

We human beings have been exploring the border between freedom and unfreedom for a very long time. Once, the alternative to freedom was not imprisonment but death. In the millennia we spent as hunter-gatherers, we had neither passwords nor prisons. Everyone in your small group knew and accepted you, though strangers were suspect. No one got put in jail because there were no buildings to serve that purpose. If a person became a threat to the group—for instance, if he became psychotic and expressed a desire to eat people—it would be the duty of the group to kill him, whereas nowadays it would be the duty of the group to lock him up, in order to keep others from harm. A justice system with an incarceration option depends on permanent architecture: you can't throw someone into a dungeon unless you have one.

After the advent of agriculture, the alternative to freedom became not death but slavery. It was now more desirable to enslave the threats to your group than to kill them. That way, they could be set to work tilling your soil, thus creating a surplus for you and making you rich. Sampson isn't tossed off a cliff, as were the captured male Trojans in the Homeric epics. Instead, he is blinded and set to work grinding grain like a donkey.

Of course, once the profitability of slaves had been recognized, the rule of supply and demand created a thriving market for slaves. You could find yourself enslaved not only by being on the losing end of a war, but by being in the wrong place at the wrong time: in the path of a slave-raiding party, for instance.

In the medieval period, everyone in the upper percentages wanted a castle, and every castle had a dungeon: dark, dismal, cold, hopeless, and rat-infested, or such is their filmic image. Dungeons were status symbols: everyone who was anyone had one. They had multiple uses: you could keep witches in them until it was time to burn them; you could shackle criminals in them, though it was often more economical to just hang them; and you could put rivals to the throne in them until you could fabricate enough evidence to proclaim them traitors and chop off their heads. And dungeons could be valuable wealth-creators, since holding foreign nobles for ransom could be lucrative. The trade was simple: you, the dungeon-possessor, got a lump sum of cash, and your prisoner got his freedom. In the reverse version, you paid a foreign dungeon-owner to sequester the political enemy of your choice.

And so it went, for hundreds of years, up to the modern age. In the nineteenth century, freedom and unfreedom began to assume their present-day forms. "Freedom" had become reified by the eighteenth-century Enlightenment: it was what the embattled farmers of the American Revolution were supposed to have been fighting for, though in practical terms they were fighting for the freedom of not paying taxes to Britain. The French revolutionaries started out with liberty, equality, and fraternity, a noble ideal that included freedom from the aristocrats, though in the short term it ended in tears, thousands of severed heads, and Napoleon.

But once Byron got hold of freedom, there was no turning back: freedom as an idea was here to stay. His Prisoner of Chillon was romantic because he didn't have freedom; that dubious character Fletcher Christian mutinied against Captain Bligh—in Byron's version—as a gesture against tyranny and a bid for freedom. And Byron himself lost his life while fighting, more or less, for the Greeks in their attempt to regain their own political freedom. Not "Dieu et mon droit" but "Freedom" was engraved on the banner waved by many a nineteenth- and twentieth-century revolutionary: slaves' freedom from slavery in the American South, South Americans' freedom from Spain, Russians' freedom from the tsar, workers' freedom from capitalist exploitation, women's freedom from patriarchal systems in which they had the rights of children but the responsibilities of adults. And, eventually, freedom from Nazism and Iron Curtain Communism.

Freedom to write, freedom to publish, freedom of speech: all are still being fought for in many countries in the world. Their martyrs are numerous.

With so many so willing to die in its name, why have citizens in many Western countries been willing to surrender their hard-won freedoms with barely more than a squeak? Usually it's fear. And fear can come in many forms: sometimes it comes down to the fear of not having a pay cheque. As long as the trains run on time and you yourself are employed, why make a fuss if a few people here and there are being strung up by their thumbs?

And by the time the thumb-stringing really gets going, fear of another kind sets in. You can protect your thumbs only by staying below the surface of the frog pond: don't stick your head up or croak too loudly, and, you are assured, as long as you don't do anything "wrong"—a shifting category—nothing bad will happen to you.

Until it does.

And since the free press will already have been suppressed, and since any independent judiciary will already have been dismantled, and since any independent writers, singers, and artists will already have been squashed, there will be no one left to defend you. If there's one thing we ought to know by now, it's that absolutist systems with no accountability and no checks and balances generate monstrous abuses of power. That seems to be an infallible rule.

But all of that may seem a little old-fashioned. It harks back to the mid-twentieth century, with its brutalism, its strutting dictators, its mass military spectacles, its crude in-your-face uniforms. The citizen-control methods of modern Western governments are much more low-profile: less jackboot than gumboot. Our leaders are applying the methods of agribusiness cattle-raising to us: ear-tag, barcode, number, sort, record. And cull, of course.

That's where the prison system comes in: shorn of its short-lived idealism—no longer a reformatory where criminals are to be reformed, no longer a penitentiary where they are to repent—it has become a warehouse where people are stashed. In its for-profit mode, it has also become a gizmo for creating more criminals, all the better to fill its available slots and extract money from taxpayers to foot the bill for it.

In the United States, young Black men are disproportionately represented in the prison population; in Canada, it's young First Nations men. Are we incapable of thinking up anything more effective, and at the same time less costly, such as better education and better job creation? But maybe it serves the powers that be to foster the conditions that create scary people and have them running around, so we ourselves will see the logic of paying to lock them up.

Digital technology has made it easier than ever to treat people like domesticated animals farmed for profit. You can no longer rent a car or a hotel room or buy much of anything without a credit card, which leaves a digital trail wherever it goes. You're told you need a social security card, a health card, a driver's licence, a bank card, a bunch of passwords. You need an "identity," and that identity is digital. All your numbers and passwords—all the data that identifies you—is supposed to be private, but as we know by now, the digital world leaks like a sieve, and security on the Internet is only as good as the next mastermind hacker or inside-job data thief. The Kremlin has gone back to using typewriters for a good reason: it's a lot easier to smuggle a memory stick out of a secure area than it is to make off with a big stack of papers.

So, what to do? In William Gibson's Neuromancer trilogy, most of the citizens are ear-tagged just like us, but some are able to exist under the radar by virtue of having no official record. Either they've wiped it or altered it, or they've avoided having one in the first place. But it would take a lot of agility and possibly a reservoir of basic survival skills for anyone to live without the required identity. Under a bridge, maybe; in a house, not.

The majority of us are double-plus unfree: our "freedom to" is limited to approved and supervised activities, and our "freedom from" doesn't keep us free from a great many things that can end up killing us, with our bathtubs being just the beginning. Freedom from toxic chemicals in the air and water? Freedom from floods, droughts, and famines? Freedom from defective automobiles? Freedom from the badly prescribed drugs that are killing hundreds of thousands of people a year? Don't hold your breath.

It's not all bad, however. All technology is a double-edged tool, and the very Internet that has too many data-leaking holes in it also allows words to travel quickly. It's easier to reveal abuses of power than it once was; it's easier to sign petitions and to protest. Though even that freedom is double-edged: the petition you sign may be used by your own government in evidence against you.

One of Aesop's fables concerns the frogs. They told the gods they wanted a king, and the gods threw down a log to be their ruler. It floated here and there and didn't do anything, and for a while they were content. But then they began complaining because they wanted a more active king. The gods, annoyed, sent them a stork, which ate them up.

Our problem is that our Western governments, increasingly, are an unpleasant combination of both the Log King and the Stork King. They're good at asserting their own freedom to spy and control, though bad at allowing their citizens as much freedom as they formerly enjoyed. Good at devising spy laws, bad at protecting us from the consequences of them, including false positives. Who says you are who you are? Whoever can alter your data.

Though our digital technologies have made life super-convenient for us—just tap and it's yours, whatever it is—maybe it's time for us to recapture some of the territory we've ceded. Time to pull the blinds, exclude the snoops, recapture the notion of privacy. Go offline.

Any volunteers? Right. I thought not. It won't be easy.

Buttons or Bows?

>>><<<

(2015)

Some novelists feed their characters, others don't. Dickens, for instance, revels in lavish feasts, whereas Dashiell Hammett allows drink only. Some go in for furniture, or paintings, or architecture; others ignore these in favour of musical instruments, floral arrangements, or dogs. Pets and menus, bathtubs and curtains, buildings and gardens, all reflect the psyches of their owners: or at least they do in books.

It's the same with clothes. For some authors a hat is only a hat, full stop. But for others, a glove, a feather, or a handbag are weighted with significance. Where would Henry James be without the wardrobes, especially those of his lavender-gloved female characters? Or Sherlock Holmes without his keen observation of boots and velveteen sleeves?

I notice the clothes in the fiction I read. If someone's wearing a dress I want to know what colour it is, and that's just the beginning. Is it in fashion or out of date? Seductive plunging neckline or chaste bow at the chin? What would be worn under it—shift, slip, crinoline, whalebone? Is the wearer overdressed for the occasion? Is she possibly a man, and if so, can we tell? In any case, does the dress make her, or him, more attractive, or more annoying, or perhaps laughable? And what about the shoes?

And, most importantly: Are the period details correct? A female character wearing a white wedding dress in an age when the most highly prized colour for brides was black will be deeply wounding to the clothes-conscious reader. "But two-way stretch girdles weren't invented yet!" they will cry. Then they will write a scornful letter to the author. There are whole websites consecrated to the chastising of fashion gaffes and anachronisms in fiction. "Only an idiot would confuse that bustle with a peplum!" they scold.

I've considered writing letters in that tone, though I've never written one. I've certainly received them, though not about the ready-to-wear; more about how to make butter. But the same principle applies.

I'm sure I developed my persnickety interest in fictional clothes because I grew up without having many real ones. That was during the war, when fabric was scarce. Search the magazines of those times and you'll find many articles on how to turn your worn-out blouse into a newer-looking one by reversing the collar, adding sprightly rickrack trim, and other such tricks. Materials were favoured not for their beauty but for their sturdiness: they were supposed to last. That meant they were lumpy and scratchy.

In my case, the absence of furbelows on my apparel was augmented by the fact that our family spent more than half the year in the northern Canadian woods, where skirts would have been stupid. I wore my brother's hand-me-downs, which were often brown and maroon. For city life, I had the chunky, uncomfortable plaid skirt of the era and the knitted cardigan given to pilling, and two dresses for warmer weather. Why would you need any more? One could be washed while the other was being worn, was the reasoning of my mother, who hated shopping for clothes and avoided it when possible.

But then, despite my mother, I got seduced. Not only were there birthday parties at which the little guests were expected to appear decked out like the Infanta of Castile in ruffles and hair bows; there were also fairy tales, in many of which garments were essential to the plot. We relished the scene in which Cinderella triumphs over her persecutors by casting off her disguise of rags and appearing as her true, gorgeous inner self with the aid of a diamond-covered gown. We still relish that scene. Is that all it takes? A dress? Bring on the fairy godmothers!

At the same time, I was introduced to the life of Hollywood glamour, as reflected in the world of paper dolls. These were of movie stars of the 1940s, such as Veronica Lake. The stars had many outfits: smart suits with matching hats that they could wear shopping, more decorated frocks for afternoon social events, cocktail dresses teamed with tiny veiled hats—not that I knew what a cocktail was—one-piece bathing suits worn with enormous sunhats while lounging beside swimming pools drinking cooling drinks. Sometimes the stars might even play tennis, but they didn't do this often on my time because the tennis clothes were boring. Mostly they went to evening gatherings, pretty as a picture in sparkly bias-cut evening gowns, long gloves up to their elbows. The gloves were especially difficult to attach with the folding paper tabs, but they were necessary. In a pinch, Elmer's Glue could be used to stick them on, but then it would be hard to get them off. Several arms were inadvertently amputated.

What the movie stars did once they got to the evening gatherings was beyond my ken, but they always needed a male escort to do it. He came with his underwear firmly in place—scant hints of genitalia—and he had a limited wardrobe: a black dinner jacket, a couple of daytime suits, and some embarrassing sportswear. In other words, he was no fun to dress. Take the crooning out of the crooners and the dancing out of Fred Astaire, and what do you have but a bunch of identical guys puttin' on their top hats? Men didn't return to the peacock days of the eighteenth century until the advent of rock 'n' roll and the hippies. But that was too late for my paper-doll period.

As the 1940s turned into the 1950s, Dior's New Look took over. This was billed as The Return of the Feminine. Gone were the serviceable, no-nonsense tweed suits, the squarish padded shoulders, to be replaced with bouffant skirts belled out with crinolines and wispy fabrics such as tulle. The word *dainty* was used often. Songs about buttons and bows were popular, the boys were home and room had to be made for them, and the baby boom was on.

By this time, I was wielding a sewing machine and making my own outfits, like many of my generation who had saved up our babysitting money and then blew it on vestments. We sewed partly because it was cheaper, but also so we could have things that weren't the same as everyone else's: the options in those days were more limited. Some of my productions were more successful than others, and several of my concepts were far too original to have occurred to a girl more thoroughly socialized than myself. ("Original," in the Toronto of those days, meant "bizarre," just as "different" was a criticism.) Did I really dye a length of factory cotton orange, print it with linoblock trilobites, and sew it into a dirndl skirt? Yes, I did. Did any of my high-school classmates find this peculiar? Without a doubt.

That was in 1956, when strapless formals were all the rage. These had their shape wired in, so the cloth breasts jutted out regardless of what was inside them. Mishaps could occur. A too-vigorous rock or roll might cause popping out; if the dress wasn't tight enough, one could be twirled around inside it so the wired front was at the back, as happened to a friend of mine. Worst of all, there could be a gap between dress and self. The other boy on a double date attended by my spouse drank too freely from the mickey in the glove compartment, and, at the post-dance midnight restaurant meal, threw up down his partner's gap. Tears from her, groans from him. So ended a budding romance.

I didn't attempt to sew a strapless—I knew my limits—but I did concoct a pink tulle formal with a bodice studded with fake seed pearls. This frock was bunchy though moderately acceptable and, according to my younger sister, had a prolonged afterlife as a set of cleaning cloths. My mother was unsentimental about fabric-related events. She'd let us ruin her cut-velvet evening gown of the 1930s by playing dressups in it. How *could* she!

Which brings me to my writing, or rather to the clothing of the characters in my writing. Such clothing always involves research— a moderate amount in the case of recent history, though even then it's best to do some cross-checking. If you're writing about the future, you might seem to have an open field, but even then the outfits must fit their context. Who can forget the zippicamiknicks in Aldous Huxley's *Brave New World* or the red sash of the Anti-Sex League in Orwell's *Nineteen Eighty-Four*?

The past is another country, and its clothes are frozen in time. The farther back, the more research is needed. Where to begin? In the earlier twentieth century, magazines and mail-order catalogues are invaluable; so are newspapers, especially their social pages, in which the clothing of every notable at a wedding or gala is described. (Not so with funerals, though the same people are often present.) Pattern books are handy, and old photographs can be useful too, though paintings are often better: once portraits became the fashion, the sitters usually wanted their finery depicted in sumptuous detail.

For *Alias Grace,* set in the mid-nineteenth century and largely in the Kingston Penitentiary, I and my researchers combed through fashion plates and written records, and consulted archivists: What sorts of boots did the women wear, to cope with the snow? Did they have red flannel petticoats? And what about the penitentiary uniforms? Blue-and-white stripes, we eventually discovered, but it took some digging.

Women in the nineteenth century were frequently lectured on the frivolity of paying too much attention to dress in lieu of doing good works. But how much attention was too much? You needed to pay some attention if you had a position to keep up. Respectable wives in England went to the Ascot races to examine the elegantly dressed high-class courtesans so they could copy their outfits. Respectable matrons of New York—Edith Wharton tells us—bought their gowns in Paris, then stored them for a season so they would not be too immorally fashionable. Reputations could stand or fall on what you wore.

And, in earlier days, heads could roll. In the Bible, the penalty for wearing a veil if you were a slave was death. God is interested not only in fig leaves, suits made of animal skins, and cross-dressing—he didn't like it—but also in where to put the tassels and in the mixing of wool with linen. In this, God and my 1956 home economics teacher had something in common, as she always suspected.

It's a very old human interest, self-decoration. From tattoos to wigs to earrings to bustles to Victoria's Secret, we've been festooning our bodies for a long time. We may not be what we wear, but what we wear is a handy key to who we think we are. In a novel, it's crucial. We love Sherlock, not only for his mind, but for his deerstalker.

So if such details interest you too, feel vindicated. And if I ever get the two-way stretch girdle wrong, by all means write me that letter.

Gabrielle Roy

>>><<<

IN NINE PARTS

(2016)

1. PREAMBLE

I read my first work by Gabrielle Roy when I was sixteen. It was 1956. I was in my last year at a suburban Toronto high school.

The Second World War had ended barely a decade earlier, yet to us it felt like ancient history. Many things about that war, including the Holocaust, had been deliberately buried. The Cold War was under way; West Germany was an important ally and needed to be treated with tact. The U.S.S.R.—such an essential partner in the war—was now the enemy, and Smiling Uncle Joe Stalin had become Evil Big Brother. A whole sheaf of wartime attitudes and memes had been tossed out along with the rationing books. The postwar cornucopia of consumer goods was in high spew.

At the beginning of the 1950s, propaganda images of domestic bliss had been promoted to hustle women out of the workforce, making way for the men returning from the war. The baby boom was in full swing; and four kids, an automatic washer, and a split-level bungalow was the ideal pushed by advertisers and politicians alike. Although Simone de Beauvoir's *Le Deuxième Sexe* was published in 1949 and translated in 1953, second-wave feminism was nowhere to be seen, or not by us high-school students. (The book did not gain traction with our generation until Betty Friedan's *The Feminine Mystique* appeared in 1963. Moreover, we felt that these books described our mothers and grandmothers, not us.)

Nor were the boys of our age bedevilled by the woes of the men in the grey flannel suits, veterans used to a lot more adrenalin than a nine-to-five could provide. These men were already being lured away from their bungalows and wives into Playboy Bunnyland by their fellow vet Hugh Hefner.

By comparison, we teenagers of the 1950s were floating in what might be called the Early Betty and Veronica Age. Archie Comics still described a reality we could identify as ours: old-maid school-teachers; balding and comical principals; and girls who made pans of brownies in home economics so boys taking shop could make yum-yum noises and rub their stomachs. Sex was Archie with a heart drawn above his head. That was as far as things went because love and marriage went together like a horse and carriage. Nobody had got around, yet, to asking the horse about its opinion.

Meanwhile, in the wider world, annihilation by atomic bomb hovered as a fearful possibility, and McCarthyism had made any talk of social welfare or workers' rights sound almost treasonably Communist. Since the Hungarian Revolution had just been quashed by Soviet tanks, we all knew what a bad thing Communism might be. Catchwords that had been all the rage in the 1930s and the 1940s were now out. You couldn't say "working class" or even "world peace" without attracting suspicious glances. In the world of B movies, invasions of Martians who would take over your brain and turn you against your fellow citizens were much in vogue: outer space was full of Communists, evidently, but so was inner space. They were everywhere.

Thus, Gabrielle Roy's masterpiece novel of 1945, *Bonheur d'Occasion,* must have seemed like dangerous fare to the nervous educators of the 1950s. Not only did it blurt out "the working class" right on its 1947 American-edition flyleaf, but it focused closely on economic and social inequalities, and its most idealistic character looked forward to a "just society." After Roy, we'd have to wait for Pierre Trudeau's leadership speech in 1968 to hear this phrase given such pride of place again. (It's odd to remember this now, when the themes of the "1 per cent" income equalization and job creation have taken centre stage once more, but that's how it was in the timorous 1950s.)

2. GABRIELLE ROY IN THE HANDS OF MME WIACEK

The Cold War politics of the day may explain why it was Gabrielle Roy's *La Petite Poule d'Eau* that was on my high-school curriculum rather than *Bonheur d'Occasion*.

Roy's novel was a set text for the French-literature final examination, and those finals determined whether a student would go to university. We élèves pored over every word under the guidance of our meticulous teacher, Madame Wiacek. As her name might suggest, Madame Wiacek was neither French nor Québécois; she was Polish—French being, at that time, the second language of choice for educated Poles.

Thus it was that a roomful of Canadian anglophones with terrible accents were studying French through a book written by a francophone from Manitoba, under the often amused tutelage of a woman who'd escaped both the Nazis and the Russians, immigrated to Canada, and somehow fetched up in a middle-class and very mundane postwar suburb of Toronto.

The most alarming event on the horizon was not likely to be an invasion of storm troopers or commissars, but the Friday-night hop, at which a bunch of adolescents rocked and rolled around the gymnasium under the supervision of the German teacher, who was Bulgarian, and the Latin teacher, who was of Indian descent by way of Trinidad. This ethnic mix of students and teachers was not untypical: our high school fancied itself as Scottish, though some students were Chinese and a number of them were Armenian. This incongruous mixture was very Canadian, and would have been fully appreciated by Gabrielle Roy herself—for among the many areas of Canadian life that she explored, long before this exploration became fashionable, was its ethnic multiplicity.

The approach we took to Gabrielle Roy's book was intensely French. We practised the classic explication du texte—a close reading of the work itself. We unravelled the sentence structures of the text but discovered little about its author. In English studies too, New Criticism was the favoured method, so biography was barely glanced at: we learned everything about *The Mayor of Casterbridge* but nothing about Thomas Hardy's life (possibly just as well, considering its gloom).

This absence of biography was normal for me at the time, but it seems very curious now—especially since the story of Gabrielle Roy is just as interesting as the story of Luzina Tousignant, the heroine of *La Petite Poule d'Eau.* Who was Gabrielle Roy? How did she become a writer? And why was her work chosen for a high-school curriculum otherwise dominated by European authors, in both French and English? Dead male European authors, I might add. There were a couple of women among the English ones, but they too were dead.

Yet here was a living female Canadian author, still alive, right on our curriculum. The astonishing fact passed without comment. The dreaded dictée hogged all our attention in our French class, and matters such as gender and nationality and class and colonialism and the bizarre circumstances of individual artists' lives were hidden in the wings, preparing to make their appearance onstage over the next decade.

But the unknown wise and good who selected Gabrielle Roy must have had their reasons. How did Gabrielle Roy pass their scrutiny?

3. GABRIELLE ROY WAS VERY FAMOUS

The short answer is that Gabrielle Roy was very famous. We weren't told about this fame of hers, but her fame was well known to the generation of teachers who'd chosen her.

The book that had made her so famous was *Bonheur d'Occasion,* her first novel. The French original was published in Montreal in 1945, just as the Second World War was drawing to a close. A translation, entitled *The Tin Flute,* appeared in English in 1947, and was adopted as the monthly selection by the Literary Guild of America—at that time a major force in publishing. The bestselling first print run was seven hundred thousand, a number that would be almost unheard of today, especially for a literary novel. There followed a triumph in France, where this book was the first Canadian novel to win the prestigious Prix Femina. It also won the Canadian Governor General's Award.

A film contract was signed, translation rights were sold in twelve languages, and Gabrielle Roy became a literary celebrity—so much so that she returned to Manitoba to escape from the demands being made upon her by the press and her admirers. The scale of her success was unprecedented for a Canadian writer, surpassing even that of Gwethalyn Graham, whose 1944 novel, *Earth and High Heaven,* was the first Canadian book to top the *New York Times* bestseller chart.

4. A CINDERELLA STORY, MORE OR LESS

Part of Roy's appeal was her rags-to-riches Cinderella story. But Gabrielle Roy had no fairy godmother; she'd come up the hard way, and most Canadians could empathize with that, having come up the hard way themselves. Moreover, the hard way was in literary vogue: the roaring twenties gave us tales of the rich and profligate, such as *The Great Gatsby,* but the dirty thirties had been characterized by such iconic poor-people books as John Steinbeck's *The Grapes of Wrath.* Plutocrats were out, except in romance novels; "the masses" were in. Not only Gabrielle Roy's novel, but her life, was in tune with the times.

Roy was born in Saint Boniface, a largely francophone district of Winnipeg. Her parents were both immigrants to Manitoba, attracted by the boom times following Confederation. Her father was originally from the Acadian community of New Brunswick; her mother was from Quebec. Politically Léon Roy was a Liberal, and when Wilfred Laurier's Liberals gained power in 1896, he was employed by the federal government as an immigration agent, helping foreign incomers settle in the province. (But live by the government, die by the government: when the Conservatives won the election of 1915, M. Roy was fired, six months short of a pension.)

Although Roy's family wasn't wealthy, it was never dirt poor. Before he lost his job, M. Roy was able to build a large house on Rue Deschambault, in a newly developed section of Saint Boniface. It was this house that became the focus of Roy's semi-autobiographical series of stories, the 1955 *Rue Deschambault* (translated as *Street of Riches*).

Gabrielle was the youngest of eleven children, of whom eight were living. Her year of birth was 1909, the same as my mother's. Thus, by the time of Roy's extraordinary fame, she was just over forty. She was five when the First World War broke out, nine when it ended, and ten when the 1919 Spanish flu epidemic swept the planet, killing twenty million worldwide, including fifty thousand Canadians—which, in a population of eight and a third million people, was substantial.

During Roy's childhood, smallpox was still a killer, as were tuberculosis, diphtheria, whooping cough, red measles, tetanus, and polio. Infant mortality rates were high, as were maternal death rates. Both having a baby and being a baby were riskier than they are now, and this is worth noting, since babies feature largely in Roy's work.

Also in 1919 the Winnipeg General Strike took place—perhaps the single most important event in the history of Canadian labour. Roy's political leanings—Liberal, egalitarian, sympathetic toward the exploited—were formed early in life, not only by the events around her, but by her family's attitude toward them.

Roy's family was francophone, but due to a legislative quirk she received a bilingual education. When Manitoba was established as a province in 1870, it was bilingual. However, over the decades, the status of French as an official language had declined, and in 1916, when Gabrielle Roy was seven, Manitoba passed a law making English the only language of instruction in public schools. (This move was deeply resented by francophones, who saw it as a gross betrayal of the province's founding principles.) But Roy attended the nun-run Académie Saint-Joseph for twelve years, where she was educated in both English and French. Thus not only was she fluently bilingual, but she had access to the great literatures of both languages. For a future novelist, this was a tremendous advantage.

The direction Roy took after receiving her grade-twelve diploma was a common one for young women of her era. She went to Normal School—a crash course for young teachers—and became a teacher in rural public schools. The job choices for young women were not numerous, especially during the Depression years, which began in 1929 when Roy was twenty. Roy then obtained a teaching job at an English-language school in Winnipeg, so she was able to live at her parents' home.

Roy saved up her teaching money, but unlike many young women, she did not then get married. Instead, she went to Europe with the intention of becoming a professional actress.

During her school-teaching years, Roy had been acting, in both French and English. The companies were of the kind that abounded in the Canada of those days—semi-amateur "little theatres"—and Roy acted with both the Cercle Molière and the Winnipeg Little Theatre. She was passionate about acting and, due to some favourable critical reception, thought she might make a career out of it. Looking at photos of her as a young woman, it's easy to see why: she had the high cheekbones and chiselled features of the screen beauties of the 1930s. At the same time, she was writing and had managed to get some pieces published in periodicals both local and national.

In 1937, she was ready to make her move. It was a move that Canadians and indeed Americans bent on an artistic career of any kind—painting, acting, music, writing—had been making for decades. You needed to expand your horizons; you needed to travel to Europe, where art was taken seriously, or so went the myth. (As this was still the pattern in the early 1960s when I myself was a young artist, I understand it well.)

Despite hostility from her family—as an unmarried daughter, wasn't it her duty to stay at home and take care of her aged, widowed mother?—off to Europe Roy duly went. Her first stop was Paris, where she stayed only a couple of weeks—I speculate that she had some problems with her "provincial" accent and the resulting snobbery, which North American francophones have been known to experience. Then she went to England. In those days the British Empire still existed, and it was fairly easy for Canadians to get into Britain. In London, Roy mingled with other young expatriates, including friends from Manitoba. She also enrolled in the Guildhall School of Music and Drama, which had added "Drama" to its name only two years previously.

Guildhall was not the top drama school in England, but even so it must have been demanding for Roy. It's hard to imagine what the experience must have been like for someone of Roy's intense and ambitious character. Amateur theatre in Canada was one thing, but it would have been more difficult in England, land of actors, for Roy to maintain her acting dream. In each of the cultural capitals

of her world—Paris, London—Roy would have been swiftly identified as being from the margins; indeed, the margins of the margins.
Manitoba—where was that? In fact, *Canada*—where was *that*? Up
to the 1970s, when I myself experienced it, this was the attitude of
English people to colonial upstarts. (It was not the attitude in Scotland, Ireland, or Wales, but that's not where Roy travelled.)

So, while doing the usual young-tourist things—the visits to the
museums, to the theatres, to the countryside—Roy fell back on her
second string: writing. A talent for mimicry can come in handy in
fiction just as it does on the stage. She already had some previous
publication experience, and she managed to place three pieces in an
important Paris magazine. It was in England, paradoxically, that she
became convinced of her vocation as a writer, and of her chances of
success.

It was now 1939. As many foresaw, a second world war was on
the way. Roy made one last visit to France, this time to the countryside, then sailed back to Canada in April. Despite more family
pressure—having had her fling, shouldn't she *now* be supporting her
aged mother?—she did not return to Saint Boniface. Instead, she
settled in Montreal, where she began the long, hard, dedicated grind
that would result, five years later, in the great success of *Bonheur
d'Occasion*.

5. MONTREAL, SIN CITY

Montreal at that time was the only Canadian city comparable to New
York City. It was the financial capital of Canada—bustling, cosmo-
politan, multilingual, and sophisticated, with impressive architecture
both ancient and Victorian, and a lively nightclub scene frequented
by A-list jazz musicians. It was also Sin City, known for its freely
flowing liquor, its many prostitutes, and its civic corruption.

Toronto was small and provincial by comparison: Protestant-
dominated, repressed, and stiff with "blue laws" that dictated such
things as who could drink what and when (almost nobody, almost
nowhere). Ottawa, although the capital of the country, was thought
to be even duller than Toronto. Vancouver then was a smallish port,
as was Halifax. Winnipeg had made its bid for glory toward the end

of the nineteenth century—the completion of the trans-Canadian railway made it a staging point for Western products such as wheat and cattle—but the glory had not lasted. Calgary and Edmonton were still small bumps on the railway. But Montreal was in full bloom, even though it was a festering lily rather than a spotless rose.

And there was Gabrielle Roy, inspecting it with a critical outsider's eye. She had to work hard to make a living, as she was a freelancer, not an employee of a newspaper like Mavis Gallant, who was working for the *Montreal Standard* at points during this period. In the war years of the early 1940s, Roy wrote for several periodicals, including *Le Jour* and *La Revue moderne*. She also wrote for *Le Bulletin des agricultures,* which, notwithstanding its title and rural readership, was a general-interest magazine. For it she wrote several long series of what we would now call "investigative journalism." For these various magazines she was also writing "reportages"— non-fiction about current events—as well as descriptive pieces, which could contain impressions as well as observations. In addition, she was contributing essays, which would contain well-argued opinions.

These projects took Roy into the intimate life of the city, especially its seamier side. She was able to take a keen look at Montreal, especially its lowest layer, where she saw abject, dead-end misery up close. Though she herself had grown up in modest circumstances, she'd never lived in an urban slum. Her own family had experienced some belt-tightening, especially after the death of her father, but nothing compared to the hardscrabble life she was now witnessing.

Following Hugh MacLennan's 1945 novel *Two Solitudes,* it had become fashionable to think of Canada as divided into two kinds of people—francophones and anglophones—who did not communicate with each other. But Montreal contained a third solitude: the Jewish community. This last group was soon to be given in-depth literary treatment by Mordecai Richler, a teenager growing up in the Saint Urbain district while Roy was writing her first novel. And, like Richler, Roy identified yet another layer of solitude, since the extreme poverty she saw first-hand in the Saint-Henri slums just down the hill from rich and privileged Westmount was fully as isolating as ethnicity and religion. The great divide in *Bonheur d'Occasion* is not only linguistic. It's a class divide.

6. *BONHEUR D'OCCASION*, ITS APPEAL AND STRENGTHS

Bonheur d'Occasion was a novel that made radical departures from tradition while weaving in other strands familiar to readers in both French and English. It challenged received opinions, including patriotism, religious piety, the position of women, and the expectations of what was still called, unselfconsciously, "the working class."

The book was ahead of its time, but not so far ahead that it left its readers behind. It was unsparing in its observations, but not overly judgmental about its characters. It described hard times and hard people, but it allowed the occasional dollop of empathy to soften its gaze.

The title, *Bonheur d'Occasion,* has several layers of meaning in French: *bonheur* is "happiness," but though *d'occasion* can mean "used" or "second-hand," it can also mean "bargain," "chance," or "opportunity." So, a shopworn happiness that is also a happy chance. This describes the determining events in the lives of the novel's main characters, who snatch at whatever small, tawdry opportunities fate makes available to them.

The English publishers wisely concluded that they couldn't cram all of these meanings into a snappy title. They fell back on *The Tin Flute,* which points to a significant object in the novel: the tin flute is a toy passionately desired by little Daniel Lacasse, which, although cheap, is nonetheless too expensive for his impoverished mother. He finally gets his longed-for flute only when he's dying in the hospital of what is described as "leukemia," but by then he's no longer interested in it. And so it goes, for quite a few of the characters in this densely populated book.

All novels come from their own time. For *Bonheur d'Occasion,* this is wartime. Money is chinking, but it's not chinking for everyone: the effects of the Great Depression are still being felt, and many lives have been warped by it.

Roy rarely names her characters without having a semi-hidden meaning in mind. You'll be told by name-tracing ancestry sites that the name Lacasse—the family at the novel's core—comes from a Gaulish word for "oak," that sturdy and useful tree, and may also refer to a box-maker. But *casser* is the verb "to break." The Lacasse family contains some oaks at least sturdy enough to survive despite what they've been through, but they're nonetheless trapped in a box. They're also broken: they limp rather than sprint. Even so, they're losing ground.

The father of the twelve Lacasse children—eleven when the book opens, ten when one of them dies, but eleven again when another one is born—is named Azarius. This isn't a common name, even in the French Canada of that time. It's the name of a sedative herb, but it's also the name of a Biblical character. In the French version of the Bible, Azariah is the name given to one of three youths put into the fiery furnace in the Book of Daniel.

In English translations, the Prayer of Azaraiah is omitted as apocryphal, but it appears in Catholic versions after Daniel 3:23. Part of it goes like this: "And thou didst deliver us into the hands of lawless enemies, most hateful forsakers of God, and to an unjust king, and the most wicked in all the world. And now we cannot open our mouths, we are become a shame and a reproach to thy servants; and to them that worship thee. Yet deliver us not up wholly."

Gabrielle Roy's character names have a tendency toward irony, so Azarius Lacasse is no Biblical hero. Instead, he's an impractical dreamer who goes from one job to another, always with the idea that he's going to make it big with some new scheme. He spends a lot of time shooting the breeze with other men from Saint-Henri, coming in late, and getting fired. As his eldest daughter, Florentine, puts it, he never has much luck.

But if I'm right about the derivation of his name, we see the head of the Lacasse family undergoing an ordeal by fire at the hands of a wicked and unjust king. In the context of the novel, the unjust king would be Montreal's wealthy and powerful—the manipulators of the social system who, in wartime, ask everything from the men of Saint-Henri, including their lives, but deal out only injustice and inequality in return. One Saint-Henri man who has enlisted in the army puts the case. Finding himself in Westmount, home of the wealthy English, he muses:

Looking up toward the high fences, the winding gravel walks, the sumptuous facades of the houses, he wondered: *Do they give all they have to give?*

The rich, polished stone glittered like steel, hard, indecipherable. And suddenly he felt the enormity of his presumption and of his innocence. . . . "Nothing on earth is to be had cheaper than your life. We others, stone, iron, steel, silver and gold, we're the things that cost dear."

If these unjust kings require their arms, legs, and lives from the men of Saint-Henri, what do they require of the women? In a word: babies. Not just any babies: babies born in wedlock, since society had no great wish to support orphanages.

In Quebec, this was the age of la revanche de berceaux—the revenge of the cradles. The term originated in Quebec before the First World War, the theory being that if French Canada could succeed in breeding faster than the English, they could out-populate them and thus avenge the fall of New France and the subsequent anglophone domination. Thus motherhood—especially prolific motherhood— was officially promoted and idealized, whipped on by both the Church and the civic authorities in Quebec. Families of ten, twelve, fourteen or more children were praised, and their mothers were seen to be doing their duty to the francophone Catholic community.

Those who paid with their bodies, their health, and the health of their children were the women of the fertile poor—the rural poor, who got a fictional going-over somewhat later by Marie-Claire Blais in her 1965 novel *Une Saison dans la Vie d'Emmanuel*, but especially the urban poor, who lived in slum conditions even more crowded than those on bare-bones farms. Babies were born with minimal care and ceremony: public health care had not yet been instituted, and hospitals were dreaded—partly because of the expense, but also because of the humiliation. While hospitals might waive their fees for the poor, such patients were looked down on as charity cases. In Saint-Henri, babies were more likely to be delivered by midwives at home than in hospitals by doctors.

In this, as in much else, the family's mother, Rose-Anna Lacasse, is typical: she avoids hospitals. Rose-Anna is a maternal name, for

Rose is the *rosa mystica,* a term for the Virgin Mary, and Anna is Saint Anne, mother of the Virgin. Rose-Anna's entire life is centered on her family. She wears herself out slaving to put food on the table and keep a roof over the head of her brood, though the family is always hanging by a thread. They live packed in like sardines, barely making ends meet, and are kicked from one substandard dwelling to another—dwellings sought out by Rose-Anna.

Rose-Anna doesn't get much thanks for her efforts: she's exploited by the older children, especially the mooching oldest son, Eugène, and also resented by them when she asks them to contribute to the family's expenses.

Every once in a while, Rose-Anna breaks down and delivers an outpouring of misery: The family is falling apart, there's nowhere she can turn, what can be done? She can't pay enough attention to the younger children because there are simply too many of them. When she finally takes little Daniel to the hospital because of the big purple bruises on his legs, the doctor upbraids her with a lecture about malnutrition. No wonder the pre-adolescent daughter Yvonne says, when asked if she's looking forward to growing older and getting married, that, on the contrary, she intends to be a nun. A religious vocation was almost the only alternative to a life of constant childbearing—unless, of course, you could afford to go to Normal School and become a schoolteacher.

The novel's other main female character is Rose-Anna's eldest child, Florentine. Again, she is not named thoughtlessly. That word's primary meaning is "blossoming," and Florentine is indeed a pretty girl of nineteen. But a florentine is also a flat, brittle pastry, and these adjectives describe Florentine's shape and manner: she's very thin, and she puts up a haughty, dismissive front to disguise her fear and insecurity.

A Florentine is also an inhabitant of Florence, which suggests Savonarola's famous "Bonfire of the Vanities," and Florentine's main characteristic is her shallow vanity. She exists by reflection: her own reflection in mirrors, and the reflection of herself in the eyes of other people. She works at the lunch counter of the "five and dime," and although she gives some of her earnings to her mother, she uses the rest to buy adornments: cheap makeup, cheap perfume, cheap trinkets. Her daydreams involve leading men on and then rejecting them, but she tries this once too often and finds herself falling in love; although it's a love that's mixed with pride and avarice, because what she really wants is to conquer and possess.

As in *Wuthering Heights,* and indeed as in the *True Romance* magazines popular in the 1940s, she has two suitors. One of them is cast in the Linton mould—a cut above Florentine socially, idealistic, and a nice guy, but not a man to whom she is drawn sexually. The other is a quasi-Byronic, cynical, passion-inspiring no-goodnik, like Heathcliff. Here the plots diverge, for in *Wuthering Heights* the no-goodnik is devoted to the heroine, while in *Bonheur d'Occasion* he has his way with her and then skips town.

Florentine finds that her first slip from virtue—which is described more like a semi-rape—has left her pregnant. The man involved is suggestively named: Jean Lévesque. In Quebec, the name Jean is always in reference to John the Baptist—a hermit and a Herodias-denouncing misogynist. The name Lévesque is "bishop." As we are told by another character, Jean doesn't like women much. So, no hope from him, even if Florentine could locate him; which, humiliatingly, she can't.

Terror is the word used by Roy to describe Florentine's state of mind when she discovers her condition. She's frantic: disgrace and ruin are staring her in the face. Should her pregnancy become known, her family's last shreds of self-respect would be destroyed. And where could she turn? There was no social support for unmarried mothers at that time. It would be almost impossible for her to get a (highly illegal) abortion; indeed, the thought doesn't even cross Florentine's mind.

Pregnant girls might be packed off to a "home for unwed mothers," usually run by a church; the neighbours would be told they'd gone to visit an aunt, but everyone knew what that meant. Their babies would be removed from them at birth, and either offered for adoption or placed in an orphanage. The consequent loss of respectability would affect a girl's ability to get a job, and she might even end up as a low-rent prostitute of the kind that some of the novel's men are in the habit of frequenting. No wonder Florentine is distraught.

Seduced and abandoned, sometimes pregnant, sometimes not, the list of such fictional girls in nineteenth-century novels is long, as is the list of consequences: poorhouses, madness, prostitution, starvation, suicide. Such women had to be punished. Even if a girl had not actually "fallen" but had been trapped in compromising circumstances, the result would be the same: Maggie Tulliver in George Eliot's *The Mill on the Floss* is just as "ruined" as Tess of the d'Urbervilles, and so is Lily Bart in Edith Wharton's *The House of Mirth*.

But tough little Florentine has a strong will to survive and devises a solution for herself. Without telling anyone of her plight, she goes after her other suitor—nice but not sexy—and hooks him into marriage, even though she doesn't love him. Tellingly, her saviour is called Emmanuel. He's in the army and about to go overseas, so she acquires not only a father for the child, but a war-wife allowance that will enable her to live in relative comfort. Salvation comes to her through the war. Her happiness may be second-rate, but at least it's something. And she buys a new coat.

One of Roy's accomplishments in *Bonheur d'Occasion* is her rejection of received pieties. Not for her the noble, good-hearted peasant: Rose-Anna's mother, who still lives the rural life, is a cold-hearted, criticizing monster, although generous with food. Not for Roy, either, the virtuous poor: these people are too hard-pressed for virtue. (At one moment, when Rose-Anna is praying and might, in another, earlier novel, have had a vision of a saint, she has instead a vision of a huge roll of dollar bills.) Rose-Anna's dogged perseverance is amazing, but she's also a dreary pain in the neck.

The only character who might be called morally virtuous is the modestly middle-class Emmanuel. But he's deluded by his own idealism, especially when it comes to Florentine. He makes her acquaintance only because he's slumming: the poor sap is afflicted with a social conscience, which leads him to hang out with the no-hopers of Saint-Henri, and to marry down. Not unsurprisingly, his own family is not pleased by the match.

Roy's refusal to buy into earlier views of "the poor" while at the same time suggesting that they were owed a better deal was certainly part of the novel's success. And its moment of publication was propitious: the war was ending, and those who had survived it were ready to consider a fairer distribution of wealth.

But perhaps the biggest contribution that *Bonheur d'Occasion* made to its society was in the area of women's rights. Roy doesn't use the language of feminism; in fact, first-wave get-the-vote feminism was by that time outmoded, and the language of the sexually liberated second wave had not yet been invented. So Roy must show rather than tell, and what she shows is a situation that is both cruel and unjust. How can a human being be expected to give birth to, feed, and support so many children, with almost no help at all? Quebeckers took a good look at the province's own policies through the eyes of Roy, as did hundreds of thousands of readers outside Quebec, and they were appalled.

Even before the second wave of feminism got under way in English North America, it was already under way, in a different form, in Quebec. The Quiet Revolution of the 1960s broke the grip of the Church on women's reproduction. The daughters of the dozen-child families refused to emulate their mothers. It's no accident that the feminist movement in Quebec was earlier, stronger, and more vociferous than anywhere else in North America: there was more to react against. From having had the highest birth rate on the continent, Quebec moved within decades to having the lowest. This has caused other problems, but that's another story.

7. SECOND NOVEL SYNDROME

It's not always a blessing for a writer to have an astonishing success with a first novel: expectations for the second one can be paralyzing. And when a novel has hit the keynotes of its own time so exactly, what to do when that time has passed? By the end of the 1940s, when the excitement over *Bonheur d'Occasion* had died down, the anti-Communist reaction had set in. Roy couldn't return to the subject matter that had made her fortune. The two novels Gabrielle Roy wrote after *Bonheur d'Occasion* were both "little people" novels, but the little people were not from urban slums in Montreal.

The first was *La Petite Poule d'Eau,* the text I sweated over in 1956. (The translation was titled *Where Nests the Water-Hen,* which makes the book sound flowery and Tennysonian, which it decidedly is not.) For her setting, Roy turned to the Petite Poule d'Eau region in Manitoba, where she'd taught briefly before her European excursion.

As with *Bonheur d'Occasion,* the French title is much more appropriate. *Poule* means "hen," and invokes the Biblical hen who gathers her chickens together. It's a motherly word, and aptly describes Luzina Tousignant, its heroine. And it's *La Petite Poule d'Eau,* not *La Grande Poule d'Eau:* this world is little, not big.

Luzina, like Azarius, is an uncommon name. My guess is that Roy chose it for its component *Luz,* meaning "light." Our Lady of Light is an epithet of the Virgin Mary, and Luzina is a light-bringer, for her efforts are focused on bringing education to her very remote corner of Manitoba so that her children can pursue a better life than hers. (They do, but the price she pays is that they leave her.)

La Petite Poule de'Eau is a sweet book, mild and nostalgic in comparison with *Bonheur d'Occasion.* You can see why the Ontario curriculum-setters of the 1950s would have decided—quite apart from its social-justice views—that the first book was not healthy fare for teenagers. Florentine's unwanted pregnancy would have led to outraged letters from parents, sniggering in the classroom, and embarrassment for Madame Wiacek.

Not that *La Petite Poule d'Eau* was without its pregnancies: its yearly pregnancies. This was a terrifying prospect for the young female readers of my generation in those days before effective birth control. Would we end up dropping babies like kittens? But Luzina regards her pregnancies with equanimity, for they give her a chance to travel, expand her horizons, and go shopping in a city.

Roy's next book of this period was *Alexandre Chenevert* (1954). It too is about a little person, but he's little in so many ways that readers have to stretch to find him interesting. Roy's attempt is heroic: place a constricted individual in a constricted situation, then bombard him with the noise of postwar modernity—advertisements everywhere, constant bad news in the papers. Alexandre doesn't enjoy anything—not his marriage, nor his one vacation to the countryside, which ends with nervous boredom. To make his life complete, he then gets cancer and dies a painful death. Only at the end of the book does he have a vision of human sympathy.

I tried hard with *Alexandre Chenevert*. Perhaps I could connect it with Tolstoy's *The Death of Ivan Ilych*, but it would suffer by comparison. Or I could tie it in with Marshall McLuhan—the global village, of which Alexandre is unwillingly a part, and the interest in advertisements, explored earlier and more humorously in McLuhan's 1951 book, *The Mechanical Bride*. But finally, after pausing to applaud the attempt, the empathy, the writing, the closely observed detail, I must turn briskly to the next stage of Roy's career. It is a lot more compelling, for it concerns the formation and role of the artist.

8. PORTRAITS OF THE ARTIST

Over the eleven years between 1955 and 1966, Roy published three books that explore the process of becoming an artist: *Rue Deschambault* (1955), translated as *Street of Riches; La Montagne Secrète* (1961), translated as *The Hidden Mountain;* and *La Route d'Altamont* (1966), translated as *The Road Past Altamont.*

The second book of this trio—*La Montagne Secrète*—is about the spiritual growth of a trapper and self-taught painter, Pierre Cadorai, whose subject and milieu is the boreal forest of Canada. The model was the Swiss-born painter René Richard, who, like Roy, had spent time on the prairies and also in the North, and who became her friend when he was already an established artist and she an established writer. It's perhaps not much of a leap to suggest that the admirable and adventurous coureur de bois figure of earlier francophone Canadian literature, seeker and capturer of beavers, has morphed into the admirable and adventurous artist figure, seeker and capturer of beauty, that Roy depicts.

Again, the book is of its time: Farley Mowat, with *People of the Deer* (1952), had already kicked off a new look at the northern and natural themes that had preoccupied earlier generations of writers and painters. But Roy was less fascinated with the North, as such, than with the aesthetic and mystical experiences that her hero experiences in these surroundings—and the process by which his experiences are transformed into art.

The two books flanking *The Hidden Mountain* belong to a noteworthy literary family that we might call "Portrait of the Artist as a

Young Girl." This motif is opened in *Street of Riches* and expanded somewhat—though obliquely—in *The Road Past Altamont,* as Roy picks up the thread of journey-as-story and the transmission of narrative gifts from one person, and generation, to another.

These books are part of a larger tradition: the female writer as her own subject. Women had been writing for some time, but it was only with the popularity of the *Bildungsroman*—the novel of formation or education—that they began to write fictions about the formative years of female writers. (None of Jane Austen's heroines is a writer, for instance. Nor are any of George Eliot's.)

Frequently, but not always, these semi-autobiographical fictions are disguised as "girls' books." The grandmother of these artistic literary girls may well be Jo, of *Little Women* fame (1868). And one of her granddaughters is certainly Sybylla Melvyn of the Australian Miles Franklin's novel *My Brilliant Career* (1901). Another is L.M. Montgomery's Emily, of the Emily of New Moon series (1923). Emily, in turn, was an inspiration to Alice Munro, who produced her own version of the genesis of a female writer, *The Lives of Girls and Women.* Margaret Laurence's variations can be found in her story collection, *A Bird in the House* (1970), and again in *The Diviners* (1974). Mavis Gallant's account of her own formation is perhaps most compactly contained in her Linnet Muir stories. In francophone Canada, the female writer perhaps most occupied with the process of becoming a female writer has been Marie-Claire Blais.

Why so many in Canada? Three possible factors may have encouraged artistically inclined young Canadian women to try their hand at writing in the first half of the twentieth century. One was the narrow range of other options. School teaching, secretarial work, nursing, home economics in its various forms, or dressmaking: that was about it. (Some jobs were opening up in journalism, though not on the news desks.) Another factor was the closeness of much of Canada to frontier conditions, and the resulting attitudes toward artistic pursuits. Men should handle practicalities: farming, fishing, engineering, prospecting, logging, medicine, the law. Art—flower painting, amateur acting, or a dabbling in verse—was an acceptable hobby for women, as long as they weren't serious about it. And writing was something you could do at home in your spare time.

But the third factor was the presence of women writers, in the world but also in Canada, who were already both successful and visible. In England, there were Virginia Woolf and Katherine Mansfield; in the United States, Edith Wharton, Margaret Mitchell, Katherine Anne Porter, Clare Boothe Luce, and Pearl S. Buck, this last a winner of the Nobel Prize. In Canada, L.M. Montgomery and Mazo de la Roche. And in France, Colette—a national institution, and frequently the subject of her own writing. Writing might not have been actively encouraged for girls, but it was not seen as completely impossible for them because many other women had succeeded at it.

The writerly coming-of-age stories in *Rue Deschambault* are set in the second and third decades of the twentieth century, when Roy was a young child, then an older child, and then a teenager. On the surface of it, the stories—at least the ones in the first part of the collection—aren't about writing at all, but about various incidents that take place in and around the family house in Saint Boniface, where the semi-autobiographical protagonist "Christine" is growing up.

The street is heterogeneous: There are two African-Canadian boarders, an Italian immigrant family, a woebegone Dutch suitor. Then there are the incoming settlers Christine's father is helping: Doukhobors and Ruthenians. This is far from being a tightly enclosed francophone community. Instead it is—like the book itself—loosely structured, shifting, multilingual, and filled with stories both happy and tragic. This is multiculturalism at its most generous.

Toward the end of the book, in a story called "The Voice of the Pools," young Christine, now sixteen, climbs up to the attic room where she has done so much reading and looks out the window. In this fictionalized version (for Roy proposed several others over the years), this is the moment at which the writerly vocation strikes.

> I then saw, not what I should later become, but that I must set
> forth on my way to becoming it. It seemed to me that I was
> at once in the attic and also far away—in the loneliness of the
> future; and that from yonder, committed at so great a distance,
> I was showing myself the road. . . . And so I had the idea of
> writing. What and why I knew not at all. I would write. It

was like a sudden love. . . . Having as yet nothing to say. . . .
I wanted to have something to say.

She announces this discovery to her long-suffering mother, who
reacts the way you might expect: "Maman seemed upset."

As *mamans* are. But this Maman goes on to say quite a mouthful:

"Writing," she told me sadly, "is hard. It must be the most
exacting business in the world . . . if it is to be true, you
understand! Is it not like cutting yourself in two . . . one half
trying to live, the other watching, weighing?"

And she went on: "First the gift is needed; if you have not
that, it's heartbreak; but if you have it, it's perhaps equally
terrible. . . . For we say the gift; but perhaps it would be better
to say the command. And here is a very strange gift . . . not
wholly human. I think other people never forgive it. This gift
is a little like a stroke of ill luck which withdraws others, which
cuts us off from almost everyone . . ."

Ah, the poète maudit, doomed by the poisonous gift. It was indeed
the age, if not of the doomed writer, then at least of the consecrated
one: the priest of art, forging the uncreated conscience of his race,
like Joyce's Stephen Dedalus. If you were a woman artist, so much
the worse: no helpful wife for you, you'd be on your own. Maman
doesn't include gender in her response, and neither does Christine;
but considering the time of writing, that's what would have been
hovering unsaid.

However, young Christine isn't buying Maman's warning wholesale.

I still hoped that I could have everything: both a warm
and true life, like a shelter . . . and also time to capture its
reverberations . . . time to withhold myself a little along the
road, and then to catch up with the others, to rejoin them and
cry joyously, "Here I am, and here is what I've found for you
along the way! . . . Have you waited for me? . . . Aren't you
waiting for me? . . . Oh, do wait for me!"

It's not a certainty, this pleasant dual future. Or not in the story. Though Gabrielle Roy did manage to have it all, after a fashion, in her life.

9. GABRIELLE ROY: MESSENGER OF THE FUTURE

Gabrielle Roy took the names of her characters seriously, so let me conclude with a small riff on her own name. Roy is a king: it sets the standard high. But Gabrielle comes from the Archangel Gabriel, messenger of messengers. Gabriel delivers "good" messages—to the Virgin Mary, the news that she's going to have an unexpected baby, but not just any old baby—and also "bad" messages—here comes the end of the world.

What is the role of the writer? Every age, and indeed every writer, has something different in mind. For Roy, in *Bonheur d'Occasion*, it was the annunciation of the future to the present. It's pleasing to think of her turning up at Rose-Anna's moment of worst despair and saying, "The future is going to be better."

In her other books, there's a different mission. She opens the curtains on windows people did not suspect were there—a remote corner of Manitoba, the ordinary life of an ordinary man, the lost but teeming past of her natal province, the many journeys of an artist—and asks readers to look through. Then—whatever the smallness, harshness, or oddness of the view—to understand, and then to empathize. For the Angel Gabriel is above all the angel of communication, and communication was a skill Roy valued highly.

The 2004 Canadian twenty-dollar bill has a quotation from Gabrielle Roy on the back, in both French and English: "Nous connaitrons-nous seulement un peu nous-memes sans les arts?" "Could we ever know each other in the slightest without the arts?"

No, we could not. As we contemplate our politically splintered society, as we reach the limits of data-collecting and the divisions and specializations of science, and as we finally turn back toward a more holistic view of human being, Roy's vision has more relevance to us than ever.

Shakespeare and Me

>>><<<

A TEMPESTUOUS LOVE STORY

(2016)

Whenever people ask me that daunting question, "Who's your favourite author?" I always say "Shakespeare." There are some foxy reasons for that: first, nobody can really argue with it, at least within the English-language category. So much of what we know about plots, characters, the stage, fairies, and inventive swear words comes from Shakespeare. Second, if you name a living author, the other living authors will be mad at you because it isn't them, but Shakespeare is dead. True, the other dead authors may be mad at you too, but even they probably won't cavil much about Shakespeare being your number one choice. Third, Shakespeare's ambiguous. Not only do we know very little if anything about what he really thought, felt, and believed, but the plays themselves are slippery as eels. Just when you think you've got it cornered, your cherished interpretation slips out through an unseen loophole and you're left scratching your head.

For that reason, Shakespeare is infinitely interpretable—and he has indeed been infinitely interpreted. We've had a fascist *Richard III*, we've had a Canadian First Nations *Macbeth*, we've had a *Tempest* set in the Arctic, we've had another *Tempest* with a female Prospero called Prospera, starring Helen Mirren. In the eighteenth century, they much preferred a *King Lear* in which Cordelia doesn't die and everything comes out all right. They also had a *Tempest* opera then, which was the version almost always performed in that century. It used only a third of Shakespeare's original text, Caliban was given a sister called Sycorax, Miranda had a sister called Dorinda, and there was an extra young man—so Dorinda would have someone to marry. He was kept locked in a cave by Prospero because it was thought that if he ever saw a woman he would die. I'm sure we've all known guys like that.

Point being, people have been redoing Shakespeare for a long time, often with odd results.

And I too have redone Shakespeare, also with odd results. In honour of Shakespeare's anniversary—birth or death, you may ask, as I did, and the answer is "death"—we are now being given the Hogarth Shakespeare project, whereby a dozen or so authors of many different ilks were asked to choose a play by Shakespeare and revisit it in the form of a prose novel. This novel could be as tightly or as loosely based on the play as the author wished.

The play I chose is *The Tempest,* and the novel I have written is called *Hag-Seed*—which is one of the names Prospero uses when he's cursing at his enslaved so-called monster, Caliban.

Before going on to explain to you why I made a few of the choices I did when writing *Hag-Seed,* I'll tell you about some of my earlier encounters with Shakespeare. Down we go, into the dark backward and abysm of time to my youth, pre-history, which took place shortly after the last Ice Age.

In those days, female poets were called poetesses, and girls took home economics and boys took shop, though both could take Latin. That is when I went to high school—it was Leaside High School in a suburban, white-bread area of Toronto. And that is where I first encountered Shakespeare.

There was a set curriculum for all five years of all high schools in the province of Ontario, Canada. We Canadians were residing within the mindset of the British Empire—to which we had belonged for a couple of centuries—and thus, for English literature, the curriculum featured some things you most likely wouldn't be able to drag the kids through today. *Two* novels by Thomas Hardy in five years? Really? Good luck with that! And *The Mill on the Floss,* a serious-business novel by George Eliot. There was a lot of nineteenth-century English literature because there was no sex in it, or not right on the page, though some of the books had some hot action in the margins. But those parts were never explained in class. You were supposed to know about them in a vague way, just as you were supposed to know that there were bad men in the shrubbery of the Toronto public parks without knowing exactly why they were bad.

We also took at least one Shakespeare play a year. Which was the first? *Julius Caesar*: simple plot, assassination, battle scenes, definitely no sex either on or off the page, and thus suitable for teenagers, in the eyes of our educators. But over the course of the years we also took *Twelfth Night, The Merchant of Venice, Hamlet.* And *Macbeth.* It seems to me that we took *Romeo and Juliet* and *A Midsummer Night's Dream* as well, but I may be confusing them with college: perhaps the powers that be were smarter than to introduce impressionable teenagers to the idea of killing yourself for young love. We had to memorize various speeches from the plays we studied and write them out on exams, punctuation-perfect; not that Shakespeare himself paid much attention to punctuation except as a way of indicating how the speeches should be delivered by the actors.

Memorizing things was once a widespread practice in schools; then it was dropped, as it was thought to be too constricting to the growing mind. But I notice it's been making a comeback, and none too soon. And it is so helpful in daily life. Who would not wish to be able to recite, in the doctor's waiting room, "Tomorrow and tomorrow and tomorrow / Creeps in this petty pace from day to day / To the last syllable of recorded time"?

And, while watching the various political shenanigans of today, it is always soothing to be able to murmur:

Why, man, he doth bestride the narrow world
Like a Colossus, and we petty men
Walk under his huge legs and peep about
To find ourselves dishonourable graves,
And wonder whether that's his hair indeed,
Or a mere semblance glued upon his head.
Men at some time are masters of their fates,
But less in this our age of data-mining.
The fault, dear Brutus, is not in our stars
But in ourselves, that we are pencil pushers,
For we're not rich enough to fund elections,

And must make do with what is foisted on us.
Alack the day, that we should see this hour!

I could go on in this vein for weeks. Once caught in the riptide of iambic pentameter, it's hard to stop.

I saw my first Shakespeare plays onstage at this very same high school. In the 1950s there was a Shakespearean theatrical enterprise in Toronto called the Earle Grey Players—a small troupe of English actors who had come to Canada in the 1940s, when the arts were not exactly a national priority, and had got marooned. They used to go around and perform in high schools. They would do whatever play was on the senior curriculum that year, which guaranteed them an attentive audience of nail-gnawing, anxiety-ridden students who would shortly be writing exams about the play in question. Mr. Earle Grey played the male leads, and Mrs. Earle Grey played the female ones: Gertrude, Calpurnia, Lady Macbeth. If you were a theatrically inclined youngster, you could be an extra in the play— a crowd member, a soldier—but you had to bring your own costume: a plaid throw rug for *Macbeth,* a bedsheet for *Julius Caesar.* For most of us, this was our first experience of Shakespeare off the page—and lucky we were to have it, though we made fun of it at the time: we put on skits in which Hamlet became Omelette, and we cackled like the witches in *Macbeth* and offered one another Eye of Newt sandwiches, and other such pleasantries typical of the youthful mind at play.

Of course I had to put the Earle Grey Players into a novel. There they are in *Cat's Eye* (1989), Chapter 44. They're doing *Macbeth.* I felt they needed to be immortalized, partly because I love semi-amateur theatricals. They are a good test of Shakespeare's viability as a playwright: he can withstand almost any performance, even when Macbeth's head (being a cabbage wrapped up in a tea towel) bounces into the orchestra pit, as I saw it do once. The reason it bounced was that the props person noticed that the cabbage they'd been using for Macbeth's head was getting stale and soft, so she replaced it with a new, hard, bouncy cabbage. But the cabbage was supposed to be soft, so that it would land with a satisfying thunk and then stay in place. I put that episode (of course) into *Cat's Eye* as well. Why make things up when life offers itself to you so bounteously?

In the same decade—the 1950s—the Stratford Shakespearean Festival was just beginning in the propitiously named town of Stratford, Ontario, which even has a river called the Avon. Its creation was at first resisted by the town leaders—they seemed to think it would be lowering to the general tone of the place, which was renowned at that time as a major train-switching centre and important hub of the pig-farming industry. You wouldn't want a lot of raffish artsy-fartsy types cluttering up the place. But artistic instincts prevailed, and the festival is now a major source of income for the town; though pigs are still important too. If there are any fans of the highly-recommended-by-me three-season TV series *Slings and Arrows,* you may recognize the pig-truck motif. Not that the fictional Burbage Festival is in any way the equivalent of the real Stratford Festival, but just sayin'.

We try to go to the real Stratford Festival every year. I've seen some of the best Shakespeare productions ever at it. A highlight was Christopher Plummer as Prospero in *The Tempest,* though *King Lear* starring Colm Feore was equally good.

The festival has been running now for sixty-three years, which seems incredible. The first director was Tyrone Guthrie, the first plays were put on in a giant tent, and the initial offering was *Richard III,* starring Alec Guinness, back in 1953. What I would give now to have seen that production! But alas, I was only thirteen, and obsessing over felt circle skirts with telephones embroidered on them and lipsticks called Fire and Ice. Such things as *Richard III* were as yet far beyond me.

Shortly after that, *Othello* was staged, also in the big tent. I didn't see that one either, but my spouse, Graeme Gibson—then about nineteen—was there with his grandfather, who was in his nineties and quite deaf. As Othello tiptoed toward the sleeping Desdemona, hands outstretched in pre-strangling position, Graeme's grandfather said—in what he thought was a whisper but which was actually a sonic boom—**"This is where he does her in."**

The tent quivered. Othello paused in mid-tiptoe. Under the coverlet, Desdemona shook visibly. Then Othello mastered the situation and himself, and carried on strangling. Now that's acting!

Shakespeare pops up here and there in my work over the years. Not only in *Cat's Eye*. There's a shorter piece called "Gertrude Talks Back," in which poor Gertrude gets to reply to Hamlet's scolding of her in the famous "Look on this picture" scene. Turns out it isn't that easy being the mother of a sulky teenage son, especially one with so many unwashed black socks; or the wife of a sanctimonious husband either. And Horatio gets a prolonged afterlife in a piece called "Horatio's Version." These are to be found in the collections *Good Bones* and *The Tent*.

And Richard III comes roaring back in my recent short fiction collection, *Stone Mattress*. The story is "Revenant"; the central character is Gavin, a dashing young poet in the 1960s, now a crabby elderly one married to Reynolds, a much younger woman.

I love Richard III as a character. He's a classic trickster figure who shares his murderous japes and pranks with us, the audience—just how closely he shared them can be seen if you go to the Globe Theatre reconstruction in London and realize that the audience was near enough to the actors so that they were talking to YOU, face to face, eyeball to eyeball. Like all tricksters, Richard is too clever for his own good. As indeed is Gavin. I love Gavin too: he's unpleasant, but he's still alive and kicking, and raging against the dying of the light; and as John Keats remarked, Shakespeare got as much pleasure from creating an Iago—a very bad person—as he did from creating an Imogen—a very good person. And so do I. People who object to works of literature because the characters in them are not people you would want to marry or have for a room-mate have entirely missed the point.

Here are Gavin and Reynolds going to a production of *Richard III*—an outdoor production, in a park—Reynolds with optimism and practicality, Gavin with grumpiness:

> The park was pullulating with activity. Kids played Frisbee in the background, babies yowled, dogs barked. Gavin pored over the program notes. Pretentious crap, as usual. The play was late starting: some spasm in the lighting system, they were told. The mosquitoes were gathering; Gavin swatted at them;

Reynolds produced the Deep Woods Off. Some fool in a scarlet unitard and pig's ears blew a trumpet to get them all to shut up, and after a minor explosion and a figure in a ruff sprinting off in the direction of the refreshment kiosk—in search of what? What had they forgotten?—the play began.

There was a prelude showing a film clip of Richard the Third's skeleton being dug up from underneath a parking lot—an event that had in fact taken place, Gavin saw it on the television news. It was Richard all right, complete with DNA evidence and many injuries to the skull. The prelude was projected onto a piece of white fabric that looked like a bedsheet, and probably was one—arts budgets being what they were, as Gavin commented to Reynolds, sotto voce. Reynolds dug him with her elbow. "Your voice is louder than you think," she whispered.

The sound track led them to understand—over a crackling loudspeaker and in lousy iambic pentameter Elizabethan pastiche—that the entire drama they were about to see was unfolding post mortem from inside Richard's battered skull. Zoom to a hole in the skull, and then right on through it to the inside of the cranium. And blackout.

Whereupon the bedsheet was whisked away and there was Richard in the floodlights, all set to caper and posture, to flounce and denounce. On his back was a preposterously large hump, decorated in a jester's red and yellow stripes. . . . The largeness of the hump was deliberate: the inner core of the play ("As opposed to the outer core," Gavin had snorted to himself) was all about the props. These were symbols of Richard's unconscious, which accounted for their enlargement. The director's thinking must have been that if the audience members were staring at outsized thrones and humps and whatnot and wondering what the fuck they were doing in this play, it wouldn't bother them so much that they couldn't hear the words.

So in addition to his gigantic, varicoloured, metonymous hump, Richard had a kingly robe with a sixteen-foot-long train attached to it, carried by two pageboys wearing outsized

boar's heads because Richard's coat of arms had a boar on it.
There was a huge butt of malmsey for Clarence to be drowned
in, and a couple of swords that were as tall as the actors.
For the smothering of the princes in the Tower, performed
in dumbshow like the play within the play in *Hamlet,* two
enormous pillows were borne in on stretchers like corpses or
roasted suckling pigs, with pillowcases that matched the motley
of Richard's hump, just in case the audience missed the point.

I've never seen exactly that production, but if it were on offer I'd go like a shot.

Now, finally, my contribution to the Hogarth Shakespeare project. Jo Nesbø is doing *Macbeth,* Jeanette Winterson has done *The Winter's Tale,* Anne Tyler has taken on *The Taming of the Shrew,* and Howard Jacobson has tackled *The Merchant of Venice.* And I grabbed *The Tempest.* It was my first choice, by miles.

Having grabbed it, I had misgivings. Revisiting a Shakespeare play in the form of a novel is a daunting challenge: Shakespeare is a giant, and without question has made the greatest contribution to the English language, to theatre, and to English literature of any writer, ever. He is also mercurial, many-layered, universal in his empathies, slippery as an eel, and a notorious shape-shifter, taking on fresh forms and variations and interpretations with every new production and in every new age. Grasping Shakespeare is like nailing jelly to a wall. As for rewriting Shakespeare: What sacrilege! Anyone attempting *that* is bound to get a load of buckshot in the nether regions from outraged Shakespeare purists.

Nonetheless, it would not be Shakespearean not to try—Shakespeare himself having been a well-known re-formulator of previous stories and plots.

I'd thought about *The Tempest* before, and written about it as well. In my book about writers and writing—called, oddly enough, *A Writer on Writing*—there's a chapter on the artist as magician and/or imposter called "Temptation: Prospero, the Wizard of Oz, Mephisto & Co." All of them are illusionists, as artists are.

Of Prospero—a good magician, more or less—like the Wizard of Oz, but not, like him, a fraud—I say, in part:

Prospero uses his arts—magic arts, arts of illusion—not just for entertainment, though he does some of that as well, but for the purposes of moral and social improvement.

That being said, it must also be said that Prospero plays God. If you don't happen to agree with him—as Caliban doesn't—you'd call him a tyrant, as Caliban does. With just a slight twist, Prospero might be the Grand Inquisitor, torturing people for their own good. You might also call him a usurper—he's stolen the island from Caliban, just as his own brother has stolen the dukedom from him; and you might call him a sorcerer, as Caliban also terms him. We—the audience—are inclined to give him the benefit of the doubt, and to see him as a benevolent despot. Or we are inclined most of the time. But Caliban is not without insight:

Without his arc, Prospero would be unable to rule. It's this that gives him his power. As Caliban points out, minus his books he's nothing. So an element of fraud is present in this magician figure, right from the beginning: altogether, he's an ambiguous gentleman. Well, of course he's ambiguous—he's an artist, after all. At the end of the play Prospero speaks the Epilogue, both in his own character and in that of the actor that plays him; and also in that of the author who has created him, yet another behind-the-scenes tyrannical controller of the action. Consider the words in which Prospero, alias the actor who plays him, alias Shakespeare who wrote his lines, begs the indulgence of the audience: "As you from crimes would pardoned be, / Let your indulgence set me free." It wasn't the last time that arc and crime were ever equated. Prospero knows he's been up to something, and that something is a little guilt-making.

That epilogue has always bothered me. What does Prospero feel so guilty about?

The first thing I did when starting this project was to reread the play. Then I read it again. Then I got my hands on all the films and filmed productions of it that I could, and watched them. Then I read the footnotes in the very helpful Oxford Classics version, because there were some things I really needed to know. About food, to begin with. What, for instance, is a pig-nut?

This year being the four hundredth anniversary of Shakespeare's death, I'm sure someone will come out with a Playbook Cookbook. What did the Macbeths serve at the feast interrupted by Banquo's ghost? What were Sir John Falstaff's favourite foods? (Many. Starchy.) When Sir Toby Belch, in *Twelfth Night*, refers to "cakes and ale," what did he have in mind?

Perhaps the cakes were "Maids of Honour," a kind of Tudor cheesecake. As for the ale, it would have been made from barley, and brewed by an "ale-wife": everything was micro-brewery then.

I always like to know what the characters eat—if anything—in fiction and plays. There's quite a lot of food mentioned in *The Tempest*, though it's mostly food that would require some very creative cooking.

Caliban, whom the other characters treat as a slave or monster, has grown up on the island. He pursues a foraging lifestyle, relying on—according to him—fish, crabs, berries, pig-nuts (a kind of plant with underground nodules on it, I discovered), jays' nests—possibly for the eggs—filberts, marmosets—a sort of monkey, which one can assume he ate, though maybe he also made hats out of them—and scamels, though we aren't sure exactly what "scamels" were. So that is what the deposed Duke of Milan, Prospero, and his daughter, Miranda, have been eating during the twelve years they've spent on the island. It's very basic: no pepper or butter, for instance. Or bread. You can see why Prospero would want to get back to Milan as soon as possible.

There's more food in *The Tempest*, though it's a magic illusion. It's in the scene where the miscreants—Prospero's usurping brother, Antonio; Alonso, the King of Naples; and Alonso's brother, Sebastian, who wants to kill him—are accosted by "several strange shapes bringing in a banquet," who invite them to eat.

We think of a "banquet" as what the Tudors would have recognized as a "feast"—a lavish, formal sit-down affair. But as Ruth Goodman's *How to Be a Tudor* informs us, a banquet was originally more like a cocktail reception: light fare, eaten while strolling around. If you were very up-to-date, you'd carry your own little monogrammed fork for snack-spearing.

As Shakespeare's characters prepare to tuck in, the elemental spirit, Ariel, disguised as a winged harpy, appears to the sound of thunder and the banquet vanishes. Ariel berates the sinners for their misdeeds, and they are then be-spelled by Prospero and go mad.

We've all been to parties like that. You've got the smoked salmon canapé halfway to your mouth when someone from your past appears, chews you out about your awfulness, and proceeds to drive you crazy. Keep that in mind about banquets.

Meanwhile, you can amuse yourself with this question: What did Shakespeare's *Tempest* "banquet" look like? Remember: No tiny potatoes yet. Also, no tomatoes, so mini-pizzas are out. Oh, and no coffee. Sorry. You're stuck with the cakes and ale.

Having done some elementary research, I had to make a few primary decisions. Where would my novel be set? The play is about illusions, as we know. And it's about vengeance versus mercy, like so many moments in Shakespeare. But it's also about prisons. When you come to think of it, just about everyone in the play is imprisoned one way or another at some moment in time. So that is why I set it in a prison.

The Tempest is the story of a magician and former Duke of Milan, set afloat with his infant daughter, Miranda, after a coup by his treacherous brother and the King of Naples. When an auspicious star brings his enemies within his reach twelve years later, he raises an illusory tempest with the aid of the air-spirit, Ariel. His enemies, his old helper Gonzalo, and Ferdinand, son of Alonso, end up onshore and are manipulated in various magical ways by Prospero via Ariel, with the upshot that Ferdinand and Miranda fall in love and the enemies are entranced, tortured, and at length forgiven. Meanwhile, Caliban has joined two lowlifes—a drunken butler and a jester—and the three of them plan to murder Prospero, but are punished by Prospero's goblins. At the end, Ariel is set free, everyone sails off to Naples, and Prospero steps out of his own play and asks to be released from it: perhaps the most puzzling ending to any Shakespeare play.

The Tempest is fiendishly complex, with several holes in the plot and some of the most gorgeous blank verse Shakespeare ever wrote. Over time, it's had wildly varying interpretations. Is the island magical in itself? Is it a prison? Is it a place of trial? Is Prospero wise and kind, or a tetchy old crank? Is Miranda sweet and pure, or a more savvy, tougher girl who knows about wombs and abuses and vilifies Caliban? Is Caliban himself the Freudian Id? Is he bad by nature? Is he Prospero's dark shadow? Is he Natural Man? Is he a victim of colonial powers? We've had all those Calibans, and more.

The Tempest is also a musical: it has more songs and dances and music in it than any other Shakespeare play. The main musician is Ariel, but Caliban also has musical talents.

But above all, *The Tempest* is a play about a producer/director/playwright putting on a play—namely, the action that takes place on the island, complete with special effects—that contains another play, the masque of the goddesses. Of all Shakespeare's plays, this one is most obviously about plays, directing, and acting.

How to do justice to all these elements in a modern novel? Is it even possible? That's what I attempted to find out.

Hag-Seed is set in the year 2013, in Canada, in a region somewhat close to the actual Stratford Shakespeare Festival. It opens with Act 1, Scene 1 of a video of *The Tempest* that's been made in a prison and is being watched onscreen by an unseen audience inside the prison. Suddenly there are sounds of a prison riot. Lockdown!

Cut to the backstory. Twelve years earlier, Felix Phillips, artistic director of the Makeshiweg Theatre Festival, was ousted from his position by Tony, his second-in-command, and Tony's pal Sal O'Nally, a politician. Felix has been living in exile in a countryside shanty. He half believes that the spirit of his only beloved child, Miranda—who died at the age of three—is with him, and is now fifteen. To ease his solitude, he's taken a position as a drama teacher at the Fletcher Correctional Institute, and has been putting on Shakespeare plays there. (Note: Similar prison programs do in fact exist.)

When an "auspicious star"—here, a twinkly female character with a lot of influence—brings his enemies within his reach, Felix stages *The Tempest* in his prison, thereby hoping to entrap them, enchant them, and get both his revenge and his old position back. He has the aid of a young hacker inmate, who uses digital technology to great effect. As no prisoner wants to play a girl, Felix hires a real actress to play Miranda. Meanwhile, the spirit-girl Miranda, fascinated with the play, decides to join in on it.

As with *The Tempest,* at the end the action is projected into the future, as the inmate student actors submit their reports about what they think will happen to the main characters once they're aboard the ship to Naples. Hint: It's not all good.

There you have it, in a pig-nut shell.

Marie-Claire Blais

>>><<<

THE ONE WHO BLEW EVERYTHING UP

(2016)

I read my first book by Marie-Claire Blais in 1961. I was twenty-one; it was my fourth and final year at Victoria College, University of Toronto. I was in a course called "English Language and Literature," which took the student from Anglo-Saxon to T.S. Eliot, covering everything in between. At the very end, as a sort of dessert, we were allowed a course in the modern novel, and at the very end of that, as a sort of double espresso, we were given two books by Canadians: *The Double Hook* by Sheila Watson and *Mad Shadows,* which was the English-translation title of *La Belle Bête* by Marie-Claire Blais.

We didn't study Canadian literature as such in Eng Lang and Lit, so these books weren't on the course because they were specifically Canadian. I think they were chosen because of their unconventional forms. In the case of *The Double Hook,* with its terse intercut short sequences, you might say "modernist." But what label could possibly be applied to *Mad Shadows*? It escaped definition. It, too, had short sequences that were intercut, but the tone was very different. Instead of the laconic plainsong of Sheila Watson, it gave us a superheated baroque in which every emotion and every adjective was cranked up to maximum volume.

It had a cover design in which a beautiful face with something wrong with the eyes was shown with red paint or possibly blood dripping down all over it. This book didn't have love, it had LOVE LOVE LOVE! It didn't have hate, it had HATE HATE HATE! Above all, it had obsessive jealousy, intense narcissism on the part of everyone in it, and a crazed wish to destroy on the part of its female protagonist. Strong stuff for the fourth year of Eng Lang and Lit!

How to describe the plot? Now that I have seen Jean Cocteau's film *La Belle et La Bête*, I have more context for its heightened surrealism; but in any case, it was a demonic riff on the old Perrault tale *Beauty and the Beast*. In that story, Beauty is as attractive as her name, and the ugly Beast almost dies for love of her, but love finally triumphs when Beauty says she will marry the Beast. Fireworks are set off, and the Beast is transformed into a handsome prince.

No such luck in *La Belle Bête*, where beauty and beastliness are one. A beautiful but idiotic son called Patrice (from *patrician*, incorporating the root word for "father," thus allied to male privilege) and an intelligent but ugly and enraged daughter, Isabelle-Marie (incorporating the word *belle*), live with a self-regarding mother who dotes only on the son. Jealousy motivates the daughter; stupidity blinds the mother.

These people don't think: they feel, and the daughter with a white-hot intensity. The epigraph is from Baudelaire's *Les Fleurs du Mal;* the theme, insofar as there is one, is about the futility of desire, the impossibility of ever having what you long for. The doomed heroine longs to be beautiful so that other people will love her, but the closest she comes is a romance with a blind man: she can be beautiful as long as she is unseen. (Could the author have read *Frankenstein*?) But when the blind man miraculously regains his sight, he runs away from her in horror. Love does not redeem.

At the end, as in *La Belle et La Bête*, fireworks are set off, but they take the form of a fire started by Isabelle-Marie. The house burns, the mother is incinerated, the heroine heads for the train tracks— intending, we assume, to do herself in—and the beautiful boy, now ugly because his sister has stuck his head into a vat of boiling water, drowns seeking his own once-beautiful reflection; like Narcissus, it's the only thing he's ever loved.

I was fascinated by both course books, but *Mad Shadows* was especially intriguing to me because I intended to be a writer and its author was only a month and a half older than I was. Mind you, she'd written *La Belle Bête* when she was only nineteen, and it was published in French when she was twenty, so she had a head start. Thanks in part to Edmund Wilson, a highly influential American literary critic who had written rhapsodically about her, Marie-Claire

Blais leapt into international literary prominence at an age at which the rest of us were still floundering around in our apprentice work.

In those days Blais was sometimes compared with Françoise Sagan, another youthful prodigy, but the two were radically different. Sagan was of the *triste* school of modernist French writers: disenchantment set the tone. Blais on the other hand went in for enchantment. Time and again her characters would seem to be under a spell, in the grip of a compulsion, driven by forces they don't understand. For a Sagan character, sin was a recreation, but for a Blais character sin was real, and could be mortal. "Gothic sensibility," you might say; but in the work of Blais, Gothicism and realism are close to being one and the same.

She spoke from that seething, fermenting, francophone-Canadian sensibility—formed by decades of repression by the Duplessis mini-dictatorship and also by the Church with its policy of the *revanche des berceaux,* with its mandated fifteen-child families. These forces had already shaped Gabrielle Roy's *Bonheur d'Occasion,* and were shortly to manifest themselves in Anne Hébert's brilliant 1970 novel, *Kamouraska.* In one sense, *Mad Shadows* and Blais's other early novels are the last gasp of the ancien régime, but in another sense they're the first trumpet sounding the advent of the "Quiet Revolution." (It was quiet only in the sense that nobody chopped off heads. Otherwise it was quite noisy.)

As for Marie-Claire Blais, she seemed determined to blow the lid off. No cows were to be sacred. She had such a reputation for intensity in those early years that few considered that she was actually—and increasingly, as the 1960s wore on—quite funny. She was taking the piss out of received ideas and accepted tropes, and having a rollicking time with language while doing it. She simply refused to buy into any orthodoxies, and that included the orthodoxies of the separatist movement when they came along at the beginning of the 1970s. Her 1973 novel, *Un Joualonais, sa Joualonie (St. Lawrence Blues),* was her riposte to the diktat that required all proper Quebec novels to be written in joual. And it was written in joual, while at the same time slyly taking the stuffing out of the idea that only one sort of language should be permitted in a novel.

———

A stunning success with a first novel can be a problem for a writer. How to duplicate it? Where to go next? Many get frozen in their tracks, worried about a decline and bedevilled by the inevitable attacks that follow a first success, but Marie-Claire Blais seemed scarcely to pause for breath. She published books in 1960, 1962, 1963, and 1965, then in 1966, 1968 (two), 1969 (two), and 1970. That's a prodigious output, and it was just her first decade. She barely slowed down in the ensuing forty years; meanwhile she gathered literary awards like Little Red Riding Hood picking daisies.

Of the books from that first decade, I—and many others— particularly like *Une Saison dans la Vie d'Emmanuel* (*A Season in the Life of Emmanuel*).

The figure of the virtuous peasant, toiling against adversity but loyal to the land, had been a staple of Québécois literature for some time, but here again Marie-Claire Blais was bent on upsetting the apple cart and standing received tropes on their heads. Emmanuel is a newborn baby, but no Saviour he. He's dropped like a kitten, after which his mother goes out to milk the cows, and his formidable, cold, mean-hearted, heavy-handed Grandmother Antoinette takes hold of him and reads him a lecture about how disgusting newborn babies are. Not exactly your standard Nativity scene. Then in comes a horde of other children—how many? Fifteen, sixteen?—we're never quite sure—and the grandmother tosses them lumps of sugar and whacks them out of her way as if they're chickens or pigs.

There follows a romp through every violation of the pieties you can imagine. Small-minded anti-literate parents, evil clergy folk, larcenous adolescents, horrible seminaries, tubercular geniuses, suicides dangling from trees, constant hunger and cold, girls tossed out of convents and fetching up in brothels, while over all the grandmother is issuing decrees and deciding fates like Cruella de Vil. This banquet of subversion is done up in an impudent and energetic language that teeters constantly on the edge of being out of control while maintaining its own exact modulations. *A Season in the Life of Emmanuel* consolidated Marie-Claire Blais's national and international reputation, while at the same time outraging a fair number of people in Quebec.

How to sum up a career like this? It's quite simply impossible. The richness, the variety, the inventiveness, the intensity are unusual in Québécois literature, or Canadian literature, or indeed any literature. Marie-Claire Blais is *sui generis*—member of no clique, subscriber to no religion except that of art, constant explorer. "The wind bloweth where it listeth, and thou hearest the sound thereof, but canst not tell whence it cometh, and whither it goeth: so is every one that is born of the Spirit," says Jesus (John 3:8), and so it has been with Marie-Claire Blais. She has followed her spirit, and her work has been the result. It's impossible to imagine our literature without her.

Kiss of the Fur Queen

>>><<<

(2016)

Published in 1998, *Kiss of the Fur Queen* by Tomson Highway topped the best-seller list for many weeks. It was a pioneering work, as it dealt with two subjects that up to that time were not widely spoken about: the abuses, both physical and sexual, that took place at the residential schools set up for First Nations children, and gay lifestyles and identities among First Nations peoples. This novel was among the first books to tackle such long-repressed and inflammatory subjects, particularly the residential schools abuses. That story has been unfolding in the eyes of the public for over a decade now, but it may fairly be said that Tomson Highway wrote the first chapter.

Highway was no stranger to pioneering and innovation. He was early on the scene as a playwright—*The Rez Sisters* made a big splash in 1986, many other plays followed, and Highway was the artistic director of Native Earth Performing Arts from 1986 to 1992. These were risky ventures, and they cut a pathway that many others have followed.

But why did this kind of activity seem so new, so unprecedented in the 1980s? In the 1960s, there were hardly any works by First Nations poets, playwrights, or fiction writers. The painter Norval Morrisseau had become known in the 1970s, but in literature the age of John Richardson's *Wacousta* and Pauline Johnson's narrative poetry was long gone. No one had arrived to fill that gap in written work by First Nations artists, and the residential schools system—dedicated to expunging anything "Native" from the minds of the young—is certainly partly responsible. How can you write what you know if what you know is an erasure?

It was Highway's genius to tell the story of that erasure: what it was like to live through, what effects it had on those who suffered it, and how—despite that created and painful blank—older traditions, beliefs, and long-familiar figures could still make their way back to the surface of consciousness. "The return of the repressed" is a psychological term, but now—in the early twenty-first century—it might as well also be a sociological-anthropological one, as many diverse groups and communities work busily at digging up what previous generations worked so hard to bury. Those who do the first unearthings are not always thanked. More often they may be criticized—they have spoken the unspeakable, they have mentioned the unmentionable, they have violated a code of silence. Also they have brought shame, for in these situations it may be blame that attaches to the perpetrators, but it is shame that attaches to the victims. So it is with rape, and these children were raped.

Kiss of the Fur Queen—with its glancing reference to that other well-known gay work, the 1985 *Kiss of the Spider Woman*—is the semi-autobiographical account of two Cree brothers, taken from their family and sent off to the abusive priests. It was the law that children had to go to schools, and when communities did not have schools, residential schools were the only choice open to them. The brothers' names were changed and the process of forced erasure was begun. Luckily they had a guardian: the trickster deity, one of whose names is Weesageechak (from which the Grey Jay gets its northern nickname, "whiskeyjack"). This deity is genderless and can take any form it pleases. In Highway's novel, for instance, it speaks as a fox, whereas in his two "rez" plays—the second being 1989's *Dry Lips Oughta Move to Kapuskasing*—the name is Nanabush: male in one play, female in another.

One of Highway's points is that the theft or obliteration of a language is also the theft or obliteration of a whole way of viewing reality, for Cree has a gender-neutral article that can be used of sentient beings, and English does not.

It has taken over twenty years for Highway's work to truly come into its time. It was well ahead of that time, but right now it is more relevant than ever.

We Hang by a Thread

>>><<<

(2016)

I am very pleased to be speaking this morning to such an enthusiastic gathering of people interested in legal education for women.

I was intending to talk to you about the trial of Grace Marks here in Toronto in 1843, as described in my novel *Alias Grace,* and about that trial in the context of legal rights for women in that century and in ours—while at the same time tossing in some of the research I did for my earlier novel *The Handmaid's Tale,* currently being shot as a TV series, with a cameo appearance by Moi. All of which would have been fun and games because we are no longer in 1843, are we? Nor are we heading toward the theocratic, woman-controlling world of *The Handmaid's Tale*—are we? But this is October 19, 2016, and the United States election is a mere twenty days away; and during the campaign we have seen an outpouring of misogyny not witnessed since the witchcraft trials of the seventeenth century, accompanied by an altogether serious online effort aimed at repealing the 19th Amendment—the amendment to the U.S. Constitution that gave women in the United States the right to vote. You have to pinch yourself to make sure you're awake.

This is a reminder to us that the hard-won rights for women and girls that many of us now take for granted could be snatched away at any moment. Culturally, those rights are very shallowly embedded—by which I mean that they haven't been around that long, historically, and that they are not fervently believed in by everyone in the culture. It seems that the male candidate for president of the United States, for one, does not believe in them. That's a pretty interesting role model for boys and men. The sexual assault statistics in that country and in our own are also telling, as are the kinds of stories from women and girls that have poured forth on Twitter under the hashtag #notokay.

As you may ask or indeed wonder, did any such thing ever happen to me, personally? Wearily I reply, Of course. Strange as it may seem, I too was once a teenage girl and then a young woman, which means I too was once a potential target—of gropers and exposure artists, in train stations and such—though, lucky me, I avoided the actual rapists, and no one ever put a date-rape drug into my drink in a bar. (Those drugs hadn't been invented yet.) But I was not always the supposedly revered elderly icon or scary witchy granny figure you see before you today. I did not always have a battalion of invisible imps and goblins to come to my aid in the form of 1.29 million Twitter followers. True, some of them are robots, and some of these robots send me tweets saying that they miss my dick and would like to chat about it, accompanying this invitation with pictures of young ladies in states of undress who are obviously not the senders of the tweets.

We hang by a thread, even in the so-called advanced West. It wouldn't take that much to roll back recent legal entitlements for women and send us right back to 1843, or even earlier. The old saying—attributed to abolitionist Wendell Phillips—is right: Eternal vigilance is the price of liberty. The Handmaids in my book are free *from* rape, narrowly defined. But they are not free *to* do very much at all, such as have a job, dress as they wish, and read. If everyone were free *to* do whatever they wanted, I'm afraid women would not fare very well, since however wonderful they are, they are usually no match for a posse of hooligans intent on gang rape, or even group grope.

How therefore do we balance freedom to and freedom from? Where is the line between you living your life—doing what you want, which today includes coming to breakfasts hosted by the Women's Legal Education and Action Fund (LEAF)—and someone else's freedom to mess you up? Historically, that is a very long story, and, as we are seeing, it is definitely To Be Continued.

Who knew this election would be fought so far below the belts? Women's belts. As usual, Canadian noses will be pressed anxiously to the window as our neighbours vote because, as the saying goes, when Washington has a cold, Canada sneezes. We'll want to know whether it's time to hide the silver, not to mention the young girls. Get some bear spray! Better still, get an old-style 1950s Playtex rubber panty-girdle! Even for—and I quote an Australian legislator—a "repulsive slug," with a grope like an octopus, that would be a challenge! One grab and the groper would sprong right off!

That said, today we are commemorating yesterday's Persons Day—the achievement of legal Personhood for at least some women in this country, a mere eighty-seven years ago. That achievement was the result of a long, long, long campaign, joined at the hip with other hard-fought campaigns—for women's right to higher education, said to be overtaxing for the weeny female brain and shrivelling to female reproductive organs; for women's right to wear bloomer suits and ride around immorally on bicycles—the end of civilization!—and for women's right to shed their constricting corsets, without which their weak spines might collapse and they would flop around on the floor like jellyfish. More materially, for women's right to own and control their own money and property once they were married, and for their right to hold jobs and earn wages.

Throughout the nineteenth century, most women in Western legal systems were adults in respect to responsibilities but minors in respect to many rights. In the case of a rare divorce—for a woman was discredited by a divorce, even if it was in no way her fault—the husband almost always got custody of the children, no matter how brutal and horrible he may have been. You were not supposed to actually murder your wife, but short of that you had almost free rein in the domestic sphere, and the wife had little recourse. The nineteenth century, with its well-known Victorian family values, was also an age of rampant prostitution and widespread child abuse, including extreme corporal punishment, deadly exploitative child labour, the drugging of infants with opiates marketed as patent medicines, and some interesting theories about child nutrition: meat would make kids too animalistic and energetic, fruit would ruin their digestive systems. They ought to be fed only white things: white bread, white milk puddings, white starches. This nutritional system was followed even in well-to-do households, not to mention boarding schools and orphanages like that of Oliver Twist. No wonder so many children of those times were pale, sickly, rickety, and too good for this world, which they frequently left early.

As for women's reproductive rights, as they are now called, they were officially non-existent. Even the use of analgesics during childbirth was preached against by many clergymen because women were supposed to suffer in childbirth: it said so in the Bible. Abortion was illegal but quite widely practised, by one means or another: unmarried women of the working classes who got pregnant and were not then supported by the man would likely find their child in an orphanage and themselves out on the street working as prostitutes. As sexually transmitted diseases were widespread, as was tuberculosis, they would probably not live long. Those girls coughing themselves to death in operas—Mimi in *La Bohème*, Violetta in *La Traviata*—had a strong basis in fact.

This is the background of my novel *Alias Grace*, which begins in the 1840s—a time of face-concealing bonnets—when a high value was put on female modesty and propriety. The novel is based on the real Grace Marks, a young Irish servant. In the summer of 1843, near what was then the small village of Richmond Hill in Upper Canada— now Ontario—two people were murdered: Thomas Kinnear, a well-off Scottish remittance gentleman in his forties, and his housekeeper and mistress Nancy Montgomery, who was twenty-three and pregnant at the time. The supposed murderers were James McDermott, Kinnear's Irish manservant—who was in his early twenties—and Grace Marks, the maid-of-all-work, who had just turned sixteen. The two of them had run away on a steamer to Lewiston in the United States, taking with them a number of valuables, but they had been followed by a friend of the murdered Kinnear and found in a hotel— though they were not sleeping in the same room—and brought back by force to Canada, where they were quickly put on trial for the murder of Kinnear. A shocking feature was that Grace appeared at the trial wearing one of the murdered woman's dresses. Well, it was a nice dress, and you wouldn't have wanted it to go to waste.

Since both of them were convicted for the murder of Kinnear—

McDermott for the actual shooting, Grace as an accomplice—the murder of Nancy Montgomery was never tried.

However, in view of the excellent character references given Grace by several of her former male employers, and in view of her youth and her plea that she had only run away with McDermott because he had threatened to kill her if she didn't, her sentence was commuted to life imprisonment. On the scaffold, just before he was hanged, James McDermott accused Grace Marks of having helped him to strangle Nancy Montgomery. After he was dead, there was only one person left who knew the truth of the matter, and she never told.

Did she or didn't she? We have never known—which was one of the reasons I was interested in Grace as the subject of a novel. In addition, the reporting on the case and the writing about it was very divided on the subject of Grace's guilt or innocence. It is often the case when a female person and a male person have been involved in a murder. Usually commentators are agreed on the subject of him—he done it—but split about her. Either she is an innocent involved against her will, threatened and coerced, or she is the instigator—a deeply evil and conniving Jezebel who egged him on, possibly with the lure of sex. Both of these versions of Grace were presented by the press, with considerable embellishments. Opinion appeared to divide along sectarian lines: For Anglican conservatives, Grace was guilty, as it was very bad form to be involved in the murder of your employer. For the Methodist political reformers, she was innocent—a put-upon and possibly feeble-minded young girl who was terrified for her own life. People, then as now, projected upon her all of their age's assumptions about women—their weakness, their potential depravity, their innate stupidity, or on the other hand their sly and devious cunning. As is usually the case, particularly with women on trial and particularly in the nineteenth century, it was a woman's entire character that was being judged, and especially her supposed sexual activity—did she or did she not sleep with McDermott? We'll never know that either. Although they couldn't agree on the colour of her hair, all commentators say that she was very good-looking. Had that not been true, the trial would probably not have attracted so much notoriety.

As for the motive, that too came in several versions. Some of the neighbours proposed that Grace was jealous of Nancy because she was in love with Mr. Kinnear, and put McDermott up to it by promising him sexual favours. Others said that, no, it was Nancy, Kinnear's mistress, who was jealous of Grace—she was older, she was pregnant, and might soon become a problem for Kinnear; whereas the young and attractive Grace was right there, possibly ready to step into her shoes. What is certainly true, however, is that neither of these women—Grace and Nancy—had very many options. They didn't have money, they didn't have a high social position, and they were entirely dependent on the whims of their employer. Had the murders not happened, Grace would have been able to get another position, most likely—there was a demand for servants—but, if dismissed by Kinnear, Nancy might not have had many choices: she was known to be his mistress, and thus would have had a poor reputation. Maybe she would have gone to the United States, where her past would not have been known.

That is where Grace ended up, after spending a quarter of a century in the Kingston Penitentiary, with a sojourn in the Toronto Lunatic Asylum. She was released in the general amnesty declared to celebrate Confederation, and crossed into the United States; we lose track of her after that, though people continued to write about her until the end of the century. She has some of the fascination of the women accused of witchcraft.

What is it about women? Why have they been so scary to men, throughout the ages? Are these frightened men like L. Frank Baum, who made his Wizard of Oz a fraud, but gave his witches real magic? Or like Rider Haggard, who created a superheroine called She who had the ability to electrocute you? Has it been a case of oppressors' guilt—knowing the wrongs you've perpetrated historically, do you fear the return of the repressed? Maybe that's why Hillary Clinton has attracted all that witch and devil imagery. Maybe we should rename her Hillary of Arc. Joan of Arc fought for her country, she was successful, but she was too strong, too uppity, and no woman could do those things on her own really, so she must have been in league with Dark Forces. Burn her at the stake!, which they did.

Time will reveal the outcome. It's almost Hallowe'en, a hinge moment when, traditionally, the doors between worlds swing open and secrets are revealed; after that comes Guy Fawkes Day, reminding us of the army of invisible hackers that lurk in the shadows. And after that comes November 8, when the fatal votes will be cast, and then will come we know not what. The repeal of the Nineteenth Amendment, perhaps; and then—who can tell because these things are catching—maybe some such unpersoning effort in Canada.

But as of today, we are still persons. Thank you to those who fought to gain that status for women. It's more agreeable to be a person than not to be one. And it's more helpful to society at large to be a person than to be merely a chattel or piece of ass. Celebrate your personhood, and while you're at it, give some thought to helping those young female people who are educating themselves in the law—all the better to defend your personhood, if push comes to shove. Or if shove comes to grope. Yes, in our country, all women are persons in title, but some women have a better shot at actualizing that personhood than others do.

PART IV

>><<

2017 TO 2019

HOW SLIPPERY IS THE SLOPE?

What Art Under Trump?

>><<

(2017)

Of what use is art? It's a question often asked in societies where money is the prime measure of worth, usually by people who do not understand art—and therefore dislike it and the artists who make it. Now, however, the question is being posed by artists themselves.

For American writers and other artists, there's a distinct chill in the air. Strongmen have a well-earned reputation for suppression and for demanding fawning tributes: "Suck up or shut up" has been their rule. During the Cold War, many writers, filmmakers, and playwrights received visits from the FBI on suspicion of "un-American activities." Will that history be repeated? Will self-censorship set in? Could we be entering an age of samizdat in the United States, with manuscripts circulating secretly because publishing them would mean inviting reprisal? That sounds extreme, but considering America's own history—and the wave of authoritarian governments sweeping the globe—it's not out of the question.

In the face of such uncertainties and fears, the creative communities of the United States are nervously urging one another not to surrender without a fight: Don't give up! Write your book! Make your art!

But what to write or make? Fifty years from now, what will be said about the art and writing of this era? The Great Depression was immortalized by John Steinbeck's *Grapes of Wrath,* which described in detail what the Dust Bowl years felt like to those living through them at the lowest level of American society. Arthur Miller's play *The Crucible* provided an apt metaphor for McCarthyism, with its witch hunts and mass accusations. Klaus Mann's 1936 novel *Mephisto,* about the rise of a famous actor, showed absolute power corrupting an artist absolutely—a fitting story during the reign of Hitler. What sorts of novels, poems, films, television series, video games, paintings, music, or graphic novels will adequately reflect America's next decade?

We don't have any idea yet. We can't: nothing is predictable except unpredictability. It's probably fair to say, however, that Donald Trump's interest in the arts, gauged on a scale from 1 to 100, is somewhere between zero and negative 10—lower than any president in the past fifty years. Some of those presidents didn't give a hoot about the arts, but at least they found it politic to pretend. Trump won't. In fact, he may not even notice they're there.

This might, in fact, work to our advantage. Stalin and Hitler took an interest in the arts and considered themselves experts and arbiters, which was very bad news for the writers and artists whose styles displeased the authorities. These got packed off to the gulag or condemned as degenerate. Hopefully, most creative people will find themselves flying under the radar, so insignificant as to escape detection.

The United States has no gulags. It prefers to express displeasure through behind-the-scenes blackballing: the screenwriter's phone doesn't ring, as it didn't for the Hollywood Ten; the musician's songs go unplayed, as Buffy Sainte-Marie's were during the Vietnam War, because of her song "Universal Soldier"; the writer's book fails to find a publisher, as was the case, for many years, with Marilyn French's *From Eve to Dawn: A History of Women in the World*. A change in the overall cultural climate may well be expected, with rewards of various kinds flowing to those willing to ride along in the wake of the incumbent powerboat, and quiet punishments meted out to those who refuse. Those reprisals may take the form of noxious POTUS tweets—like the recent one in which Trump kicked his *Celebrity Apprentice* successor, Arnold Schwarzenegger, right in the ratings—or vulgar public denunciations, like his dismissal of Meryl Streep after her Golden Globes speech implicitly criticized Trump as a bully.

And what will happen to freedom of speech, that hallmark of

American democracy? Will the very idea become a euphemism for hate speech and Internet bullying, a hammer to whack "political correctness"? That has already begun. If it intensifies, will those defending the concept of free speech then be attacked from the left as collaborators with Fascists?

Surely we can look to the artists to uphold our better values! Don't they represent the most noble features of the human spirit? Not necessarily. Creative people come in many makes and models. Some are merely paid entertainers, opportunists out to make a million bucks. Some have more sinister agendas. There's nothing inherently sacred about films and pictures and writers and books. *Mein Kampf* was a book.

Plenty of creative people in the past have rolled over for the powerful. In fact, they're especially subject to authoritarian pressures because, as isolated individuals, they're very easy to pick off. No armed militia of painters protects them; no underground mafia of screenwriters will put a horse's head in your bed if you cross them. Those under attack may be defended verbally by other artists, but such defence counts for little if a ruthless establishment is bent on their destruction. The pen is mightier than the sword, but only in retrospect: at the time of combat, those with the swords generally win. But this is America; it has a long and honourable history of resistance. And its multivoiced and multifaceted variety will itself be some defence.

There will, of course, be protest movements, and artists and writers will be urged to join them. It will be their moral duty—or so they will be told—to lend their voices to the cause. (Artists are always being lectured on their moral duty, a fate other professionals—dentists, for example—generally avoid.) But it's tricky telling creative people what to create or demanding that their art serve a high-minded agenda crafted by others. Those among them who follow such hortatory instructions are likely to produce mere propaganda or two-dimensional allegory—tedious sermonizing either way. The art galleries of the mediocre are wallpapered with good intentions.

What then? What sort of genuine artistic response might be possible? Maybe social satire. Perhaps someone will attempt the equivalent of Jonathan Swift's *A Modest Proposal,* which suggested the consumption of babies as an economic solution to Irish poverty. But satire, alas, tends to fall flat when reality exceeds even the wildest exaggerations of the imagination—as it is increasingly doing today.

Science fiction, fantasy, and speculative fiction have often been used to register protest in times of political pressure. They have told the truth, but told it slant, as Yevgeny Zamyatin did in his 1924 novel *We,* which anticipated the Soviet repressions to come. Many American writers took to science fiction in the McCarthy years because it allowed them to criticize their society without being too easily spotted by the powers intent on quashing criticism.

Some will produce "witness art," like those artists who have responded to great catastrophes: wars, earthquakes, genocides. Surely the journal-keepers are already at work, inscribing events and their responses to them, like those who kept accounts of the Black Death until they themselves succumbed to it; or like Anne Frank, writing her diary from her attic hiding place; or like Samuel Pepys, who wrote down what happened during the Great Fire of London. Works of simple witnessing can be intensely powerful, like Nawal El Saadawi's *Memoirs from the Women's Prison,* about her time behind bars in Anwar Sadat's Egypt, or Yan Lianke's *The Four Books,* which chronicles the famines and mass deaths in China during the Great Leap Forward. American artists and writers have seldom been shy about exploring the fissures and cracks in their own country. Let's hope that if democracy implodes and free speech is suppressed, someone will record the process as it unfolds.

In the short run, perhaps all we can expect from artists is only what we have always expected. As once-solid certainties crumble, it may be enough to cultivate your own artistic garden—to do what you can as well as you can for as long as you can do it; to create alternate worlds that offer both temporary escapes and moments of insight; to open windows in the given world that allow us to see outside it.

With the Trump era upon us, it's the artists and writers who can remind us, in times of crisis or panic, that each one of us is more than just a vote, a statistic. Lives may be deformed by politics—and many certainly have been—but we are not, finally, the sum of our politicians. Throughout history, it has been hope for artistic work that expresses, for this time and place, as powerfully and eloquently as possible, what it is to be human.

The Illustrated Man

>>><<<

INTRODUCTION

(2017)

What is it about horror stories, ghost tales, science fiction, fantasy, and other such wonder tales that is especially enthralling to young readers? Is it at that age that we first become aware of our inner monsters? Is it a collective nostalgia for folk tales and magic? Is it a form of psychic exorcism? Are we thumbing our noses at Death?

In the 1950s, teenage bibliophiles were not yet called "young adults," but we were mainlining weirdness all the same. Adults evidently knew about our tastes: a book-of-the-month scheme for high-schoolers, of which I was a member in 1953 when I was thirteen, served up for our first selection a classic, the now somewhat forgotten horror-thriller *Donovan's Brain*. The brain in question was nourished on brain food and kept in a large fish tank by overly optimistic scientists who'd hoped it would solve the problems of the universe. Instead, it was planning to take over the world. Worse, it had electrical powers. There were a lot of malevolent brains on the loose in those days.

Not surprisingly, considering my predilections, I came across and devoured Ray Bradbury's 1951 classic *The Illustrated Man* around this time. Did I buy it in the drugstore for twenty-five cents—what I made per hour for babysitting? Did I check it out from the library? Did I stumble upon it while babysitting? I can't remember. But I read it. The title and cover illustration would have been enough to grip me—back then, nobody you were likely to know would have had a tattoo of any kind, and the idea of someone who was tattooed all over his body—let alone tattooed with pictures that would come to life and tell their stories—was bizarre enough to merit my adolescent attention.

The early 1950s was a high point for Ray Bradbury. In the 1940s, paperback publishing had transformed reading in the United States in much the same way that e-books altered it in the early twenty-first century: by offering cheapness and convenience. A paperback cost a tenth of a hardback, and you didn't have to go into an intimidating bookstore to get one; you bought paperbacks in the drugstore, the same place you bought comic books and magazines. The paperback industry made its profits by printing and selling in volume—thus the term *mass market*—and it used lurid covers to reassure the kind of reader who might otherwise have feared a book that looked too high-falutin' and "literary." Every cover promised sex 'n' scandal, or sex 'n' death, or sex 'n' aliens, or sex 'n' horror: the attrition rate for blondes in skimpy clothing was high. Ray Bradbury never went in much for the sex part: the horror, the death, and the aliens were more his line.

The demand for paperbacks was very high, the paperback racks screamed for a flow of new materials, and paperback publishers recycled classics and literary authors with covers that made them look like true crime stories or romance novels. As a teen, I read Hemingway, Faulkner, James A. Michener, and many other highly regarded authors that way, and so did hundreds of thousands of other people.

Some literary authors flinched at appearing on this platform—they feared their art would be degraded—but not Bradbury. Although *The Illustrated Man* first appeared as a Doubleday hardback with an artistic modernist design, it was out the next year in a Bantam paperback, complete with a bulging-eyed horror-face cover. Bradbury had built his career through magazines and radio, so he understood mass-market paperback publication as a valuable means of reaching additional readers. A book might appear first as a hardback, but people like me—young people—would almost inevitably read it in paperback, as we read Huxley and Orwell and H.G. Wells, all of whom Ray Bradbury himself had read. But his first love was horror, and his own early writing was heavily weighted to the dark side, even when it wasn't about the gruesome non-dead. There aren't many happy endings in his work.

Any writer who delves as deeply into horror as Ray Bradbury did has a complex relationship with mortality, and it's not surprising to learn that Ray Bradbury as a child was worried that he would die at any moment. "When I look back now," he says in his small essay "Take Me Home," "I realize what a trial I must have been to my friends and relatives. It was one frenzy after one elation after one enthusiasm after one hysteria after another. I was always yelling and running somewhere, because I was afraid life was going to be over that very afternoon."

But the flip side of the mortality coin is immortality. At the age of twelve, Bradbury had a definitive encounter with a stage magician called Mr. Electrico, one of the sideshow acts at a travelling circus. Mr. Electrico had a unique act: he sat in an electrified chair, thus in turn electrifying a sword he held, with which he in turn electrified the spectators, making their hair stand on end and sparks come out of their ears. He electrified young Bradbury in this manner, while shouting, "Live forever!"

The boy had to go to a funeral the next day, a close encounter with real death that led him to seek out Mr. Electrico once more to find out how this *living forever* thing was to be done. The old carney showed him around what used to be called the freak show—complete with a tattooed man who was later to morph into the title figure of *The Illustrated Man*—and then told him that he, Ray, contained the soul of Mr. Electrico's best friend, who had died in the Great War. This must have made an impression on young Ray, because right after his baptism by electricity at the hands of Mr. Electrico he started writing; nor did he stop until his own death.

How do you live forever? Through other people, it seemed: those whose souls turned up in your body. And through other voices, the voices that spoke through you. And through your written words, the code for those voices. At the end of *Fahrenheit 451,* the hero finds—in a world of destroyed books—a group of people who have become the vanished books by memorizing them: a perfect embodiment for the knot of mysteries presented to young Ray by Mr. Electrico.

Right after Ray Bradbury died I was talking with a poet. "He was the first writer I read all of," said this man. "When I was twelve or thirteen. I read every single book—I sought them out. I read them cover to cover." I said I thought that a lot of writers—and a lot of readers—had had the same experience, and that they were writers and readers of the most diverse kinds: poets and prose writers and readers, of all ages and of all kinds of literature, from pulp adventure to highbrow experiment.

What accounts for Bradbury's reach? And—a difficult question, but one that critics and interviewers are always asking—where would you locate him on the categorizing map of literature, or even in bookstores, where books must now be shelved according to their "genre"?

Such distinctions would have annoyed Ray Bradbury. He was formed by the "golden age" of science fiction and wonder tales— usually thought of as the 1930s—and built his career, initially, on the main platform that existed then and for several decades thereafter: an extensive popular-magazine market for short fiction. Though he would end by appearing in the respected *New Yorker,* he began in 1938 by publishing in an amateur fan magazine, then in his own magazine, *Futura Fantasies.* Then he published in the pulps, including *Super Science Stories* and *Weird Tales.*

You could make a living that way if you wrote a lot, and if you wrote different kinds of stories, and Bradbury did manage to make a living. He wrote every day, and once vowed to write a story a week— a feat he accomplished. His income was helped along by adaptations for the comics, then by screen and TV versions. He worked his way up to the glossies, including *Playboy* and *Esquire;* he also published full-length books. Writing was both his vocation—he was called to it, and wrote intuitively—and his self-supporting career, and he was proud of both of these aspects. He ducked classification and genre corrals as much as he could: as far as he was concerned he was a taleteller, a writer of fiction, and the tales and the fiction did not need to have watertight-compartment labels.

The term *science fiction* made him nervous: he did not want to be shut up in a box. He thought of science fiction as being about things that could really happen, whereas he mostly wrote about the impossible. He, in his turn, made hard science fiction purists nervous, since he used their paraphernalia—spaceships, other planets, sleights of hand involving physics theory—for what he called "fantasy." Mars as he treats it is not a place described with scientific accuracy or even much consistency, but a state of mind, and he recycles it for whatever he needs at the moment. Spaceships are not miracles of technology but psychic conveyances, serving the same purpose as Dorothy's whirlwind-borne house in *The Wonderful Wizard of Oz,* or Ransom's unlikely flying-coffin aircraft in C.S. Lewis's *Silent Planet* trilogy, or the trance of the traditional shaman: they get you to the Otherworld.

In his best work, Bradbury sinks a taproot right down into the dark, Gothic core of America. It's no accident that he was descended from Mary Bradbury, convicted as a witch in 1692 during the notorious Salem witchcraft trials, for, among other things, assuming the form of a blue boar. (She was not hanged, since her execution was delayed until the craze was over.) The Salem trials are a seminal trope in American history, one that has repeated itself over and over in various forms—both literary and political—throughout the years. At its heart is the notion of the doubleness of life: you are not who you are but have a secret and probably evil twin. More importantly, the neighbours are not who you think they are. They might be witches, in the seventeenth century, or people who will falsely accuse you of being a witch; or traitors, in the eighteenth century, at the time of the Revolution; or Communists, in the twentieth; or people who will stone you to death, in Shirley Jackson's "The Lottery"; or terrorists, in the twenty-first century.

All who knew Bradbury testify to his enthusiasm, his openness, his generosity toward others. To the outside world he presented a combination of eager, wonder-filled boy and kindly uncle. But his imagination had surely been kidnapped in babyhood by some darker force—Edgar Allan Poe primarily, whom he read avidly at the age of eight.

Poe's "William Wilson" opposes two twinned selves, and Bradbury can almost be said to have acted them out: the bright self, all sunshine and front porches and lemonade; and the dark one, the one who could imagine a frisky dog digging up an undead corpse and leading it home to visit his master, a bedridden little boy. Bradbury is full of surprises, but they are seldom nice ones for his characters.

Who can you trust? Almost nobody. Or nobody who claims a Norman Rockwellian normality, which is bound to be a facade.

But nostalgia for the same Rockwellian normality is very real in Bradbury's work, with the detail lovingly rendered. He was born in 1920 in Waukegan, Illinois, and it is this town and this time—the 1920s and 1930s of his youth—that appears again and again in his work, sometimes on Earth, sometimes on Mars. You can't go home again, said Thomas Wolfe—another American nostalgist—but you can retrieve the past by writing about it, as Wolfe and Bradbury both did. However, in Bradbury's work the charm lasts only until midnight strikes and your hometown buddies and family members reveal themselves as Martians who are about to murder you. The shadow of the black-shrouded clock from Poe's "The Masque of the Red Death" is never far from Bradbury's world: time is the enemy.

The Illustrated Man—like Bradbury's earlier *The Martian Chronicles* (1950)—is a collection of previously published stories held together somewhat loosely by a framing conceit. In the case of *The Illustrated Man*, this conceit is the title character, a refugee from a freak show. He has been tattooed by a magic time-travelling woman who has given the pictures on his skin the ability to foretell the future, which allows Bradbury to mingle "futuristic" stories with things in them that hadn't been invented yet, like robot wives, with other stories that might take place in a very near future and contained no gizmos that did not then exist. The man's tattoos play Scheherazade to Death's murderous king: as long as the tattoos are narrating their stories, the tattooed man himself is still alive. Things don't end as well for the man as for Scheherazade, however: the last tattoo predicts the man's own death. Indeed, this is—overall—a foreboding collection.

When I try to remember which of these stories made the most impression on me as a teenager, there is one clear standout: "The Veldt." In this story—now a classic—two children, mischievously named Peter and Wendy, have been provided with a playroom that can portray on its four walls any setting the children program. Their favourite is an African veldt, with lions in the background. Their parents become concerned because the kids are coming to prefer this non-real play area to real life, and to them. They decide to put a stop to the veldt. But then—as such facsimiles tend to, in Bradbury's work—the veldt becomes conscious of their intention and finishes them off.

Of the other stories, some are slight, some more impressive, some reruns of earlier themes that still interested him, some forerunners of literary things to come, both for himself and for others. *The Stepford Wives* is surely foreshadowed by his story "Marionettes, Inc.," in which a pair of spouses, to fool and evade their partners, have robot replicas made of themselves that—needless to say—get out of control. "The Exiles" predates *Fahrenheit 451* and channels one of Bradbury's anxieties—warranted in those clamped-down, suspicious McCarthyesque days—having to do with the banning and destruction of literature. "The Visitor" echoes an earlier story, "The Martian"—in both, an individual with special talents (shape-changing, telepathy) is destroyed by the frantic desires of those who want what he has. (Is this a comment on writers and fandom? Perhaps.) "The City," like the story "The Third Expedition" in *The Martian Chronicles,* is one of those alluring traps for travelling astronauts we kids learned from Bradbury to beware, as well as being a clever use of biological warfare. "The Other Foot" is a severe look at racism in which Mars has been colonized yet again, this time by Black people who are prepared to give a very cool segregationist welcome to the last inhabitants of a destroyed Earth, who are about to arrive on Mars, and who happen to be white. In "The Fire Balloons," the Martians appear again, this time as beautiful forms of pure energy, who, lacking bodies, do not need Earth's form of missionary salvation.

Just from that sampling, you can see that Bradbury had a lot on his mind, or possibly a lot *in* his mind. His wide range of interests, his boundless curiosity, his versatility, his inventiveness, and his fascination with human nature, warts and all, are on full display in *The Illustrated Man*—as is his astonishing productivity. When we think of American writing in the second half of the twentieth century, it would be impossible not to include Ray Bradbury. Anyone writing wonder tales now—and I include dystopias, which are in a flourishing state at present—owes him a considerable debt.

Am I a Bad Feminist?

>>><<<

(2018)

It seems that I am a "Bad Feminist." I can add that to the other things I've been accused of since 1972, such as climbing to fame up a pyramid of decapitated men's heads (a lefty journal), of being a dominatrix bent on the subjugation of men (a righty one, complete with an illustration of me in leather boots and a whip), and of being an awful person who can annihilate—with her magic White Witch powers—anyone critical of her at Toronto dinner tables. I'm so scary! And now, it seems, I am conducting a War on Women, like the misogynistic, rape-enabling Bad Feminist that I am.

What would a Good Feminist look like, in the eyes of my accusers?

My fundamental position is that women are human beings, with the full range of saintly and demonic behaviours this entails, including criminal ones. They're not angels, incapable of wrongdoing. If they were, we wouldn't need a legal system for such accusations, since they would all be true.

Nor do I believe that women are children, incapable of agency or of making moral decisions. If they were, we're back to the nineteenth century, and women should not own property, have credit cards, have access to higher education, control their own reproduction, or vote. There are powerful groups in North America pushing this agenda, but they are not usually considered feminists.

Furthermore, I believe that in order to have civil and human rights for women, there have to be civil and human rights, period, including the right to fundamental justice, just as for women to have the vote, there has to be a vote. Do Good Feminists believe that only women should have such rights? Surely not. That would be to flip the coin on the old state of affairs in which only men had such rights.

So let us suppose that my Good Feminist accusers, and the Bad Feminist that is me, agree on the above points. Where do we diverge? And how did I get into such hot water with the Good Feminists?

In November of 2016, I signed—as a matter of principle, as I have signed many petitions—an Open Letter called UBC Accountable, which calls for holding the University of British Columbia account-able for its failed process in its treatment of one of its former employ-ees, Steven Galloway, the former chair of the department of creative writing, as well as its treatment of those who became ancillary com-plainants in the case. Specifically, several years ago, the university went public in national media before there was an inquiry, and even before the accused was allowed to know the details of the accusation. Before he could find them out, he had to sign a confidentiality agree-ment. The public—including me—was left with the impression that this man was a violent serial rapist, and everyone was free to attack him publicly, since under the agreement he had signed, he couldn't say anything to defend himself. A barrage of invective followed.

But then, after an inquiry by a judge that went on for months, with multiple witnesses and interviews, the judge said there had been no sexual assault, according to a statement released by Mr. Galloway through his lawyer. The employee got fired anyway. Every-one was surprised, including me. His faculty association launched a grievance, which is continuing, and until it is over, the public still cannot have access to the judge's report or her reasoning from the evidence presented. The not-guilty verdict displeased some people. They continued to attack. It was at this point that details of UBC's flawed process began to circulate, and the UBC Accountable letter came into being.

A fair-minded person would now withhold judgment as to guilt until the report and the evidence are available for us to see. We are grown-ups: we can make up our own minds, one way or the other. The signatories of the UBC Accountable letter have always taken this position. My critics have not because they have already made up their minds. Are these Good Feminists fair-minded people? If not, they are just feeding into the very old narrative that holds women to be incapable of fairness or of considered judgment, and they are giving the opponents of women yet another reason to deny them positions of decision-making in the world.

A digression: Witch talk. Another point against me is that I compared the UBC proceedings to the Salem witchcraft trials, in which a person was guilty because accused, since the rules of evidence were such that you could not be found innocent. My Good Feminist accusers take exception to this comparison. They think I was comparing them to the teenage Salem witchfinders and calling them hysterical little girls. I was alluding instead to the structure in place at the trials themselves.

There are, at present, three kinds of "witch" language. (1) Calling someone a witch, as applied lavishly to Hillary Clinton during the recent election. (2) "Witch hunt," used to imply that someone is looking for something that doesn't exist. (3) The structure of the Salem witchcraft trials, in which you were guilty because accused. I was talking about the third use.

This structure—guilty because accused—has applied in many more episodes in human history than Salem. It tends to kick in during the "Terror and Virtue" phase of revolutions—something has gone wrong, and there must be a purge, as in the French Revolution, Stalin's purges in the U.S.S.R., the Red Guard period in China, the reign of the Generals in Argentina, and the early days of the Iranian Revolution. The list is long and Left and Right have both indulged. Before "Terror and Virtue" is over, a great many have fallen by the wayside. Note that I am not saying that there are no traitors or whatever the target group may be; simply that in such times, the usual rules of evidence are bypassed.

Such things are always done in the name of ushering in a better world. Sometimes they do usher one in, for a time anyway. Sometimes they are used as an excuse for new forms of oppression. As for vigilante justice—condemnation without a trial—it begins as a response to a lack of justice—either the system is corrupt, as in pre-revolutionary France, or there isn't one, as in the Wild West—so people take things into their own hands. But understandable and temporary vigilante justice can morph into a culturally solidified lynch-mob habit, in which the available mode of justice is thrown out the window, and extra-legal power structures are put into place and maintained. The Cosa Nostra, for instance, began as a resistance to political tyranny.

The #MeToo moment is a symptom of a broken legal system. All too frequently, women and other sexual-abuse complainants couldn't get a fair hearing through institutions—including corporate structures—so they used a new tool: the Internet. Stars fell from the skies. This has been very effective, and has been seen as a massive wake-up call. But what next? The legal system can be fixed, or our society could dispose of it. Institutions, corporations, and workplaces can houseclean, or they can expect more stars to fall, and also a lot of asteroids.

If the legal system is bypassed because it is seen as ineffectual, what will take its place? Who will be the new power brokers? It won't be the Bad Feminists like me. We are acceptable neither to Right nor to Left. In times of extremes, extremists win. Their ideology becomes a religion, anyone who doesn't puppet their views is seen as an apostate, a heretic, or a traitor, and moderates in the middle are annihilated. Fiction writers are particularly suspect because they write about human beings, and people are morally ambiguous. The aim of ideology is to eliminate ambiguity.

The UBC Accountable letter is also a symptom—a symptom of the failure of the University of British Columbia and its flawed process. This should have been a matter addressed by Canadian Civil Liberties or B.C. Civil Liberties. Maybe these organizations will now put up their hands. Since the letter has now become a censorship issue—with calls being made to erase the site and the many thoughtful words of its writers—perhaps PEN Canada, PEN International, Canadian Journalists for Free Expression (CJFE), and Index on Censorship may also have a view.

The letter said from the beginning that UBC failed the accused and the complainants both. I would add that it failed the taxpaying public, who fund UBC to the tune of $600 million a year. We would like to know how our money was spent in this instance. Donors to UBC—and it receives *billions* of dollars in private donations—also have a right to know.

In this whole affair, writers have been set against one another, especially since the letter was distorted by its attackers and vilified as a War on Women. But at this time, I call upon all—both the Good Feminists and the Bad Feminists like me—to drop their unproductive squabbling, join forces, and direct the spotlight where it should have been all along—at UBC. Two of the ancillary complainants have now spoken out against UBC's process in this affair. For that, they should be thanked.

Once UBC has begun an independent inquiry into its own actions—such as the one conducted recently at Wilfrid Laurier University—and has pledged to make that inquiry public, the UBC Accountable site will have served its purpose. That purpose was never to squash women. Why have accountability and transparency been framed as antithetical to women's rights?

We Lost Ursula Le Guin
When We Needed Her Most

>>><<<

(2018)

When I finally got the brilliant and renowned writer Ursula K. Le Guin all to myself on a stage in Portland, some years ago, I asked her the question I'd always been longing to ask: "Where do the ones who walk away from Omelas go?" Tricky question! She changed the subject.

Omelas is one of Le Guin's fictional "thought experiments": a perfect city where everyone has a lovely time, but everyone also knows that the city's fate rests upon a single child who is kept in a dungeon and horribly mistreated. Without this child, the city will fall. Think slavery in the world of ancient Greece and Rome, think the antebellum South, think people under colonial rule, think England in the nineteenth century. That miserable child in Omelas is a close relative of the poverty-stricken but threatening children who clutch at the skirts of the Ghost of Christmas Present in Charles Dickens's *A Christmas Carol.* Their names are Ignorance and Want, and they are very pertinent today.

A wealthy city sustained by the mistreated—this is what the ones who are walking away from Omelas are walking away from. My question was, therefore: Where in the world could we find a society in which the happiness of some does not depend on the misery of others? How do we build Omelas, minus the tortured child?

Neither Ursula K. Le Guin nor I knew, but it was a question that Le Guin spent her lifetime trying to answer, and the worlds she so skillfully created in the attempt are many, varied, and entrancing. As an anarchist, she would have wanted a self-governing society, with gender and racial equality. She would have wanted respect for life forms other than human. She would have wanted a child-friendly society, as opposed to one that imposes childbirth but does not care about the mothers or the actual children. Or so I surmise from her writing.

Le Guin was born in 1929: a child in the Depression, a teenager in the Second World War, then at college right after the war, in that moment that seemed so filled with the spirit of renewal. She went to Radcliffe, a liminal space then: it was Harvard but not really, its women allowed some participation but not full access. She would have strolled past the dining hall, where—she would have been told—the male students used to pelt with buns any female who dared to show her face. (Once she became a writer—a science fiction writer, among other things—the men defending that particular tree house continued the exclusionary bun-pelting. She took note, and was not amused.)

After Radcliffe she went to graduate school, studying French and Italian literature. She was taught to think, as they used to say, like a man: widely, curiously, rigorously. But after she married and left academia, she found herself in a society that treated her and all women—from a legal point of view—like an irresponsible thirteen-year-old. For those who'd been taught they were grown-ups, this was like trying to seal a volcano inside a tin can. It was this generation of American women who fuelled much of the second-wave feminism of the late 1960s and 1970s, which was when that particular tin can exploded. This was a time of high energy for Le Guin the writer.

But political thought and activity was just one facet of this astonishingly talented woman's multifaceted life and work. The Earthsea trilogy, for instance, is a memorable exploration of the relationship between life and death: without the darkness, no light; and mortality allows all that is alive to be. The darkness includes the hidden and less pleasant sides of our selves—our fears, our pride, our envy. Ged, its hero, must face his shadow self before it devours him. Only then will he become whole. In the process, he must contend with the wisdom of dragons: ambiguous and not our wisdom, but wisdom nonetheless.

Recently, I found myself talking with a much younger woman

who was mourning the loss of a friend. "Read the Earthsea trilogy," I suggested. "It will help." She did, and it did.

But now Ursula K. Le Guin has died.

When I heard that, I had an absurd vision based on the scene in *A Wizard of Earthsea,* in which the mage Ged tries to summon the spirit of a child back from the land of the dead. There was Ursula, moving calmly away down a hill of whispering sand under the unchanging stars; and there was me, distraught and running after her and calling: "No! Come back! We need you here and now!"

Especially now, in the land of normalized p—y-grabbing, the rollback of women's rights on so many fronts but especially in health care and contraception, and the effort to squeeze women out of the workplace by those who, having failed to compete through skill and intellectual superiority, have weaponized their penises.

She had seen a similar explosion of women's anger in the early 1970s, at the time of the second-wave feminist movement. She knew where outrage came from: suppressed anger. In the 1960s and 1970s, that anger came from many directions, but in general from being treated as lesser—much lesser—even though the work done and the contribution made were as great, or greater. One of the first catchphrases of the day was "Housework is work." One of the most resented quotations came from the civil rights movement: "The only place for a woman in the Movement is on her back."

Anger was something that long puzzled Le Guin. In her 2014 essay "About Anger," she writes:

> Anger is a useful, perhaps indispensable tool in motivating resistance to injustice. But I think it is a weapon—a tool useful only in combat and self-defence. . . . Anger points powerfully to the denial of rights, but the exercise of rights can't live and thrive on anger. It lives and thrives on the dogged pursuit of justice. . . . Valued as an end in itself, it loses its goal. It fuels not positive activism but regression, obsession, vengeance, self-righteousness.

The long-term goal, the dogged pursuit of justice—that took up a lot of her thought and time.

We can't call Ursula K. Le Guin back from the land of the unchanging stars, but happily she left us her multifaceted work, her hard-earned wisdom, and her fundamental optimism. Her sane, smart, crafty, and lyrical voice is more necessary now than ever.

For it, and for her, we should be thankful.

Three Tarot Cards

>>><<<

(2018)

It is a great pleasure to be delivering this year's *lectio magistralis*. I love Florence and am very happy to be here, but this kind invitation has also been the cause of some puzzlement on my part. I was told I could talk to you about whatever I liked as long as it had something to do with writing. But what can I possibly say about writing in general that others have not said before, or which I myself haven't said before, which, in my own case did not amount to very much? For what can be said with any authority about writing in general? No one idea of it seems to cover the case.

For example: Writing is a line of black marks on the page, or else on the washroom wall, placed in those locations by countless numbers of people. Writing is a way of recording the human voice, though it is not the only way. Writing is falling out of fashion, or else it is not, depending on who's telling you. Writing is most often a form of storytelling, and storytelling is one of the earliest of human inventions, and arguably the most important one; we learn much more easily through stories than through, for instance, charts and graphs. Writing was devised in Mesopotamia as a way of keeping temple inventories of commodities such as wheat. Writing was once feared as a secret known only to scribes and magicians, and still carries a whiff of warning: I recently received a coffee cup inscribed with the word WORD, and the subscription "Handle with care." Writing has been forged, and used to destroy people, as in the case of Mary, Queen of Scots. Writing has also been used to save people threatened with execution: behold, the written and signed pardon, arriving just in time! Writing has been used to blackmail and extort;

it has also been used to bring hope and joy. Handwriting was taught widely in the nineteenth century because capitalism needed a lot of clerks who could read and write in order to keep track of wealth, and of who owed what to whom.

Oh, but you didn't mean writing, small-w, you say. You meant Writing, capital letter! You meant *literary* writing, or at least written works of some degree of elevation. You meant, possibly, the sort of writing I myself have been known to commit from time to time. I say "commit" advisedly—one commits an act, but one also commits a crime, and writing of the literary sort is an act, but it can also be viewed as a crime. Many have been jailed or sent to their deaths merely because of their writing. Sacrilege and treachery have been among the verdicts; whereas among the literary critics—who are themselves writers, let us not forget—bad taste as well as bad writing have been among the accusations.

Beware of writing, we might say! Perhaps one ought to show discretion, and never record anything on paper. But in my case it is far too late for that.

Because human beings are symbol makers and like to organize their symbols in comprehensible ways, I will now attempt to look at some aspects of writing through three Tarot cards: La Papesse, or The Female Pope; The Wheel of Fortune; and La Balance, or Justice.

And because human beings are storytellers, and have been for tens of thousands of years, I will begin with three stories: The first story: "How I Became a Writer (sort of)." The second story: "How I Once Employed the Tarot Deck in a Rudimentary Fiction-Writing Class in Edmonton, Alberta, Canada, in the Year 1969/1970." And the third story: "How I Was Given a Copy of the Visconti Tarot Deck, in Milano, Italy, in the Year 2017."

THE FIRST STORY: "HOW I BECAME A WRITER (SORT OF)"

Here is the context. In the late 1950s and early 1960s—that distant planet I am well placed to describe to you, having been alive and already somewhat grown up by then—there were no cellphones. More than that: there were no personal computers, or social media, or any Internet. There were not even any fax machines. Electric typewriters were just being invented; I did not acquire one until 1967. There were no pantyhose. There were no caffè lattes, or not in North America: lattes had not yet made a stealth attack from Europe and infiltrated the collective bloodstream. There were very few—if any—people who were female in STEM studies, which means Science, Technology, Engineering, and Math.

If you were in medicine and a woman, you were most likely a nurse. If in law—unlikely—you were a law clerk. If you were a woman in politics—at least in North America—you were a freak, and treated as such.

Most novelists and poets in the 1950s and early 1960s were male. There was only one school of creative writing then. It was in Iowa. There were no such schools in Toronto, Canada, which is where I began to be a writer. Any skills I may have come by during my long and peculiar trajectory have been self-taught, with help—I am pleased to acknowledge—from my friends, first readers, agents, and editors. But it took me quite a while to acquire these skills: first I had to write something. And a lot of what I wrote in the beginning was quite bad. So it is with most writers.

In 1957, having already assimilated some of the core texts that have been so useful to me ever since—the Bible, *The Iliad, The Odyssey,* the *Aeneid,* any folk tales I could get hold of from around the world, *The Thousand and One Nights,* a great many detective and science fiction novels, a huge stash of comic books, a lot of Shakespeare and nineteenth-century novels—though not yet Dante, Cervantes, or much Chaucer—I entered university. The humanities were having a boom time of sorts then, or at least they were more respected than they are now. They had, indeed—and in some circles—filled a void that was being created in the space once occupied by religion. They seemed to offer spiritual uplift, or personal enrichment, or nebulous enhancement. They were supposed to be—in some way that was never very well defined—morally Good For You.

There was a downside to this view, as there is to everything human. The Soviet Union, in the 1920s and 1930s and later, had taken this kind of moralizing analysis to an extreme—certain poets and writers could not even be published there, having been declared "degenerate" and thus harmful to society. So dangerous was the great Russian poet Anna Akhmatova thought to be that she was banned from publication in the U.S.S.R. for decades. Her astonishing poem "Requiem"—about what it felt like to live through Stalin's terror and his purges in the 1930s—was composed in fragments, which were then memorized by Akhmatova's trusted friends. Any record in writing was burned: to have been caught with the evidence might well have meant a death sentence for Akhmatova. When Stalin was finally dead and glasnost had at last arrived, the fragments of the poem were reassembled and the poem was published.

Imagine risking your life to preserve a poem or a work of fiction or a record of what has happened! But people do. Just recently, a book of short stories about life in a very repressive regime was smuggled out of North Korea. It is called *The Accusation*. The author used a pseudonym—Bandi, meaning "Firefly." Think about that. A tiny insect, sending out frail pulses of light in the darkness.

This is the writer as witness, as messenger—a time-honoured role. I recall that use of the voice from the Book of Job—said to be one of the most ancient in the collection of texts we know as the Bible. The voice is the voice of the messenger who comes to Job, describing the catastrophes that have destroyed his children. He says: "I only have escaped alone to tell thee." This is one of the things that imaginative literature can do in times of trial and trouble—it can bear witness.

However, when too much moral scrutiny is brought to bear on art by forces outside it that claim to be acting to protect society, you invariably get censorship, and you even get things like the obscenity trial of Flaubert's groundbreaking novel, *Madame Bovary*. This very moral view of literature—nothing should be published that would scandalize—was typical of the Victorian age—an age that matched its virtuous high-mindedness with the largest population of courtesans, street prostitutes and children sold into the sex trade that London has ever seen. But we have never been free of it, this idea that novels and poems and artworks in general have to be judged according to whether or not they are Good For You, by the standards of whoever is doing the judging.

In our age, this kind of moralizing is likely to manifest as an examination of artistic items that frames them merely as a subset of the entertainment business, or else as some kind of secretion—like a pearl around an irritating grain of sand—or as detritus, like a shed snake skin or a collection of toenail clippings produced by the culture at large, and worth studying only as a symptom of all the things that were wrong with the author's psyche or her or his worldview or his or her socio-economic position or her or his philosophy, or aesthetic, or set of prejudices.

It is no longer the contemplation of the artistic object that is said to be good for us: it is the critical destruction of it. What a relief—another tainted cultural object consigned to the dustbin of history, as we more enlightened beings proceed along the Yellow Brick Road to the Emerald City of Oz, where everyone is happy and well behaved, or—as Saint Augustine, inventor of sex as the original sin, would have it—the City of God. In our age, this high-minded judgmentalism of ours (from which I myself am by no means exempt, I hasten to add) runs in tandem with a saturation level of violent pornography unheard of and indeed impossible in earlier times. Human beings and human societies are nothing if not contradictory, as you may have noticed.

But I digress. There I was, then, in 1957, at the age of seventeen. Toronto in 1948—the year I moved into it—had a population of roughly 680,000. It was known as "Toronto the Good," or sometimes "Toronto the Blue," in reference to its blue laws—no drinking in establishments where people might see you from the street, for instance, and never on Sundays. On Sundays the entertainment was going down to the railway switching yards to watch the trains being shunted around.

Today things have reversed somewhat: Toronto is now considered to be the most multicultural city in the world. Who in 1948 could have thought that such a thing would happen? The word *multicultural* hadn't even been invented then! In 1961, when I was a young writer, the advice I was given by those few stalwarts already in the arts was, basically, "Get out of Toronto." Or they would expand on that: "Get out of Canada." Canada then had few published writers, no film industry, and no music industry. The arts were something you imported, supposing you had a yen for them: wood was what you exported. Canada was considered sterile ground for the creative or entrepreneurial mind, and indeed for almost every form of endeavour except logging and mining, and fish. As one of the few recognized pundits we'd produced at that time said, memorably: "Americans like to make money. Canadians like to count it."

That pundit was Northrop Frye, thanks to whom I went to Harvard graduate school instead of to Paris, where I had been intending to work as a waitress, live in a garret, write masterpieces in my spare time, smoke cigarettes—Gitanes, by choice, but no hope there, as I was allergic to them—drink absinthe—similarly no hope, since when alcoholized I threw up, an unpoetic thing to do—get tuberculosis, the romantic disease of choice, as in operas. I did know about operas, thanks to the radio, and to the Saturday-afternoon broadcasts live from the Metropolitan Opera Company in New York City.

I chose Harvard and a graduate English degree over Paris and dying from tuberculosis because Frye was of the opinion that I would probably get more writing done as a student than as a waitress—we called them waitresses then, not "servers"—and he was right, as I found out later when I actually did become a waitress. Clearing away the half-eaten food of strangers is a good weight-loss technique, incidentally. I lost ten pounds. But that's another story.

All this time I was writing. I finally published my first novel in 1969. Which brings me to:

THE SECOND STORY: "HOW I ONCE EMPLOYED THE TAROT DECK IN A RUDIMENTARY FICTION-WRITING CLASS IN EDMONTON, ALBERTA, CANADA, IN THE YEAR 1969/1970"

If you weren't born yet in 1970, don't worry: a lot of people weren't.

I lived in Edmonton, Alberta, in the years 1968 to 1970. I was supposed to be finishing my Harvard Ph.D. thesis in Victorian literature, which had to do with powerful supernatural female figures and their relationship to the Wordsworthian and the Darwinian views of Nature, but at a moment during these two years I got waylaid by the film business and started writing scripts, and I never did get back to the thesis about the supernatural females.

There was a rudimentary fiction-writing class being offered at the University of Edmonton then, and I was asked to teach in it, being by that time a published poet. The students were undergraduates, and terrified of the page. To help them out, and to give them something to focus their attention, I brought my Tarot pack to the class and asked them to choose one of the major arcana—the cards with named pictures—or else one of the face cards—the minor arcana—the King, Queen, Chevalier or Horseman, and Page—from the four suits, which, in Tarot, are Cups, Swords, Wands, and Coins. (In ordinary card decks, these have become Hearts, Spades, Clubs, and Diamonds.) Happily, the Tarot deck contains a number of powerful female cards as well as male ones, so there was plenty of choice for all.

This worked quite well as a way of triggering episodes of writing, as did the telling of folk tales as prompts for stories. One of the students wrote quite a good version of the Fitcher's Bird variant of the Bluebeard story from the point of view of the magic egg, which betrays two of the heroine's sisters by getting blood on it, but not the third sister, who puts it on a shelf before entering the bloody chamber.

Why did I know about the Tarot cards? They were in vogue in the time of T.S. Eliot, who mentions them in his classic poem *The Waste Land*. A minor novelist of the period—Charles Williams, a member of the Tolkien circle—even wrote a novel based around them called *The Greater Trumps*. So I'd learned about the Tarot through studying twentieth-century literature. I'd had a copy of the Marseilles deck in my possession for some time, and was in the habit of casting fortunes with it, until it got a little too accurate for comfort.

I had also recently learned astrology and palmistry, under the following circumstances: I was living in an Edmonton house that was divided in two, and in the other half of it lived a Dutch historian of art called Jetske Sybyzma, who was studying Hieronymus Bosch. She had a theory—since recognized—that his paintings contained astrological symbols, and so she had studied astrology and books about astrology in order to interpret these symbols. With astrology went palmistry, since that system too was connected to the planets, and the arrangement of hands, fingers, and rings in Renaissance portraits can tell us a lot about the subject of the portrait.

During the long, dark, cold Edmonton nights, when it was hazardous to venture outside because of the ice, and also the ice fog—crystals of ice that could get into your lungs and cut them open—as a way of passing the time, Jetske taught me what she knew about reading hands and casting horoscopes. The Tarot pack, too, is connected with these astrological systems. Which brings me to:

THE THIRD STORY: "HOW I WAS GIVEN A COPY OF THE VISCONTI TAROT DECK, IN MILANO, ITALY, IN THE YEAR 2017"

Toward the end of 2017, I attended the Noir in Festival, which is dedicated to noir films and novels, and which takes place in Milano and Como. There I received the Raymond Chandler Award, which was very pleasing to me, since Raymond Chandler's works were among the detective novels I had read as a young person. During our visit to Como, we went up in the funicular to the town of Brunate and saw—in the church there—the famous picture of the female Pope, which has been variously identified, but which is supposed to be connected to the story of Santa Guglielma—the founder of a gender-equal religious sect who prophesied the advent of a female Pope.

This prophecy was, understandably, not popular with the official Church, and especially not with the Inquisition. Guglielma took refuge at the top of the Brunate mountain, and—said our guide—the inquisitors were too lazy to climb up there, so they never caught her; though they subsequently dug up her bones and burned them at the stake.

The Visconti-Sforza Tarot deck was commissioned more than a hundred years later, and the second card in the deck—La Papesse, The Female Pope, which has had its name changed in some Tarot versions to The High Priestess—is said to have been included in honour of Santa Guglielma and her sect. Who can tell? But so goes the story.

After our visit to Brunate and our conversation about the female Pope, the publisher's representative—Matteo Columbo, who is himself a magician of sorts—presented me with a copy of the beautiful Visconti-Sforza Tarot deck, which contains the designs on which all subsequent versions of the deck are based.

I have chosen three cards to represent three aspects of the novel. They will correspond roughly to the beginning, the middle, and the end.

The first card is La Papesse, or The High Priestess. In fortune casting, it signifies the occult and mysterious, underground forces at work, and secrets. I draw your attention to it in relation to the writing of novels—because every novel is in some sense a mystery novel. If there are no secrets at the beginning of the book—and if the author shows her hand too early ("showing your hand" is another metaphor from card games)—we readers will not be intrigued enough to read on.

We want to learn more. We expect a certain amount of misdirection from the author: we hope to discover that things and people are not as we were at first led to believe. We expect the hidden to be revealed by the end of the story, and if it is not, we can become quite annoyed.

The Female Pope or High Priestess card is governed, in astrological terms, by the moon, which by medieval times had acquired a somewhat dubious reputation. It can stand for intuition, but it can also stand for change, impermanence, and illusion. The Moon card in the Tarot deck shows—among other things—reflections in the water. There is the moon, and there is the reflection of the moon. The reflection is an illusion: you cannot seize the moon by jumping into the lake.

And novels too are reflections and illusions. As an author, you must work as hard as you can to make your illusion a convincing one. I am not disparaging novel-writing by saying this. Truth of a kind can appear—and often does appear—through reflections and illusions. As Emily Dickinson ordered poets to do, novels tell the truth, but tell it slant. She also said, "The Truth must dazzle gradually." Moonlight and indirection, not the full noon-time glare all at once. This is good advice for novel writers.

My next Tarot card is also governed by the moon. It is called: The

Wheel of Fortune. I have chosen it to represent the middle of the novel.

Because a story always consists of a sequence of events—this happens, then this happens, then this happens—and the events of the story take place in a certain order, the composition of a novel must always involve considerations of time. As Leon Edel, the biographer of Henry James, once said, if it's a novel there will be a clock in it.

Or, we might add, some other way of marking the passage of time. Sundials mark time circularly by marking the circle made by the sun. Clocks—the analogue version—are circular: the hands go around, and then the next day they go around again. The phases of the moon mark time—new moon, full moon, old moon, dark moon, and then the sequence repeats. Calendars in their usual paper form are, however, linear—March 2018 is torn off and discarded, and, although each year repeats the months and the cycle of the seasons, the years themselves will not repeat. We will never see 1812 again, except in historical films and science fiction time-travel fantasies.

If time is linear, where is the beginning and where is the end? A question it is useless to ask if time is circular.

How will the novelist conceive of time? How will it be arranged within the narrative? The codex book form within which most novels are embedded is linear—that is, the pages are numbered in sequence—but the way time is handled within this linear arrangement is not necessarily linear. The time element might for instance resemble a circle—at the end, the central character finds him- or herself back in a situation similar to the one from which he started out, though she would not necessarily be the same age at the end, unless it is a story that contains supernatural or unnatural features. Or time might be arranged to tell parallel stories that take place at the same time, but that then intersect. Or we might find ourselves dealing with multiple flashbacks.

The story—what happens—and the structure—how to tell the reader what happens—may be the same, or they may be different. If the same, the story begins at the beginning and goes along until it comes to the end, where it stops. If different, the point of entry will not be the same as the beginning of the story. For instance, in *The*

Iliad, the point of entry finds Achilles sulking in his tent, after which we learn why he is sulking in his tent, and then why he comes out of his tent and what he does then.

In *A Christmas Carol* by Charles Dickens, the point of entry is miserly old Scrooge having a miserable time of it on Christmas Eve, during which he is visited by the ghost of his dead partner, and after which we are shown three separate time pockets—Scrooge's past, his present, and his possible future—each of which tells us readers more about his life, while telling Scrooge more about himself. Time then stops and reverses, and he is allowed to live Christmas Day all over again, this time much more merrily.

In Emily Brontë's novel *Wuthering Heights,* the point of entry (the beginning of the story) is very far along in the actual novel (the sequence of events). The female protagonist, Catherine, is long dead; her obsessed and morally dubious adorer, Heathcliff, is middle-aged; and their story—the story we are about to hear—is told through the voices of two other people entirely: a gentleman who wants to rent a property owned by Heathcliff, and Nelly, the former hired help in the household of the central characters, who knows quite a lot of the story, though not everything.

Those are several of the many ways in which time in a novel may be arranged.

By way of experiment, let's try a few variations on a familiar tale, *Little Red Riding Hood.*

1. Simple linear version. Once upon a time, there was a little girl whose mother had made her a beautiful red cloak with a hood, and so the girl was called Little Red Riding Hood. One day, her mother said to her, "I have prepared a basket of nourishing treats for your grandmother, who is ailing, and who lives on the other side of the forest. You must take it to her, but be careful not to stray from the path, for there are wolves who live in the forest . . ." And you know the rest.

2. *In medias res.* Little Red Riding Hood was so happy! The birds were singing, the sun was shining, and the wildflowers were in bloom! What a good idea—to pick a bouquet for her grandmother! But contrary to instructions she had received

before this story begins, Little Red Riding Hood had strayed from the path, and suddenly, out from behind a tree stepped a polite but decidedly hairy gentleman with very white and pointy teeth. "Good day, little girl," he said. "What are you doing?" "I am picking a bouquet for my grandmother, who lives on the other side of the forest," said Little Red Riding Hood. And you know the rest.

3. Retrospective, with flashbacks. Looking back, Little Red Riding Hood's grandmother shuddered every time she remembered the horrible day she had spent inside the stomach of the wolf. It had been very dark in there, and decidedly acidic, and there were a number of plastic bags that the wolf had eaten by mistake, as well as the remains of several ham sandwiches. The grandmother much preferred watercress sandwiches. But the worst part of her ordeal was having to listen silently while the wolf dressed up in her nightgown and nightcap and then did an impersonation of her. Such a bad impersonation! And all to entrap her beloved grandchild, Little Red Riding Hood! But then, luckily, along came . . ." And you know the rest.

Or we might take a more sinister view—the view taken as a rule by detective thrillers—and begin with the corpse. But whose corpse? In one version of the story, both the grandmother and the wolf bite the dust, but in another version it is only the wolf. Why not tell the story both ways and let the reader choose? Many have done this, including the authors of *Write Your Own Adventure Stories,* and also Charlotte Brontë, in her novel *Villette.* In such a case there is not a single order of events, there are two.

Or, in the case of multiple narrators, there are a number of orders of events. This is the scheme proposed by the Kurosawa film *Rashomon,* so famously that the title has become short form among writers for this kind of multiple-stranded approach in which each account contradicts the others. "Ah. Pulling a *Rashomon,*" they might say, nodding wisely.

Some fictional structures resemble jigsaw puzzles—many pieces that are seen by the end to fit artfully together. Others resemble the child's game of Clue—the writer sprinkles clues, the reader tries to spot them. But whatever the story and whatever the structure, there is always—in any act of storytelling, and in any act of fiction—an assumed interplay between the spinner of the tale and the unraveller and interpreter of it—the listener or reader.

The Wheel of Fortune Tarot card has to do with time. There is a well-known television show in America called *Wheel of Fortune,* and both the television show and the Tarot card derive their name and symbolism from the Roman goddess Fortuna, or the goddess of luck. The Romans prayed to Fortuna in the hope she would favour them and bring them material wealth. She was, however, notorious for being fickle and unpredictable, as gamblers were well placed to know. It is she—otherwise known as Lady Luck—who is being invoked in the sprightly gambling song-and-dance number in the 1950s musical comedy *Guys and Dolls* called "Luck, Be a Lady Tonight," in which a character is rolling the dice. He implores Lady Luck to behave in a ladylike fashion and stick with him, rather than wandering off as she so frequently does.

The fickleness of the goddess Fortuna is the feature highlighted in the opening song of Carl Orff's voice cantata, *Carmina Burana.* The Latin words begin like this:

O Fortuna / Velut luna / Statu variabilis / Semper crescis / Aut decrescis; / Vita detestabilis / Nunc obdurat / Et tunc curat / Ludo mentis aciem, / Egestatem, Potestatem / Dissolvit ut glaciem. / Sors immanis / Et inanis, / Rota tu volubilis / Status malus / Vana salus / Semper dissolubilis . . .

O Fortuna, you are fickle as the moon, always waxing and waning; this miserable life first wrecks, then cures at a whim; poverty and power melt like ice. Fate, you monster of emptiness, you malevolent whirling wheel—happiness is in vain, and always fades away.

Lady Luck and her sometimes malevolent whirling Wheel of Fortune made it into medieval and early Renaissance symbolism, and thus into the fortune-telling Tarot cards. Fortuna was well known to Shakespeare, for instance. I needed to spend some time recently thinking about this goddess because she has an important part in *The Tempest*. The central figure, the magician Prospero—we know by his name that he is the darling of Fortune—has been down on his luck for twelve years, having been usurped by his treacherous brother, set adrift in a leaky boat, and marooned on an island. There he would have stayed, except for the actions of—I quote—"an auspicious star," who is linked with the goddess Fortuna—here known as "Bountiful Fortune, my dear lady." It is thanks to this influence that Prospero's enemies are brought within range of his magic powers and he is able to stage the illusion of the tempest that begins the play.

I was immersed in this material because—as part of the Hogarth Shakespeare Project—I was writing a modern-novel rendering of the play, which has since been published as *Hag-Seed:* one of the bad names that the earth-creature, Caliban, is called.

Each element in the play had to be represented in my novel—but what was I to do about "Auspicious Star" and "Bountiful Fortune, my dear lady"? The action could not start without them, or her, but in the original play they are not characters as such. My solution was to provide an influential woman called Estelle, who wears sparkly jewellery and has a twinkly manner—that takes care of the "star" elements—and is given to wearing wardrobe items with wheels and fruits and flowers on them, since Fortuna's emblems are the wheel and the cornucopia, or Horn of Plenty, which is what you hope Fortuna will bring you. It is due to Estelle, acting behind the scenes, that my hero's enemies are brought within his reach.

In more simple Tarot packs, such as the Marseilles deck, the Wheel of Fortune has lost its goddess, but in the earlier Visconti deck Fortuna is fully present. She is shown turning her wheel, and, as it turns, people are rising up on the left-hand side of it (thus on the right hand of Fortune). One temporarily fortunate individual is shown at the top wearing a crown, but others—who used to be at the top—are being thrown off to Fortuna's left or crushed beneath the wheel at the bottom.

This is where we get the term *revolution.* A revolution involves a turning of the wheel—whereby those on the bottom mount to the top, and those at the top are deposed. This kind of wheel-turning does not promise equality, by the way—merely a major place-change, with luck for some and unluck for others. And, since every human symbol has a negative version of itself, the wheel also became a particularly unpleasant medieval torture device known as . . . The Wheel.

Human societies are ever changing; thus there is no such thing as being on the wrong side of history—if history means who's in political power and who's not, and who's in intellectual fashion and who's not, because history of that kind doesn't have sides. History is not an inevitable linear progression. It doesn't start with Genesis and go on to Revelation, at the end of which the City of God appears and everything is fine forever. There is no inevitability in the course of human power and fashion: what looks like the right side of history today may well be cast as the wrong side of it tomorrow, but then the right side of it again the day after tomorrow.

In the writing of novels, the place of the goddess Fortuna is taken by the novelist. It is she or he who arranges time and turns the wheel, elevating some characters to happiness, deposing others or even killing them off. Perhaps time in the novel is always a combination of wheel and road: the wheel revolves, and fortunes—in love and life—are made and unmade, but all the while the wheel is travelling along the road and time is progressing in a linear fashion as well. When you are writing a novel, you have to watch the clock and the calendar—was there enough time for X to sneak into the greenhouse and murder Y? But you also have to keep an eye on the moon, which, we already know, signifies illusion.

Fortune is like the moon: *Semper crescis, aut decrescis.* Ever waxing and waning.

My third card is Justicia, or The Balance. I have chosen it to represent the ending of the novel.

Not much in the way of justice can be expected of the goddess Fortuna and her fickle wheel, but the Tarot does contain such a concept, represented by the card called La Balance—the two-armed scales—or Justicia, the goddess of justice. Again, this is a Roman goddess—the familiar figure you sometimes see outside court-houses, carrying a sword in one hand to signify punishment and a two-armed scales in the other, signifying the weighing of evidence and therefore a just verdict. As you might expect, the goddess of justice is governed by the astrological sign of Libra, or the Balance. Sometimes Justicia has a blindfold, to show that she does not play favourites and cannot be bribed. But in the Visconti Tarot deck, she does not wear a blindfold. She sees everything.

The goddess of justice dates from Roman times—which is how she got into the Tarot—but her two-handed scales is a lot older. In ancient Egypt, after you died you went to the Afterworld, where your heart was weighed against the feather of the goddess of truth or right acting. If your heart was found wanting, it was tossed to a super-natural crocodile and devoured. You could cheat by having a coffin charm put into your coffin—another useful function for writing—but the god Thoth, who had the head of an ibis and was the scribe god, might be standing by with a written list of all your good and bad actions.

In Tarot fortune-casting, this card signifies a positive resolution for you if you yourself have acted kindly and fairly. If not, you need to pay attention—for, with La Balance, how you have acted toward others will be balanced by how fate acts toward you. The action of this card is not at all like that of the Wheel of Fortune: quite the reverse. It says that there is a moral pattern, and that you are part of it. It is a card that concerns itself not with things in process—the middle of a novel, let us say—but with outcomes—resolutions and endings.

The sequence of cards now shows the patterning of novels. For the beginning of a novel, the Female Pope or High Priestess, with her secrets and hints; for the middle, the Wheel of Fortune, with its unrolling of time and events and the ever-changing fortunes of the characters; and for the ending, Justicia, or The Balance, when—we hope—the characters will receive the fates they deserve—good fates for the good characters, bad fates for the bad ones.

That is certainly what we wished as children, and folk tales as a rule are happy to oblige. Cinderella, being a good character, receives a much-improved fortune in the form of a nice rich man who wan-ders by on a horse and has a shoe fetish—well, at least it's better than poking about in the ashes—and Little Red Riding Hood is rescued from the wolf. How unhappy we would be if things worked out otherwise, and Little Red Riding Hood became simply a tasty wolf meal!

But we live in an ironic age, Dear Reader. Sometimes the endings to our novels are not so simple. In fact, most of the time they are not so simple. There are many other cards in the deck—The Falling Tower, for instance, which is catastrophic, or the Hanged Man, which promises illumination but only if you spend some time dangling from a tree upside down. Or the Magician, a good card to have if you are an artist. We might meditate on some of these other cards as possible guides for the writing of a novel.

But whatever cards we choose, the goddess of justice with her balance is always present somewhere in our minds, telling us, if not that events in our novel have turned out as they should, at least how they ought to have turned out. As a rule, we know when things are fair and when they are not fair. We wish they were fair, but they are not always. That, alas, is real life. Or, in a novel, the illusion of real life.

And now it is time for me to fold up my deck of cards and slip it into the pocket of my magician's jacket. Is the Magician in the Tarot deck a mere juggler? Sometimes. Novelists have their tricks. They pull rabbits out of hats quite frequently. But at a deeper level, the Magician card is about positive transformation. And so, we hope, is the novel. "Your book changed my life," people frequently say to novelists. At this point, it is best not to ask them how. That is a question for the reader to answer.

For the writer must now move on to the composition of a new novel, and thus back to the beginning—to the card of the High Priestess and her fresh batch of secrets, hints, and intuitions. Like the god Hermes, she is the opener of doors. What will come next? We long to know, but with a story, we can only find out by following the pathway of the Wheel—ever twisting, ever turning—into the forest, which, as ever, contains wolves, and rising and falling fortunes, and illusions, but which might have a little justice at the end.

A Slave State?

>>><<<

(2018)

Nobody likes abortion, even when safe and legal. It's not what any woman would choose for a happy time on Saturday night. But nobody likes women bleeding to death on the bathroom floor from illegal abortions either. What to do?

Perhaps a different way of approaching the question would be to ask: What kind of country do you want to live in? One in which every individual is free to make decisions concerning his or her health and body, or one in which half the population is free and the other half is enslaved?

Women who cannot make their own decisions about whether or not to have babies are enslaved because the state claims ownership of their bodies and the right to dictate the use to which their bodies must be put. The only similar circumstance for men is conscription into an army. In both cases there is risk to the individual's life, but an army conscript is at least provided with food, clothing, and lodging. Even criminals in prisons have a right to those things. If the state is mandating enforced childbirth, why should it not pay for prenatal care, for the birth itself, for postnatal care, and—for babies who are not sold off to richer families—for the cost of bringing up the child?

And if the state is very fond of babies, why not honour the women who have the most babies by respecting them and lifting them out of poverty? If women are providing a needed service to the state—albeit against their wills—surely they should be paid for their labour. If the goal is more babies, I am sure many women would oblige if properly recompensed. Otherwise, they are inclined to follow the natural law: placental mammals will abort in the face of resource scarcity.

But I doubt that the state is willing to go so far as to provide the needed resources. Instead, it just wants to reinforce the usual cheap trick: force women to have babies, and then make them pay. And pay. And pay. As I said, slavery.

If one chooses to have a baby, that is of course a different matter. The baby is a gift, given by life itself. But to be a gift a thing must be freely given and freely received. A gift can also be rejected. A gift that cannot be rejected is not a gift, but a symptom of tyranny.

We say that women "give birth." And mothers who have chosen to be mothers do give birth, and feel it as a gift. But if they have not chosen, birth is not a gift they give; it is an extortion from them against their wills.

No one is forcing women to have abortions. No one either should force them to undergo childbirth. Enforce childbirth if you wish, Argentina, but at least call that enforcing by what it is. It is slavery: the claim to own and control another's body, and to profit by that claim.

Oryx and Crake

>>><<<

INTRODUCTION

(2018)

"*Oryx and Crake*? But what does it mean?" my publishers asked when I told them the title of the novel I had just finished. "Oryx and Crake are the names of two bioforms that are extinct by the time of the novel," I said. "They are also the names of the central characters." "But by the time the novel begins, they're dead," said the publishers. "That's the point," said I. "Or one of them." (Another point, which I did not mention, is that this title sounds quite a lot like frogs singing in a pond. Try pronouncing it three times, thus: *Oryx oryx oryx. Crake crake crake.* You see?)

As the publishers were still not convinced, I told them that *R, Y, X,* and *K* were power letters, and that no title that contained all of them could possibly be without virtue. Did they believe me? It is hard to say. But *Oryx and Crake* has remained the name of the novel to this very day.

It is also the one of the two novels written by me that is most likely to be taught in schools to adolescents. Evidently, teachers have responded to the power of the magic letters. Or to something.

In addition to which, *Oryx and Crake* is the first of my novels—and thus, at the time, the only one—to have a male narrator throughout. Yes, I was tired of being asked why I "always" wrote about women. I didn't, always. But this book was a monolith. True to the axioms of gendered literary criticism, as soon as the book was published I was asked why I hadn't used a female narrator. Pobody's nerfect.

Here is how it all came to pass. I began writing *Oryx and Crake* in March 2001. I was in Australia, and had just finished a book tour there for *The Blind Assassin,* my previous novel. Then I'd spent some time bird-watching in the monsoon rainforest of Arnhem Land, where I'd also visited several open-sided cave complexes where Aboriginal peoples had lived in harmony with their environment, in an unchanging culture, for forty or fifty thousand years.

After that, our birding group went to Philip Gregory's Cassowary House, near Cairns. As birders and naturalists were in the habit of doing even then—and had been doing for decades—we found ourselves discussing the high rate of extinctions that had been taking place in the natural world due to the fact that human beings were altering that world at an accelerating rate. How long would there still be cassowaries—those extraordinary flightless birds that looked like blue, purple, and pink dinosaurs and could disembowel you with one claw? A number of these were stalking the grounds of Cassowary House, eating cut-up bananas and gobbling up any pies unwisely left on windowsills to cool. How long would the red-necked crakes scuttling about in the underbrush be able to survive? Not long, was the general opinion among us.

And what about *Homo sapiens sapiens*? Would our species continue to destroy the biological system from which it had emerged—and which continued to sustain it—thus assuring its quick march to oblivion? Would it stop, consider its reckless ways, and manage to reverse them? Would it be able to invent itself out of the corner into which its own inventions had painted it? Or—having developed the biotechnological means of obliterating itself, perhaps by an engineered supervirus, and having discovered also the means to alter the human genome—would it decide to replace itself with a kinder, less greedy, and less rapacious version of itself, designed by some philanthropist or deranged individual bent on world betterment? Was there a prophet and/or mad scientist lurking among us who was getting ready to push the Reset button?

It was while watching the red-necked crakes from the Cassowary House balcony that the plan of *Oryx and Crake* appeared to me almost in its entirety. I began making notes on it that night. I felt too tired to begin another novel so soon after the last one, but when a story clamours with such insistence, you can't postpone it.

Every novel has a long prelude in the writer's life—what she or he has seen, experienced, read, and pondered—and *Oryx and Crake* was no exception. I'd been considering dystopic "what if" scenarios, and also species extinctions, for a long time. Several of my close relatives are scientists, and the main topic at the annual family Christmas dinner—while the turkey is being dissected, rather than carved—is likely to be intestinal parasites or sex hormones in mice—or, more recently, the invention of the CRISPR gene-editing tool, already being considered for the kind of "Gene Genie" commercial venture that appears in *Oryx and Crake*. My recreational reading is likely to be pop science of the Stephen Jay Gould or *Scientific American* type, partly so I'll be able to keep up with the family dialogue.

I'd been clipping small items from the back pages of newspapers for years, and noting with alarm that trends derided ten years ago as paranoid fantasies had become possibilities, then actualities. And so it is with *Oryx and Crake*: the growing of human organs in pigs, only a possibility when I wrote the book, is now an actuality. "Chickie-Nobs" were an invention back then, but "lab meat" is now with us. The self-healing function of cat purring—the science of which was in its infancy when I was writing the book—is now fairly widely accepted. And yet more discoveries and inventions are on the way.

But which will get there first—the brave new world of biotech and AI and solar energy, or the collapse of the high-tech society that produces and enables them? The rules of biology are as inexorable as those of physics: run out of food and water and you die. No animal can exhaust its resource base and hope to survive. Human civilizations are subject to the same law, and the catastrophes caused by climate change are already—in part—causing havoc among us.

Like *The Handmaid's Tale*, *Oryx and Crake* is a speculative fiction—in the line of descent from Orwell's *Nineteen Eighty-Four*—not a traditional science fiction in the line of H.G. Wells's *War of the Worlds*. It contains no intergalactic space travel, no teleportation, no Martians. As with *The Handmaid's Tale*, it invents nothing we haven't already invented or started to invent. Every novel begins with a "what if," and then sets forth its axioms. The "what if" of *Oryx and Crake* is simply: What if we continue down the road we're already on? How slippery is the slope? What are our saving graces? Who's got the will to stop us? Might we be able to bioengineer ourselves out of the train wreck we seem already to have set in motion?

Oryx and Crake is a jolly, fun-filled romp in which almost the entire human race has been annihilated, before which it has split into two parts: a technocracy and an anarchy. But there is a ray of hope: a group of quasi-humans who have been genetically engineered so that they will never suffer from the ills that plague *Homo sapiens sapiens*. In other words, they are designer people.

The designer people, or Crakers—so they are known in the book—have several accessories I wouldn't mind having myself: built-in insect repellent, automatic sunblock, and the ability to digest leaves, like rabbits. They don't need clothes or agriculture or the territory to grow food and fabric materials, and therefore they don't have territorial wars.

They also have several traits that would indeed be improvements of a sort, though most of us wouldn't like them. These include seasonal mating—like that of most other mammals—during which certain parts of their bodies turn blue, as with baboons—so there is no more romantic rejection or rape. Everyone has sex, and to add a little romantic touch, the male Crakers do some singing and dancing courtship moves. Many animals do this, my favourite being the silverfish: if the male silverfish's dance is accepted by the female, he hands her a sperm packet, end of story. When I told this to my accountant, he said, "I have clients who would kill for that."

The male Crakers also present a gift of flowers—just as male penguins present the female penguin with a stone. I thought of adding a bowerbird feature, having observed some bowerbirds in Australia, but that got complex, and involved male rivalries—which Crake wishes to eliminate—so that was dropped: the male Crakers do not steal blue plastic clothes pegs from one another, unlike bowerbirds. But the Crakers have sex in groups, like cats, so there are no anxieties over who is the real dad.

The Crakers are peaceful, gentle, vegetarian, and kind. Alas, our *Homo sapiens sapiens* relic—whose name is Jimmy—finds them mind-numbingly boring. As storytelling animals—which human beings are—we are fatally addicted to drama.

"Perfect storms" occur when a number of different forces coincide, and so it is with the perfect storms of human history. As novelist Alistair MacLeod has said, writers write about what worries them, and the world of *Oryx and Crake* is what worries me at present. It's not merely a question of our Frankensteinean innovations—most human inventions are neutral tools, deriving their negative and positive moral charges from the uses we make of them, and a number of those uses have been applaudable; though it is true that even "good" inventions are likely to have unintended consequences. Lowering the death rate without increasing the food supply will get you famines, social upheavals, and wars, every time.

Novels don't provide answers: they leave that to the how-to books. Instead, novels ask questions.

The first one in *Oryx and Crake* is probably, "Can we be trusted with ourselves?" For no matter how high the tech, *Homo sapiens sapiens* remains at heart what he's been for tens of thousands of years—the same emotions, the same preoccupations, the same good, bad, and ugly. We're a mixed bag, we humans.

But suppose we could eliminate the bad and the ugly, how would we do it? And would the result still be human? And if such creatures lacked aggression and the killer instinct, like Jonathan Swift's virtuous-horse Houyhnhnms in *Gulliver's Travels*, wouldn't they be quickly rendered extinct, as so many First Nations peoples were after their encounter with sixteenth- and seventeenth-century Europeans? Is it enough that some of us are quite nice, reasonably decent people, like Gulliver himself—and like Jimmy in *Oryx and Crake*? Jimmy has "a good heart." Will our good hearts be sufficient to save us, or will something else be required?

In order to protect the new, more beautiful, and ethically better model of us we are now increasingly capable of creating, and also to preserve the biosphere we ourselves are so rapidly destroying, wouldn't we have to do away with our present model of human being? You'd think so.

Crake thinks so too. And he does it.

Greetings, Earthlings! What Are These Human Rights of Which You Speak?

>>><<<

(2018)

Greetings, Earthlings!

I am very pleased to be here among you, although I admit that many of your ways still seem bizarre to me, despite the extensive research I have done on you.

I come from a planet in a galaxy far, far away and in another genre. The name of my planet is unpronounceable by you, since you lack the necessary vocal structures—which led us to view you for many millennia as lacking in intelligent life—but I have translated this name, very approximately, as "Mashupzyx." It seems to be a rule with you that the names of alien planets must contain the letters Z, Y, and X, and I have accommodated this rule in my translation.

Our physical forms on Mashupzyx would be puzzling and possibly even alarming to you—you would no doubt see us as a blend of octopus, giant sea slug, and salt and pepper shaker. So, to calm your nerves, I have assumed the form of a short, elderly, frazzle-headed female human person from the country of Canada. I thought this would be more comforting for you than the pterodactyl, mastodon, sea crocodile, gorgon, oversized cockroach, or giant rat of Sumatra that I also tried out. But I realized that, should I appear before you as any of them and begin making a speech, you might all run shrieking from the auditorium, and shortly there would be military helicopters, ray guns, flame-throwing drones, torches and pitchforks, silver bullets, and goodness knows what else! It would have been so untidy!

But in self-defence, I would have had to order the destruction of all of you, for which I would have felt at least some remorse, since you have produced some quite good musicians during your short period of existence. On Mashupzyx, we are partial to Mozart. If you see us coming in destructive mode, looking like oversized cockroaches or airborne crocodiles, play some Mozart.

You can see that I have done my due diligence on Earth folk and their lethal habits. I am aware of your xenophobia and alarmism, and also your capacity for chaos, since we have an extensive library of your films and television shows on Mashupzyx. In these films and television shows, you frequently run away shrieking—I have to observe that the word *monster* is overused among you. Then, after the shrieking phase, you take up weaponry. I wished to avoid this.

So, all things considered, I felt the old-lady disguise was best. I even thought of putting on a flowered apron as an extra little touch. You human people usually find old ladies harmless—although annoying—and expect them to smile benignly at you and then give you cookies, as well as wise advice that you frivolously disregard; that is, when you are not accusing the old ladies of causing the bubonic plague and frying them at the stake as witches.

But never mind the witches episode. Surely you would never do anything like that nowadays! Maybe shoot some people in synagogues, or human-traffic some ten-year-olds, or wrench hundreds of two-year-olds away from their parents and stick them into cages, or . . . but let us emphasize the positive!

Here I am, then, in my old-lady outfit, ready to explore the answer to the question: What are these human rights of which you speak? It is not a question that makes any sense to us on Mashupzyx, since on our planet we have no need for such things as specially delineated *rights*. All of us, although we are by no means identical to one another, are equal in the social and legal senses, unlike—it sadly appears—yourselves. You need these "human rights" items spelled out, for the simple reason that a lot of you haven't got them.

Some of you believe that this inequality is a bad thing. Others of you actually *enjoy* the prospect of others having less, and being considered *worth* less, than yourselves!

Humanity has its darker side.

But we cannot even begin on the question of these missing human rights until we have interrogated an even more basic question, namely: What are these *humans*?

There are several answers to that, depending on whom you ask.

I first asked a person called "Hamlet." Some think this Hamlet individual did not actually exist, but he seems to be better known and more respected than many so-called real people, and therefore I take him to be an authority of sorts on human beings. He had this to say:

> What a piece of work is a man! How noble in reason, how infinite in faculty! In form and moving how express and admirable! In action how like an angel, in apprehension how like a god! The beauty of the world. The paragon of animals. And yet to me, what is this quintessence of dust? Man delights not me; no, nor woman neither; though by your smiling you seem to say so.

So humankind is seen by Hamlet as having many good qualities: smart, capable of reason, graceful, the performer of angelically virtuous and powerful works, and with an overview of the world that is godlike. Not only that, but the "man" is good-looking, and tip-top in the hierarchy of the animal kingdom. (Hamlet says nothing about the inferiority of human teeth; but then, he is not a dentist.) However, despite all these qualities, humans are essentially mere dust. So he doesn't find them very joy-making.

Anyone reading world history—the fate of the millions killed in, for instance, the sum total of the First and Second World Wars, Korea, Vietnam, Cambodia, Rwanda, Afghanistan, Iraq, Syria, and on and on—would be inclined to agree with Hamlet's gloomier view. Human beings do have an alarming tendency to butcher others of their kind. Only ants and rats, and to a lesser extent, one kind of chimpanzee, display quite such an interest in group territorial aggression, and in reducing fellow members of their species to a non-living condition. We inhabitants of Mashupzyx feel sorry for you. You cause one another such grief and pain, and a lot of you never seem to have much fun at all.

That is one way of looking at humankind. I also investigated the answers of those people you call "scientists." Their province appears to be truth in the form of factual evidence-based knowledge. They like to create hypotheses, test them through repeatable experiments, and derive theories from these. Theories are different from laws of nature, it appears: if an exception is found to a theory, further experiments must be done, and the theory may be disproven or changed. Laws of nature, however, are immutable: there can be no exception to a law of nature. Many among you do not understand this, and state as "laws of nature" ideas that are not laws of nature at all. And that would include the so-called "law of nature" explanation of why the woman kind of human ought to be treated worse than the man kind.

Which brings us to Hamlet's quip at the end of his speech: "Man delights not me, nor woman neither, though by your smiling you would seem to say so." It took me a while to get my temporary old-lady head around this. (On Mashupzyx, we do not have heads, as such.) When speaking of "man," Hamlet is speaking of human qualities in general, but when he switches what you humans call "gender," or sometimes "sexual identity," he is implying copulatory activity.

This seems to be a widespread habit among you Earthlings: you can't think of women without thinking of sex, usually in some kind of humorous or demeaning way. The word *woman* causes Hamlet's pals to smile. Nudge, nudge, wink, wink, as a certain class of English male person used to say about anything to do with goings-on of an amorous nature.

But on Mashupzyx we do not have a female gender, as such. As I've mentioned, we are more akin to a blend of octopus, giant sea slug, and salt and pepper shaker. We have multiple appendages, and several of them on each of us contain cross-pollinating granules—these being the appendages that resemble salt and pepper shakers. When we wish to procreate, we entwine each other in our many arms, and apply either the "salt" appendage or the "pepper" one to the other individual's corresponding appendage. Numerous individuals can take part in this activity all at once. It saves time. And no one need ever feel jealous or left out. When it comes to procreation, it's sort of like—in your world—folk dancing. All are welcome!

Biologists have pointed out that humans are more closely related to the common chimpanzee (*Pan troglodytes*)—sharing 98 per cent or more of its genetic footprint—and have based many hypotheses upon this. Chimpanzee groups appear to be dominated by aggressive males, except when they aren't, and have been known to use tools, boss females around, and make war. Patriarchal, you might say. But there is another kind of chimpanzee—the bonobo (*Pan paniscus*)—that is equally closely related. The bonobos rule through matriarchal groups, solve tensions by making love, and bite off the fingers of troublesome males. It seems that human beings have some choice of close animal relatives, and thus not everything about them is biologically predetermined.

In the Western tradition—to which you yourselves belong—the patriarchal chimp model has prevailed in recent times, by which I mean the past four or five thousand years. It is perhaps due to your method of procreating that you decided many thousands of years ago that those you deemed "women" were inferior to your other kind, and did not deserve to be treated as well. But paradoxically, in even earlier times—the times before that—women were honoured for that very same birth-giving capability. What changed? When did women become viewed as lesser?

Those among you called "anthropologists" have been very busy in that respect. The immutable "it is because it is" "law of nature" justification was tossed out some time ago, except in pockets of resistance such as certain regions of the United States, and also in Russia, and also in . . . but the list would be embarrassingly long, now that I consider it. But it was correct to toss out this justification. No, Dear Humans: women are not by nature stupider. They do not by nature have less endurance. They are not necessarily less rational, or more emotional—they commit, for instance, far fewer crimes of passion and fewer suicides than men, both of these things having their roots in hyper-emotionalism.

Men shed fewer tears, it is true. But they shed more blood. So in the wet-dry contrast, you might say that men are wetter. And on Mashupzyx, we do say that.

It is also true that, in the hunter-gatherer era, men—never having been known to get pregnant—were tasked with chasing down the gazelles, insofar as they *were* chased down, since heavily pregnant women do not make good sprinters, but most food for the family and community was provided by the botanical skills and the gathering expertise of women, since gazelles do not grow on every tree.

And that is why men do not pick up their socks from the floor once they have taken them off: men simply do not see these socks, having evolved to notice only animals that are moving. Whereas women can easily distinguish the socks from the background of floor carpet, having evolved to gather mushrooms—which the discarded socks closely resemble in form, and sometimes in texture and aroma. At least, that is what we from Mashupzyx have concluded.

If the socks could be equipped with tiny solar lights that would flash on and off, the men would be able to see them, and of course—being unselfish and altruistic—would then scoop them off the floor and put them into the laundry basket, and one more major cause of human unhappiness would be eliminated!

Back to gender inequality. The anthropologists are now telling us that they trace the beginning of the unequal treatment of women to the early Bronze Age, which coincides both with the growing of wheat and a rise in organized warfare. They've been digging up bones from that period, and are finding that the men were eating both meat and wheat, but the women were eating only wheat, and thus developing bone deficiencies. And therefore becoming smaller and weaker, compared to their hunter-gatherer forebears.

Alas, Earthlings—it was a vicious circle. Rulers promoted the growing of wheat because it all ripened at once, and was thus easy to tax. But to grow wheat you need arable land. Invading your neighbours and taking away *their* arable land thus became tempting; but for that you needed an army, and for an army you needed a food substance that could be stored in large quantities, such as wheat.

The heavy weapons and bronze armour of the foot soldiers and chariot-driven spear hurlers of those days—the ancient Greeks, the Trojan warriors, and so forth—required a lot of upper body strength, which men had more of. But among the horse-riding, nomadic Scythians, farther east and north, lightish bows were the weapon of choice, and these can be handled quite easily by women. Among the Scythians there were women warriors, who wore trousers—horrors!—and shot arrows, and were honoured military heroes.

(Yes, it's real: they've been excavating the Scythian tombs.) Thus giving rise to the myth of the Amazons, to Artemis the moon goddess with her silver bow, to Susan the skilled archer in the Narnia books, and to Katniss Everdeen in *The Hunger Games*.

Nothing pestered the classical Greek male imagination more than the Amazons. The Amazons were at once their biggest dream—a woman equal to men, and thus worthy of real love! Theseus married one!—and their worst nightmare—a woman equal to men! What if they win? At anything? But especially, what if they win in warfare?

But I digress.

When you'd conquered a lot of land, you needed people to work that land, such as peasant children—produced from women—or else slaves, whether stolen, defeated in battle, or born into slavery. The women, the children, and the slaves were all deemed to have fewer rights than men because they were by nature inferior. Well, you would be tempted to say that, wouldn't you? If those people could vote, they would have voted themselves out of slavery. And since the ancient Mediterranean system ran on slavery, you couldn't have that.

Thus came the idea that some people had—by nature—fewer rights than others because they were lesser by nature. But there are no such laws of nature. We Mashupzyxtians have made a thorough investigation of it. As I have said, a law of nature admits of no exceptions: if there is an exception, the law is no longer a law. You humans have an expression, "the exception that proves the rule," but this does not hold for evidence-based, demonstrable laws of nature. There were too many smart, skilled women, and too many smart, skilled slaves, to justify inferiority as a *true* law of nature. Men addled their brains thinking up other reasons why various kinds of people were inferior: perhaps they were dishonourable and ignoble. But isn't it dishonourable and ignoble to cheat on your own so-called laws of nature?

We Mashupzyxtians have two questions that we like to ask of anything. Is it true? And: Is it fair? If it is not true that some people are by nature inferior to others, is it fair that they should be treated as if they are?

After many millennia of treating some people as by nature inferior, but nevertheless gradually extending the franchise—or the participation in full citizenship—from kings to nobles, from nobles to male landowners, from male landowners to male inhabitants, you human beings—or some of you—finally got it into your heads that human rights should be universal.

That move came after the horrors of two world wars and the revelations about the concentration camps and genocides conducted by the Nazi regime in the 1930s and the 1940s. The Universal Declaration of Human Rights was proclaimed in 1948 at the United Nations—another of your sporadic attempts to curtail your own blood-shedding propensities.

Here are some human words about it, lifted from the website of the Australian Human Rights Commission. (As an aside, I have to say that the Internet and websites have been invaluable to us Mashupzyxtians in our efforts to understand you. Some of us have made a study of politics, which we initially confused with cat videos. I think we've got that cleared up now, but for a while we were following something called Grumpy Cat, under the impression that it was the president of one of your larger countries.

To resume: The Universal Declaration of Human Rights. I quote:

> The Universal Declaration begins by recognising that "the inherent dignity of all members of the human family is the foundation of freedom, justice and peace in the world."
>
> It declares that human rights are universal—to be enjoyed by all people, no matter who they are or where they live.
>
> The Universal Declaration includes civil and political rights, like the right to life, liberty, free speech and privacy. It also includes economic, social and cultural rights, like the right to social security, health and education.

You may find the full text of the Universal Declaration on the website, if you can tear yourself away from the cat videos. You can also find the Convention on the Elimination of All Forms of Discrimination Against Women of 1981—a belated confirmation of the views of Olympe de Gouges, who hopefully presented a Declaration of the Rights of Women during the French Revolution, was accused of treason against the state, and was beheaded for her presumption; after which the Revolution excluded women from political activity.

And you may also find the United Nations Declaration on the Rights of Indigenous Peoples of 2007. So you see, little by little, you here on Earth have at least been making gestures toward the happy state of equality we enjoy on Mashupzyx. Good for you!

But, Earthlings, some words of warning. First, all of these Declarations and Conventions are ideals. Even in countries that have signed on to them, they have not been fully implemented. If they are not to remain merely words, more efforts must be made. And note: The more inequality there is, the more abuse.

Second, rights do not fall out of heaven. They are not a divine given. They have been battled for over centuries, and they have also been battled against. This is an ongoing tug-of-war. It's never over. Cain is always picking up a rock; Abel is always being slain. Greed, jealousy, the quest for power . . . when has *Homo sapiens sapiens* been without them? A stable society has at least some means of coping with these propensities. An unstable one uncorks the inner demons.

Third, organized and well-funded forces are now at work against these fragile human rights. There are some among you who are bored with the blandness of quasi-democracies, and wish to resurrect the totalitarianisms of the twentieth century. To this I would say: Beware. It may seem like a jolly idea at the beginning, what with all the marching and cosplay and the feeling that you are serving a Fearless Leader who will tell you the truth, unlike any of those in the past; but these things have never ended well, especially for the citizens.

Totalitarianisms act in much the same ways no matter what they call themselves. Their aim is total, unchallenged power; their means include the telling of lies, the bigger the better; the silencing of the independent press—by, for instance, strangling and then dismembering journalists—as well as the imprisonment or murder of any artists and writers who don't happen to agree with them; the doing away with an independent judiciary, thus making law-enforcement simply an arm of the government, exercising unjust laws that the totalitarian government has devised; the using of extra-legal means of suppression, such as assassinations, the inciting of mobs to violent attacks on identifiable groups, and the organizing of denunciations intended to destroy rivals, solidify power, and keep the population in a state of fear. Once the denunciation machine is up to full steam, it has tremendous momentum: in order to avoid being the next one to be denounced, you yourself are tempted to become a denouncer. And many have succumbed to this temptation in the past.

Why do these kinds of regimes get going? How do they seize power?

They get going initially in periods of chaos—usually economic— and through a sense of injustice in the population, or a large enough section of it. Such times favour the rise of anarchy, with mob violence and lynchings and kangaroo courts, succeeded typically—when people can't live in chaos anymore—by warlords and strongmen. These gather a following by directing anger at a target group, such as lepers, witches, Tutsis, AIDS sufferers, Mexicans, refugees, and the like.

Naysayers must be squashed, needless to emphasize. And the middle ground must be eliminated: those standing on it represent fairness, decency, moderation, and common sense, and when radical, irrational belief is required, say the strongmen, we can't have any of that. Driven by the fear of being found hypocritical, impure, or unworthy, extremists push one another to further and further extremes.

Do I need to tell you that extremists use democracy's own cherished tools against it? Voting, for instance. Voting is so useful when you can manipulate people into voting for your Leader—and then that elected person uses his power to co-opt or subvert the free-vote system the next time around.

Extremists will also try to monkey with what is known as free speech—the right to voice political opinions without being jailed, the right of the press to investigate and print the truth without reprisals. At the moment, in America, it's those of the Right who are trumpeting "free speech"—which does not in fact mean the right to say absolutely whatever you want, however untruthful, wherever you want to say it, and does not protect you from another right—the individual's right to defend his or her good name against damaging lies.

But the Left has foolishly taken the bait thrown out by the Right, and is busily trying to shut down certain manifestations of speech that it doesn't like. One should be careful of forging such weapons: they are certain to be used against you. Do you agree with the political muzzling of climate science and toxicity research? Do you deride evidence-based journalism and evidence-based policies? Do you applaud the smashing up of newspapers and the beating up and murdering of journalists? Do you shout "hooray" when the press is called—pace Stalin—"the enemy of the people"? If so, line up over here, in the queue marked "dictatorship." The line forms either to the left or to the right. But, as they say about dead people, they all end up in the same box.

Not that we use boxes as such, on our planet. Our funeral ceremonies consist of . . . but I will leave that for another time. Let us just say that a certain amount of mashupzyxtophagy is involved. Waste not, want not. None of us is ever exactly dead. Just . . . dispersed.

To end on a note of hope—Mashupzyxtians love notes of hope—you are not living in a totalitarian dictatorship now—or yet. Please avoid it.

Earthlings, you need not go down the divisive path of suspicion and hatred. You can instead identify as fellow human beings, and try to understand and face your common human problems together.

And you do have some large problems to solve! For instance, unless you regulate the temperature and chemical makeup of your planet, you will all be shitting plastic before long, your oceans will die, and then you won't be able to breathe, and it will be Goodbye, *Homo sapiens sapiens*. We'll be sorry to see you go. You have some good points. We do like Mozart. But we can save the scores, and play the music ourselves.

It need not be thus. The choice is yours.

My time here is up, and my mission to you has been accomplished; because, as you have guessed by now, this was never merely a voyage of investigation. We wish you well—if we had fingers, they would be crossed—and we are standing by in outer space to do something or other, we aren't sure what, in case you really mess up in a major way. It might involve ray guns.

We hope you'll be able to think of some good solutions by yourselves, however. You're pretty smart, after all.

Now I must shed my disguise of elderly short female person, glow with an incandescent light, sprout multiple pseudopod-like appendages, and shoot up into the stratosphere . . . bound for a planet in a galaxy far, far away, and in another genre.

Earthlings, behave yourselves! Have fun when possible! Avoid totalitarianisms! Enjoy the cat videos! Read up on human rights! Eat lots of kale! Get rid of single-use plastic!

Farewell . . . until we meet again.

Payback

>>><<<

INTRODUCTION TO NEW EDITION

(2019)

Although my Massey Lectures, collectively titled *Payback: Debt and the Shadow Side of Wealth,* were greeted as prophetic when they first appeared in the fall of 2008, I did not foresee the publication of them at that time, which coincided with the great financial meltdown. So much for my prophetic powers. But here is how I came by that undeserved reputation, in this instance.

By the early 2000s, I'd spent some years dodging various invitations to give the prestigious CBC Massey Lectures, which were inaugurated in 1961 to provide a forum on radio where "major contemporary thinkers could address important issues of our time." Those lectures are a lot of work! First you must write the lectures. Then you must turn the lectures into a book, which must be somewhat longer than the lectures themselves. Then you must deliver the lectures, one after another, in five different widely spaced cities across Canada, pausing only long enough to put on and remove your long underwear, as fall weather can be variable. Finally you must edit the lectures down to size for the radio broadcast.

This inflating and depuffing routine poses challenges, not only to one's skills but to one's ego—if the lectures should now be made shorter, having previously been made longer, how much faith can you place in the infallibility of each of your golden words?

So every time I was asked to deliver the Massey Lectures, I politely declined. "Thanks very much, but I'll be washing my hair," I said in effect. "And I'll be washing it next year too, and also the year after that, and . . ." Here I must explain the metaphor. It's from the 1950s, and it was what you were supposed to say in order to sidestep a date you didn't want to go on.

And so time passed—a time when I was always washing my hair when the subject of my delivering the Massey Lectures came up. But then Fate intervened. The Massey Lectures had traditionally been published by House of Anansi Press, a small literary company I'd kicked some founding money into back in the 1960s, whose board I'd subsequently served on while editing some of its books, and for which I'd written a tome called *Survival,* as part of the ongoing effort to prop up its finances. Anansi is now a mid-sized and very respectable press, but in 2002, it was in dire straits. It had been bought by a larger Canadian publisher, Stoddart, a while earlier, but now Stoddart itself was about to go down the drain, and Anansi would be gurgling into oblivion along with it.

In the nick of time, a man named Scott Griffin—who'd needed to be pried out of his Superman costume when a child—swooped in and bought Anansi, plucking it from the Slough of Despond, carrying its limp form to the shore, and restoring its breath of life with a judicious injection of cold cash. But meanwhile the Massey Lectures invitational circle had prudently decided to remove the lecture series from Anansi and bestow it on a larger and more solvent company.

Many were the wailings and dismal were the dirges! Couldn't I *do* something? A wart-removing potion, a curse or charm, an invocation to the moon? Something with an asp? I did not then and do not now have supernatural powers, but I gave it my best shot. I sat down and composed a zinger, in my best Anne of Green Gables tantrum mode, to this effect:

If you take the Masseys away from House of Anansi, I will never, never, never give the Massey Lectures, ever! (Stomp of foot.)

They didn't take the Masseys away from Anansi. Probably nothing to do with me, but you can see what would of necessity follow. And it did.

Expletive! I exclaimed. *Now I have to actually give the (expletive deleted) Massey Lectures!*

It was a fine example of the theme I was shortly to find myself exploring: on the face of it, they had done me a favour. I owed them. I had to repay them.

So I said I would give the Massey Lectures, without knowing what I would give them about. I fidgeted, I procrastinated, I pondered, weak and weary, over many a quaint and curious volume of forgotten lore.

Eventually I found myself circling around a set of questions that were bound to occur to anyone who had studied the nineteenth-century authors at any length. Heathcliff goes away poor and comes back rich: how? (Not in any good way, we'll be bound.) Will Chad Newsome of *The Ambassadors* leave his accomplished and refined French mistress and return to manage the vulgar but profitable family business in New England? (We guess yes.) Would Madame Bovary have got away with adultery if she'd been better at double-entry bookkeeping and had not run into debt? (Without question, say we.) Every nineteenth-century novel you crack open may delude you at first with tales of love and romance, but at the core of each one lies a bank account. Or the lack of one.

When I announced to the expectant Massey board that I had chosen my topic and it was Debt, I am told they blenched and huddled.

They thought I was going to write about Economics. They were much relieved when I explained that, no, my subject was simply the way human beings have thought about what is owed, who owes it, and how it should be repaid—the balancing of the scales, in religion, literature, the criminal underworld, the revenge tragedy, and in nature, an area in which we have, alas, vastly overdrawn our account.

The invitational committee wiped the beads of perspiration from their brows, and I submitted an outline and vanished down the rabbit hole of research. There was plenty of time. It was only 2007, and the lectures weren't due to be delivered until the fall of 2009.

Then Fate struck again. At the beginning of 2008, the Massey folk came to me in the guise of supplicants. Their 2008 lecturer would not be ready in time, so could I *please, please, please* deliver my own lectures a year early?

It was February. I would have to have the text of the book done by June, so it could be published in time for October, when the lecture tour would start. It was a tall order.

"Give me a couple of researchers," I said, rolling up my sleeves. What are sleeves for if you can't roll them up?

Five months and many hours of keyboard-pounding later, we were sort of ready. Yet more perspiration was wiped from brows.

Then Fate struck a third time. Just as the book was published and the lecture tour began—in Newfoundland, as it happened—the Big Financial Meltdown and Crisis occurred. And mine was the only book out there that was—on the face of it—about this topic. "How did you know?" asked various admiring hedge-fund managers. Useless to reply that I hadn't known: there was the evidence, laid out in the form of a book.

I do not have a crystal ball. If I really could predict the future, I'd have cornered the stock market long ago.

Memory of Fire

>>><<<

INTRODUCTION

(2019)

I first encountered Eduardo Galeano in 1981, at an Amnesty International conference in Toronto called "The Writer and Human Rights." I still have the poster, which features a winged horse.

To set the scene: The Cold War was still ongoing, and would not end until the Berlin Wall came down in 1989. The period of the Red Guards in China, during which 300,000 people had died, was only fourteen years in the past. Pol Pot's reign in Cambodia, which killed a quarter of the population, had ended a mere two years previously.

In Latin America, instability and violence were the rule, not the exception. Argentina was still under the right-wing rule of the generals, who "disappeared" some 30,000 people: kidnapping them, torturing them, throwing them out of planes into the ocean. In the case of women, raping them, and if they were pregnant, giving their babies to the families of fellow generals before throwing the women themselves out of planes. In El Salvador, civil war was raging, with many atrocities. In Chile, the 1973 coup d'état led by Pinochet and supported by the United States had been followed by a period of extreme violence—torture, killings, and disappearances. In Peru, the Communist Shining Path had launched its violent campaign just the year before.

I myself had joined Amnesty International at the time of the October Crisis in Canada, in 1970. The crisis had begun when members of the Front de Libération du Québec (FLQ) kidnapped James Cross, the British trade commissioner in Montreal, and later kidnapped and killed Pierre Laporte, the Minister of Labor. As a member of Amnesty, it was not possible to ignore the many flagrant violations of rights that were happening, or to be ignorant of the special treatment handed out to writers and artists. My interest in these matters was not theoretical: it was obvious that regimes bent on repression—whether on the left or on the right—had a particular interest in silencing independent voices. That meant artists and media outlets, such as radio, television, and newspapers.

I later became involved in the building of the English-Canadian PEN Centre—with a specific interest in the Writers in Prison program that helped writers who had been jailed because of something they had written—but that was in the future. In 1981, my focus was Amnesty.

The conference was what you might have expected, given the times: serious, concerned, urgent, but oddly dream-like: here we were in Canada, where nobody was being thrown out of planes, talking about what writers might or could do in the face of such horrors. Susan Sontag was there: thanks to the Russian émigré poet Joseph Brodsky, she'd just discovered that Stalin had not been Santa Claus—a fact known already to many present—and wanted us to send a telegram to Fidel Castro beginning "You murderer." (It is not really the best way of getting people out of jail in absolutist regimes.)

In the midst of all the turmoil, there was Galeano—cool, calm, observant. There were some empty chairs on the stage, each representing a disappeared person; one of them was for Galeano's best friend. I can't remember what he said, but it must have made an impression on me because I read *Memory of Fire* when it appeared in English translation in 1986. I was enormously impressed by it—so much so that I found myself using a quotation from its first volume, *Genesis,* as an epigraph for my 1988 novel, *Cat's Eye.* It reads:

> When the Tukanas cut off her head, the old woman collected her own blood in her hands and blew it towards the sun.
> "My soul enters you, too!" she shouted.
> Since then anyone who kills receives in his body, without wanting or knowing it, the soul of his victim.

It's a motif that runs throughout *Memory of Fire:* the murderer and the murdered, the oppressor and the oppressed, the conqueror and the conquered, the enslaver and the enslaved, the torturer and the tortured—these partners are joined at the hip, neither can escape the memory of what has occurred between them, and ultimately those who have perpetrated crimes and atrocities will suffer in some way from their acts.

Memory of Fire is history of a sort—the history of the Americas, so rich, many-layered, violent, lush, suggestive, and excessive. It is "history" in that the events recounted did actually happen. But it is not standard history. It is more like choreography or music: short vignettes, succinct riffs, facts embodied as embroidered verbal gestures. How variegated this world was, or is, as it unrolls through time. How cruel and often stupid the behaviours of those shown in it: harsh colonizers, defiant Maroons, hunters of escaped slaves. Nor are the animals omitted: crocodiles lurk, disguised as logs; female spiders devour their mates, at leisure and with relish.

There is nothing else like *Memory of Fire*. To read it is to be taken on an electrifying trip through a semi-hallucinatory, centuries-long, masterfully constructed Tunnel of Horrors that is harshly lit, lurid, and overcoloured but also deeply convincing. Did people really do such things? Are they really still doing them?

Welcome to the unreal real world. You will learn much, you will marvel often, and though you may be shocked and appalled—as Eduardo Galeano surely expected—you will never be bored.

Tell. The. Truth.

>>><<<

(2019)

Thank you very much for awarding me the unique honour of the CHS Burke Medal. I feel exceptionally flattered! And it is highly pleasing to me that Trinity College Dublin's Historical Society is a debating society! I was once a member of a college debating society—though not one with a pedigree as ancient as this one's—in the snow-swept wilderness of Toronto, Canada.

Some words of wisdom are expected from me on this occasion, it being an accepted fallacy that all people become wiser as they grow older. So here are a few substitutes for words of wisdom that I have come up with for you.

Here is my first observation: An emotion does not justify an action. Some seem to have lost sight of this. "We are very angry," they say. So far so honest. But this feeling, however sincere, does not in itself justify what you may do as a result. If anger were sufficient justification, all those men who kill their wives or girlfriends in fits of jealous rage would not be convicted of homicide. Anger can motivate an action, but it does not of itself excuse it.

In some countries, so-called crimes of passion committed by men get lower sentences. And anger itself was once highly gendered. In the 1950s, it was a putdown to say, "Oh, she's just an angry woman"; or, more tellingly, "She's just angry because she's not a man."

Here is my second word-cluster. It has to do with truth. In our age of fake news and Internet bots, truth is a stuff that can be difficult to come by. Isn't there "no real truth"? we are asked. Isn't it merely a question of which closed thought bubble you wish to take shelter in? But all this online sleight of hand doesn't mean that the facts of a situation do not exist. And the expression "speak truth to power" means nothing if there is no truth. I support mainstream media because they fact-check—most of the time—and if they get it wrong and print something that is untrue and damaging, they can be sued—unlike fly-by-night websites that appear and disappear like fireflies. There is a move afoot to demand that Facebook send a correction to everyone who has received a piece of fake news. I support this move. Corrections do work. Much of the time.

When my latest novel, *The Testaments,* was published, one reviewer found it old-fashioned: how quaint was the notion that the revelation of rotten secrets from inside a regime might help to bring it down. In the United States, the truth seemed to be making no difference in the polls. However, things changed quite suddenly with the appearance of some whistleblowers who were blowing new and disturbing tunes on their whistles. And people *have* started listening because these tunes seem to be true.

If you head into a career as a journalist, or a non-fiction writer, or even a fiction writer placing your story within the real world, please heed the advice of those such as Jodi Kantor, Megan Twohey, and Ronan Farrow, writing about powerful men exposed by female whistleblowers—men such as Harvey Weinstein. Do the research. Cross-check everything for accuracy. Make sure you've got the facts. Otherwise you risk going down in flames, like the experienced journalist Sabrina Erdely, whose *Rolling Stone* story about a rape was not cross-checked, and which ended up costing that publication upwards of US$4.5 million in damages because what it had printed was not true. Just because a thing ought to be true—just because you mean well—just because it fits your ideology—just because it would be very convenient in the general scheme of things if it *were* true—doesn't mean it *is* true. You need to be prepared to back up your facts because if you say something that is not popular, you will surely be attacked. Or to quote George Orwell: "If liberty means anything at all, it means the right to tell people what they do not want to hear." And to quote him again: three words: Tell. The. Truth.

My third nugget of wisdom has to do with power. A line from a poem of mine is often cited: "A word after a word after a word / Is power." Yes, as far as it goes. But what is power? In and of itself, power is morally neutral. There's nothing that says it is good, there's nothing that says it is bad. Electricity can light your lamp or it can burn down your house; and so it is with human power. And power over yourself is different from power over others. Nor—supposing you have some power to act—can you always know the end results of your actions. Causes often have unforeseen effects. To quote Samuel Beckett: "That's how it is on this bitch of an earth." Once you acquire power—I'm assuming that you will acquire some because I am such a screaming optimist—I trust that you will use it well. Or as well as possible, under the circumstances.

This is a debating society. It runs on words. Words after words after words, spoken—we hope—powerfully. Grammatically complex languages—languages that allow us to speak of long-past times before we were born, and of futures that may exist after our deaths—these languages are perhaps our first truly human technologies. We've been given our languages by our human ancestors, stretching as far back as we can know. Use these languages truthfully, use them fairly. And if you do that, you will also be using them powerfully, in the best sense.

Our words are now in your hands.

PART V

>><<

2020 TO 2021

THOUGHT AND MEMORY

Growing Up in Quarantineland

>>><<<

(2020)

There are two kinds of nightmares. The first is the bad dream you've had many times before. You find yourself in a very familiar, sinister place: the creepy cellar, the murderous hotel, the dark forest. But since it's a nightmare you've experienced before, your focus is sharpened admirably: the pointed stick worked against the monster last time, so let's try again.

In the second nightmare, everything that ought to be familiar is strange. You're lost, there are no directions, and you don't know what to do.

It seems we're living through both kinds at the moment, but which will resonate most with you will depend on your age. The second nightmare is a good fit for the young, who have never experienced anything like this before. What's happening? they cry. Life is ruined! Nothing will ever be normal again! I can't stand it!

But, for old folks like me, it's the first nightmare that is plaguing our sleep once more: we've been here before, or if not here, somewhere eerily like it.

Any child growing up in Canada in the 1940s, at a time before there were vaccines for a horde of deadly diseases, was familiar with quarantine signs. They were yellow and they appeared on the front doors of houses. They said things such as DIPHTHERIA and SCARLET FEVER and WHOOPING COUGH. Milkmen—there were still milkmen in those years, sometimes with horse-drawn wagons—and bread men, ditto, and even icemen, and certainly postmen (and yes, they were all men) had to leave things on the front doorsteps. We kids would stand outside in the snow—for me, it was always winter in cities, as the rest of the time my family was up in the woods—gazing at the mysterious signs and wondering what gruesome things were going on inside the houses. Children were very susceptible to these diseases, especially diphtheria—I had four little cousins who died of it—so once in a while a classmate would disappear, sometimes to return, sometimes not.

You were absolutely not supposed to go to public swimming pools in the summer, we were told, because there might be an outbreak of polio. Carnivals then had freak shows, and quite often one of the attractions would be The Girl in the Iron Lung, who was stuck inside a metallic tube and who could not move, even to breathe: the Iron Lung did her breathing for her, with a gasping sound that was amplified over the P.A. system.

As for lesser diseases such as chicken pox, tonsillitis, mumps, and the common kind of measles, kids were just expected to get them, and they did. When you were ill you were, of necessity, at home and in bed, and when you were recovering you risked boredom. No TV or video games; what you were given instead, in addition to the ginger ale and grape juice, was a pile of old magazines, a scrapbook, and scissors and paste. You cut out the more interesting pictures and pasted them into the scrapbook. One Lysol ad showed a woman up to her waist in water labelled "DOUBT, INHIBITIONS, IGNORANCE, MISGIVINGS," with the caption: "Too Late to Cry Out in Anguish!"

ME: "Why is she crying out in anguish?"
MOTHER: "I need to hang out the wash."

Magazine ads showed germs hiding everywhere, especially in sinks and toilets, equipped with devilish horns and malignant, evil little faces. Soap, toothpaste, mouthwash, drain cleaner, and household bleach were what you needed, and in vast quantities. Germs caused many illnesses, but they also caused personal tragedies such as halitosis—"Always a bridesmaid, never a bride," the ad mourned because the lovely lady in the pretty dress and the sad face had Bad Breath—and B.O., which meant Body Odour. Horrors! It was worse than a disease! As the 1940s shifted into the 1950s and adolescence swept over us, we went around sniffing our underarms and investing our babysitting money in deodorants and floral-scented cologne, because Even Your Best Friend Wouldn't Tell You.

Then there were feet. What could be done about feet? Various powders might be used. But, judging from the general classroom aroma, frequently they were not.

The worst thing about the nasty germs that were causing all of these diseases, not to mention smells, was that they were invisible. Nothing is scarier than an enemy you can't see.

Invisible enemies have a long history. In 1693, the New England religious leader Cotton Mather published *Wonders of the Invisible World,* a defence of his belief in witchcraft and demons. Not long after the seventeenth century ended, he also supported the introduction of inoculation against smallpox to New England. Demons = invisible. Cause of smallpox also = invisible. It all fits! Inoculation almost got him lynched, as it involved rubbing material from an infected pock into a cut in your arm, which was vigorously counter-intuitive for his countrymen at that time.

From inoculation came, eventually, vaccination, and then the hunt was on to identify the pathogens responsible for each of the killer diseases pestering humankind. The microscope made many things possible, and one by one, vaccines for common illnesses were developed. People were born into a world that felt safe from germs, or at least a lot safer than it had ever been. Rather than expecting to get a certain number of illnesses as a matter of course, newer generations now considered themselves exempt. Then along came AIDS and confidence was shaken, but only for a time. Treatments were developed, lives were prolonged, and that danger too receded to the level of background noise.

But in the long view, plagues have been a recurring factor in human history. Bacteria and viruses have killed a great many more people than wars ever did. The mortality rate for the Black Death in Europe is estimated at 50 per cent; the death rate from pathogens introduced by Europeans to the inhabitants of the Americas, who had no immunity to them, is estimated at between 80 per cent and 90 per cent. Millions and millions died from the Spanish flu. From the point of view of a virus or a bacterium, you are not a fascinating individual with a memorable life story. You are merely a possible matrix in which a microbe can make more microbes.

In interludes between pandemics, we like to think it's all over. Epidemiologists have never thought that. They're always waiting for the next one.

In 2003, I published *Oryx and Crake,* which revolves around a lethal pandemic, although a man-made one. (In a sense, all are man-made: if we didn't domesticate animals and eat certain kinds of wild ones, our chances of contracting new, species-leaping viruses would go way down.)

Was I always fated to write such a book? Possibly. My parents had both been through the Spanish flu in 1919 and their memories of it were vivid. In the 1950s, when I was supposed to be doing my high-school homework, I was reading sci fi, such as H.G. Wells's *War of the Worlds,* in which the invading Martians are defeated not by warfare but by microbes from Planet Earth, to which they have no immunity. Or I was reading fantasy, such as T.H. White's *The Sword in the Stone,* in which good wizard Merlin defeats bad witch Madam Mim in a shape-changing battle by becoming a number of disease germs, which topple Mim's monster dragon. Simultaneously I was reading Hans Zinsser's classic, *Rats, Lice and History,* about how outbreaks of disease affect us.

So, when we were studying Byron's poem "The Destruction of Sennacherib," in which an Assyrian army is destroyed overnight, I did not ask myself which Angel of the Lord had been sent. Instead, I wondered, "Which disease?" When Ingmar Bergman's classic film *The Seventh Seal* hit Canadian screens in 1958 complete with gruesome scenes of the Black Death, I was more than ready for it.

Oryx and Crake did not attract any criticism from biologists telling me not to be silly because such a thing could never happen. They knew it could. Because, in some form or another, it already had.

So here we are again, I thought when the present pandemic began: drowning in Doubt, Ignorance, and Misgivings, surrounded by invisible evil germs that may be lying in wait anywhere, except that this time they aren't shown in pictures as imps with horns but as colourful and attractive tufted pompoms. But like those whimsical things that look cute at first but can take over your body in sci fi films, these pompoms can kill.

What to do? In my 2008 book *Payback,* I gathered together the six reactions people had to the Black Death while it was unfolding. They were:

1. Protect yourself.
2. Give up and party, which could include drunkenness and theft.
3. Help others.
4. Blame. (Lepers, gypsies, witches, and Jews were all blamed for spreading the plague.)
5. Bear witness.
6. Go about your life.

It's not one or the other. I don't suggest No. 2. Or No. 4—giving up and blaming are not helpful—but protecting yourself, thereby helping others, or bearing witness by keeping a journal, or going about your life as much as you can with the aid of online support systems—these are possible now in a way that they were not in the fourteenth century.

So plaster a virtual quarantine sign on your door, don't let strangers in, consider yourself a potential plague vector, watch *Invasion of the Body Snatchers* (again) or *The Seventh Seal* (again). And get out the scissors and paste, analogue or digital, or the pen and paper, ditto. If you yourself are not ill, the pandemic may have given you a gift! That gift is time. Always meant to write a novel or take up clog-dancing? Now's your chance.

And take heart! Humanity's been through it before. There will be an Other Side, eventually. We just need to make it through this part, between Before and After. As novelists know, the middle section is the hardest to figure out. But it can be done.

The Equivalents

>>><<<

(2020)

In the fall of 1961, when I was twenty-one, I entered Harvard Radcliffe as a graduate student. What was I even doing there? I didn't want to be a professor; I wanted to be a writer. But everyone knew you couldn't support yourself that way, so I disguised myself in tweed and set out to acquire some credentials. I'd been told by a male poet that you really had to be a truck driver so as to understand life, but there wasn't much hope of that for me, so teaching it would have to be.

I lived in a large, wooden three-storey graduate women's residence on Appian Way that I later used as a quasi-model for the Commander's house in *The Handmaid's Tale*. Toms, creeping and peeping, decorated the building like barnacles on a whale. You'd look up from your desk and there would be a pair of men's feet, right on your window ledge. There was one communal phone, and any incoming call was likely to be an obscene one. These attentions were viewed by the authorities as minor annoyances, like midges. You were supposed to pay no attention.

There were a lot of things to which you were supposed to pay no attention. The English department didn't hire women as a matter of principle, though it was happy enough to teach them; but this was not mentioned in polite company. The prevailing view was that it was laudable to educate women enough that they could make intelligent conversation with their husbands' business colleagues, but anything beyond that would make them "neurotic." (Freud was a big influence on the 1950s push to cage women into their homes and bodies, and "neurotic" was akin to "leprous.")

So graduate women were neurotic by definition, and they were at Harvard on sufferance. In fact, women in American public life were there on sufferance. In the 1950s, women were informed in numerous ways that their role was now to be a supporting one. They were to ditch their wartime Rosie the Riveter overalls and their independent incomes, act helpless and cute like Lucille Ball, and fulfill their femininity through having children, renouncing thought, and deferring to their husbands. Men who did not want to be Type A hyperachievers were failed men, and women who did want that were failed women. So went the story.

This brainwashing had its heaviest impact on the generation before mine—those who were young mothers in the 1950s. My own cohort had dodged that bullet, having been teenage rock 'n' rollers, after which the more bohemian frequented coffee houses featuring folk singing and poetry. For the females among us, being a housewife was not our inevitable fate. Instead, we could engage in free love and be dedicated artists—though somehow you couldn't be both a housewife and a dedicated artist. Or could you? That particular narrative was in flux.

It was at this juncture, when the views of women set in place so rigidly in the 1950s were wavering, that Mary Ingraham Bunting, the president of Radcliffe, managed to set up the Radcliffe Institute for Independent Study. It was aimed at gifted women whose careers had been hampered by marriage and children, and who might benefit from a reset. The institute—which Bunting called "my messy experiment"—would give such women some time, a little money, and a room of their own. Above all, it would give them one another: fellow human beings who could understand what they were up against and take them seriously.

The Equivalents is the fascinating story of this messy experiment. The institute welcomed its initial group of twenty-three fellows in September 1961. Expectations were low and accommodations were modest. No one foresaw that this understated endeavour would become an important seedbed for the explosive second-wave women's movement that surged into public view at the end of the 1960s.

The book reads like a novel, and an intense one at that: the characters include Sylvia Plath and Anne Sexton, both of whom would become key writers of their era, both of whom would die by suicide; Maxine Kumin, who would go on to win a Pulitzer; Robert Lowell, who taught Plath and Sexton, and was already hailed as the founder of "confessional" poetry; Tillie Olsen, whose institute stay would result in her best-known book, *Silences,* about the forces that kept women from creating; and Betty Friedan, soon to publish *The Feminine Mystique,* which would galvanize hordes of discontented women who'd tried and failed to be Stepford Wives.

Who knew that Friedan and Bunting had once been collaborators? Friedan was in on the institute's planning and Bunting helped Friedan develop *The Feminine Mystique,* though ultimately Bunting proved too genteel for Friedan and Friedan too loud for Bunting. The former wished to rearrange the furniture; the latter came close to wanting to set fire to the house.

How did Mrs. Bunting get the reluctant nod from Harvard's old boys' club? Short answer: She was familiar with the territory and, like the sirens, she knew what song to sing. The Cold War was in space and the Soviets were outbraining the U.S.A., partly by harnessing talented woman power. Shouldn't the United States mobilize its own smart females? Two dozen women given a little money and office space might not sound like much of a mobilization, but as it turned out, they set off a chain reaction.

The first institute fellows were up against their own double identity. They were housewives and thus dismissible, but they were also talented—published poets and fiction writers, recognized painters and sculptors. A man could be a genius and unstable and also widely revered, as Robert Lowell was; but for a woman, "genius" was likely to be parsed as "nut case" and also "bad mother"—a much more devastating label than "bad father." *The Equivalents* explores the contradictory forces at work in the women of this bridge generation: too vital and ambitious for the 1950s doll's house, but too early for the full-throttle feminism of the 1970s.

The Equivalents delves deep into the complex lives of these women. Using letters, recorded material from the period, interviews, and biographies, Maggie Doherty explores their friendships, rivalries, and jealousies, their marriages, their crises, their anxieties and fears, and also their moments of exhilaration and triumph. The relationship between Sexton and her fellow poet Kumin is especially touching, though it could not, in the end, keep Sexton in the land of the living.

Doherty conveys the electricities and entanglements of this first experiment, but she doesn't dodge its limitations. As she follows the story through the 1960s, she includes Alice Walker and her "womanist" activities on behalf of Black women, whose problems were quite different from those of the middle-class white women who by and large populated the institute: the feminine mystique decried by Friedan had never applied to them. Olsen, as a working-class Communist, was an outsider of a different sort.

Most of this group did not identify as "feminists" of the kind that appeared at the end of the 1960s. Although their work was taken up by younger agitators, they wanted to be artists, not activists. As the decade rolled out, with the civil rights movement, the anti-war protests, and the arrival of lesbian activism, divisions appeared—not only between new and different forms of feminism but between erstwhile close friends who had bonded at the institute. "Poets in their youth begin in gladness," Wordsworth said. "But thereof comes in the end despondency and madness." Madness for some, and certainly despondency for others. What had become of those early hopes, those twin-soul friendships?

The Equivalents is an observant, thoughtful, and energetic account of a decade viewed through the lens of the institute. Doherty strives to make the reader understand the conditions—material, spiritual, and intellectual—in which these women struggled to define themselves and to channel their art. The past is always another country, but we can visit it as tourists, and it's useful to have such a thorough guide.

Doherty closes with a comparison of that era with today's. What has changed for women over sixty years, what remains the same, and what is worse? Was all that struggle and angst and creative turmoil for nothing? She doesn't think so, and neither do I. I once lived in that distant country, and I'm grateful to the author of *The Equivalents* for reminding me that I have no wish to return.

Inseparable

>>><<<

INTRODUCTION

(2020)

How exciting to learn that Simone de Beauvoir, grandmother of second-wave feminism, had written a novel that had never been published! In French it was called *Les Inseparables* and was said by the journal *Les Libraires* to be a story that "follows with emotion and clarity the passionate friendship between two rebellious young women." Of course I wanted to read it, but then I was asked to write an introduction to the English translation.

My initial reaction was panic. This was a throwback: as a young person, I was terrified of Simone de Beauvoir. I went to university at the end of the 1950s and the beginning of the 1960s, when, among the black-turtleneck-wearing, heavy-eyelinered cognoscenti—admittedly not numerous in the Toronto of those days—the French existentialists were worshipped as minor gods. Camus, how revered! How eagerly we read his grim novels! Beckett, how adored! His plays, especially *Waiting for Godot,* were favourites of college drama clubs. Ionesco and the Theatre of the Absurd, how puzzling! Yet his plays too were often performed among us (and some, such as *Rhinoceros*—a metaphor for Fascist takeovers—are increasingly pertinent).

Sartre, how bafflingly smart, though not what you'd call cute. Who hadn't quoted "Hell is other people"? Did we recognize that the corollary would have to be "Heaven is solitude"? No, we did not. Did we forgive him for having sucked up to Stalinism for so many years? Yes, we did, more or less, because he'd denounced the invasion of Hungary by the U.S.S.R. in 1956, and had written an incandescent introduction to Henri Alleg's *The Question* (1958), an account of

Alleg's brutal torture at the hands of the French military during the Algerian War—a book banned in France by the government, but available to us in the boonies, as I read it in 1961.

But among all these intimidating existentialist luminaries there was only one female person: Simone de Beauvoir. How frighteningly tough she must be, I thought, to be holding her own among the super-intellectual steely-brained Parisian Olympians! It was a time when women who aspired to be more than embodiments of assigned gender roles felt they had to comport themselves like macho men—coldly, with avowed self-interest—while seizing the initiative, even the sexual initiative. A bon mot here, a slapping away of a wandering hand there, an insouciant affair, or two, or twenty, followed by cigarettes, as in films . . . I never would have been up to it, struggling as I was with the lesser demands of the college debating club. In addition to which, smoking made me cough. As for those dowdy wartime suits with the durability and the shoulder pads, those would have been far too high a price to pay for a seat at the café table.

Why was Simone de Beauvoir so frightening to me? Easy for you to ask: you have the benefit of distance—dead people are less innately scary than living ones, especially if they've been cut down to size by biographers, ever alert to flaws—whereas for me, Beauvoir was a giant contemporary. There was the twenty-year-old me in provincial Toronto, dreaming of running away to Paris to compose masterpieces in a garret while working as a waitress, and there were the existentialists, holding court at Le Dôme Café in Montparnasse, writing for *Les Temps Modernes,* and sneering at the likes of mousy me. I could imagine what they might say. "Bourgeoise," they would begin, flicking the ashes off their Gitanes. Worse: Canadian. "Quelques arpents de neige," they would quote Voltaire. Moreover, a Canadian from the backwoods. And the worst kind of backwoods Canadian: an anglo. The dismissive contempt! The sophisticated disdain! There is no snobbism quite like French snobbism, especially that of the Left. (The Left of the mid-twentieth century, that is; I am sure no such thing would happen now.)

But then I grew somewhat older, and I actually went to Paris, where I was not rejected by existentialists—I couldn't find any, as I couldn't afford to eat in Parisian cafés—and shortly after that I was in Vancouver, where I finally read *The Second Sex* from cover to cover, in the washroom so no one would see me doing it. (The year was 1964, and second-wave feminism had not yet arrived in the hinterlands of North America.)

At this point, some of my terror was replaced by pity. What a strict upbringing had been imposed upon the young Simone. How constrained she had felt, in her supervised body and frilly girl's clothing and rigidly prescribed social behaviour. It seemed that there were advantages to being a backwoods Canadian girl, after all: free from censorious nuns and demanding sets of highish-society relatives, I could run around in trousers—better than skirts, considering the mosquitoes—and paddle my own canoe, and, once in high school, attend sock hops and go rollicking off to drive-in movies with slightly disreputable boyfriends. Such unconstrained and indeed unladylike comportment would never have been permitted to the young Simone. The strictness was for her own good, or so she would have been told. If she violated the rules of her class, ruin would await her and disgrace would be the lot of her family.

It's worth reminding ourselves that France did not grant the vote to women until 1944, and then only through a law signed by de Gaulle in exile. That's almost twenty-five years after most Canadian women gained the same right. So Beauvoir grew up hearing that women in effect were unworthy of having a say in the public life of the nation. She would have been thirty-six before she could vote, and then only in theory, since the Germans were still in control of France at that time.

Once she came of age during the 1920s, Simone de Beauvoir reacted strongly against her corseted background. I, a being much less corseted, did not feel that the conditions described in *The Second Sex* applied to all women. Some of the book rang true to me, to be sure. Though by no means all of it.

In addition, there was the generation gap: I was born in 1939, whereas Simone de Beauvoir was born in 1908, a year before my mother. They were of the same cohort, though worlds apart. My mother grew up in rural Nova Scotia, where she was a tomboy, a horseback rider, and a speed skater. (Try to picture Simone de Beauvoir speed-skating and you will grasp the difference.) Both had lived through the First World War as children and the Second World War as adults, though France was at the centre of both, and Canada— though its wartime military losses were greatly out of proportion to its population—was never bombed and never occupied. The hardness, the flintiness, the unflinching stare at the uglier sides of existence that we find in Beauvoir are not unconnected to France's ordeals. Enduring these two wars, with their privations, dangers, anxieties, political infighting, and betrayals: that passage through Hell would have taken its toll.

Thus my mother lacked the flinty gaze, having instead a cheerful, roll-up-your-sleeves, don't-whine practicality that would have seemed offensively naive to any mid-century Parisian. Overcome by the oppressiveness of existence? Faced with a large rock that Sisyphus must roll uphill, only to have it roll down again? Plagued by the existential tension between justice and freedom? Striving for inner authenticity, or indeed for meaning? Worried by how many men you'd have to sleep with in order to wipe the stain of the haute bourgeoisie from yourself forever? "Take a nice brisk walk in the fresh air," my mother would have said, "and you'll feel a lot better." When I was waxing too depressingly intellectual and/or morose, this was her advice to me.

My mother wouldn't have been very interested in the more abstract and philosophical portions of *The Second Sex*, but I expect she would have been intrigued by much of Simone de Beauvoir's other writing. From this distance it's arguable that Beauvoir's freshest and most immediate work comes directly from her own experience. Again and again she felt drawn back to her childhood, her youth, her young adulthood—exploring her own formation, her complex feelings, her sensations of the time. The best-known example is perhaps the first volume of her autobiography, *Memoirs d'une Jeune Fille Rangée* (1958), but the same material appears in stories and novels. She was, in a sense, haunted by herself. Whose invisible but heavy footfall was that, coming inexorably up the dark stairway? It usually turned out to be hers. The ghost of her former self, or selves, was ever present.

And now we have a wellspring of sorts: *Inseparable*, unpublished until now. It recounts what was perhaps the single most influential experience of Beauvoir's life: her relationship with "Zaza"—the Andrée of the novel—a many-layered and intense friendship that ended with Zaza's early and tragic death.

Beauvoir wrote this book in 1954, five years after publishing *The Second Sex,* and made the mistake of showing it to Sartre. He judged most works by political standards and could not grasp its significance; for a materialist Marxist this was odd, as the book is intensely descriptive of the physical and social conditions of its two young female characters. At that time the only means of production taken seriously had to do with factories and agriculture, not the unpaid and undervalued labour of women. Sartre dismissed this work as inconsequential. Beauvoir wrote of it in her memoir that it "seemed to have no inner necessity and failed to hold the reader's interest." This *appears* to have been a quote from Sartre, one with which Beauvoir *appears* to have agreed at the time.

Well, Dear Reader, M. Sartre was wrong, at least from this Dear Reader's perspective. I suppose that if you're keen on abstractions such as the Perfection of Humankind and Total Justice and Equality, you won't like novels much, since all novels are about individual people and their circumstances; and you particularly won't like novels written by your lady love about events that have taken place before you yourself have manifested in her life, and that feature an important, talented, and adored Other who happens to be female. The inner life of young girls of the bourgeoisie? How trivial. Pouf. Enough with this small-scale pathos, Simone. Turn your well-honed mind to more serious matters.

Ah, but, M. Sartre, we reply from the twenty-first century, these *are* serious matters. Without Zaza, without the passionate devotion between the two of them, without Zaza's encouragement of Beauvoir's intellectual ambitions and her desire to break free of the conventions of her time, without Simone de Beauvoir's view of the crushing expectations placed on Zaza as a woman by her family and her society—expectations that, in Beauvoir's view, literally squeezed the life out of Zaza, despite her mind, her strength, her wit, her will—would there have been a *Second Sex*? And without that pivotal book, what else would not have followed?

Furthermore, how many versions of Zazas are living on the earth right now—bright, talented, capable women, some oppressed by the laws of their nations, others through poverty or discrimination within supposedly more gender-equal countries? *Inseparable* is particular to its own time and place—all novels are—but it transcends its own time and place as well.

Read it and weep, Dear Reader. The author herself weeps, at the outset: this is how the story begins, with tears. It seems that, despite her forbidding exterior, Beauvoir never stopped weeping for the lost Zaza. Perhaps she herself worked so hard to become who she was as a sort of memorial: Beauvoir must express herself to the utmost because Zaza could not.

We

>>><<<

INTRODUCTION

(2020)

I didn't read Yevgeny Zamyatin's remarkable novel *We* until the 1990s, many years after I'd written *The Handmaid's Tale*. How could I have missed one of the most important dystopias of the twentieth century, and one that was a direct influence on George Orwell's *Nineteen Eighty-Four*—which was a direct influence on me?

Perhaps I missed it because I was an Orwell reader but not an Orwell scholar, and a science fiction reader but not a science fiction scholar. When I did finally come across *We,* I was amazed by it. And now, reading it again in this fresh, intense translation by Bela Shayevich, I am amazed all over again.

So much in *We* seems prophetic: the attempt to abolish the individual by merging all citizens with the state; the surveillance of almost every act and thought, in part through the charming giant pink ears that quiveringly listen to every utterance; the "liquidation" of dissenters—in Lenin's writing of 1918, "liquidation" is metaphorical, but in *We* it's literal, as those to be liquidated are in fact transformed into liquid; the erection of a border wall that serves not just to prevent invasion but to keep citizens inside; the creation of a larger-than-life, all-knowing, all-wise Big Brotherish Benefactor who may be simply an image or a simulacrum—all these details foreshadowed things to come. So did the use of letters and numbers rather than names: Hitler's extermination camps had not yet engraved numbers on their inhabitants, and we of this age had not yet become the fodder for algorithms. Stalin had yet to forge the cult of his own personality, the Berlin Wall was decades in the future, electronic bugging had not been developed, Stalin's show trials and mass purges would not take place for a decade—yet here is the general plan of later dictatorships and surveillance capitalisms, laid out in *We* as if in a blueprint.

Zamyatin was writing *We* in 1920–1921, while the civil war that followed the Bolshevik-dominated October Revolution was still ongoing. Zamyatin himself, having been a member of the movement before 1905, was an Old Bolshevik (a group slated for liquidation by Stalin in the 1930s because they stuck to their original democratic-Communist ideals instead of going along with Comrade Stalin's autocracy)—but now that the Bolsheviks were winning the civil war, Zamyatin didn't like the way things were going. The original communal committees were becoming mere rubber-stampers for the power elite who had emerged under Lenin and would be solidified by Stalin. Was this equality? Was this the flowering of the individual's gifts and talents that had been so romantically proposed by the earlier party?

In his 1921 essay, "I Am Afraid," Zamyatin said, "True literature can exist only when it is created, not by diligent and reliable officials, but by madmen, hermits, heretics, dreamers, rebels and sceptics." In this he was a child of the Romantic movement, as was the revolution itself. But the "diligent and reliable officials," having seen which way the Leninist-Stalinist wind was blowing, were already busying themselves with censorship, issuing decrees about preferable subjects and styles, and pulling out the unorthodox weeds. This is always a dangerous exercise in a totalitarianism, since weeds and flowers are likely to change places in the blink of an autocrat's eye.

We can be viewed in part as a utopia: the goal of the One State is universal happiness, and it argues that since you can't be both happy and free, freedom has to go. The "rights" over which people were making such a fuss in the nineteenth century (and over which they continue to make such a fuss now) are viewed as ridiculous: if the One State has everything under control and is acting for the greatest possible happiness of everyone, who needs rights?

We follows a long line of nineteenth-century utopias that also proposed recipes for universal happiness. So many literary utopias were written in the nineteenth century that Gilbert and Sullivan created an operatic parody of them called *Utopia, Limited*. A few highlights are Bulwer-Lytton's *The Coming Race* (a superior human race lives underneath Norway, with an advanced technology, inflatable wings, reason over passion, and females who are bigger and stronger than males); *News from Nowhere* by William Morris (socialist and equal, with arts and crafts, artistic clothing, and every female a Pre-Raphaelite stunner); and *A Crystal Age* by W.H. Hudson, in which people not only have beauty and artistic clothing, but are rendered happy, like the Shakers, through having no interest in sex whatsoever.

The later nineteenth century was obsessed with "the woman problem" and "the new woman," and not a single utopia—and then not a single dystopia—could refrain from tinkering with existing conventions concerning sex. Nor could the U.S.S.R. Its early attempts to abolish the family, to raise children collectively, to allow instant divorce, and, in a few cities, to decree it a crime for a woman to refuse to have sex with a male Communist (nice try, guys!) created such a farcical and shambolic misery that Stalin backpedalled furiously in the 1930s.

But Zamyatin was writing in the early, fermenting period, and it is this cluster of attitudes and policies that *We* satirizes. Though people live in literal glass houses, with all of their actions transparent, they lower their blinds modestly for the hour of sex, booked in advance via pink ticket and duly recorded by an older woman in the foyer of each apartment building, according to regulations. But though everyone has sex, only women who meet certain physical specifications are allowed to have children: eugenics was considered "progressive" at this time.

As in Jack London's 1908 novel, *The Iron Heel*—a dystopia hoping for a utopian future—and also in Orwell's *Nineteen Eighty-Four*, the driving forces of dissent in *We* are female. D-503, the male protagonist, begins as a dedicated member of the One State, preparing to send a rocket into the universe with the aim of sharing the One State's recipe for perfect happiness with worlds unknown. Dystopian characters are prone to journal-writing, and D-503 intends his journal for the universe. But soon the plot thickens, and so does D's prose. Has he been dipping into Edgar Allan Poe in his more lurid moments? Or the German Gothic Romantics? Or Baudelaire? Possibly. Or his author has.

The cause of this emotional disruption is sex. If only D could stick to his scheduled sexual appointments and his pink tickets! But he cannot. Enter I-330, an angular, individualistic secret bohemian and alcohol-drinking dissident who seduces him in a hidden love nest and leads him to question the One State. She is in sharp contrast to O-90, a round, compliant woman who's forbidden to have children because she's too short, and who is D's registered pink-ticket sexual partner. O can stand for a circle—completion and fullness—or for an empty zero, and Zamyatin chooses both. At first we think O-90 is a nullity, but when she becomes pregnant despite the official veto, she surprises us.

Much has been written about the difference between I-cultures and We-cultures. In an I-culture such as the United States, individuality and personal choice are almost a religion. No accident there. America was initiated by Puritans, and in Protestantism it's the individual soul vis-à-vis God that's important, not membership in a universal Church. Puritans were big journal-writers, recording every spiritual blip and bleep: you have to believe in the high value of your soul to do that. "Find your voice" is a mantra in North American writing schools, and that means your unique voice. "Free speech" is taken to mean you can say anything you like.

In We-cultures, on the contrary, why do you need that kind of voice? It's belonging to a group that's valued: one should act in the interests of social harmony. "Free speech" means you can say anything you like, but what you like will naturally be constrained by the effects it may have on others, and who will decide that? The "we" will. But when does a "we" become a mob? Is D's description of everyone going for a walk in unified lockstep a dream or a nightmare? When does the so-harmonious, so-unified "we" become a Nazi rally? This is the cultural crossfire we are caught in today.

Any human being is surely both: an I, special, discrete; and a We, part of a family, a country, a culture. In the best of worlds, the We—the group—values the I for its uniqueness, and the I knows itself through its relationships with others. If the balance is understood and respected—or so we fondly believe—there need not be a conflict.

But the One State has upset the balance: it has tried to obliterate the I, which nonetheless stubbornly persists. Hence poor D-503's torments. D's arguments with himself are Zamyatin's arguments with the emerging conformity and voice-stifling of the early U.S.S.R. What was happening to the bright vision held out by the utopias of the nineteenth century, and indeed by Communism itself? What had gone so wrong?

When Orwell wrote *Nineteen Eighty-Four*, Stalin's purges and liquidations had already happened, Hitler had come and gone, the extent to which a person could be reduced and distorted by torture was known, so his vision is much darker than Zamyatin's. Zamyatin's two heroines are staunch, like Jack London's, whereas Orwell's Julia capitulates and betrays almost immediately. Zamyatin's character S-4711 is a secret service operative, but his number gives away his alter ego: 4711 is the name of a cologne that originated in the German city of Cologne, which in the year 1288 staged a successful democratic revolt against church and state authorities, and became a Free Imperial City. Yes, S-4711 is actually a dissident, bent on revolt. Whereas in *Nineteen Eighty-Four*, O'Brien pretends to be a dissident but is actually a member of the state police.

Zamyatin holds out the possibility of escape: beyond the Wall is a natural world where there are free "barbarian" human beings, covered with—could it be fur? For Orwell, no one in the world of *Nineteen Eighty-Four* can leave that world, though he does permit a distant future in which the repressive society no longer exists.

We was written at a particular moment in history—the moment when the utopia promised by Communism was fading into dystopia; when, in the name of making everyone happy, heretics would be accused of thoughtcrime, disagreement with an autocrat would be equated with disloyalty to the revolution, show trials would proliferate, and liquidation would become the order of the day. How could Zamyatin have seen the future so clearly? He didn't, of course. He saw the present, and what was already lurking in its shadows.

"Men's courses will foreshadow certain ends, to which, if persevered in, they must lead," says Ebenezer Scrooge in *A Christmas*

Carol. "But if the courses be departed from, the ends will change." *We* was a warning to its own place and time—one that was not heeded because it was not heard: the "diligent and reliable officials" and their censorship of Zamyatin took care of that. The courses were not departed from. Millions and millions died.

Is it also a warning to us, in our time? If it is, what sort of warning? Are we listening?

The Writing of *The Testaments*

>>><<<

(2020)

Greetings! It is a great honour to have been asked to deliver this year's Belle van Zuylen Lecture. I am so sorry I could not be there in person, but as we all have to these days, I'm making do with what is available. I only hope you will not get too bored, as it's quite stressful to watch people talking for very long on a screen, but I will do my best under the circumstances.

Under the circumstances: always a limiting factor for anyone, anywhere: the circumstances. Learning about Belle van Zuylen led me to realize what an extraordinary person of the female persuasion she was, but also how formed by her circumstances. Had she not been born into a well-to-do aristocratic family, she would not have had an education. If she had not had an education, she would not have been a writer, nor would she have become acquainted with many of the Enlightenment minds of the later eighteenth century; nor would she have been liberal in her outlook—*liberal* as that term was once understood—nor would she have had a critical attitude toward the more retrograde elements in the European nobility, nor would she have held a generally favourable view of the reforms proposed during the French Revolution.

But if she had been in France at the time of that revolution, and especially during the Terror, which caused many heads to roll, her own head may well have come off; since to be of a well-to-do aristocratic family, to have had a broad education, and to be known as Isabelle de Charrière by marriage—a definitely upper-class surname—would have been next door to a death sentence. Nor would her liberal views have saved her: Olympe de Gouges, the author of *Declaration of the Rights of Woman and of the Female Citizen* (1791), which claimed for women a small portion of the kinds of rights that revolutionary men were claiming for themselves in 1789, ended up being accused of sedition and treason and beheaded by the guillotine.

After her death, she was used as a warning to other women—"the impudent Olympe de Gouges, who was the first woman to start up women's political clubs, who abandoned the cares of her home, to meddle in the affairs of the Republic, and whose head fell under the avenging blade of the law," as one man tut-tutted while mansplaining to a group of uppity women. In fact, Olympe de Gouges had not started up any women's political clubs, she had merely inspired them after her death; but in such partisan affairs, and under the pressure of moral panics, an insistence on the exact truth is considered pedantic. *Impudent* is the key word here: it comes from the Latin "pudere," meaning to be ashamed, so impudent means, among other things, shameless and immodest—terms almost always used of women but not of men. Madame de Gouges's requests were seen as immodest and shameless, like a brazen, body-exposing dress; and this kind of rhetoric persisted throughout the nineteenth century whenever impudent women raised their hands in support of greater equality.

Why such a pushback? Alas, Jean-Jacques Rousseau—one of the intellectual progenitors of the French Revolution, and much read by Belle van Zuylen—had a view of women that confined them to the home sphere and to service in the needs of others, in a way that would not have been considered out of place in Nazi Germany. So Madame de Gouges's request for a little more equality could be seen as undermining the foundations of the brave new world that the revolution saw itself as building. Despite their key role during the revolution, after it women were needed to produce and raise the next generation of male republican Frenchmen, and that's all they were needed for. So off with her head. (This pattern was repeated almost exactly during the course of the Russian Revolution, and indeed during the aftermath of the Second World War in England and North America. Thanks for your help, ladies; now scurry back to your nests and stay there because that's where you really belong. And please, no impudence.)

Belle van Zuylen is said to have said that French aristocrats had learned nothing from the French Revolution, but those aristocratic political refugees whom she came to know in Switzerland had learned at least one thing: If aristocratic heads are rolling, and if you happen to be an aristocrat, run away! Run away very fast! Your good intentions and even your good actions—supposing you have any to your credit—will not save you because at such times it's not who you think you are as an individual, or even the good deeds you believe you have done, that will count for you or against you. It's who other people think you are—those now pulling the strings or lowering the blade—and it will be "sentence first and verdict afterwards"—the reference is to the bloodthirsty and tyrannical Queen of Hearts in *Alice's Adventures in Wonderland*—since, during a moral panic of any kind, to be accused is to be convicted and then to be punished. The facts cease to matter, and the judicial process, if any, becomes a matter of rubber stamps. This is a pattern humankind has repeated many times over the course of its history. When there is a crisis, whether real or imagined, culprits—whether real or imagined— must be found and eliminated.

Lucky Belle van Zuylen, to be living in Switzerland during all that dangerous uproar. She died in 1805, the year after Napoleon crowned himself emperor, thus abolishing the Republic that the Revolution had established and signalling the end—at least temporarily—of Enlightenment ideals. Things actually got worse for the rights of women once Napoleon came in. The post-revolution government had decriminalized abortion, but Napoleon recriminalized it. He also legalized slavery again, which the revolution had abolished, and his deputies committed sadistic mass atrocities in Haiti and Guadaloupe that rival anything the twentieth century came up with in that vein.

I wonder what Belle van Zuylen thought of Napoleon during the year she had to observe him. She would not have witnessed the worst of him—the biggest slaughters and horrors were yet to come— but she must have been very discouraged to see the collapse of her humane ideals.

I have always been suspicious of the phrase *the wrong side of history*. History doesn't progress along a clearly marked one-directional road toward the golden city of Utopia. It winds around, it reverses, very much depending on the circumstances. The Great Leap Forward can become the Great Leap Backward with astonishing rapidity, depending on the food supply, the advent of a pandemic, or the lust for power of a greedy despot. History is not a god, although it has been worshipped like one by various factions in the past. History is simply human beings doing stuff. "Where does Margaret Atwood come up with this weird shit?" one dismayed reader of *The Handmaid's Tale* asked plaintively on Twitter. But it is not I who come up with this weird shit. It is human beings, and they have come up with a large amount of shit much weirder than anything I have put into *The Handmaid's Tale* or *The Testaments*. Novelists have to pull back on the horror. If they put in all the weird shit that actually happens, no one but a psychopathic sadist would be able to read it.

Which brings us to the writing of *The Testaments,* the subject of today's lecture. *The Testaments* was published in September of 2019, and is the sequel to my novel *The Handmaid's Tale.*

I wrote *The Handmaid's Tale* in the early 1980s, at the beginning of a right-wing pushback against some earlier movements. One of these was the New Deal—crafted during the Depression, and under which America saw not only the beginning of a pre-war recovery from the Depression and then a postwar boom time during the late 1940s and the 1950s, but also an equalizing movement in incomes. Not equal, but equalizing. The Reagan years began to flip that—removing regulations, taking off the brakes, and distributing money upwards rather than sideways and downwards. The "trickle-down effect" was supposed to share the wealth, but it did not. There wasn't much of a trickle; instead there was a dam.

That was only one facet of the pushback. Another was the rise of the religious right, and its determination to reverse the changes wrought by the second-wave women's movement of the 1970s; in particular, these people wanted to control women's bodies. Welcome back, Napoleon, and a slew of others who have tried to do the same, including Nicolae Ceaușescu of Romania, who decreed that women of childbearing age had to have four children or state the reason why. This came with mandatory monthly pregnancy tests and penalties, and resulted in female suicides and overcrowded orphanages, as many women lacked the wherewithal to feed that many children. In the United States, the main push was to outlaw any form of birth control. Not that this was coupled with assistance to those actually forced into childbearing against their wills. The Vikings were a step up the ladder: you got into Valhalla if you died either in battle or in childbirth. Even Saint Paul, that hairy old misogynist, held that women could be redeemed through childbirth. Not so the American religious right.

So, *The Handmaid's Tale* was written in response to questions I was asking myself about what would happen if these people gained power, and what they would do. Pretty much what they were saying they would do. Women should be in the home, and the way to guarantee that was to deprive them of jobs and money. They should serve the needs of men, as Rousseau had said they should; otherwise, they had no use.

The Handmaid's Tale seemed rather far-fetched in 1985, even to me.

But never say never. Time moved on. The Iron Curtain fell. The triumph of capitalism was announced. In the early 1990s, the end of history was proclaimed, somewhat prematurely. With the attack on the Twin Towers in New York on 9/11 of 2001, history rumbled into action again, this time in a different direction. In 2008, the world economy suffered a meltdown due to reckless economic policies. These kinds of scary events led to a desire for greater safety and security on the part of the citizenry: right-wing policies suddenly had a bit more appeal. Chaos and threat precede dictators: the dictator or the totalitarian government proposes itself as an answer to clear and present dangers.

Such elements have a habit of causing more chaos and threat as a way of frightening people and angering them, blaming the chaos and threat on other people—people who must be suppressed or eliminated—and proposing themselves as the answer to the problem. We alone can fix it, they say. We have a plan. We will restore the right order of society. Things will be better under our leadership. Those who are not with us are against us. It's compelling, that message. It has its charms, especially if you are frightened or angry.

Such was the message being megaphoned in the summer of 2016, when I began writing *The Testaments.* It was also the moment when we began filming *The Handmaid's Tale* Hulu/MGM television series, in which I make a cameo appearance as an enforcer. That was a very peculiar moment in my life—to find myself inside a story I myself had created, acting out the part of a character to whom, in real life, I would have been strongly opposed. Or I think I would have been strongly opposed. But what form might such opposition have taken? In a real totalitarianism, those who strongly oppose, and who get found out, are shot.

Ever since *The Handmaid's Tale* was published, readers had been asking me what happened to its central character at the end. "I don't know," I would say. "Maybe she got out. Maybe she was captured. What do you think?" Would I ever write a sequel? "No," I would say. "I would not be able to re-create that narrative voice."

But now here I was in 2016, embarking on a sequel. I still could not re-create that narrative voice. In an online course on writing that I recorded several years ago, I said that one might always consider a story from the different points of view of those within it. Also, one need not begin at the beginning. *Little Red Riding Hood,* for instance, might begin, "It was dark inside the wolf."

And that is how *The Handmaid's Tale* begins—it is dark inside the wolf, the wolf being the regime of Gilead—and that is also how *The Testaments* begins. It's dark inside the wolf, but this time the wolf is Aunt Lydia, who heads up the Aunts, charged with keeping the women and girls of Gilead in order, and the darkness inside the wolf is the secrecy—and also the box of other people's secrets—inside Aunt Lydia's head.

At the end of *The Handmaid's Tale,* we visit an academic symposium held a couple of hundred years after the Gilead regime is over—thus telling us that it is indeed over. This is what becomes of the past once it is past: it's transformed into a history book, or it becomes a play or an historical novel or a film or a television series, or it becomes a museum exhibition, or a statue, or a painting; or it becomes a subject for academic study, and symposiums are held about it, and animated discussions take place.

Material for the present, in other words. As Thomas King has remarked, history isn't what happened—it's the stories we tell about what happened. How we interpret and present what happened. And that interpretation and presentation is always taking place in the now of the speaker or interpreter because where else can it take place? Therefore the past as we know it is always changing. Some parts of it are buried, but then dug up again. Some are spun positively, and then spun negatively. Statues are erected to admired or important figures, and then they are pulled down. I myself have lived through a number of statue take-downs, including those in the former Soviet Union, and that of the Shah of Iran, and currently those of various Confederate generals in the United States.

So *The Testaments* begins with the unveiling of a statue. It is a statue of Aunt Lydia. Granted, it's in an obscure location—she is, after all, a woman, and women by and large do not get statues in Gilead—but it is nonetheless a statue.

I won't tell you what has become of it by the time of the next symposium on Gileadean studies at the end of *The Testaments,* except to say that this is what does become of statues when old and disliked regimes are swept away and new orders take over. How many Roman and Greek statues of gods were mutilated by Christians, once they got power? Lots.

The beginnings of totalitarianisms are fascinating—their instigators never present themselves as evil plotters who will wreck your life but as heralds of a new and better society—and their crumblings are equally fascinating. The rapidity with which the Berlin Wall came down was staggering. Very few had expected it. So in 2016, at a time during which we'd been witnessing a turn toward authoritarianisms, both in Europe and elsewhere, I wanted to explore, at least in fiction, a turning in the other direction; a veering toward freedom, not away from it. Do totalitarianisms collapse from within, once they have become corrupt and have failed to deliver a golden future? Do they collapse through civil war, or through invasion from without, or through resistance to them on the part of their citizens, or through power struggles among their own elites? There are no universal failsafe recipes, though some or all of these factors may play a part.

Obsessed as I have been with the Second World War, I have also been obsessed with collaboration. Among the citizens of the countries invaded by Germany, there were collaborators. In the U.S.S.R., some who had come to realize that the regime was flawed and corrupt and had betrayed its own origin story nevertheless went along with it and helped it. Why?

The reasons for collaboration are several: a person may be a true believer, and stay in a corrupt regime hoping to steer it back to its original and surely virtuous path. A person may be very afraid: go along with it or go down to the grave, is the usual formulation. A person may be ambitious: if there's only one game in town you'd better play it if you want to advance, and thus to benefit materially. Or a person may feel that they can do so much more good from within a regime than by trying to oppose it from without. I think of Himmler's masseur, Kersten, who would get Himmler up on the massage table, cure his mysterious pains, and then persuade him to save people from the Gestapo. "If it weren't for me," such people tell themselves, "it would have been so much worse. Under the circumstances, I acted well." And there is always some truth to that, though the circumstances can be very limiting and the sphere of action that's possible may be extremely small. If, that is, you wish to remain alive.

Manuscripts written in secret and then hidden or smuggled out have also fascinated me for a long time. They are numerous—from Anne Frank's diary to Curzio Malaparte's *Kaputt*. Why do people risk their lives to act as recording angels? Why indeed? Do they really have faith that we in the future—once it is our present—will receive their message, and will understand it, and care about it? It seems they do have such faith.

It's my own faith that when there is a tyrannical regime, there will be a resistance movement against it. And so it is in both *The Handmaid's Tale* and *The Testaments*. The resistance movement against Gilead is called MayDay, after the call for help used by ships and airplanes in distress in the Second World War. It's from the French *m'aider*—help me. I note that this is also the cry of the fly with a tiny man's head on it in the horror film *The Fly*. "Help me!" he calls in a teeny buzzing little voice. Is that what cries for help sound like when they come to us across a huge gulf of time? But can we go back in time and actually help the one who calls to us? No. But we can listen, and we can acknowledge the message.

In addition to taking us into the darkness inside the wolf of Aunt

Lydia's mind, *The Testaments* is also narrated by two much younger women—the first of whom has grown up inside Gilead and knows no other reality, the second of whom has grown up across the border in Canada. I am old enough to have known and spoken with several actual resistance members from the Second World War who managed not to get caught and shot—from Poland, from France, and also from Holland—and as I'm sure you know, many of them were very young at the time—under the age of twenty. And so it is in *The Testaments.*

The major writing time of the book stretched from 2016 to 2019. The story unfolded as reality changed around me, and it also unfolded as the television series rolled out. Season One began in April 2017, when I was perhaps a quarter of the way through my writing. Season Two launched in 2018, and Season Three in 2019. The shooting of Season Four was delayed by COVID-19, but it will begin in a few weeks. Thus the writing of the book proceeded in parallel with the television series, but luckily for me, sixteen years into the future: I knew what might become of the characters before the television writers did. I also had the advantage of reading the scripts through various stages. "You can't kill that person!" I would say. "They are still alive in the future—that is, in the novel I'm writing. I need them!" It was a curious experience—living in the future of a bunch of people who don't actually exist, or not in the usual meaning of that word.

And we are all having curious experiences now, in this unprecedented year.

At some point, this time of ours might be the subject of an academic symposium. That would not be a terrible outcome: it presupposes that there will still be people in the future, and that they will still have attention to devote to the reinterpretation of history, and that freedom of speech and intellectual activity will still exist in some form. It's not the meanest of hopes: at least we won't be destroyed by robots, or by planetary meltdown, or by a virus that is 100 per cent lethal, and that we really can't control.

I write books about possible unpleasant futures in the hope that we will not allow these futures into reality. Under the circumstances, we're doing moderately well, more or less, or some of us are. I only hope that the wave of authoritarian political behaviour we have been witnessing will retreat, and that our collective circumstances will not get worse. There's fear and there's hope: the two are not unconnected.

Under what circumstances do we wish to live? Perhaps this is the real question we should be asking ourselves. It's dark inside the wolf, yes; but it's light outside the wolf. So, how can we get there?

The Bedside Book of Birds

>>><<<

FOREWORD

(2020)

In 2001, when Graeme Gibson had already been collecting bird stories and images for over ten years, the two of us went to a Viking dress-up party as Odin's Ravens. The names of these ravens were Huginn and Muninn—Thought and Memory—and they flew around the world during the day, returning in the evening to perch on Odin's shoulders and tell him what they had seen. This is how Odin became so wise: he listened to the birds.

To disguise ourselves as ravens we wore black, with black gloves, and beaks made of black construction paper. I was Memory and Graeme was Thought. He said he couldn't be Memory because he didn't have a good one, and that was why he kept such copious journals: they were a hedge against forgetting. He relied on these journals for the anecdotes about his encounters with birds that he included in *The Bedside Book of Birds:* they were recorded by him at the time they happened, fresh from reality.

Graeme's history with birdwatching was a long and passionate one. It was a pursuit we shared, though if birdwatching were a religion, I'd have been the blasé communicant who'd grown up in it and performed its rituals because that's what our people do, and Graeme would have been the new convert, smitten with blinding light on the road to Damascus. Every new bird was a revelation to him. He wasn't much interested in making lists of the birds he'd seen, though he did make such lists as an aid to memory. Instead, it was the experience of the particular, singular bird that enthralled him: this one, just here, just now. A red-tailed hawk! Look at that! Nothing could be more magnificent!

At such moments I'd see even common birds anew, as I was viewing them through his eyes. Our shared life was propelled in part by his enthusiasm. This enthusiasm segued into conservation activities, then to Graeme's leading bird trips, then to his co-founding of the Pelee Island Bird Observatory, then to his work with Nature Canada and BirdLife International.

And it led also to his crafting of *The Bedside Book of Birds*. He wasn't writing a field guide about classification and identification, or a how-to-bird book, or a Big Year personal birding record: what he was after was the many ways birds have affected people, throughout many centuries and across all cultures. Humans have been imaging birds ever since we've been human. They've been world-egg creators, helpers, messengers, and guides; they've been symbols of hope and aspiration; they've also been demonic presences and harbingers of doom. As has been said, the angels got their wings from the birds, but the devils got their claws. With birds, it's not all pure larksong.

Wherever we went and whatever he was reading, Graeme collected: myths about birds, folk tales about birds, paintings and drawings and sculptures featuring birds, bird poems, excerpts from works of fiction, accounts by biologists and travellers. A miscellany is a kind of scrapbook, and the scrapbook he was assembling was very large. The most painful part of his labour was cutting it down to a manageable size.

Although no publisher had been interested when he first proposed this book back in the 1990s—it was an odd duck, a love letter of sorts, and it couldn't be easily classified—when it finally appeared in 2005 it was a smash hit, somewhat to Graeme's bemusement. He was lucky in having an excellent designer, C.S. Richardson, and lucky too in that the ancient forest-friendly paper he insisted on having took the coloured ink so well. The result was a joy to the eye as well as an entertainment for the mind and a stimulant for the soul. Graeme being Graeme, he promptly gave away the profits: birds had been a gift to him, and gifts must be passed on.

Graeme never lost his delight in birds. In the last year of his life—

when, due to the progress of his vascular dementia, he could no longer read or write—he still liked to watch the birds going about their vibrant lives. Our backyard feeder and our birdbath were attracting only sparrows and robins and grackles and the occasional pigeon, but he didn't care: every bird was worthy of attention. "I no longer know their names," he told a friend of ours. "But then, they don't know my name either."

Perpetual Motion and *Gentleman Death*

>>><<<

INTRODUCTION

(2020)

The first time I sat down to talk with Graeme Gibson, in 1970, I read his hand, as I was in the habit of doing for strangers in those reckless days. "Everything is connected to everything else," I said sagely. "Your intellectual and creative selves are continuous with your life-line and your fate line. It's all one." And so it was, and so it would be.

Fleeing the city and the complexities of a crumbled marriage, Graeme moved to a rented farm near Beeton, Ontario, that year. I visited off and on, and then off, and then on. We were both working with the newly founded small publisher House of Anansi Press— I say "working" loosely because it was a young writers' press and nobody got paid very much. I was editing Graeme's book *Eleven Canadian Novelists*—radio interviews with writers that he'd done for Robert Weaver's CBC show *Anthology*. It was my job to hack a pathway through the transcripts: they'd been typed up by a woman who turned out to be somewhat deaf, so I had to guess what the writers might actually have said.

When we weren't busying ourselves with such publishing tasks, we were trying to arrange a life together. The man who owned the Beeton farmhouse wanted us to buy it, but someone had cut a piece out of the main beam of the old barn and stuck it over the fireplace— meaning that the barn would soon collapse—so we looked elsewhere. We didn't have much money, but we finally found something we could afford: an 1835 farmhouse, uninhabited, uninsulated, and, unknown to us at the time of purchase, haunted.

Having raised the sagging floor and discovered a big pile of well-rotted manure in the barn suitable for a vegetable garden, we settled down to write, more or less. Graeme was at the same time organizing the Writers' Union of Canada and taking various literary odd jobs to make a semblance of an income, and on weekends and holidays we usually had a houseful of hungry people: his teenage sons, their friends, and friends of ours on restful outings from the city, all of them joined midway through the 1970s by our newborn daughter. We had two stoves: a wood-burner, on which a cauldron of something was eternally simmering; and an electric one, with an oven suitable for reviving half-dead lambs. We had a washing machine of sorts but no dryer. Various of our preserved foods exploded in the root cellar. I won't go into the matter of the sauerkraut, except to say that we should have made it outdoors.

In the midst of this intermittent chaos, Graeme wrote on, somewhat more than I did at the time. His first novel, *Five Legs* (1969), had done surprisingly well for such an experimental work; his second, *Communion* (1971), was a succès d'estime, but at the end of it he'd killed off Felix, the young man who'd first appeared in *Five Legs*. Now he was casting around for his next focal point. During this period, several proto-novels came and went: they would be started in a fire of optimism, then shelved when they failed to engage him fully. He was an all-or-nothing kind of man.

Graeme was a person not only of enthusiasms but also of moral imperatives. He decided that since we had a hundred acres of weedy farmland, it was our duty to farm it. He didn't want to be a city person lolling about idly in the country; he wanted the immersive experience. Needless to say, neither of us had ever spent time on a farm before. At auctions he acquired a second-hand baler and a harrow to go with the old tractor that had come with the property. What we grew on our rolling acres was alfalfa. Graeme later said that farming was driving around until something broke, then driving around to find the part to fix it, then driving around . . .

We also accumulated an assortment of non-human beings. "What kind of animals should we have?" Graeme had asked an old farmer at the outset. "None" was the answer. Then, after a pause: "If you're gonna have livestock, you're gonna have dead stock." And so it was, and so it would be. Things died. Sometimes we ate them.

We had chickens, for which Graeme built a henhouse and an

enclosed yard; an old horse, which the poet Paulette Jiles had persuaded us to rescue; some ducks because we had a pond and what was a pond without ducks? Another horse, to keep the first one company; some jumping cows whose escapes were the marvel of the neighbourhood; and a couple of geese that got stepped on by the cows and then eaten; and then—why?—some sheep, which had a habit of dying of gid or almost drowning in the pond; and, to round off this Noah's Ark, a pair of peacocks.

The peacocks were for my birthday. They added unearthly screams to the ambience, which by now was quite Gothic. I won't describe our attempt to raise chicks in an incubator—you have to get the temperature just right, and we didn't, and Frankenchicks is what came out—nor the sad tale of the male peacock, who was deprived of his peahen by a blood-drinking weasel and went mad and became a mass murderer of the hens.

Thus began *Perpetual Motion*, Graeme's tale of pioneer farming set in a house strangely like the one we were living in and on a piece of land oddly like ours. The protagonist, Robert Fraser, is a man of enthusiasms, like Graeme, and his frustrations and crackpot obsessions have at least a cousinly relationship to Graeme's. So do the blackflies and thunderstorms and recalcitrant cows that plague him.

But although some of the incidents and details are immediately recognizable to me, not everything in the book came from personal experience. Graeme combed through dictionaries of slang and unconventional usage to make sure his characters were using words they really would have used, unpleasant though modern tastes might find some of these. He consulted local histories—what was going on in and around Shelburne, Ontario, in the early to mid-nineteenth century? What had the people who'd settled the area been like—those from whom many in Ontario were descended, including Graeme? Not always very savoury, the novel tells us.

The digging up of the bones of extinct giant animals and the exhibiting of them was a much-publicized pursuit in the nineteenth century, and Southern Ontario was a hot spot for mammoths, Graeme discovered. So it's not anachronistic that Robert Fraser unearths such a skeleton, nor that he hopes to profit by it. Public interest was high, as was controversy: Such animals were a challenge to the prevailing

Biblical narrative. Were these beasts dragons that had perished in Noah's Flood, and if not, what were they? Fraser's excavated mammoth bones set the keynote for the novel; as the mammoth went, so might we overweening humans go, was the subtext.

Then there was the history of the perpetual motion machine, that alluring but impossible Holy Grail sought by many inventors in those times, and the huge flights of passenger pigeons—so damaging to crops—and the money that could be made from slaughtering them. The search for perpetual motion and the extinction of the passenger pigeon were based on the seemingly incurable human hope that there is indeed a free lunch eternally available on this earth. Nature's bounty—here in the form of pigeons—will never run out. The first law of thermodynamics can be cheated. It's a delusion, but one that persists to this day.

The Gibsonian style is difficult to describe. Hesitations in speech and thought, doublethink, expletives and spluttering, the tics and tricks of verbal communication and the failures to communicate: these are present to a greater or lesser extent in all of Graeme's fictions. Farce and antic dispositions and human stupidity and nobility and futility and tragedy are never far apart, though tempered with a sort of loony cheerfulness. The last word in *Perpetual Motion* is *moon*, a Western symbol for illusion and deception. But despite the explosion of his crazed machine, Robert Fraser does not give up; he continues the "desolate search" for something that—try as he might, plausible though he may sound in his efforts to convince others— does not exist.

Graeme almost didn't finish *Perpetual Motion* because three-quarters of the way through it he nearly died. In mid-November of 1979, I was in Windsor, Ontario, doing a book event, and when I got back to my hotel room there was a message waiting for me. It was from our friend and neighbour Peter Pearson—the filmmaker— who was standing watch in the hospital in Alliston, Ontario. Graeme was in the operating room. He had a ruptured duodenal ulcer, which, given a few more hours, would have put an end to him. Eight weeks later, though still wobbly, he was back on the fictional track. He worked on the novel during the two or three months he spent in Scotland while I was holding down the farm with help. Shortly after this, we moved back to the city, a choice for which Graeme's near-death and weakened condition were only some of the reasons. *Perpetual Motion* was finished, and published in 1982, with translations into French, Spanish, German, and, as I recall, Polish.

Graeme's near-death was a hint of what was to happen in his life during the 1980s. His father, Brigadier-General T.G. Gibson, died in the middle of the decade, and his younger brother, Alan Gibson—a film and television director in England—followed in 1987. (His mother had died earlier, in the mid-1960s.) These deaths, his own near-miss, and the fact that in the natural course of events he himself would be next in his family to go—a fact of which he was more than aware—were the impetus behind his fourth and final novel, *Gentleman Death* (1993).

It's a curious book; but then, which of his books is not? It begins with a novel being written half-heartedly by a moderately successful novelist strangely like Graeme. This comically unsatisfactory novel bears more than a passing resemblance to some of those that Graeme himself had cast aside. The real-life novelist is called Robert Fraser, like the protagonist of *Perpetual Motion,* and is clearly a descendant. Does novel-writing have the same place in the mental life of Robert Fraser the Second as the search for a perpetual motion machine had in the life of Robert Fraser the First? Is it too a delusion, a clutch at the moon? Possibly.

Robert Fraser's novel weaves in and out of Robert Fraser's life, and his memories and dreams inform both. The memories of his childhood during the Second World War are absolutely Graeme's. His mother's struggles as a woman left to cope with two boys during the early 1940s, her depressions after her hospital visits to soldiers mangled by the war, his own fears about his overseas father as the fathers of his friends were killed one after another—we in the family remember him describing these events in much the same words as those used by Robert Fraser. The illness and death of his beloved brother, his grief and loss—these too are in the book. His battles with his father, then his caretaking as that father ages, becomes frail, and starts seeing people who aren't there—all of it happened as described. Robert's quizzical attempt to come to terms with mortality, his experience of ghosts, and his dreams of the departed, his recognition of the death's head behind his own face—these too were Graeme's. They are also widely shared human experiences, although each of us encounters them in a unique way.

No spoilers, but Graeme's protagonist does achieve an equilibrium of sorts. Living in the past, however unhappy that past may have been, is a protection against the knowledge of our own mortality, since in our past we ourselves are always alive, no matter how many around us have died; and to live in the present is to accept our inevitable death. Yet if you aren't alive to the present, how can you live your life to the full? Death the Gentleman waits for us all, not outside us but within us: our secret sharer, and in a sense our friend, for what would life be if we were doomed to live forever? "Here it is at last, the distinguished thing," Henry James is said to have said on his deathbed, a quotation with which Graeme was familiar. Robert Fraser is not completely Graeme, of course; but, as I'd said when I'd first met him, his creative life and his real life were one.

Caught in Time's Current

>>><<<

(2020)

I can say with a measure of certainty—having consulted my poor excuse for a journal—that my poem "Dearly" was written in the third week of August 2017, on a back street of Stratford, Ontario, Canada, with either a pencil or a rollerball (I'd have to check that) on some piece of paper that may have been anything from an old envelope to a shopping list to a notebook page; I'd have to check that as well, but I'm guessing notebook. The language is early twenty-first-century Canadian English, which accounts for the phrase *less of a shit,* which would never have been used in, for instance, Tennyson's *In Memoriam;* though something like it might have appeared in one of Chaucer's more vernacular tales—*lesse of a shitte,* perhaps. This poem was then taken out of a drawer, its handwriting more or less deciphered by me, and typed as a digital document in December 2017. I know that part from the date and time identifier on the document.

The poem was composed much as described at the beginning of it. I was indeed making my way along the sidewalk, rather slowly. My knees were in poor condition due to my having recently spent five hours in a twisted position in the back seat of a car with a one-and-a-half-year-old, with a bunch of luggage piled on top of me. (Improved now, thanks. Or the knees are.) I was in fact carrying half a cup of coffee in a takeout cup with a regrettable plastic lid. (Better options are available now, thanks to the justifiable uproar over plastic pollution.) Slow walking leads to rumination, which leads to poetry. Park benches are my friends, and it wasn't raining. Scribbling ensued.

Why was I walking alone, and not with Graeme—with whom I'd walked many hundreds of miles, ever since 1971, in places as diverse as mainland Scotland, Orkney, Cuba, Norfolk, the mid-north mixed-forest Canada, southern France, the Canadian Arctic, and the Northwest Territories? Walking had been one of our chief joys—that and canoeing—until his knees started to go, earlier than mine. So he was at the bed and breakfast in Stratford that we had been going to for some years, and I had hobbled out for supplies, fuelling myself with caffeine along the way.

We were in Stratford on our annual visit to see a mix of Shakespeare, musicals, and surprises. Was I also giving a talk? Probably, since I'd just published *Hag-Seed,* set, not coincidentally, at a festival that bears more than a passing resemblance to the Stratford, Ontario, one. Watching Shakespeare, researching Shakespeare, writing about Shakespeare—it's a short leap to the contemplation of obsolete words, words that are fading, the malleability of language, all language—*gay* used to mean *happy,* and it once referred to the demimonde—and from that to the slipstream of time itself. We're caught in time's current. It moves. It leaves things behind.

That's the foreground. In the near distance, Graeme had received a diagnosis of dementia in 2012, so we were five years into it. In August of 2017 it was still moving slowly enough, but the clock was ticking. We knew the what, but we didn't know the when.

We'd talked about this a lot. We tried not to spend too much time under a pall of gloom.

We managed to do a lot of the things we wanted to do, and squeezed out enough happiness from hour to hour. Graeme was premourned: all the poems about him in the book *Dearly* were written before he actually died.

At the same time, we were dealing with the Hulu/MGM television series of *The Handmaid's Tale*—it had launched in April 2017—and that in itself had been a blockbusting phenomenon. Its multiple wins at the Emmys were still in the future, as was the launch of the excellent miniseries made of *Alias Grace*—but both of them were still on my mind. Both were also backlit by the lurid glow cast by the 2016 presidential election, which I'd experienced like those nightmare movies where you're expecting a girl to jump out of a cake and instead it's the Joker. Had Clinton won the election, *The Hand-maid's Tale* TV series would have been framed as a bullet dodged. As things were, the viewership was not only very high but very horrified. However, few expected at this point that the efforts to undermine the foundations of American democracy—an independent functioning media, a judiciary separate from the executive branch, and a military that owes its loyalty to the country as embodied in the Constitution, not to some king or junta or dictator—would go as far as they were to go by November 2020.

Alias Grace, based on a real double murder in the mid-nineteenth century, was also about to chime eerily, not only with the pussy-grabber-in-chief but also with the #MeToo uprising. The miniseries launched in September, the Harvey Weinstein allegations surfaced in October. But none of that had happened yet as I was limping along the street, meditating on the fading word *dearly.*

What else was I doing in August 2017? I'd started my novel *The Testaments* about a year before—before the election, but in the lead-up to it. We already knew, back in 1985, that the world of Gilead came to an end, but we did not know how. I was in the initial or "mud pie" phase of exploring the possibilities, although I had sent a one-pager to my publishers in February.

You can't work easily on a novel while watching two plays a day. You can, however, scribble poetry. And so I did.

Here, then, is "Dearly": a poem that's part of its own zeitgeist, while claiming not to be part of it. It's not exactly a memento mori, more like a memento vita.

To quote Ursula K. Le Guin (whose obituary I would shortly write, though that, too, had not yet happened), "Only in dark the light. Only in dying life."

Poems—like everything else—are created in a particular time (2000 BC, AD 800, the fourteenth century, 1858, the First World War, and so on). They're also written in a place (Mesopotamia, Britain, France, Japan, Russia); and beyond that, in a location where the writer happens to be (in a study, on a lawn, in bed, in a trench, in a café, on an airplane). They are often composed orally, then written down on a surface (clay, papyrus, vellum, paper, digital screen), with a writing implement of some kind (stylus, brush, quill pen, steel nib, pencil, rollerball, computer), and in a particular language (Ancient Egyptian, Old English, Catalan, Chinese, Spanish, Haida).

Beliefs about what a poem is supposed to be (praising the gods, extolling the charms of a beloved, celebrating warlike heroism, praising dukes and duchesses, tearing strips off the power elite, meditating on nature and its creatures and botany, calling on the commoners to rebel, hailing the Great Leap Forward, saying blunt things about your ex and/or the patriarchy) vary widely. The ways in which the poem is supposed to accomplish its task (in exalted language, with musical accompaniment, in rhyming couplets, in free verse, in sonnets, with tropes drawn from the word-hoard, with a judicious number of dialect, slang, and swear words, extempore at a slam event) are equally numerous and subject to fashion.

The intended audience may range from your fellow goddess priestesses, to the king and court of the moment, to your intellectual workers' self-criticism group, to your fellow troubadours, to fashionable society, to your fellow beatniks, to your Creative Writing 101 class, to your online fans, to—as Emily Dickinson put it—your fellow nobodies. Who can get exiled, shot, or censored for saying what has also veered wildly from time to time and from place to place. In a dictatorship, uneasy lies the bard that bears the frown: the wrong words in the wrong place can get you into a heap of trouble.

So it is with every poem: poems are embedded in their time and place. They can't renounce their roots. But, with luck, they may also transcend them. All that means, however, is that readers who come along later may appreciate them, though doubtless not in the exact way that was first intended. Hymns to the Great and Terrible Mesopotamian Goddess Inanna are fascinating—to me at least—but they don't cause the marrow to melt in my bones as they might have done for an ancient listener: I don't think Inanna may appear at any moment and level a few mountains, though I could always be wrong about that.

Despite the way the Romantics went on about timeless fame and writing for the ages, there's no "forever" in such matters. Reputations and styles rise and fall, books get spurned and burned, then unearthed and recycled, and today's singer for eternity is likely to end up as the day after tomorrow's fire starter, just at the day after tomorrow's fire starter may be snatched from the flames, extolled, and embossed on a plinth. There's a reason the Wheel of Fortune in the Tarot pack is, in fact, a wheel. What goes round comes round, at least sometimes. It's not called the Inevitable Straight Road Pathway to Fortune. There isn't one.

That advance warning having been issued, I'll quote the postman in the film *Il Postino,* who's nicked Neruda's poems and ascribed them to himself in order to serenade his love. "Poetry doesn't belong to those who write it," he says. "It belongs to those who need it." Indeed, after the poem has passed out of the hands of the one who's written it down, and after that person may have departed from time and space and be wafting around as atoms, who else can a poem belong to?

For whom does the bell toll? For you, Dear Reader. Who is the poem for? Also for you.

DEARLY

It's an old word, fading now.
Dearly did I wish.
Dearly did I long for.
I loved him dearly.

I make my way along the sidewalk
mindfully, because of my wrecked knees
about which I give less of a shit
than you may imagine
since there are other things, more important—
wait for it, you'll see—

bearing half a coffee
in a paper cup with—
dearly do I regret it—
a plastic lid—
trying to remember what words once meant.

Dearly.
How was it used?
Dearly beloved.
Dearly beloved, we are gathered.
Dearly beloved, we are gathered here
in this forgotten photo album
I came across recently.

Fading now,
the sepias, the black and whites, the colour prints,
everyone so much younger.
The Polaroids.
What is a Polaroid? asks the newborn.
Newborn a decade ago.

How to explain?
You took the picture and then it came out the top.
The top of what?
It's that baffled look I see a lot.
So hard to describe
the smallest details of how—
all these dearly gathered together—
of how we used to live.
We wrapped up garbage
in newspaper tied with string.
What is newspaper?
You see what I mean.

String though, we still have string.
It links things together.
A string of pearls.
That's what they would say.

How to keep track of the days?
Each one shining, each one alone,
each one then gone.
I've kept some of them in a drawer on paper,

those days, fading now.
Beads can be used for counting.
As in rosaries.
But I don't like stones around my neck.

Along this street there are many flowers,
fading now because it is August
and dusty, and heading into fall.
Soon the chrysanthemums will bloom,
flowers of the dead, in France.
Don't think this is morbid.
It's just reality.

So hard to describe the smallest details of flowers.
This is a stamen, nothing to do with men.
This is a pistil, nothing to do with guns.
It's the smallest details that foil translators
and myself too, trying to describe.
See what I mean.
You can wander away. You can get lost.
Words can do that.

Dearly beloved, gathered here together
in this closed drawer,
fading now, I miss you.
I miss the missing, those who left earlier.
I miss even those who are still here.
I miss you all dearly.
Dearly do I sorrow for you.

Sorrow: *that's another word*
you don't hear much any more.
I sorrow dearly.

Big Science

>>><<<

(2021)

"Here come the planes. They're American planes!"

Musicologists and the less young will recognize those lines, which are from Laurie Anderson's 1981 unlikely voice-synthesizer hit "O Superman." This song, if it is one—try humming it in the shower—led to Anderson's first multi-song album, 1982's *Big Science*.

Big Science is now being reissued at a very timely moment: America is reinventing itself again. It's a self-rescue mission, and just in time: democracy, we have been led to believe, has been snatched from the jaws of autocracy, maybe. A New Deal, leading to a fairer distribution of wealth and an ultimately liveable planet, is on the way, possibly. Racism dating back centuries is being addressed, hopefully. Let's hope these helicopters don't crash.

I didn't understand, back in 1981, that "O Superman" was about the mission to retrieve embattled Americans during the Iranian revolution and the hostage crisis, in which fifty-two U.S. diplomats were held by Iran for more than a year. Anderson herself has said that the song is directly related to Operation Eagle Claw, a military rescue operation that failed: a failure that included a helicopter crash. This catastrophe demonstrated that the American military-industrial Superman was not invincible, and that the automation and electronics mentioned in the song would not always win. The helicopter crash, said Anderson, was the initial inspiration for the song or performance piece. When "O Superman" became a hit, first in the U.K. and then elsewhere, Anderson claims to have been astonished. What were the chances? Very slim, you would have said ahead of time.

You can always remember what you were doing at certain key moments in your life. Such moments are different for everyone. Some of my moments have been attached to public tragedies: when Kennedy was assassinated, I was working at a market research company in downtown Toronto; when 9/11 struck, I was in the Toronto airport, thinking I was about to fly to New York. Some of my moments have been weather-related: witnessing hurricanes, caught in ice storms. And some have been musical. I was four, sitting in an armchair in Sault Ste. Marie ineptly sewing my stuffed bear into its clothes, when I first heard "Mairzy Doats" on the radio. "Blue Moon" came to me sung by a live band, while I was oozing across a high-school dance floor in the clinch favoured in those days. Bob Dylan revealed himself to me in 1964, curly-headed and be-mouth-organed, on a Boston stage with barefoot Joan Baez, queen of the folkies.

Jump cut. It was 1981. Time had passed. Unsurprisingly, I was older. Surprisingly—or it would have been a surprise to me in 1964—I now had a partner and a child, not to mention two cats and a house. Ronald Reagan had just been elected president, and the morning he was promising for America was going to be a lot different from the new age of hippiedom and feminism we'd been living through in the 1970s.

So, 1981. We had the radio on while cooking dinner, when an eerie sound came pulsating over the airwaves.

"What was that thing?" I said. It was not the sort of music, or even sound, that you ordinarily heard on the radio; or anywhere else, come to think of it. The closest to it was when, back in the days of record players and vinyls, we teenagers used to play 45s on 33 speed because it sounded funny. A soprano could be reduced to a slow, zombie-like baritone growl, and often had been.

What I'd just heard, however, wasn't funny. "This is your mother," says a chirpy midwestern voice on an answering machine. "Are you coming home?" But it isn't your mother. It's "the hand, the hand that takes." It's a construct. It's something out of a sci fi movie, such as *Invasion of the Body Snatchers*: it looks human but it's not human, which is both creepy and sinister. Worse, it's your only hope, Mom and Dad and God and justice and force having proved lacking.

"That thing" I'd been mesmerized by was "O Superman." As you can see, I've never forgotten it. It was not like anything else, and Laurie Anderson was not like anyone else either.

Or anyone you would ordinarily think of as a pop musician. Up until her breakout single, she'd been an avant-garde performance artist and inventor, trained initially in the visual arts, and collaborating with like-minded artists such as William Burroughs and John Cage. The 1970s—remembered not only for wide ties, long coats and high boots, and the ethnic look, but also for active second-wave feminism—was a period of high energy for performance art events. These were evanescent by nature, emphasizing process over product. They had roots that went back to Dada in the teens of the twentieth century, to Group Zero, a late 1950s attempt to create something new from the rubble of the Second World War, and to Fluxus, active in the 1960s and 1970s.

Anderson's large project in *Big Science* was a critical and anxious examination of the United States, though not exactly from without. She was born in 1947, and was thus ten in 1957, old enough to have witnessed the surge of new material objects that had flooded American homes in that decade, fifteen in 1962 during a highly active period of the civil rights movement, and twenty in 1967, when campus unrest and anti–Vietnam War protests were in full swing. The upending of norms, for a person of that age, must have seemed normal.

But although New York became her cultural base camp, Anderson was not a big-city girl. She grew up in Illinois, the heart of the heart of America. She came by her perky Mom voice and her "Howdy stranger" tropes honestly. She was a refugee, not to America but from within America: a Mom-and-apple-pie America, an America of the past that was being rapidly transformed by material inventions, and by the freeways, malls, and drive-in banks cited in the song "Big Science" as landmarks on the road to town. What might be bulldozed next? How much of the natural matrix would be left? Was America's worship of technology about to obliterate America? And, more largely, in what consisted our humanity?

As the twentieth century has morphed into the twenty-first, as the consequences of the destruction of the natural world have become devastatingly clear, as analogue has been superseded by digital, as the possibilities for surveillance have increased a hundredfold, and as the ruthless hive mind of the Borg has been approximated through online media, Anderson's anxious and unsettling probings have taken on an aura of the prophetic. Do you want to be a human being anymore? Are you one now? What even is that? Or should you just allow yourself to be held in the long electronic petrochemical arms of your false mother?

Big Science has never been more pertinent than it is right now. Have a listen. Confront the urgent questions. Feel the chill.

Barry Lopez

>>><<<

(2021)

I first met Barry Lopez decades ago, on a trip to Alaska. "Welcome to Alaska," people said, "where the women are men and the men are animals." It might have been a joke, but there was some truth to it, and a truth that was somewhat familiar to me. I grew up in the north and Alaska is the north. Tough women.

But if you're going to be an animal, it matters which animal. It's one thing to be a weasel, another to be a wolf. If you pick wolf, you most likely have Barry to thank. Loyal to their pack, smart, resourceful, survival-oriented, and good-looking as well: What's not to like? Well, there's being slaughtered from helicopters. That doesn't happen to weasels. There is that.

Graeme and I were already great fans of Barry's work. *Of Wolves and Men* (1978) was a breakthrough, as was *Arctic Dreams* (1986). To meet Barry was to feel we were entering a sphere where a language was spoken that had been fading away—the language of our inseparable connection with the natural world—yet here was a speaker who was renewing it. Barry was a prophet in the wilderness, not that he would have called it a wilderness. A lonely speaker then—he must often have wondered whether anyone was truly listening—he is an essential speaker now. Though many of his contemporaries in the 1970s and 1980s may not—by and large—have understood the urgency of his message, the young people of such worldwide movements as Extinction Rebellion grasp it very well. Every breath we inhale comes from Nature; kill it and we kill ourselves. The oceans are the lungs of the planet, and the northern oceans are the key to that system, a system that has made Earth a Goldilocks planet for eons.

Now that the man-made Sixth Great Extinction is upon us and the Arctic is melting, the centrality of Barry's writing is self-evident. We lose our connection with the matrix that sustains us at our peril, and that peril is approaching faster than once anticipated. Let us hope that Barry Lopez will not prove to be a singer of the loved and the lost. The loved "blue marble," the loved wild—if they are irreparably lost, so will we be. Reading Barry's work—rereading it—is to remind ourselves how very great—and how immeasurably stupid— that loss would be.

Thank you, Barry.

The Sea Trilogy

>>><<<

INTRODUCTION

(2021)

The oceans are the living heart and lungs of our planet. They produce most of the oxygen in our atmosphere, and through their circulating currents they control climate. Without healthy oceans, we land-dwelling, air-breathing mid-sized primates will die.

The republication of the marine biologist Rachel Carson's first three books—*Under the Sea-Wind, The Sea Around Us,* and *The Edge of the Sea*—marks a new, widespread recognition of these facts. When Carson was writing these books, in the late 1930s, the 1940s, and the 1950s, a number of things that are now realities in our world had not yet happened. There were warning signs, but these warnings were only glimmers. Few were aware that we had entered the age of the Sixth Great Extinction. The nascent climate crisis had not impacted public consciousness. Large-scale industrial fishing was just beginning, and the cod stocks of the Grand Banks of Newfoundland had not yet crashed due to overfishing. Other fish populations were not being decimated due to devastating bycatch. The regenerative biosystems of the continental shelves had not yet been wrecked by draggers. The coral reefs were not yet bleaching. "Ghost nets" made of plastic rope were not yet drifting around in the oceans, entangling and killing fish, dolphins, and whales. No countries had set up marine-protected areas because why would you need such a thing? Wasn't the sea an ever-renewing source of bounty, there for humankind's taking? You didn't need to pay attention to its ecosystems because why would you? The sea could take care of itself. It was too big to fail. As Lord Byron wrote:

Roll on, thou deep and dark blue Ocean—roll!
Ten thousand fleets sweep over thee in vain;
Man marks the earth with ruin—his control
Stops with the shore . . .

That may have been true in the nineteenth century, in the age of wooden sailing ships. But today, in the era of oil, plastics, pesticides, and rampant industrial overfishing, it is no longer true. If Carson were alive today, she would be the first to be underlining the dangers of human ocean-killing.

Rachel Carson is a pivotal figure of the twentieth century. Those of us who care about preserving a viable planet for its many forms of life—our own species included—would not be where we are without her, and those millions currently suffering from the effects of pollution, from the climate crisis and its associated famines, fires, and floods, and resource wars, would also not be where they are if more decision-makers had listened to her and acted upon her insights.

By "pivotal," I mean that people thought one way before her essential 1962 book, *Silent Spring*, and they thought another way after it. She stood her ground, and defended her evidence-based conclusions. As we are now living in a new era of science denial and a refusal to face facts—not only those about climate heating and the biosphere-killing effects of new insecticides and herbicides, but about more immediately human concerns such as vaccination and vote-counting—the know-nothing, hostile reactions to her revelations should not surprise us.

Silent Spring was Carson's fourth book. The first, *Under the Sea-Wind*, was published in 1941—not a propitious year for publishing anything that wasn't about current politics, since the Second World War was under way and the United States was about to actively enter it. This book—a lyrical and charming exercise in the type of animal-centred nature writing pioneered by Ernest Thompson Seton of *Wild Animals I Have Known* and Henry Williamson of *Tarka the Otter* and *Salar the Salmon*—would probably today be marketed as young adult or children's literature, though Carson's intended audience was broader. She aimed to raise awareness about the interconnectedness of life through following the life stories of three individual organisms: a sanderling, a mackerel, and an eel.

Stories people tell about other life forms or objects are inevitably anthropomorphic—even "The Life of a Pencil" and Hans Christian Andersen's tale about a Christmas tree are like that—so it's no use dissing Carson in that respect. Once you embark on plots concerning individuals with points of view, humanizing them will be the result, whether you dress your animal characters up in frocks and sailor hats, like Beatrix Potter, or let them swim naked, like Carson's eel. On the plus side, this technique helps readers empathize with other life forms. On the minus side, eels don't really have human names, nor do otters or wolves, so some Easter Bunnying is inevitably going on. But the delight in the sea's many mysteries and gifts are well worth the read, though such a story written today would have to include the man-made perils the organisms would now face: habitat destruction, pollution, the threat of extinction. Anguilla the Eel would doubtless have to struggle with a plastic bag, and Silverbar the Sanderling's migration would be more like that of the curlews, in Fred Bodsworth's tragic novel of that name.

Carson's next book, *The Sea Around Us,* was published in 1951— the year after postwar austerity seemed finally over, and was a huge success. It's not a fictionalized account, but a factual one, combining history and pre-history and geology and biology in a secular and celebratory hymn to the ocean. Many were eager to follow its author beneath the waves, into the ultramarine depths. Remember Captain Nemo, of Jules Verne's *Twenty Thousand Leagues Under the Sea?* Maybe you don't, but in 1951, many readers did. Under the sea was a realm of adventure and wonder, and how thrilling it was to be taken on a tour by such a well-informed and enthusiastic guide! No mermaids, but on the other hand, marvels even greater. It was this book that put Rachel Carson on the national and international map.

The Edge of the Sea, the third in Carson's sea trilogy, came in 1955. This is the book with which I identified most closely then, when I was fifteen. It's about beachcombing, something I myself had done a lot of along the coast of the Bay of Fundy during visits to my Nova Scotian relatives in the postwar summers of the late 1940s and early

1950s. The tide pools and caves and flora and starfish and gastropods of that shore were the same as those across the bay, so the first third of *The Edge of the Sea* was speaking about creatures I myself had seen. I still can't pass a rock pool at low tide without looking in to see what might possibly be in there.

In all three of these books there is one underlying refrain: *Look. See. Observe. Learn. Wonder. Question. Conclude.* Rachel Carson taught people to look at the sea, and to think about the sea, in fresh ways. She brought the same habits of mind to the observations of bird life—to the dwindling bird life she was noticing—that led to *Silent Spring.* Without her work on the oceans, she would not have developed the tools that enabled her investigation of the effects of pesticides. And without the fame and the platform that her sea trilogy had brought her, no one would have listened to her alarming message, once she had delivered it. And if no one had listened to it, there would no longer be any eagles, or peregrines, or—eventually—woodland warblers.

Rachel Carson is one of the major grandparents of environmental movements today. We human beings owe her a vast debt, and if we make it to the twenty-second century as a species it will be due in part to her. It's a huge pleasure to welcome this new edition of her sea trilogy. Thank you, Saint Rachel, wherever you may be.

Acknowledgements

>>><<<

My thanks first to my many readers of these essays and occasional pieces over the years, and for the responses that have come my way.

Thanks to my sister and first editor, Ruth Atwood, who helped with the first and second weedings—plowing doggedly through the fields of verbiage, pruning an unmanageable number of short pieces down to a reasonable size. And to Lucia Cino, who sourced the originals and tracked down the printed versions, finding things that—quite frankly—I'd forgotten I'd written. During COVID, this was not the easiest of tasks, as libraries were closed—including the Thomas Fisher Rare Book Library at the University of Toronto, which contains many of the manuscripts. Thanks to the librarians, for helpfulness beyond the call of duty.

Thanks to the editors of the many magazines and newspapers I've worked with for many years; and to my book editors on both sides of the Atlantic, whose thoughtfulness and enthusiasm have been so encouraging. This group includes Becky Hardie of Penguin Random House UK, Louise Dennys and Martha Kanya-Forstner of Penguin Random House Canada, Lee Boudreaux and LuAnn Walther of Penguin Random House US. Heather Sangster of Strong Finish again acted as the demon copy editor who picks every nit, including those yet unhatched. Jess Atwood Gibson attempts to save me from myself, not always successfully.

Thanks to my now-retired agents, Phoebe Larmore and Vivienne Schuster; to the tireless Karolina Sutton of Curtis Brown; and to Caitlin Leydon, Claire Nozieres, Sophie Baker, Jodi Fabbri, and Katie Harrison, who so deftly handle foreign rights.

Thanks also to those who keep me trundling through time and who remind me what day it is, including Lucia Cino of O.W. Toad Limited and Penny Kavanaugh; to V.J. Bauer, who designs and tends the website; and to Mike Stoyan and Sheldon Shoib, to Donald Bennett, to Bob Clark and Dave Cole.

To Coleen Quinn, who makes sure I get out of the Writing Burrow and onto the open road; to Xiaolan Zhao and Vicky Dong; to Matthew Gibson, who fixes stuff; and to the Shock Doctors, for keeping the lights on, and to Evelyn Heskin, Ted Humphreys, Deanna Adams, and Randy Gardner, who help make the Writing Burrows habitable.

And as always to Graeme Gibson, who was with us for most of the years in which these pieces were written. He always laughed at the jokes.

Credits

>>><<<

We would like to credit the following sources of the work contained in this volume:

PART I: 2004 TO 2009 | WHAT WILL HAPPEN NEXT?

"Scientific Romancing." Presented as the Kesterton Lecture, School of Journalism and Communication, Carleton University, Ottawa, ON, Jan. 22, 2004.
    p. 9: "Orwell and Me," *Guardian*, June 16, 2003.

"*Frozen in Time*: Introduction." First published as the introduction to Owen Beattie and John Geiger, *Frozen in Time: The Fate of the Franklin Expedition* (Vancouver: Greystone Books, 2004), 1–8.

"*From Eve to Dawn*." First published as book review "*From Eve to Dawn* by Marilyn French," *Times* (UK), Aug. 21, 2004. Subsequently published as the foreword to Marilyn French, *From Eve to Dawn: A History of Women, Vol. 1* (New York: Feminist Press, 2008), ix–xiv.

"Polonia." First published as "Polonia: In Response to 'What Advice Would You Give the Young?'" In *Dropped Threads 3: Beyond the Small Circle,* ed. Marjorie Anderson (Toronto: Vintage Canada, 2006), 9–18.
    pp. 29–30: Lord Polonius dialogue, in William Shakespeare, *The Tragedy of Hamlet, Prince of Denmark,* Act I, Scene 3 (London: Globe Edition, 1864).

"Somebody's Daughter." Written in 2005 for the UNESCO Literacy for Life program and first published in *The Alphabet of Hope: Writers for Literacy* (Paris: United Nations Educational, Scientific and Cultural Organization, 2007), 13–16.
    p. 32: Bryher (Annie Winifred Ellerman), *The Heart to Artemis: A Writer's Memoirs* (Middletown, CT: Paris Press / Wesleyan University Press, 2006), 14.

"Five Visits to the Word-Hoard." Presented as the Bill Duthie Memorial Lecture, Vancouver International Writers Festival, Vancouver, BC, Oct. 13, 2005. First published in *Writing Life: Celebrated Canadian and International Authors on Writing and Life,* ed. Constance Rooke (Toronto: McClelland & Stewart, 2006), 10–23.
    pp. 39–40: Robertson Davies, *Fifth Business* (Toronto: Penguin Books, 1977), 38–39. • p. 40: Alice Munro, "Cortes Island," in *The Love of a Good Woman* (Toronto: Penguin Books, 1999), 143.

"*The Echo Maker*." First published as book review "In the Heart of the Heartland," *New York Review*, Dec. 21, 2006.
    p. 51: "It's about a disillusioned . . .": Jeffrey Williams, "The Last Generalist: An Interview with Richard Powers," *Cultural Logic* 2, no. 2 (Spring 1999): 16. • p. 51: "I am No One . . .": Richard Powers, *The Echo Maker* (New York: Farrar, Straus and Giroux, 2006), 64. • p. 52: "Nobody's quite what . . .": Ibid., 68. • pp. 52–53: "Love was not . . .": Ibid., 267. • p. 53: "Even the intact . . .": Ibid., 259. • pp. 53–54: "real or decoration . . .": Ibid., 108. • p. 54: "living in the age . . .": Ibid., 269. • p. 54: "Yo, Man . . .": Ibid., 103. • p. 54: "The utter estrangement . . .": Ibid., 108. • p. 55: "I am everywhere . . .": L. Frank Baum, *The Wonderful Wizard of Oz* (First published Chicago: George M. Hill Company, 1900), c. 15. • p. 57: "The outcome of . . .": Powers, *The Echo Maker,* 443. • p. 58: "Doesn't want to be . . .": Ibid., 445. • p. 58: "To find the soul . . .": Ibid., vii. • p. 59: "Just as good . . .": Ibid., 447. • p. 59: "In some ways . . .": Ibid.

"Wetlands." Speech presented at the Charles Sauriol Environmental Dinner celebrating the Canadian naturalist's early leadership in wetlands protection, Toronto and Region Conservation Foundation, Toronto, ON, Nov. 9, 2006.

"Trees of Life, Trees of Death." Presented as a lecture honouring the centennial celebration of the Faculty of Forestry, University of Toronto, Toronto, ON, Apr. 5, 2007.

p. 73: Dante Alighieri, *The Divine Comedy*, trans. H.R. Huse (1472; New York: Rinehart, 1954). • p. 74: Kenneth Grahame, *The Wind in the Willows* (New York: Charles Scribner's Sons, 1914), 52, 55.

"Ryszard Kapuściński." First published as book review "A Sense of Wonder," *Guardian*, June 9, 2007.

p. 81: Ryszard Kapuściński, *Imperium*, trans. Klara Glowczewska (New York: Vintage Books, 1995), 164. • p. 82: Ryszard Kapuściński, *Travels with Herodotus*, trans. Klara Glowczewska (New York: Alfred A. Knopf, 2007), 277.

"Anne of Green Gables." First published as the afterword to the New Canadian Library reissue of L.M. Montgomery, *Anne of Green Gables* (Toronto: New Canadian Library / McClelland & Stewart, 2008), 355–61. Subsequently published as "Nobody Ever Did Want Me," *Guardian*, Mar. 29, 2008.

"Alice Munro: An Appreciation." First published as the introduction to Alice Munro, *Carried Away: A Selection of Stories* (New York and Toronto: Everyman's Library / Alfred A. Knopf, 2006), ix–xx. An edited version was subsequently published as "Alice Munro: An Appreciation by Margaret Atwood," *Guardian*, Oct. 11, 2008.

p. 94: Alice Munro, "The Turkey Season," in *Carried Away*, 70. • p. 95: "The local paper . . .": Alice Munro, "Meneseteung," in *Carried Away*, 179. • p. 95: "Poems, even . . .": Ibid., 198. • p. 96: Alice Munro, *Lives of Girls and Women* (Toronto: McGraw-Hill Ryerson, 1971), 253. • p. 98: Ibid., 210. • p. 98: "In Hanratty . . .": Munro, "Royal Beatings," in *Carried Away*, 5. • pp. 98–99: "to see people . . .": Ibid., 12. • p. 99: "She felt ashamed . . .": Munro, "The Beggar Maid," in *Carried Away*, 52. • p. 99: "a layer of loyalty . . .": Ibid., 53. • p. 99: "I may have . . .": Munro, "Meneseteung," 202. • p. 100: Munro, "The Moons of Jupiter," in *Carried Away*, 85. • p. 101: Munro, "The Turkey Season," in *Carried Away*, 73. • p. 102: Munro, "The Beggar Maid," 30. • p. 103: Munro, *Lives of Girls and Women*, 141. • p. 103: "It is real . . .": Munro, "Differently," in *Carried Away*, 229. • p. 103: "How hard it is . . .": Munro, "The Progress of Love," in *Carried Away*, 129. • p. 104: "that made him seem . . .": Munro, "Something I've Been Meaning to Tell You," in *Something I've Been Meaning to Tell You* (Toronto: McGraw-Hill Ryerson, 1974), 3.

"Ancient Balances." First published in *Payback: Debt and the Shadow Side of Wealth*, CBC Massey Lectures series (Toronto: House of Anansi Press, 2008), 1–40. Established in 1961, the annual CBC Massey Lectures series is co-hosted by the University of Toronto's Massey College, CBC Radio, and the House of Anansi Press.

p. 117: Robert Wright, *The Moral Animal: Why We Are the Way We Are* (New York: Vintage Books, 1994), 204.

"Scrooge: An Introduction." First published as the introduction to Charles Dickens, *A Christmas Carol and Other Christmas Books*, illustrated by Arthur Rackham (London, New York, and Toronto: Everyman's Library / Alfred A. Knopf, 2009), ix–xiii.

"A Writing Life." First published as "A Writer's Life," *Guardian*, Jan. 2009.

PART II: 2010 TO 2013 | ART IS OUR NATURE

"The Writer as Political Agent? Really?" First published in a special commemorative issue of the *Index on Censorship* journal as "Don't Tell Us What to Write," *Index on Censorship* 39, no. 4 (print, Dec. 1, 2010; online, Dec. 16, 2010): 58–63.

"Literature and the Environment." Speech presented at the International PEN Congress, Tokyo, Sept. 26, 2010.

"Alice Munro." First published as "Munro the Icon," *Guardian*, May 30, 2009.

"The Gift: Introduction." First published as the foreword to the Canons reissue of Lewis Hyde, *The Gift: How the Creative Spirit Transforms the World* (Edinburgh: Canongate Canons, 2012), vii–xi.

"Bring Up the Bodies." First published as book review *"Bring Up the Bodies* by Hilary Mantel—Review," *Guardian,* May 4, 2012.

"Rachel Carson Anniversary." First published as book review "Margaret Atwood: Rachel Carson's *Silent Spring,* 50 Years On," *Guardian,* Dec. 7, 2010.

p. 165: Rachel Carson, *Silent Spring* (Boston: Houghton Mifflin, 2002), 297.

"The Futures Market: Stories We Tell About Times to Come." Presented as the Grace A. Tanner Lecture in Human Values, Southern Utah University, Cedar City, UT, Apr. 2, 2013. Subsequently published by the Grace A. Tanner Lecture in Human Values (2013): 1–24.

pp. 172–73: 2012 Calendar, *Cabinet* magazine (https://www.cabinetmagazine.org/projects /last_calendar.php). • p. 173: "Select a blue . . .": Abracadabra forum, n.d. • p. 173: "Masters of Potato Energy . . .": Wikia [now Fandom] scratchpad entry, n.d. • pp. 176–77: T.S. Eliot, "The Burial of the Dead" in *The Waste Land* (1922). • pp. 181–82: Naomi Alderman, "The Meaning of Zombies," *Granta,* Nov. 20, 2011.

"Why I Wrote *MaddAddam*." First published for Wattpad, Aug. 30, 2013.

"Seven Gothic Tales: Introduction." First published as the introduction to Isak Dinesen, *Seven Gothic Tales* (London: The Folio Society, 2013), xi–xvi. Subsequently published as "Margaret Atwood on the Show-Stopping Isak Dinesen," *Guardian,* Nov. 29, 2013.

p. 189: "I well remember . . .": Sara Stambaugh, "Isak Dinesen in America," public lecture presented at the Canadian Initiative for Nordic Studies, University of Alberta, Edmonton, AB, Oct. 28, 1998. • pp. 189–90: "as you got . . .": Isak Dinesen, "The Supper at Elsinore," in *Seven Gothic Tales,* 224. • pp. 191–92: Dinesen, "The Deluge at Norderney," in *Seven Gothic Tales,* 190.

"Doctor Sleep." First published as book review "Shine On," *New York Times,* Sept. 13, 2013.

"Doris Lessing." First published as book review "Doris Lessing: A Model for Every Writer Coming Back from the Beyond," *Guardian,* Nov. 18, 2013.

"How to Change the World?" First published in Dutch translation in *Nexus* 63 (Spring 2013), this essay is a reflection on the topic of the panel discussions at the Nexus Conference, Stadsschouwburg Amsterdam, Nexus Institute, Amsterdam, Dec. 2, 2012.

p. 204: Ugo Bardi, "Cassandra's Curse: How 'The Limits to Growth' Was Demonized," *The Oil Drum: Europe,* Mar. 9, 2008 (http://theoildrum.com/node/3551). • p. 205: Potsdam Institute for Climate Impact Research and Climate Analytics, *Turn Down the Heat: Why a 4° Centigrade Warmer World Must be Avoided* (Washington, DC: World Bank, Nov. 2012), https://openknowledge.worldbank.org/handle/10986/11860.

PART III: 2014 TO 2016 | WHICH IS TO BE MASTER

"In Translationland." Presented as the W.G. Sebald Lecture on Literary Translation, British Centre for Literary Translation, University of East Anglia, Norwich, UK, Feb. 18, 2014.

p. 218: W.G. Sebald to Michael Hulse, "Letters to a Translator," *Little Star* 5 (2014), https:// littlestarjournal.com/issues/. • p. 224: Edward Lear, "The Dong with the Luminous Nose," in *Laughable Lyrics: A Fourth Book of Nonsense Poems, Songs, Botany, Music, &c.* (London: Robert John Bush, 1877), unpag. • p. 225: "'Twas brillig . . .": Lewis Carroll, "Jabberwocky," in *Alice Through the Looking-Glass* (1871). • p. 225: "'When *I* use a word . . .": Ibid.

"On Beauty." First published as "Truth and Beauty," *Harper's Bazaar* (UK ed.), Oct. 2014, 302–5.

"The Summer of the Stromatolites." First published in *That Summer: Great Writers on Life-Changing Summers,* an online series available on *Biographile* (online), the now-defunct Penguin Random House website focused on biography, memoir, and truth in fiction, June 2014.

"Kafka: Three Encounters." Presented as part of the *In the Shadow of Kafka* series of documentaries and drama re-examining the life and legacy of Franz Kafka, BBC Radio 3, May 11, 2015.

pp. 241–42: Franz Kafka, "Excursion into the Mountains," in *The Complete Stories* (London, New York, and Toronto: The Schocken Kafka Library / Penguin Random House, 1995 [first published in English by Schocken 1946; story written between 1904 and 1912 and first published in German 1912]), 383.

"Future Library." Speech presented at the inaugural Future Library Handover Day, Oslo, May 26, 2015, for "Scribbler Moon," the first manuscript solicited by the Future Library. This public artwork project aims to collect an original work by a popular writer every year from 2014 to 2114. These one hundred manuscripts will remain unread and unpublished until 2114, when they will be printed in limited edition using paper made from one thousand trees specially planted for the project. Subsequently published online at https://www.futurelibrary .no/#/years/2014.

"Reflections on *The Handmaid's Tale*." Keynote speech presented at Tennessee Tech University, Cookeville, TN, Nov. 3, 2015.
    p. 250: "The Good Wife's Guide," *Housekeeping Monthly*, May 13, 1955. Since proven to be a spoof: www.snopes.com/fact-check/how-to-be-a-good-wife/.

"We Are Double-Plus Unfree." First published as "Margaret Atwood: We Are Double-Plus Unfree," *Guardian*, Sept. 18, 2015. Subsequently published as *Freedom*, Vintage Minis series (London: Vintage Classics / Penguin Random House UK, 2018).
    p. 259: "A Robin Red . . .": William Blake, "Auguries of Innocence," first published 1863. •
p. 259: "Sufficient to have stood . . .": John Milton, *Paradise Lost*, Book III, first published 1667.
• p. 259: "Freedom, high-day . . .": Caliban dialogue, in William Shakespeare, *The Tempest*, Act II, Scene 2 (London: Globe Edition, 1864).

"Buttons or Bows?" First published as "The Handmaid's Tulle: From Sherlock's Deerstalker to the Zippicamiknicks of 'Brave New World,' Fictional Clothes Must Always Fit, Says Margaret Atwood," *Daily Telegraph*, Feb. 14, 2015, 4–5.

"Gabrielle Roy: In Nine Parts." First published in *Legacy: How French Canadians Have Shaped North America*, ed. André Pratte and Jonathan Kay (Toronto: Signal Books / McClelland & Stewart / Penguin Random House Canada, 2016), 233–56. Copyright © 2016 Generic Productions Inc. Reprinted by permission of Signal Books / McClelland & Stewart, a division of Penguin Random House Canada Limited. All rights reserved.
    p. 282: Gabrielle Roy, *The Tin Flute*, trans. Hannah Josephson (New York: Reynal & Hitchcock, 1947). • pp. 290–91: Roy, "The Voice of the Pools," in *Street of Riches*, trans. Henry Biness (Toronto: New Canadian Library / McClelland & Stewart, 1991), 130–31. • p. 291: " 'Writing,' she told me sadly . . .": Ibid., 132. • p. 291: "I still hoped . . .": Ibid., 132–33.

"Shakespeare and Me: A Tempestuous Love Story." Presented as the keynote speech for the American Library Association Annual Conference and Exhibition, Orlando, FL, June 25, 2016.
    p. 295: "Tomorrow . . .": Macbeth dialogue, in William Shakespeare, *The Tragedy of Macbeth*, Act V, Scene 5 (London: Globe Edition, 1864). • pp. 295–96: "Why, man, he doth . . .": Cassius dialogue (with author modifications), in William Shakespeare, *The Tragedy of Julius Caesar*, Act I, Scene 2 (London: Globe Edition, 1864). • pp. 298–300: "Revenant," in *Stone Mattress* (Toronto: McClelland & Stewart, 2014), 37–39. • pp. 300–301: "Temptation: Prospero, the Wizard of Oz, Mephisto & Co.," in *Writers and Writing* (Toronto: Emblem Editions / McClelland & Stewart, 2014), 91–122. First published as *Negotiating with the Dead: A Writer on Writing* (Cambridge, UK: Cambridge University Press, 2002).

"Marie-Claire Blais: The One Who Blew Everything Up." First published in French as "Celle qui a tout fait sauter." Original English manuscript translated into French by Anne-Marie Régimbald, *Liberté*, no. 312 (Été 2016): 37–38.

"*Kiss of the Fur Queen*." First excerpted in "Ranking the Top Canadian Books of the Past 25 Years: Margaret Atwood on *Kiss of the Fur Queen*," *Maclean's*, Oct. 14, 2016. Subsequently published in *The 25 Most Influential Canadian Books of the Past 25 Years*, LRC 25th Anniversary Edition, *Literary Review of Canada*, Nov. 2016.

"We Hang by a Thread." Presented as the keynote address at a fundraiser for the Women's Legal Education and Action Fund (LEAF) Persons Day Breakfast Gala, Sheraton Centre,

Toronto, Oct. 19, 2016. LEAF National is an organization that helps to educate young female lawyers and also acts as intervenor in some legal cases. It is entirely distinct from West Coast LEAF and has taken some different policy positions.

PART IV: 2017 TO 2019 | HOW SLIPPERY IS THE SLOPE?

"What Art Under Trump?" First published in *The Nation,* Jan. 18, 2017.

"*The Illustrated Man:* Introduction." Parts of this introduction were first published as the eulogy "Margaret Atwood on Ray Bradbury," *Guardian,* June 8, 2012. Subsequently published as the introduction to Ray Bradbury, *The Illustrated Man,* illustrated by Marc Burckhardt (London: The Folio Society, 2017).

    p. 330: Ray Bradbury, "Take Me Home," *The New Yorker,* published online May 18, 2012; published in print June 4 and 11, 2012.

"Am I a Bad Feminist?" First published in the *Globe and Mail,* Jan. 13, 2018.

"We Lost Ursula Le Guin When We Needed Her Most." Parts of this essay were first published as "We Lost Ursula Le Guin When We Needed Her Most," *Washington Post,* Jan. 24, 2018, and "Ursula K Le Guin, by Margaret Atwood: 'One of the Literary Greats of the 20th Century,'" *Guardian,* Jan. 24, 2018.

    p. 342: Ursula K. Le Guin, "About Anger" (written 2014), in *No Time to Spare: Thinking About What Matters* (New York: Houghton Mifflin Harcourt, 2017), 136, 138.

"Three Tarot Cards." First presented as a *lectio magistralis* for the Santa Maddalena Foundation's Premio Gregor von Rezzori–Città di Firenze (a prize for the best work of fiction translated into Italian the previous year), Festival degli Scrittori, Florence, May 4, 2018. Subsequently published in English and Italian in *XII Edizione: 3–4–5 Maggio 2018* (Florence: The Santa Maddalena Foundation, 2018), 2–41.

    p. 356: Carl Orff, "O Fortuna," in *Carmina Burana* (cantata composed in 1935–36; premiered June 8, 1937). English translation provided by the author.

"A Slave State?" First published as the prologue ("Prologo") to Ana Correa, *Somos Belén* (Buenos Aires: Planeta, 2019), 9–12.

"*Oryx and Crake:* Introduction." First published as the introduction to *Oryx and Crake,* illustrated by Harriet Lee-Merrion (London: The Folio Society, 2019), xiii–xvii.

"Greetings, Earthlings! What Are These Human Rights of Which You Speak?" Presented as the 25th Nexus Lecture, Amsterdam, Nov. 10, 2018. Subsequently published in the journal *Nexus 81* (2019): 14–26, and in *The World as It Is in the Eyes of Margaret Atwood, Wole Soyinka, and Ai Weiwei,* vol. 2 of the Cultura Animi series (Amsterdam: Nexus Institute, 2019), 19–23.

    p. 370: Hamlet dialogue, in William Shakespeare, *The Tragedy of Hamlet, Prince of Denmark,* Act II, Scene 2 (London: Globe Edition, 1864). • p. 375: "What is the Universal Declaration of Human Rights?," Australian Human Rights Commission (online), n.d. (humanrights.gov.au/our-work/what-universal-declaration-human-rights).

"*Payback:* Introduction to the New Edition." First published as the introduction to the revised edition of *Payback: Debt and the Shadow Side of Wealth,* CBC Massey Lectures series (Toronto: House of Anansi Press, 2019), ix–xiv. Established in 1961, the annual CBC Massey Lectures series is co-hosted by the University of Toronto's Massey College, CBC Radio, and the House of Anansi Press.

"*Memory of Fire:* Introduction." Written as the introduction to a forthcoming reissue of Eduardo Galeano, *Memory of Fire* trilogy (New York: Bold Type Books, an imprint of Hachette Book Group).

    p. 385: Epigraph, in *Cat's Eye* (Toronto: McClelland & Stewart, 1988).

"Tell. The. Truth." Presented as the acceptance speech for the Burke Medal for Outstanding Contribution to Discourse through the Arts, College Historical Society of Trinity College Dublin, Dublin, Nov. 1, 2019.

PART V: 2020 TO 2021 | THOUGHT AND MEMORY

"Growing Up in Quarantineland." First published as "Growing Up in Quarantineland: Childhood Nightmares in the Age of Germs Prepared Me for Coronavirus," *Globe and Mail,* March 28, 2020.

  p. 397: Adapted from *Payback: Debt and the Shadow Side of Wealth,* CBC Massey Lectures series (Toronto: House of Anansi Press, 2008), 186.

"*The Equivalents.*" First published as book review "Margaret Atwood Reviews *The Equivalents,* About the Artists Who Seeded Second-Wave Feminism," *Globe and Mail,* May 22, 2020.

"*Inseparable:* Introduction." First published as the introduction to the English translation of Simone de Beauvoir, *Inseparable,* trans. Sarah Smith (New York: Ecco / HarperCollins, 2021). Subsequently published as "Read It and Weep: Margaret Atwood on the Intimidating, Haunting Intellect of Simone de Beauvoir," *Literary Hub,* Sept. 8, 2021.

"*We:* Introduction." First published as the introduction to a Canons new English translation of Yevgeny Zamyatin, *We,* trans. Bela Shayevich (Edinburgh: Canongate Books, 2020), 1–7. Subsequently published as "Margaret Atwood: The Forgotten Dystopia That Inspired George Orwell—and Me," *Telegraph,* Nov. 14, 2020.

  p. 409: Yevgeny Zamyatin, "I Am Afraid" (written 1921), in *A Soviet Heretic: Essays by Yevgeny Zamyatin,* trans. Mirra Ginsberg (Chicago: University of Chicago Press, 1970), 57. • pp. 412–13: Charles Dickens, *A Christmas Carol and Other Christmas Books,* illustrated by Arthur Rackham (London, New York, and Toronto: Everyman's Library / Alfred A. Knopf, 2009), 77.

"The Writing of *The Testaments.*" Presented as the 12th Belle van Zuylen Lecture, International Literature Festival Utrecht (ILFU), Utrecht, Oct. 1, 2020, via livestream from Toronto.

  p. 415: English translation (translator unknown) of French politician and Commune leader Pierre Gaspard Chaumette in a Nov. 15, 1793, Commune meeting, in *Réimpression de l'ancien Moniteur,* vol. 18 (Paris: Plon, 1860), 451.

"*The Bedside Book of Birds:* Foreword." First published as the new foreword to the reissue of Graeme Gibson, *The Bedside Book of Birds: An Avian Miscellany* (Toronto: Doubleday Canada, 2021), xii–xv.

"*Perpetual Motion* and *Gentleman Death:* Introduction." First published as the new introduction to the reissue of Graeme Gibson, *Perpetual Motion/Gentleman Death: Two Novels* (Toronto: McClelland & Stewart, 2020), 1–9. Subsequently excerpted as "Margaret Atwood Introduces Graeme Gibson's *Perpetual Motion* and *Gentleman Death,*" *Globe and Mail,* Aug. 26, 2020; updated Aug. 28, 2020.

"Caught in Time's Current." First published as "Caught in Time's Current: Margaret Atwood on Grief, Poetry, and the Past Four Years," *Guardian,* Nov. 7, 2020.

  p. 435: Epigraph, in Ursula K. Le Guin, *A Wizard of Earthsea: Book One of the Earthsea Cycle* (New York: Houghton Mifflin / Houghton Mifflin Harcourt Publishing Company, 1980). • pp. 437–39: "Dearly," in *Dearly: Poems* (Toronto: McClelland & Stewart, 2020), 118–20.

"Big Science." First published as "'It Has Never Been More Pertinent'—Margaret Atwood on the Chilling Genius of Laurie Anderson's *Big Science,*" *Guardian,* Apr. 8, 2021; updated Apr. 9, 2021.

  pp. 440, 441: Laurie Anderson, "O Superman," recorded 1981 (Single on One Ten Records, 1981); track 6 on *Big Science,* 1982 (Warner Brothers, vinyl LP).

"Barry Lopez." First published as "Thank You, Barry: Margaret Atwood," *Orion Magazine,* Dec. 29, 2020.

"The Sea Trilogy: Introduction." First published as the introduction to the Canons reissue of Rachel Carson, *The Sea Around Us* (Edinburgh: Canongate Books, 2021).

  p. 447: Lord Byron, "Canto the Fourth: CLXXIX," *Childe Harold's Pilgrimage,* originally published between 1812 and 1818.

Index

>>><<<

Margaret Atwood is the author of more than fifty books of fiction, poetry, and critical essays. Her novels include *Cat's Eye, The Robber Bride, Alias Grace, The Blind Assassin,* and the *MaddAddam* trilogy. Her 1985 classic, *The Handmaid's Tale,* was followed in 2019 by a sequel, *The Testaments,* which was a global number one bestseller and won the Booker Prize. In 2020 she published *Dearly,* her first collection of poetry in a decade.

Atwood has won numerous awards, including the Arthur C. Clarke Award for Imagination in Service to Society, the Franz Kafka Prize, the Peace Prize of the German Book Trade, the PEN USA Lifetime Achievement Award, and the Dayton Literary Peace Prize. In 2019 she was made a member of the Order of the Companions of Honour for services to literature. She has also worked as a cartoonist, illustrator, librettist, playwright, and puppeteer. She lives in Toronto, Canada.